# Computer Security

# Computer Security

## SECOND EDITION

# Dieter Gollmann

*Hamburg University of Technology*

John Wiley & Sons, Ltd

*Other Wiley Editorial Offices*

John Wiley & Sons Inc., 111 River Street, Hoboken, NJ 07030, USA

Jossey-Bass, 989 Market Street, San Francisco, CA 94103-1741, USA

Wiley-VCH Verlag GmbH, Boschstr. 12, D-69469 Weinheim, Germany

John Wiley & Sons Australia Ltd, 42 McDougall Street, Milton, Queensland 4064, Australia

John Wiley & Sons (Asia) Pte Ltd, 2 Clementi Loop #02-01, Jin Xing Distripark, Singapore 129809

John Wiley & Sons Canada Ltd, 22 Worcester Road, Etobicoke, Ontario, Canada M9W 1L1

Wiley also publishes its books in a variety of electronic formats. Some content that appears
in print may not be available in electronic books.

*Library of Congress Cataloging-in-Publication Data*

Gollmann, Dieter.
    Computer security / Dieter Gollmann. – 2nd ed.
        p. cm.
    Includes bibliographical references and index.
    ISBN-13: 978-0-470-86293-3 (pbk. : alk. paper)
    ISBN-10: 0-470-86293-9 (pbk. : alk. paper)
    1.  Computer security.    I. Title.

QA76.9.A25G65 2005
005.8 – dc22

2005026866

*British Library Cataloguing in Publication Data*

A catalogue record for this book is available from the British Library

ISBN-13: 978-0-470-86293-3
ISBN-10: 0-470-86293-9

Typeset in 9/12 Sabon by Laserwords Private Limited, Chennai, India
Printed and bound in Great Britain by Bell & Bain, Glasgow
This book is printed on acid-free paper responsibly manufactured from sustainable forestry
in which at least two trees are planted for each one used for paper production.

# Contents

# Preface

Ég geng i hring
i kringum allt, sem er.
Og utan þessa hrings
er veröld mín.

**Steinn Steinarr**

This book grew out of my lecture notes for courses taught on a one-year postgraduate program on information security. While discussing the terms of reference for an industrial placement in the first year of this program, the security manager in charge stressed the importance of stating explicitly the objectives a project is not intended to meet. So:

- this is not a handbook of computer security;
- this is not an encyclopedia of computer security;
- this is not a history of computer security.

Of course, this book will refer to events in the history of computer security. It will cover quite a bit of ground and point to further material in this area, and I hope that security practitioners will find some of the ideas and content useful. However, it was first and foremost written as a textbook on computer security. It aspires to provide students who have a background in computer science with a basis for assessing and comparing the technical merits of security products.

The paragraphs above started the Preface to the first edition of *Computer Security*, which then went on to explain my choice of topics and the structure of the book. The material in this first edition had been compiled over several years, at a time when the Internet had already been opened to commercial use and the World Wide Web had come into existence, but before the changes brought about by these events had reached the full extent we are experiencing today. In retrospect, this period from the mid to late 1990s was governed by the belief that communications security and in particular strong cryptography would make the Internet and the World Wide Web secure places to visit.

These issues were resolved and satisfactory communications security protocols are widely deployed today. However, security has refused to go away as a problem, and attention is shifting back to the end systems. Buffer overflows, and code vulnerabilities in general, have moved into the limelight. Access control is no longer enforced mainly by the operating system but also at the middleware and application layers. Code-based access control has become an alternative to traditional approaches based on user identities.

This second edition tries to do justice to these developments in computer security. New chapters on authentication in distributed systems, mobility, software security, and new paradigms in access control have been added. The chapters on Unix security, Windows 2000 security, and network security have been updated. The material on security models has been rearranged and split into two chapters. Chapter 8 shows how to construct a formal security model, in this case the Bell–LaPadula model, and how to apply it in the analysis of a computer system. Chapter 9 gives an overview of other important security models. Some issues that were fashionable at the time of writing, such as Trusted Computing, are only touched on briefly. Others, like Web Services security, have been left out, not least because this field is still evolving and technical details might become out of date too quickly.

As in the first edition, the book is focused on computer security, i.e. on technical security issues of the end systems used in today's IT applications. The decision to concentrate on technical aspects is deliberate. This is not a book on information security in general, although an introductory chapter on risk analysis and security management has been included for lecturers who want to use this book as background for a course on information security. The fact that these topics do not get more attention should not be misconstrued to imply that they are not important for computer security. On the contrary, decisions about technical security matters cannot be made without reference to the context they are applied in, and even the best technical measures are ineffective if managed badly or deployed wrongly. On the postgraduate program mentioned above, courses on technical subjects were taught alongside a course on security management that covered the non-technical security issues surrounding computer security. Even while focusing on technical matters, I would still feel I had failed if, at the end of this book, the reader would accept 'Is this system secure?' as a meaningful question before the purpose of the system had been made clear.

Throughout the book, I have tried to extract general security principles from the discussions of the various topics covered. When concrete security systems, such as the security features in Unix or Windows 2000, are presented, they serve primarily as illustrations of these general points, and are never meant as comprehensive introductions to those systems. This is due first to limitations of space; many chapters deal with topics that could easily be covered in books of their own. Second, it is due to the ever-changing nature of computer security systems; explanations of technical details are in danger of becoming out of date quickly. Finally, it is due to a frequent complaint that security practitioners know how their systems work but not what they really are good for. Hence, the book is trying to remind the reader of the latter.

I have included exercises in each chapter but cannot claim to have succeeded to my own satisfaction in all instances. In my defense, I can only claim that computer security is not simply a collection of recipes that can be demonstrated within the confinements of a typical textbook exercise. In some areas, like password security or cryptography, it is easy to construct exercises that have precise answers which can be found by going through the correct sequence of steps. Other areas are more suited to projects, essays or discussions. Although it is naturally desirable to support a course on computer security with experiments on real systems, I have not included suggestions for laboratory sessions in this book. Operating systems, database management systems or firewalls are the prime candidates for practical exercises. The actual examples will depend on the particular systems available to the lecturer. For specific systems there are often excellent books available that explain how to use the system's security mechanisms.

Because this is a textbook, I have sometimes included important material in exercises that would be expected to have a place in the main body of a handbook on computer security.

I am indebted to numerous colleagues who encouraged me to bring *Computer Security* up to date and provided feedback on the first edition, reporting what they found useful, and not so useful, in that book. Unfortunately, not all their suggestions could be accommodated in this second edition. Jason Crampton deserves special thanks for his extremely helpful and detailed recommendations and corrections for a good many chapters. Tuomas Aura and Kai Rannenberg also kindly helped with detailed advice on those chapters where I consulted their technical expertise.

Dieter Gollmann
Hamburg, August 2005

# Chapter 1

## Introduction

It is quite common for essays on the uptake of new information technology (IT) to start with a remark such as:

> Security concerns are a major reason for holding back the take-up of new information technologies, thus preventing citizens and companies from reaping the full benefits these technologies would offer.

Statements like this are made by academics writing books on security, by consultants trying to convince customers of the value of their services, by vendors of security products or by government officials in charge of security programs. Security stories play well in the media, working with powerful motifs like the fall of the mighty (Microsoft) or the fear of invisible foes (viruses and worms creeping around in the Internet).

People with an axe to grind certainly have reasons to exaggerate the dangers we are facing and it is often difficult to obtain hard evidence for assessing the real size of the problem. On the other hand, threats are real, as anyone who has been a victim of a worm or virus will confirm. Indeed, the widespread use of open communications networks like the Internet, or of cellular telephone systems, has exposed a large user population to security threats. A fundamental understanding of the potential vulnerabilities of such networks, of the core protection mechanisms and of their limitations has thus become essential for IT professionals.

This book is about computer security. The original focus of computer security was on multiuser systems. Users had to be kept apart and unauthorized users had to be stopped from modifying systems software. Today's focus is on computing devices that may figure as the end systems in a network. Many security issues stem from the fact that these devices are connected to a network and may in some way be attacked from 'untrusted' nodes. Traditional network security services protect traffic between nodes, with the task completed once a message has been safely handed over to the other side. Our problems start when the message has been received and is then processed within the end system.

Before moving to the technical content of this book, this first chapter will go over some important issues that have to be addressed when trying to implement security measures in practice. The deployment of security measures (and of IT in general) is a management decision, and technical security measures have to work hand in hand with organizational measures to be effective. Management decisions should be underpinned by some analysis of current risks and threats. Hence, we will give a brief survey of security management and of risk and threat analysis.

## OBJECTIVES

- Set the scene for our discussion of computer security.
- Give a brief introduction to security management.
- Cover the basics of risk and threat analysis.

# 1.1 ATTACKS AND ATTACKERS

Not so long after the first generation of cellular telephone systems had established a customer base, members of the British royal family found some very private phone calls reprinted in newspapers. These systems transmitted the traffic between a mobile device and a base station in the clear, so anyone with the right equipment could listen in on telephone calls. Second generation systems like GSM then included cryptographic mechanisms for protecting the radio link. Similar confidentiality concerns are raised by credit card purchases over the Internet. The basic Internet protocols provide no confidentiality protection so parties located between customer and merchant could capture card numbers and use them later for fraudulent purchases. Secure Socket Layer (SSL) was developed by Netscape to deal with this very problem.

However, the real danger may lurk somewhere else. Scanning Internet traffic for packets containing credit card numbers is an attack with a low yield. Badly protected servers at a merchant site holding a database of customer credit card numbers are a much more rewarding target. There is documented evidence that such attacks have occurred, either to obtain credit card numbers or to blackmail the merchant.

*Identity theft*, i.e. using somebody else's 'identity' (name, social security number, bank account number, etc.) to gain access to a resource or service, exploits an inherent weakness in services that use non-secret identifying information to authenticate requests.

Vulnerabilities in software accepting external user input, like Internet browsers or mail software, may allow external parties to take control of a device. Attackers may corrupt data on the device itself or use it as a stepping stone for attacks against third parties. Worms and viruses make use of overgenerous features or vulnerabilities to spread widely and overload networks and end systems with the traffic they generate. The Internet worm of November 1988 is an early well-documented example of this species (Eichin and Rochlis, 1989). Denial-of-service attacks against specific targets have started to occur in the last few years. Resilience against denial-of-service attacks has become a new criterion in the design of security protocols.

Returning to the first example, as traffic between mobile and base station was unprotected, attackers could also capture the 'secret' identifiers used to authenticate customers for charging purposes. Major road intersections were a popular place for fraudsters to lie in wait. With these identifiers, attackers could then create cloned phones and make calls that were charged to the victim's account. There was a time when reportedly up to 50% of phone calls were fraudulent in some particularly badly affected networks.

GSM uses a challenge/response protocol for subscriber authentication and does not transmit secrets in this process, so this particular attack can no longer be mounted. However, this certainly does not imply that all charging problems have been solved. Today, we see attempts to lure unwitting customers into calling back to premium rate numbers owned by the attacker, using the existing charging system to get the victim's money. This is an attack (mis)using a technical system, rather than an attack exploiting a flaw in a technical system. Countermeasures are to be found at the human level, e.g. exercising caution before answering a call back request, and in the legal system, e.g. clarifying how user consent has to be sought for subscribers to be liable for charges to their account.

In the scenarios described above the attacks came from the outside. Keeping the enemy outside the castle walls is a traditional paradigm in computer security. However, typical statistics for the sources of attacks show that attacks from insiders account for a majority of incidents and the largest proportion of damages (United Nations, 1999). There is a suggestion that attacks via the Internet might change this picture, but insider fraud remains a considerable concern in organizations and in electronic commerce transactions.

It has been said that the goal of security engineering is to raise the effort involved in an attack to a level where the costs exceed the attacker's gains. Such advice may be short sighted. Not every attacker is motivated by a wish for money. Employees who have been made redundant may want to exact revenge on their former employer. Hackers may want to demonstrate their technical expertise and draw particular satisfaction from defeating security mechanisms that have been put in their way. 'Cyber vandals' may launch attacks without much interest in their consequences. Political activists may deface the web sites of organizations they dislike.

There is similar variance in the expertise required to break into a system. In some cases insider knowledge will be required to put together a successful attack plan. In this respect, *social engineering* may be more important than technical wizardry (Mitnick and Simon, 2002). Hassling computer operators on the phone to give the caller the password to a user account is a favorite ploy. Some attacks require deep technical understanding. Other attacks have been automated and can be downloaded from web sites so that they may be executed by *script kiddies* who have little insight into the vulnerabilities or features these attacks are exploiting.

## 1.2 SECURITY

Software may crash, communication networks may go down, hardware components may fail, human operators may make mistakes. As long as these failures cannot be directly attributed to some deliberate human action they would not be classified as security issues. Accidental failures would count as *reliability* issues. Operating mistakes would be attributed to *usability* issues. Security is concerned with *intentional* failures. There may not always be a clear intent to achieve a particular goal, but there is at some stage a decision by a person to do something they are not supposed to do. As sketched above, the reasons for such actions can be manifold. The root cause of security problems is human nature.

Security practitioners know that 'security is a people problem' that cannot be solved by technology alone. The legal system has to define the boundaries of acceptable behavior through data protection and computer misuse laws. Responsibility for security within organizations, be they companies or universities, resides ultimately with management. Users have to cooperate and comply with the security rules laid down in their organization. Of course, correct deployment and operation of technical measures is also part of the overall solution.

## 1.3 SECURITY MANAGEMENT

Protecting the assets of an organization is the responsibility of management. Assets include sensitive information like product plans, customer records or financial data, and the IT infrastructure of the organization. At the same time, security measures often restrict members of the organization in their working patterns and there may be a certain temptation to flaunt security rules. This is particularly likely to happen if security instructions do not come from a superior authority but from some other branch of the organization.

It is thus strongly recommended to organize security responsibilities in an organization in a way that makes it clear that security measures have the full support of senior management. A brief *policy* document signed by the chief executive that lays down the ground rules can serve as a starting point. This document would be part of everyone's employment handbook. Then, *security awareness* programs should be organized. Not every member has to become a security expert, but all members should know:

- why security is important for themselves and for the organization;
- what is expected of each member;
- which good practices they should follow.

The mirror image of users ignoring apparently unreasonable security rules is security experts treating apparently unreasonable users as the enemy. Trying to force users to follow rules they regard as arbitrary is not an efficient approach. Studies have shown that involving users as stakeholders in the security of their organizations can make users voluntarily comply with rules rather than looking for workarounds (Adams and Sasse, 1999).

Organizations developing IT services or products have the additional task of providing security training for their developers. There is rarely a clear dividing line between the security-relevant components and the rest of a system. It thus helps if developers in general are aware of the environment a service will be deployed in and of the expected dangers, so that they can highlight the need for protection even if they do not implement the protection mechanisms themselves. Developers should also be alert to the fact that certain categories of sensitive data, e.g. personal data, have to be processed according to specific rules and regulations. Finally, developers should keep up to date with known coding vulnerabilities.

## 1.3.1 Security Policies

Security policies state what should be protected but may also indicate how this should be done. To maintain clarity in our terminology, we follow the definitions laid out in Sterne (1991) and distinguish between organizational and automated security policies. A policy has given objectives.

> **Security Policy Objective**  A statement of intent to protect an identified resource from unauthorized use.

A policy also has to explain how the objectives are to be met. This can be done first at the level of the organization.

> **Organizational Security Policy**  The set of laws, rules and practices that regulate how an organization manages, protects and distributes resources to achieve specified security policy objectives.

Within an IT system, organizational policies can be supported by technical means.

> **Automated Security Policy**  The set of restrictions and properties that specify how a computing system prevents information and computing resources from being used to violate an organizational security policy.

Automated policies address issues like the definition of access control lists or firewall settings, decisions on the services that may be run on devices and the security protocols used to protect network traffic.

## 1.3.2 Measuring Security

Measuring security is the holy grail of security engineering. To convince managers (or customers) of the benefits of a new security mechanism, wouldn't it be nice if we could measure the security of the system before and after introducing the mechanism? Indeed, it is difficult to reach well-founded management decisions if such quantitative information cannot be procured. Ideally, a *measurement* would give a quantitative result that can be compared to other measurements, not just a qualitative statement about the security of the product or system being analyzed.

- A *product* is a package of IT software, firmware and/or hardware, providing functionality designed for use or incorporation within a multiplicity of systems.
- A *system* is a specific IT installation, with a particular purpose and operational environment (CCIB, 2004a).

Measurements of a product are indicative of its potential security, but even a secure product can be deployed in an insecure manner. A notorious example is a service account whose default password is not changed. It is thus a task for security management to ensure that the security features provided are properly used. For a product, one might use the number of security flaws (bugs) detected as a measure of its security. Tracking the discovery of flaws over time may serve as the basis for predicting the time to the discovery of the next flaw. Relevant methodologies have been developed in the area of *software reliability*. These methodologies assume that the detection of flaws and the invocation of buggy code are governed by a probability distribution given a priori, or a given family of probability distributions where parameters still have to be estimated. Another proposal is to measure the *attack surface* of a product, i.e. the number of interfaces to outside callers or the number of dangerous instructions in the code (Howard, Pincus and Wing, 2003).

These proposals are measurements in the sense that they deliver quantitative results. It is open to debate whether they really measure security. How relevant is the number of security flaws? It is sufficient for an attacker to find and exploit a single flaw to compromise security. It is equally open to debate whether such metrics could be the basis for a meaningful security comparison of products, given that it is rare to find two products that serve exactly the same purpose. It has therefore been suggested that these metrics are best treated as *quality* metrics and used for monitoring the evolution of individual products.

Security metrics for a system could look at the actual configurations of the products deployed. In a system with access control features, we could look at the number of accounts with system privileges or the number of accounts with weak passwords. In a networked system, we could look at the number of open ports or at the services accessible from outside and whether the currently running versions have known vulnerabilities. Such attributes certainly give valuable *status information* but do not really give the quantitative results desired from a measurement.

Specifically for computer networks, we could measure the connectivity of nodes in a network to assess how quickly and how far attacks could spread. We could also measure the time services are unavailable after an attack, or predict recovery times and cost of recovery for a given configuration and class of attacks.

In an alternative approach, we could try to measure security by measuring the cost of mounting attacks. We could consider:

- the time an attacker has to invest in the attack, e.g. analyzing software products;
- the expenses the attacker has to incur, e.g. computing cycles or special equipment;
- the knowledge necessary to conduct the attack.

However, the cost of discovering an attack for the first time is often much larger than the cost of mounting the attack itself. Today, *attack scripts* are readily available so that attacks can be launched with very little effort or knowledge of the system vulnerabilities being exploited.

As yet another alternative, we could focus on the assets in the given system and measure the risks these assets are exposed to. Section 1.4.4 gives an overview of risk and threat analysis. In summary, desirable as security measurements are, we have at best metrics for some individual aspects of security and the search for better metrics is still an open field of research.

## 1.3.3 Standards

Prescriptive security management standards that stipulate which security measures have to be taken in an organization exist for specific industry branches. Typical examples are regulations for the financial sector[1], or rules for dealing with classified material in government departments[2].

Other management standards are best described as codes of best practice for security management. The most prominent of these standards is ISO 17799 (International Organization for Standardization, 2001). It is not a technical standard for security products or a set of evaluation criteria for products or systems. The major topics in ISO 17799 are as follows.

- Establishing organizational security policy: this document provides management direction and support on security matters.

- Organizational security infrastructure: responsibilities for security within an enterprise have to be properly organized. Management has to be able to get an accurate view of the state of security within an enterprise. Reporting structures should facilitate efficient communication and implementation of security decisions. Security has to be maintained when information services are being outsourced to third parties.

- Asset classification and control: to know what is worth protecting, and how much to spend on protection, an enterprise has to have a clear picture of its assets and of their value.

- Physical and environmental security: physical security measures (fences, locked doors, etc.) protect access to business premises or to sensitive areas (rooms) within a building. E.g. only authorized personnel get access to server rooms. These measures can prevent unauthorized access to sensitive information and theft of equipment. The likelihood of natural disasters can depend on environmental factors, e.g. is the area subject to flooding?

- Personnel security: your own personnel or contract personnel can be a source of insecurity. There should be procedures for new employees joining and for employees leaving (e.g. collect keys and entry badges, delete user accounts of leaving members.) Enforced holiday periods can stop staff hiding the traces of fraud they are committing. Background checks on new hires can be a good idea. In some sectors those checks may be required by law, but there may also be privacy laws that restrict which information an employer may seek about its employees.

- Communications and operations management: the day-to-day management of IT systems and of business processes has to ensure that security is maintained.

- Access control: access control can apply to data, services and computers. Particular attention should be applied to remote access, e.g. through the Internet or dial-in connections. Automated security policies define how access control is being enforced.

---

[1] E.g. the Payment Card Industry (PCI) Data Security Standard supported by Visa.
[2] E.g. the US policy stating that the encryption algorithm AES can be used for top-secret data with 192-bit or 256-bit keys (CNSS, 2003).

- Systems development and maintenance: security issues should be considered when an IT system is being developed. Operational security depends on proper maintenance (e.g. patching vulnerable code, updating virus scanners). IT support has to be conducted securely (how do you deal with users who have forgotten their password?) and IT projects have to be managed with security in mind (who is writing sensitive applications, who gets access to sensitive data?).

- Business continuity planning: put measures in place so that your business can cope with major failures or disasters. Measures start with keeping backups of important data kept in a different building and may go on to the provision of reserve computing facilities in a remote location. You also have to account for losing key staff members.

- Compliance. organizations have to comply with legal, regulatory and contractual obligations, as well as with standards and their own organizational security policy. The auditing process should be efficient while trying to minimize its interference with business processes. In practice, these aspects often pose a greater challenge than fielding technical security measures.

Achieving compliance with ISO 17799 can be quite an onerous task. The current state of your organization vis-à-vis the standard has to be established and any shortcomings identified have to be addressed. There exist software tools that partially automate this process, again applying best practice, only this time ensuring compliance with the standard.

## 1.4 RISK AND THREAT ANALYSIS

Many areas of engineering and business have developed their own disciplines and terminology for risk analysis. This section will give a brief overview of risk analysis for IT security. Within IT security, risk analysis is being applied:

- comprehensively for all information assets of an enterprise;
- specifically for the IT infrastructure of an enterprise;
- during the development of new products or systems, e.g. in the area of software security.

Informally, risk is the possibility that some incident or attack can cause damage to your enterprise. An attack against an IT system consists of a sequence of actions, exploiting weak points in the system, until the attacker's goals have been achieved. To assess the risk posed by the attack we have to evaluate the amount of damage being done and the likelihood of the attack occurring. This likelihood will depend on the attacker's motivation and on how easy it is to mount the attack. In turn, this will further depend on the security configuration of the system under attack.

To disentangle the various strands of investigations that have to be pursued in the process of risk analysis, we will refer to *assets*, *vulnerabilities* and *threats*, and calculate risk as a function thereof. Informally:

$$Risk = Assets \times Threats \times Vulnerabilities.$$

In the process of risk analysis, values are assigned to assets, vulnerabilities and threats. In *quantitative* risk analysis, values are taken from a mathematical domain like a probability space. For example, by assigning monetary values to assets and probabilities to threats the expected loss can be calculated. In *qualitative* risk analysis, values are taken from domains that do not have an underlying mathematical structure. Risk is calculated based on rules that capture the consolidated advice of security experts.

## 1.4.1 Assets

First, assets have to be identified and valued. In an IT system, assets include:

- hardware: laptops, servers, routers, PDAs, mobile phones, smart cards etc.;
- software: applications, operating systems, database management systems, source code, object code etc.;
- data and information: essential data for running and planning your business, design documents, digital content, data about your customers etc.;
- reputation.

Identification of assets should be a relatively straightforward systematic exercise. Valuation of assets is more of a challenge. Some assets, such as hardware, can be valued according to their monetary replacement costs. For other assets, such as data and information, this is more difficult. If your business plans are leaked to the competition or private information about your customers is leaked to the public you have to account for indirect losses due to lost business opportunities. The competition may underbid you and your customers may desert you. Even when equipment is lost or stolen you have to consider the value of the data stored on it, and the value of the services that were running on it. In such situations, assets can be valued according to their importance. As a good metric for importance, ask yourself how long your business could survive when a given asset has been damaged: a day, a week, a month?

## 1.4.2 Vulnerabilities

Vulnerabilities are weaknesses of a system that could be accidentally or intentionally exploited to damage assets. In an IT system, typical vulnerabilities are:

- accounts with system privileges where the default password, such as 'MANAGER', has not been changed;
- programs with unnecessary privileges;
- programs with known flaws;
- weak access control settings on resources, e.g. having kernel memory world writable;
- weak firewall configurations that allow access to vulnerable services.

*Vulnerability scanners* provide a systematic and automated way of identifying vulnerabilities. Their knowledge base of known vulnerabilities has to be kept up to date. Organizations like SANS or Computer Emergency Response Teams (CERTs) provide this information, as do security advisories of software companies.

Vulnerabilities can be rated according to their impact (level of criticality). A vulnerability that allows an attacker to take over a systems account is more critical than a vulnerability that gives access to an unprivileged user account. A vulnerability that allows an attacker to completely impersonate a user is more critical than a vulnerability where the user can only be impersonated in the context of a single specific service. Some scanners will also give a rating for the vulnerabilities they detect.

Terminology in IT security is notoriously imprecise, and you might find vulnerability scanners that are marketed as risk analysis tools. It is of course perfectly reasonable to use a different conceptual framework than the one sketched here, so the burden is on you to find out what any 'risk analysis tool' is actually offering, and then place it in the framework of your choice.

### 1.4.3 Threats

Threats are actions by adversaries who try to exploit vulnerabilities to damage assets. There are various ways to identify threats. We can categorize threats by the damage done to assets. For example, Microsoft's STRIDE threat model for software security lists the following categories (Howard and LeBlanc, 2002).

- Spoofing identities: the attacker pretends to be somebody else.

- Tampering with data: e.g. security settings are changed to give the attacker more privileges.

- Repudiation: a user denies having performed an action like mounting an attack, or making a purchase.

- Information disclosure: information may lose its value if it is disclosed to the wrong parties (e.g. trade secrets); your organization may face penalties if is does not properly protect information (e.g. personal information about individuals).

- Denial of service (DoS): DoS attacks can make web sites temporarily unavailable; there have been stories in the press that businesses use such attacks to harm competitors.

- Elevation of privilege: a user gains more privileges on a computer system than he/she is entitled to.

Then we can identify the source of attacks. Would the adversary be a member of your organization or an outsider, a contractor or a former member? Has the adversary direct access to your systems or is the attack launched remotely?

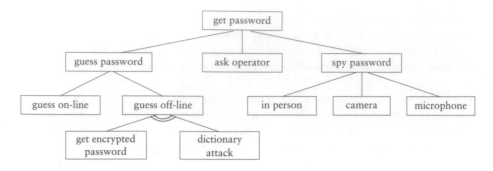

Figure 1.1: Attack Tree for Obtaining Another User's Password

We can also analyze how an attack is executed in detail. An attack may start with innocuous steps, gathering information needed to move on to gain privileges on one machine, from there jump to another machine, until the final target is reached. To get a fuller picture of potential threats, a forest of *attack trees* can be constructed. The root of an attack tree is a generic attack. The nodes in the tree are subgoals that must be achieved for the attack to succeed. Subgoals can be broken into further subgoals. There are AND-nodes and OR-nodes. To reach an AND-node, all subgoals have to be achieved. To reach an OR-node, it is enough if one subgoal is achieved. Figure 1.1 gives a basic attack tree for the attack 'get password'. A password can be obtained by guessing, or by tricking an operator to reveal it, or by spying on the user. Guessing could be on-line or off-line. For off-line guessing, the attacker needs the encrypted password and has to perform a dictionary attack. The attacker could spy on the victim in person (so-called shoulder surfing), direct a camera at the keyboard or direct a microphone at the keyboard and distinguish the keys pressed by sound.

It is possible to assign values to the edges in an attack tree. These values can indicate the estimated cost of an attack, the likelihood that it will occur, the likelihood that it will succeed or some other aspect of interest. From these values, the cheapest attack, or the most likely attack, or the attack most likely to succeed can be computed.

Attack trees are thus a formalized and structured method for analyzing threats. Threat assessments become reproducible as the overall assessment of a threat can be traced to the individual assessments of subgoals. If the final result appears implausible, the tree can be consulted to see which subgoals were most critical for the final result, and those individual valuations may be adjusted to more 'sensible' values. This remark explains why the construction of attack trees is more an art than a science. You need experience to know when to readjust your ratings for subgoals, and when to adjust your preconceived opinion of the severity of a threat. You also need experience to know when to stop breaking up subgoals into ever more subgoals, a phenomenon known in the trade as *analysis paralysis*.

Threats can be rated according to their likelihood. The likelihood depends on the difficulty of the attack, on the motivation of the attacker and on the number of potential attackers. *Attack scripts* automate attacks, making it easy to launch the attack. They are also likely to be available to a larger set of attackers. Hence, such attacks would be rated more likely than an individual hand-crafted attack.

### 1.4.4 Risk

Having rated the value of assets, the criticality of vulnerabilities and the likelihood of threats, we now face the tricky task of calculating our risks.

In quantitative risk analysis, expected losses could be computed in the framework of probability theory, based on monetary values for the assets and probabilities for the likelihood of threats. Such a method has the pleasing feature of being based on a well-established mathematical theory, but also has the considerable drawback that the ratings we obtain are often based on educated guesses. In short, the quality of the results we obtain cannot be better than the quality of the inputs provided. We could consider other mathematical frameworks, such as fuzzy theory, to make some provisions for the imprecise nature of our ratings. There are areas of risk analysis where quantitative methods work, but more often the lack of precision in the inputs does not justify a mathematical treatment.

In qualitative risk analysis:

- assets could be rated on a scale of critical – very important – important – not important;
- criticality of vulnerabilities could be rated on a scale of has to be fixed immediately – has to be fixed soon – should be fixed – fix if convenient;
- threats could be rated on a scale of very likely – likely – unlikely – very unlikely.

A finer granularity of scaling could be provided, e.g. numerical values from 1 to 10. Whatever scheme is used, guidance has to be given on how to assign ratings. The mapping of the ratings for assets, vulnerabilities and threats to risks is often given by a table drawn up to reflect the judgment of security experts. The DREAD methodology that complements STRIDE may serve as an example of a scheme for qualitative risk analysis (Howard and LeBlanc, 2002).

- Damage potential: relates to the values of the assets being affected.

- Reproducibility: one aspect of how difficult it is to launch an attack; attacks that are easy to reproduce are a greater risk than attacks that only work in specific circumstances.

- Exploitability: relates to the effort, expertise and resources required to launch an attack.

- Affected users: for software vendors, another important contributing factor to damage potential.

- Discoverability: when will the attack be detected? In the most damaging case, you will never know that your system has been compromised. (In World War II, German intelligence refused to believe that many of their encryption schemes had been broken.)

### 1.4.5 Countermeasures – Risk Mitigation

The result of a risk analysis is a prioritized list of threats, together with recommended countermeasures to mitigate risk. Risk analysis tools usually come with a knowledge base of countermeasures for the threats they can identify.

It might seem trivially true that one should first go through a risk analysis before deciding on which security measures to implement. However, there are two reasons why this ideal approach may not work. Conducting a risk analysis for a larger organization will take time, but the IT system in the organization and the world around will keep changing. So, by the time the results of the analysis are presented, they are already somewhat out of date. Moreover, the costs of a full risk analysis may be difficult to justify to management.

For these reasons, organizations may opt for *baseline protection* as an alternative. This approach analyzes the security requirements for typical cases and recommends security measures deemed adequate. One of the best known IT security baseline documents is maintained by the German Information Security Agency (BSI, 2003).

## 1.5 FURTHER READING

Anderson's book on security engineering gives an excellent insight into the full extent of the challenges faced in security (2001). A good discussion of security management, and of IT security in general, can be found in Smith (1993). A discussion on the various meanings of the term security policy is given by Sterne (1991). The observations on defining security policies in commercial organizations made by Martin Smith (1993) are still valid today. The management of information security risks is discussed by Alberts and Dorofee (2003).

## 1.6 EXERCISES

**Exercise 1.1**  Discuss further options for measuring the security of products and systems.

**Exercise 1.2**  On the computing system you are using, identify the software components that potentially could incorporate security mechanisms.

**Exercise 1.3**   Should a risk analysis of a computer center include flooding damages to computing equipment even when the center is in a high and dry location?

**Exercise 1.4**   Conduct a risk and threat analysis for a mobile phone service, taking into account that calls are transmitted over a radio link between mobile phone and base station, and that with international roaming a subscriber can use the service in so-called visited networks when traveling abroad. Consider the subscribers' and the network operators' viewpoints in your analysis.

**Exercise 1.5**   Bank customers can withdraw cash from automated teller machines (ATMs) using a cash card and a personal identification number (PIN). Conduct a risk and threat analysis for this application, both from the customers' and the banks' viewpoints.

**Exercise 1.6**   Consider the theft of a central server from a university department. Which assets could be damaged if this happens? Construct an attack tree for this threat.

# Chapter 2

# Foundations of Computer Security

We cannot start a meaningful exploration of computer security without defining the subject itself. We should not start such an exploration without some general guidelines that can help to bring order into the multitude of concepts and security mechanisms that you can encounter today. Thus, our first task is the search for a definition of computer security. To get away from discussing individual security systems in isolation, we will propose a set of general engineering principles that can guide the design of secure information processing systems. You are encouraged to keep looking out for these principles in the various security systems presented throughout this book.

## OBJECTIVES

- Approach a definition of computer security, introducing confidentiality, integrity and availability.
- Explain the fundamental dilemma of computer security.
- Mention some general design decisions that have to be made when constructing secure systems.
- Point out that computer security mechanisms have to rely on physical or organizational protection measures to be effective.

## 2.1  DEFINITIONS

In good academic tradition, we start our investigations by defining the object of our studies. At least, we will try to do so. Computer security deals with the techniques employed to maintain security within a computer system. We will not attempt to distinguish between computer systems, loosely speaking boxes with processors and memory in them, and IT systems, roughly closely coupled networks of computer systems. Technology keeps moving too fast. Modern computers are already a closely coupled network of components. Software that was once an application program can become part of the operating system. Web browsers are a recent high-profile example of this trend. Software running on your machine need not be stored on your machine. It can come from a local server, or maybe even from a web server somewhere on the Internet. Hence, you may use computer security and IT security as synonyms without risking too much confusion.

At first glance, we seem to have a clear map for the road ahead as 'security' appears to be a rather obvious concept. However, security is one of those unfortunate notions that seem to retreat further and further when you try to pin down their precise meaning. Much effort has gone into drafting definitions of computer security, and into later revisions of these definitions. The editors of these documents are almost inevitably either accused of being too narrow or of trespassing into areas of computer science outside of computer security proper.

### 2.1.1  Security

Security is about the protection of assets. This definition implies that you have to know your assets, and their value. This general observation is of course also true in computer security and we have already mentioned the role of risk analysis in section 1.4. Our focus turns now specifically to protection measures in computer systems. A rough classification of protection measures distinguishes between:

- prevention: take measures that prevent your assets from being damaged;
- detection: take measures that allow you to detect when an asset has been damaged, how it has been damaged and who has caused the damage;
- reaction: take measures that allow you to recover your assets or to recover from damage to your assets.

To illustrate this point, consider the protection of valuable items kept in your private home.

- Prevention: locks on the door and window bars make it more difficult for a burglar to break into your home. A wall round the property, or the moat of a medieval castle, adds another layer of protection.
- Detection: you will detect when something has been stolen if it is no longer there. A burglar alarm goes off when a break-in occurs. Closed circuit television can provide information that leads to the identification of an intruder.

- Reaction: you can call the police. You may decide to replace the stolen item. The police may retrieve a stolen item and be able to return it to you.

Examples from the physical world can help to explain principles in computer security. However, it is not always possible or advisable to draw parallels between physical security and computer security. Some terms are actually quite misleading when used in an IT context. To take an example closer to our area, consider the use of credit card numbers when placing orders over the Internet. A fraudster could use your credit card number to make purchases that will be charged to your card. How can you protect yourself?

- Prevention: use encryption when placing an order. Rely on the merchant to perform some checks on the caller before accepting a credit card order. Don't use your card number on the Internet.
- Detection: a transaction that you had not authorized appears on your credit card statement.
- Reaction: you can ask for a new card number. The cost of the fraudulent transaction has to be covered by the card holder, the merchant where the fraudster had made the purchase, or the card issuer.

In this example, the fraudster has 'stolen' your card number, but you still possess it. This is different from the case where your card has been stolen. As a consequence, in some legal frameworks, such as in the United Kingdom, the fraudster could not be charged for stealing your credit card number. New laws had to be passed to address a new threat.

To continue this line of enquiry, consider your options for protecting confidential information. Possibly, you will only detect that your secret has been compromised when it is disclosed. In some cases, the damage may then be irretrievable. Your competitors may have got hold of a product design you had spent years developing, reached the market before you, and be reaping all the profits while you are going out of business. In such a situation, prevention is your only sensible method of protecting your assets. This also explains why historically computer security has paid a lot of attention to preventing the disclosure of confidential information.

There is not always a direct trade-off between prevention and detection. Practice shows that the more you invest in prevention, the more you may have to invest in detection to be certain that prevention works.

## 2.1.2 Computer Security

In a first attempt to capture the notion of computer security, we examine how information assets can be compromised. The definition most frequently proposed covers three aspects:

- confidentiality: prevention of unauthorized disclosure of information;

- integrity: prevention of unauthorized modification of information;
- availability: prevention of unauthorized withholding of information or resources.

You can immediately start a discussion on the priority of these topics and make a case for reordering these items. Alternatively, you can argue that the list is incomplete—as lists are never complete—and add further points like *authenticity*, if you have communications in mind, or *accountability* and *nonrepudiation*, if your interest is in applications such as electronic commerce.

Even at this general level, you will find disagreement about the precise definition of some security aspects. Therefore, we will often give a reference for a definition so that the context it comes from becomes apparent. We will pick documents important to the history of computer security like the US *DoD Trusted Computer System Evaluation Criteria* (the Orange Book; US Department of Defense, 1987), the European *Information Technology Security Evaluation Criteria* (ITSEC; Commission of the European Communities, 1991), both covered in Chapter 10, and the International Standard ISO 7498-2 (International Organization for Standardization, 1989), the ISO/OSI security architecture for communications security, now superseded by ISO 10181, but still quite influential. The definitions above, for example, have been taken from ITSEC.

## 2.1.3 Confidentiality

Historically, security and secrecy were closely related. Even today, many people still feel that the main objective of computer security is to stop unauthorized users *reading* sensitive information. More generally, unauthorized users should not *learn* sensitive information. Confidentiality (privacy, secrecy) captures this aspect of computer security. The terms *privacy* and *secrecy* are sometimes used to distinguish between the protection of personal data (privacy) and the protection of data belonging to an organization (secrecy). Confidentiality is a well-defined concept and research in computer security has often concentrated on this topic, not least because it raised new issues that had no counterpart in physical security. Sometimes security and confidentiality are even used as synonyms.

Once you delve deeper into confidentiality issues you will face the question of whether you only want to hide the content of a document from unauthorized view, or also its existence. To see why one might take this extra step, consider traffic analysis in a communications system. The adversary simply looks at who is talking to whom how often, but not at the content of the messages passed. Even so, an observer may derive useful information about the relationship between the corresponding parties. In the context of traffic analysis, you might require the *unlinkability* of certain events. If you want to hide who is engaging in a certain action, you could ask for a property like *anonymity*.

In a world of paper documents, you could control access to a document simply by specifying the list of people who were allowed to read it. Somewhat surprisingly, it has also been found necessary to police write operations when enforcing confidentiality. You will read more on this topic in section 8.2.

### 2.1.4 Integrity

It is quite difficult to give a concise definition of integrity. In general, integrity is about making sure that everything is as it is supposed to be. (Sorry for this rather unhelpful definition but it reflects reality.) Within the confinements of computer security, we may settle for the definition quoted at the start of section 2.1.2 and declare that integrity deals with the prevention of unauthorized *writing*. When this interpretation is used with information-flow policies (Chapter 9), integrity is the dual of confidentiality and we can expect to use similar techniques to achieve both goals.

However, further issues like 'being authorized to do what one does' or 'following the correct procedures' have also been subsumed under the term integrity. This approach is taken in the influential paper by Clark and Wilson (1987), which declares integrity to be the property that:

> no user of the system, even if authorized, may be permitted to modify data items in such a way that assets or accounting records of the company are lost or corrupted.

If we define integrity to be the prevention of all unauthorized actions, then confidentiality becomes a part of integrity.

So far we have captured security by specifying the user actions that have to be controlled. From a systematic point of view, you are better off by concentrating on the *state* of the system when defining integrity. The Orange Book (US Department of Defense, 1985) definition of integrity is precisely of this nature.

> **Data Integrity** The state that exists when computerized data is the same as that in the source documents and has not been exposed to accidental or malicious alteration or destruction.

Here, integrity is a synonym for *external consistency*. The data stored in a computer system should correctly reflect some reality outside the computer system. This is of course highly desirable, but it is impossible to guarantee this property merely by mechanisms internal to the computer system.

To add to the confusion, other areas of information security have their own notions of integrity. For example, in communications security, integrity refers to the *detection* and *correction* of modification, insertion, deletion or replay of transmitted data. This includes both *intentional* manipulations and random transmission errors. You could view intentional modification as a special case of unauthorized modification, when nobody is authorized to modify. However, there is not much to gain from taking such a position because the presence, or absence, of an authorization structure has an impact on the nature of the problem that has to be solved, and on the respective security mechanisms.

Integrity is often a prerequisite for other security properties. For example, an attacker could try to circumvent confidentiality controls by modifying the operating system or an access control table referenced by the operating system. Hence, we have to protect the integrity of the operating system or the integrity of access control data structures to achieve confidentiality.

Finally, we should mention that there exist even more general definitions of integrity, which treat security and availability as parts of integrity.

## 2.1.5 Availability

We take the definition given in ISO 7498-2 (International Organization for Standardization, 1989).

> **Availability**    The property of being accessible and useable upon demand by an authorized entity.

Availability is very much a concern beyond the traditional boundaries of computer security. Engineering techniques used to improve availability often come from other areas like fault-tolerant computing. In the context of security, we want to ensure that a malicious attacker cannot prevent legitimate users from having reasonable access to their systems. That is, we want to prevent *denial of service*. Again, we refer to ISO 7498-2 for a definition.

> **Denial of Service**    The prevention of authorized access to resources or the delaying of time-critical operations.

There have now been a number of incidents of *flooding* attacks on the Internet where an attacker effectively disables a server by overwhelming it with connection requests. Figure 2.1 shows one of the first denial-of-service attacks (*smurf*). The attacker sends an ICMP echo request to the broadcast address of some network with a spoofed sender address (the victim's address). The echo request will be distributed to all nodes in that network. Each node will reply back to the spoofed sender address, flooding the victim with reply packets. The amplification provided by the broadcast address works to the attacker's advantage.

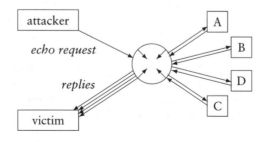

○   **Figure 2.1: A Denial-of-service Attack (Smurf)**

In many situations, availability may be the most important aspect of computer security, but there is a distinct lack of security mechanisms for handling this problem. As a matter of fact, security mechanisms that are too restrictive or too expensive can themselves lead to denial of service. Designers of security protocols now often try to avoid imbalances in workload that would allow a malicious party to overload its correspondent at little cost to itself.

## 2.1.6 Accountability

We have now covered the three traditional areas of computer security. Looking back, you can see that they all deal with different aspects of access control and put their emphasis on the *prevention* of unwelcome events. We have to accept the fact that we will hardly ever be able to prevent all improper actions. First, we may find that authorized actions can lead to a security violation. Second, we may find a flaw in our security system that allows an attacker to find a way past our controls. Therefore, you may add a new security requirement to your list: users should be held responsible for their actions. This requirement is particularly important in the emerging world of electronic commerce but you can already find it in such historic documents as the Orange Book (US Department of Defense, 1985).

> **Accountability**  Audit information must be selectively kept and protected so that actions affecting security can be traced to the responsible party.

To be able to do so, the system has to *identify* and *authenticate* users. It has to keep an *audit trail* of security-relevant events. If a security violation has occurred, information from the audit trail may help to identify the perpetrator and the steps that were taken to compromise the system.

## 2.1.7 Nonrepudiation

Nonrepudiation services provide *unforgeable evidence* that a specific action occurred. This definition is meaningful when analyzing the security services that cryptographic mechanisms can provide. Digital signatures (section 11.4) provide nonrepudiation. They are evidence that can be verified by a third party. Typical nonrepudiation services in communications security are *nonrepudiation of origin* providing evidence about the sender of a document, and *nonrepudiation of delivery*, providing evidence about the fact that a message was delivered to a specific recipient.

Discussions about nonrepudiation are prone to suffering from imprecise language. Should one talk about nonrepudiation of receipt when mail has been delivered to a mailbox? Even more fundamental misunderstandings about nonrepudiation prevail. It is sometimes said that nonrepudiation services provide 'irrefutable evidence' about some event, and that such evidence will be 'accepted by any court in the world'. It is naïve to assume that mathematical evidence can make it impossible for a person to deny involvement in a disputed event. The concept of irrefutable evidence is alien to most legal systems. We will briefly return to this topic in section 12.5.6.

## 2.1.8 Reliability

In a discussion of security, there are several reasons for mentioning other areas of computing like *reliability*, relating to (accidental) failures, and *safety*, relating to the impact of system failures on their environment, which also deal with situations where a system has to perform properly in adverse conditions. The first is an overlap in terminology. Depending on your preferred point of view, security is an aspect of reliability or vice versa. IFIP WG 10.4 has tried to escape from this dilemma by introducing *dependability* as the unifying concept and treating security, reliability, integrity and availability as aspects of dependability (Laprie, 1992).

> **Dependability**  The property of a computer system such that reliance can justifiably be placed on the service it delivers. The **service** delivered by a system is its behavior *as it is perceived* by its user(s); a **user** is another system (physical, human) which *interacts* with the former.

The second reason is that there are applications that have to address more than one issue at the same time. Consider, for example, a computer system in a safety-critical application. On occasions, the users of this system have to react to an emergency. Security controls should prevent intruders from causing accidents maliciously and may attempt to identify an intrusion by looking for unfamiliar patterns of behavior. A reaction to an emergency may also appear unfamiliar–hopefully emergencies are rare events–so intrusion detection may misread legitimate actions in a critical situation as an attack and potentially compound the problem by triggering security mechanisms that interfere with the actions of the emergency team. In general, you must not address security independently of the other requirements of the application you want to secure.

Finally, similar engineering methods are used in both areas. For example, standards for evaluating security software and for evaluating safety-critical software have many parallels and some experts expect that eventually there will be only a single standard.

## 2.1.9 Our Definition

In this book, we will adopt the following operational definition of security.

> **Computer Security**  Deals with the *prevention* and *detection* of *unauthorized* actions by users of a computer system.

With this definition, proper authorization and access control are essential to computer security. Proper authorization assumes the existence of a *security policy*, as explained in section 1.3.1. We could include the *correction* of the effects of improper actions in the definition of security but this aspect will only play a minor role in our further discussions.

The definition given describes what we do in computer security. When looking at the root causes for why we do it, we might adopt a definition like:

**Computer Security**    Concerned with the measures we can take to deal with *intentional* actions by parties behaving in some unwelcome fashion.

This definition does not mention unauthorized actions. It does not refer to attacks either but draws the boundary wider to include issues like spam mail. Sending an unsolicited email is not necessarily an attack. (If you are looking for a job, you might send your CV to companies that might find your skills useful, even if no vacancies are advertised.) Similarly, receiving an unsolicited mail need not be an unwelcome event. This will change according to the number and nature of the emails a person receives on a daily basis. When this misuse of email becomes too much of a nuisance, the fight against spam becomes a security issue.

### Lesson

The main conclusions of this introductory discussion on terminology are as follows.

1. There is no single definition of security.

2. When reading a document, be careful not to confuse your own notion of security with that used in the document.

3. A lot of time is being spent (and wasted) in trying to define unambiguous notations for security.

## 2.2 THE FUNDAMENTAL DILEMMA OF COMPUTER SECURITY

As the number of users relying on computer security has grown from a few organizations dealing with classified data to everyone connected to the Internet, the requirements on computer security have changed radically. Not least, this change has given rise to a fundamental dilemma.

*Security-unaware* users have specific security requirements but usually no security expertise.

This dilemma is clearly visible in current strategies for *security evaluation*. Informally, security evaluation checks whether a product delivers an advertised security service. Thus, the *function* of the security system has to be stated and we need *assurance* that the security controls will be effective and withstand penetration attempts.

The Orange Book (US Department of Defense, 1985) was the first guideline for evaluating computer security products (in operating systems) and has been highly influential in the development of computer security. Functionality and assurance are tied together into predefined classes. Users can only choose from this set of classes. However, the Orange Book is quite rigid and has not been overly successful in addressing the evaluation of computer networks or database management systems. Hence, there was a cry for a more flexible set of criteria.

ITSEC answered this cry. Functionality and assurance were separated to allow the specification of very specific *Targets of Evaluation (TOEs)*. The security-unaware user is now asked to make sense of specific TOEs and to compare products evaluated against different TOEs.

The fundamental dilemma of computer security appears in many disguises. Its resolution is currently the most pressing challenge in computer security. Not surprisingly, there are no easy answers.

Compared to this fundamental dilemma, the conflict between security and ease-of-use is a straightforward engineering trade-off. Security's impact on performance is manifold.

- Security mechanisms need additional computational resources. This cost can be quantified easily.

- Security interferes with the working patterns users are accustomed to. Clumsy or inappropriate security restrictions lead to loss of productivity.

- Effort has to be spent on managing security. Buyers of security systems therefore often opt for the product that has the best management features (which is often the one with the best graphical user interface).

## 2.3 DATA VS INFORMATION

Computer security is about controlling access to *information* and *resources*. However, controlling access to information can sometimes be quite difficult and is therefore often replaced by the more straightforward goal of controlling access to *data*. The distinction between data and information is subtle but it is also the root of some of the more difficult problems in security.

Data represents information. Information is the (subjective) interpretation of data.

> **Data**   Physical phenomena chosen by convention to represent certain aspects of our conceptual and real world. The meanings we assign to data are called information. Data is used to transmit and store information and to derive new information by manipulating the data according to formal rules (Brinch Hansen, 1973).

When there is a close link between information and the corresponding data, the two concepts may give very similar results. However, this is not always the case. It may be possible to transmit information over a *covert channel* (section 8.2.5). There, the data comprises 'yes' and 'no' replies to access requests while the information received comprises the contents of a sensitive file. Another example is the problem of *inference* in statistical databases (section 17.4). For a brief look at this issue, consider an Inland Revenue database of tax returns. This database is not only used by tax inspectors, who have access to individual records, but also by Treasury officials for general planning purposes. They must therefore have access to statistical summaries of tax returns but have no business in reading individual records. Assume that the database management system will allow statistical queries only on sufficiently large data-sets to protect individual records. It would still be possible to combine the results from two queries over large datasets which differ only by a single record. Thus, even without accessing the data directly, information about an individual record can be derived.

## 2.4 PRINCIPLES OF COMPUTER SECURITY

You are likely to come across statements claiming that computer security is a very complex issue, 'like rocket science'. Don't let such opinions frighten you off. If you are given the chance to implement the security features of a computer system in a systematic way, a disciplined approach to software (systems) development and a good understanding of a few essential security principles will carry you a long way. However, you certainly will struggle if you add on security to an already complex system as an afterthought, when you are constrained by design decisions that have been taken without any consideration of their security implications. Unfortunately, too often this is the case.

We will now propose a few fundamental design parameters of computer security. These design decisions provide the framework for structuring the presentations in this book. Figure 2.2 illustrates the main dimensions in the design space for computer security. The horizontal axis represents the focus of the security policy (section 2.4.1). The vertical axis represents the layer of the computer system where a protection mechanism is implemented (section 2.4.2).

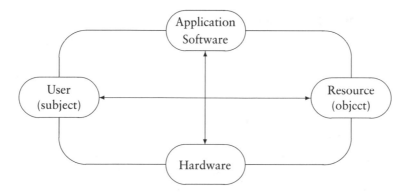

Figure 2.2:  The Dimensions of Computer Security

### 2.4.1 Focus of Control

Let us rephrase the definitions of integrity given in section 2.1.4. We could say that integrity has to do with compliance with a given set of rules. We can have rules on:

- the format and content of data items; for example, a rule could state that the balance fields in an accounts database have to contain an integer; such integrity rules define internal consistency properties and do not depend on the user accessing the data item or on the operation performed on the data item;
- the operations that may be performed on a data item; for example, a rule could state that only the operations 'open account', 'check balance', 'withdraw' and 'deposit' have access to the balance fields in an accounts database and that only bank clerks are allowed to execute 'open account'; such rules may depend on the user and on the data item;
- the users who are allowed to access a data item; for example, a rule could state that only the account holder and bank clerks have access to balance fields in an accounts database.

We have just made an important general observation and arrived at our first design decision.

> **1st Design Decision**    In a given application, should the protection mechanisms in a computer system focus on:
> - data
> - operations
> - or users?

It is a fundamental design decision which of these options to take when applying security controls. Operating systems have traditionally focused on protecting data (resources). In modern applications, it is often more relevant to control the users' actions.

### 2.4.2 The Man–Machine Scale

Figure 2.3 presents a simple layered model of a computer system. This model is only intended for general guidance. You should not expect to find all the layers in every computer system you analyze, nor should you be surprised to find systems where you can identify more than the five layers of our model.

- Users run *application programs* that have been tailored to meet quite specific application requirements.
- The application programs may make use of the *services* provided by a general purpose software package like a database management system (DBMS) or an object reference broker (ORB).
- The services run on top of the *operating system*, which performs file and memory management and controls access to resources like printers and I/O devices.

| applications |
|:---:|
| services |
| operating system |
| OS kernel |
| hardware |

○ **Figure 2.3: Layers of an IT System**

- The operating system may have a *kernel* (microkernel, hypervisor) that mediates every access to the processor and to memory.
- The *hardware*, i.e. processors and memory, physically stores and manipulates the data held in the computer system.

Security controls can sensibly be placed in any of these layers. We have now explained the dimensions of our second fundamental security principle.

**2nd Design Decision**   In which layer of the computer system should a security mechanism be placed?

When you investigate fielded security products, you will observe security mechanisms at every layer of this model, from hardware to application software. It is the task of the designer to find the right layer for each mechanism, and to find the right mechanisms for each layer.

Take a second look at our new design decision, visualizing the security mechanisms of a computer system as concentric protection rings, with hardware mechanisms in the center and application mechanisms at the outside (Figure 2.4). Mechanisms towards the center tend to be more generic, more computer oriented and more concerned with controlling access to data. Mechanisms at the outside are more likely to address individual user requirements. Combining our first two design decisions, we will refer to the *man–machine*

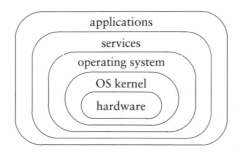

○ **Figure 2.4: The Onion Model of Protection Mechanisms**

Figure 2.5: The Man–machine Scale for Access Control Mechanisms

*scale* for placing security mechanisms (Figure 2.5). This scale is related to the distinction between data (machine oriented) and information (man oriented).

### 2.4.3 Complexity vs Assurance

Frequently, the location of a security mechanism on the man–machine scale is closely related to its complexity. To the right of the scale, you find simple generic mechanisms while applications often clamor for *feature-rich* security functions. Hence, there is yet another decision you have to take.

> 3rd **Design Decision**   Do you prefer simplicity–and higher assurance–to a feature-rich security environment?

This decision is linked to the fundamental dilemma of computer security. A simple generic mechanism may well be unable to enforce specific protection requirements, but to choose the right options in a feature-rich security environment users have to be security experts. Security-unaware users are left in a no-win situation.

To achieve a high degree of assurance, the security system has to be examined in close detail and as exhaustively as possible. Hence, there is an obvious trade-off between complexity and assurance. The higher an assurance level you aim for, the simpler your system ought to be. As an immediate consequence, you can observe that:

> feature-reach security systems and high assurance do not match easily.

It will not come as a surprise that high assurance requires adherence to systematic design practices. As a matter of fact, computer security is one of the areas that adopted formal methods early on as a tool in its quest for the highest assurance levels.

### 2.4.4 Centralized or Decentralized Controls

Within the domain of a security policy, the same controls should be enforced. If there is a single central entity in charge of security, then it is easy to achieve uniformity but this central entity may become a performance bottleneck. Conversely, a distributed solution may be more efficient but we have to take added care to guarantee that the different components enforce the policy consistently.

**4th Design Decision**    Should the tasks of defining and enforcing security be given to a central entity or should they be left to individual components in a system?

This question arises naturally in distributed systems security and you will see examples of both alternatives. However, this question is also meaningful in the context of mainframe systems as demonstrated by the mandatory and discretionary security policies of the Bell–LaPadula model covered in section 8.2.

## 2.5 THE LAYER BELOW

So far, we have briefly touched on assurance but have predominantly explored options for expressing the most appropriate security policies. It is now time to think about attackers trying to bypass our protection mechanisms. Every protection mechanism defines a *security perimeter (boundary)*. The parts of the system that can malfunction without compromising the protection mechanism lie outside this perimeter. The parts of the system that can be used to disable the protection mechanism lie within this perimeter. This observation leads to an immediate and important extension of the second design decision proposed in section 2.4.2.

**5th Design Decision**    How can you prevent an attacker getting access to a layer below the protection mechanism?

An attacker with access to the 'layer below' is in a position to subvert protection mechanisms further up. For example, if you gain systems privileges in the operating system, you are usually able to change programs or files containing the control data for security mechanisms in the services and applications layers. If you have direct access to the physical memory devices so that you can manipulate the raw data, the logical access controls of the operating system have been bypassed. Below, we give six further examples to illustrate this point. The fact that security mechanisms have a soft underbelly and are vulnerable to attacks from lower layers should be a reason for concern, but not for despair. When you reach the stage where you cannot apply computer security mechanisms or do not want to do so, you can still put in place physical or organizational security measures (Figure 2.6).

### Recovery Tools

If the logical organization of the memory is destroyed due to some physical memory fault, it is no longer possible to access files even if their physical representation is still intact. Recovery tools, like Norton Utilities, can help to restore the data by reading the (physical) memory directly and then restoring the file structure. Such a tool can, of course, be used to circumvent logical access control as it does not care for the logical memory structure.

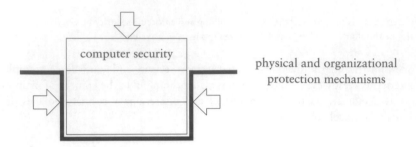

Figure 2.6: **Physical and Organizational Security Measures Controlling Access to the Layers Below**

### Unix Devices

Unix treats I/O devices and physical memory devices like files. The same access control mechanisms can therefore be applied to these devices as to files. If access permissions are defined badly, e.g. if read access is given to a disk which contains read-protected files, then an attacker can read the disk contents and reconstruct the files. You can find more information on Unix security in Chapter 6.

### Object Reuse (Release of Memory)

A single-processor multiprogramming system may execute several processes at the same time but only one process can 'own' the processor at any point in time. Whenever the operating system deactivates the running process to activate the next, a *context switch* is performed. All data necessary for the later continuation of the execution is saved and memory is allocated for the new process. *Storage residues* are data left behind in the memory area allocated to the new process. If the new process could read such storage residues, the logical separation between processes that the operating system should provide has been breached. To avoid this problem, all memory locations that are released could be overwritten with a fixed pattern or the new process could be granted read access only to locations it has already written to.

### Buffer Overruns

In a buffer overrun attack, a value is assigned to a variable that is too large for the memory buffer allocated to that variable, so that memory allocated to other variables is overwritten. This method for modifying variables that should be logically inaccessible is further explained in section 14.4.1.

### Backup

A conscientious system manager will perform regular backups. Whoever can lay their hands on the backup tape has access to all the data on the tape and logical access control is of no help. Thus, backup tapes have to be locked away safely to protect the data.

## Core Dumps

When a system crashes, it creates a *core dump* of its internal state so that the reasons for the crash can be more easily identified. If the internal state contains sensitive information, like cryptographic keys, and if core dumps are stored in files that can be read by anyone, an attacker could intentionally crash a multiuser system and look in the core dump for data belonging to other users.

## 2.6 FURTHER READING

To get a second opinion on computer security, there are a number of books you could consult. A very readable introduction to the subject is provided by Russel and Gangemi Sr. (1991). Amoroso (1994) covers the theoretical elements of computer security. A discussion of the technicalities of designing secure operating systems from the 1980s can be found in Gasser (1988) (out of print but available on the Web). Another comprehensive treatment of information security, with many valuable pointers for further reading, is presented by Pfleeger and Lawrence Pfleeger (2003).

Books on the security features of specific operating systems tend to be rather expensive, concentrate on issues relevant to someone managing such a system, like the menus to call up and the options to choose from, but do not provide too much further insight into the way security is implemented. Notable exceptions to this rule are Park's book on AS/400 (1995), which goes into technical details of the operating system and shows how code at lower layers can compromise the security provided by the operating system, and Brown's book on Windows security (2000). Good books on Unix security are by Curry (1992), Ferbrache and Shearer (1992) and Garfinkel, Spafford and Schwartz (2003). For more specific topics, you will find further pointers to sources at the end of the relevant chapters.

To appreciate the current state of an area of research, you should also be aware of its history. Two influential reports that triggered much research in computer security are by Ware (1979) and Anderson (1972). If you cannot get hold of these reports, MacKenzie and Pottinger (1997) provide a summary of the early history of computer security.

## 2.7 EXERCISES

**Exercise 2.1** Conduct a search for definitions of security concepts. Good starting points are the web sites of the US TCSEC program or the UK ITSEC Scheme.

- http://www.radium.ncsc.mil/tpep/process/faq.html
- http://www.itsec.gov.uk

Many of the major IT companies also have pages on security on their web sites.

**Exercise 2.2** Examine the relationship between unlinkability and anonymity.

**Exercise 2.3** Write a short essay discussing the difference between data and information and find your own examples to demonstrate that controlling access to data does not necessarily imply controlling access to information.

**Exercise 2.4** Medical records pose particular security problems. Assume that your medical records can be accessed on-line. On the one hand, this information is sensitive and should be protected from disclosure. On the other hand, in an emergency it is highly desirable that whoever treats you has access to your records. How would you use prevention, detection and recovery to secure your records?

**Exercise 2.5** Draft a security policy for protecting examination results kept on a computer system. Your policy should at least consider the access requirements of students, lecturers and administrators.

**Exercise 2.6** On the computing system you are using, identify the software components that could potentially incorporate security mechanisms.

**Exercise 2.7** Discuss: is a good graphical user interface an appropriate criterion for purchasing a security product?

**Exercise 2.8** Look for further examples where a security mechanism in one layer can be bypassed by an attacker who has access to a layer below.

**Exercise 2.9** Identify the security perimeters that may be applicable when analyzing personal computer (PC) security. In your analysis, consider when it is appropriate to assume that the room the PC is placed in, the PC itself or some security module within the PC, lies within the security perimeter.

# Chapter

# 3

# Identification and Authentication

In a secure system you might want to track the identities of the users requesting its services. Authentication is the process of verifying a user's identity. There exist two reasons for authenticating a user.

- The user identity is a parameter in access control decisions.
- The user identity is recorded when logging security-relevant events in an audit trail.

Chapter 15 will explain why it is not always necessary or desirable to base access control on user identities. There is a much stronger case for using identities in audit logs. This chapter deals with identification and authentication of users as it is standard in current operating systems. Authentication in distributed systems is the topic of Chapter 12.

## OBJECTIVES

- Revisit a reasonably familiar mechanism to learn some general lessons.
- Get an introduction to password protection.
- Appreciate that security mechanisms rely on administrative measures to be effective.
- Understand the dangers when using abstractions in computer security.

## 3.1 USERNAME AND PASSWORD

Literally, you make your first contact with computer security when you log on to a computer and are asked to enter your *username* and *password*. The first step is called *identification*. You announce who you are. The second step is called *authentication*. You prove that you are who you claim to be. To distinguish this use of the word 'authentication' from other interpretations, we can specifically refer to:

> **Entity Authentication**    The process of verifying a claimed identity.

Once you have entered username and password, the computer will compare your input against the entries stored in a password file. Login will succeed if you enter a valid username and the corresponding password. If username or password is incorrect, login fails. Usually, the login screen will then be displayed again and you can start your next attempt. Some systems keep a count of failed login attempts and prevent or delay further attempts when a certain threshold has been reached. To reduce the chance of an attacker using an unattended machine where another user is logged on, authentication may be demanded not only at the start of a session but also at certain intervals during the session (*repeated authentication*). You may also choose to *lock* the screen or to close a session automatically if a machine is idle for too long.

### Lesson

Repeated authentication addresses a familiar problem in computer security, known as TOCTTOU (time of check to time of use). The operating system *checks* a user's identity at the start of a session but *uses* the identity to make access control decisions later on during the session.

Once upon a time, you would have entered username and password on a screen containing a friendly welcome message and some information on the system you were about to access. Today, cautious systems managers will not make too much information available to the outside world and replace the welcome message with a warning for unauthorized persons to stay out. For example, Windows offers the option of displaying a *legal notice* dialog box. Users have to acknowledge this warning message before logon can proceed.

Today, most computer systems use identification and authentication through username and password as their first line of defense. For most users, this mechanism has become an integral part of the routine of starting a session on their computer. We have thus a mechanism that is widely accepted and not too difficult to implement. On the other hand, managing password security can be quite expensive and obtaining a valid password is a common way of gaining unauthorized access to a computer system. Let us therefore examine the actual security of passwords when used as an authentication mechanism.

We will look at the issues of:

- forgotten passwords
- password guessing
- password spoofing
- compromise of the password file.

Do not forget that the user also has an important role to play in password protection. Authentication is compromised when you reveal your password, either by telling it to someone or by writing it down and leaving it in a place where other people can find it. To alert users about password compromise or about recently attempted attacks, the system could display, after successful login, the time of the last login and the number of failed login attempts since then. Of course, we have been assuming all along that a password has been set for the user account. If the system administrator or user forgets to set the password, an attacker is spared the trouble of finding it.

## 3.2 MANAGING PASSWORDS

Passwords are meant to be secrets shared between the user and the system authenticating the user. So, how do you bootstrap a system so that the password ends up in the right places, but nowhere else? In an enterprise, users could be asked to come to an office and collect their password personally. If this is not feasible, the password could be conveyed by mail, email or phone, or entered by the user on a web page. You now have to consider who might intercept the message and, most importantly, who might actually pick it up. For example, a letter containing the password for an on-line bank account might be stolen or an impersonator may phone in asking for another user's password. How do you authenticate a remote user when the user has not got a password yet? To address these issues:

- do not give the password to the caller but call back an authorized phone number from your files, e.g. from an internal company address book;
- call back someone else, e.g. the caller's manager or local security officer;
- send passwords that are valid only for a single login request so that the user has to change immediately to a password not known by the sender;
- send mail by courier with personal delivery;
- request confirmation on a different channel to activate the user account, e.g. enter the password on a web page and send confirmation by SMS (phone).

When setting up a new user account you might tolerate some delay in getting your password. However, when you are in the middle of an important task and realize that you have forgotten your password you need an instant remedy. The procedures for resetting a password are pretty much the same as mentioned above, but now an organization has to staff a hot desk at all times requests may come in. In global organizations such a hot desk has to be available round the clock. Proper security training has to be given to personnel at the hot desk. Thus, password support can become a major cost factor.

**Lesson**

Security mechanisms may fail to give access to legitimate users. Your overall security solution should be able to handle such situations efficiently.

## 3.3 CHOOSING PASSWORDS

Password choice is a critical security issue. While you cannot eliminate the risk of an attacker guessing a valid password, you can try to keep the probability of such an event as low as possible. To see how, you have to be aware of two basic guessing strategies an attacker may follow:

- Exhaustive search (brute force): try all possible combinations of valid symbols, up to a certain length.

- Intelligent search: search through a restricted name space, e.g. try passwords that are somehow associated with a user like name, names of friends and relatives, car brand, car registration number, phone number etc., or try passwords that are generally popular. A typical example for the second approach is a *dictionary attack* trying all passwords from an online dictionary.

So, what are your defenses?

- Change default passwords: when systems are delivered, they often come with default accounts like 'system' with default passwords like 'manager'. This helps the field engineer to install the system, but if the password is left unchanged the attacker has an easy job getting into the system. In the example just given, the attacker even gets access to a particularly privileged account.

- Password length: to thwart exhaustive search, a minimal password length should be prescribed. Unfortunately, Unix systems traditionally have a *maximal* password length, set to eight characters only.

- Password format: mix upper- and lower-case symbols and include numerical and other nonalphabetical symbols in your password. The size of the password space is at least $|A|^n$ where $n$ is the minimal password length and $|A|$ is the size of the character set used for constructing passwords.

- Avoid obvious passwords: don't be surprised to find out that attackers are equipped with lists of popular passwords and be aware that dictionary attacks have extended the scope of 'obvious' quite substantially. Today, you can find an online dictionary for almost every language.

How can the system further help to improve password security?

- Password checkers: as a system manager, you can use tools that check passwords against some dictionary of 'weak' passwords and prevent users from choosing such passwords. This imitates – and preempts – dictionary attacks against the system.

- Password generation: some operating systems include password generators producing random but pronounceable passwords. Users are not allowed to pick their own password but have to adopt a password proposed by the system.

- Password aging: in many systems, expiry dates for passwords can be set, forcing users to change passwords at regular intervals. There may be additional mechanisms to prevent users from choosing previous passwords, e.g. a list of the last 10 passwords used. Of course, determined users will still be able to revert to their favorite password by making a sufficient number of changes until their old password is accepted again.

- Limit login attempts: the system can monitor unsuccessful login attempts and react by locking the user account completely or at least for a certain period of time to prevent or discourage further attempts. The time the account is locked could be increased in proportion to the number of failed attempts.

Given what has just been said, it would seem that we achieve the highest security if users have to use long passwords, mixing upper- and lower-case characters and numerical symbols, probably generated for them by the system, and changed repeatedly. Will this approach really work? Will we get the desired security in practice?

Users are unlikely to memorize long and complicated passwords. Instead, such passwords will be written down on a piece of paper that is kept close to the computer, where it is most useful both for the legitimate user and a potential intruder. It is a standard task of security managers to look out for passwords on notes posted on computer terminals. Similar considerations apply when passwords are changed very frequently. Users who find it difficult to comply with the rigor of such a password management scheme may be tempted to use passwords which can be more easily memorized, and therefore more easily guessed. They may revert quickly to their favorite password or make simple and predictable changes to this password. If you have to change the password every month, just add the month (two digits, from 01 to 12, or three characters from JAN to DEC, the choice is yours) to your chosen password and you have passwords that you can remember. Of course, an attacker who has found one of those passwords gets a good idea what to expect next.

Then you have to account for the fact that even users who take all security precautions very seriously, avoid weak passwords that can be guessed easily and do not write passwords down will inevitably now and then forget their password. This will disrupt the user's work. To obtain a new password, the user may contact a system operator. This will disrupt the system operator's work and open the way for a new attack. Bullying an operator into releasing a password is a tried and tested method of breaking into a system. Successful attacks are more often based on *social engineering* than on technical ingenuity (Mitnick and Simon, 2002).

Experience shows that people are best at memorizing passwords they use regularly. Hence, passwords work reasonably well in situations where they are entered quite frequently, but not so with systems that are used only occasionally. When changing your password, it is good advice to type it immediately several times. It is equally good advice not to change passwords before weekends or holidays.

### Lesson

You must not look at security mechanisms in isolation. Putting too much emphasis on one security mechanism may actually weaken the system, not least because users will find ways of circumventing security if they cannot do their job properly when the security mechanisms are inappropriate. With passwords, you have observed a trade-off between the complexity of passwords and the faculties of human memory.

## 3.4 SPOOFING ATTACKS

Identification and authentication through username and password provide *unilateral authentication*. A user enters a password and the computer verifies the user's identity. But does the user know who has received this password? So far, the answer is no. The user has no guarantees about the identity of the party at the other end of the line.

This is a real problem, leading to a second kind of password compromise. In a *spoofing attack*, the attacker, who may be a legitimate user, runs a program that presents a fake login screen on some terminal/workstation. An unsuspecting user comes to this terminal and tries to log in. The victim is led through what appears to be the normal login menu and is asked for username and password. These are then stored by the attacker. Execution could then be handed over to the user, or login is aborted with a (fake) error message and the spoofing program terminates. Control is returned to the operating system which now prompts the user with a genuine login request. The user tries again, succeeds on this second attempt and may remain completely unaware of the fact that the password has been compromised.

What can be done about such a spoofing attack?

- Displaying the number of failed logins may indicate to the user that such an attack has happened. If your first login fails but you are told at your second attempt that there has been no unsuccessful login attempt since your last session, you should become suspicious.

- Trusted path: guarantee that the user communicates with the operating system and not with a spoofing program. For example, Windows has a *secure attention sequence* CTRL+ALT+DEL which invokes the Windows operating system logon screen. You should press such a secure attention key when starting a session, even when the logon screen is already displayed.

- Mutual authentication: if users require stronger guarantees about the identity of the system they are communicating with, e.g. in a distributed system, the system could be required to authenticate itself to the user.

### 3.4.1 Password Caching

Beyond spoofing attacks, an intruder may have other ways of 'finding' a password. Our description of login has been quite abstract. The password travels directly from the user to the password checking routine. In reality, it will be held temporarily in intermediate storage locations like buffers, caches or even a web page. The management of these storage locations is normally beyond the control of the user and a password may be kept longer than the user has bargained for.

This issue is illustrated nicely by a problem encountered by the developers of an early web-based on-line banking service (Arceneaux, 1996). Web browsers cache information that makes it possible for users to scroll back to pages they have recently visited. To use the on-line banking service, you enter your password on a web page. You conduct your business, close the banking application, but do not terminate the browser session. The next user on the terminal can scroll back to the page with your password and log on as you. As a precaution, it is therefore, recommended to exit the browser after the banking transaction. Note that users are now asked to participate in a memory management activity they would otherwise not be involved in. This is another instance of *object reuse* (section 2.5).

**Lesson**

Abstraction is useful and dangerous at the same time. It is useful to discuss password security in abstract terms. You can examine policies on password formats or aging without knowing how passwords are processed in your IT system. It is dangerous to discuss password security only at such an abstract level though. Implementation flaws can compromise the best security policies.

## 3.5 PROTECTING THE PASSWORD FILE

To verify a user's identity, the system compares the password entered by the user against a value stored in the *password file*. Such a password file is of course an extremely attractive target for an attacker. Disclosure of the unencrypted contents of a password file or modification of its contents constitute a third possibility for password compromise. Even the disclosure of encrypted passwords may be a concern. Then dictionary attacks could be conducted off-line and protection measures like limiting the number of unsuccessful login attempts would not come into play. To protect the password file, we have the options of:

- cryptographic protection;
- access control enforced by the operating system;
- a combination of cryptographic protection and access control, possibly with further enhancements to slow down dictionary attacks.

For cryptographic protection, we do not even need an encryption algorithm. A one-way function will do the job. For now, the following working definition will do.

> **One-way Function**   A function that is relatively easy to compute but significantly harder to undo or reverse. That is, given $x$ it is easy to compute $f(x)$, but given $f(x)$ it is hard to compute $x$.

Chapter 11 has more details on one-way functions. One-way functions have been used to protect stored passwords for quite some time (Wilkes, 1968, pp. 91ff.). Instead of the password $x$, the value $f(x)$ is stored in the password file. When a user logs in and enters a password, say $x'$, the system applies the one-way function $f$ and then compares $f(x')$ with the expected value $f(x)$. If the values match, the user has been successfully authenticated. If $f$ is a proper one-way function, it is not feasible to reconstruct a password $x$ from $f(x)$. In the following, we will refer to 'encrypted' passwords even if we are actually applying a one-way function to the passwords.

The password file can't be left world-readable because of off-line dictionary attacks. In a dictionary attack, the attacker 'encrypts' all words in a dictionary and compares the results against the encrypted entries in the password file. If a match is found, the attacker knows that user's password. One-way functions can be chosen to slow down dictionary attacks. This consideration has governed the choice of the one-way function crypt(3) used in Unix systems, which repeats a slightly modified DES algorithm 25 times, using the all-zero block as start value and the password as key (Morris and Thompson, 1979). Of course, there is a slight performance penalty for legitimate users at login, but if you optimize the one-way function for speed you also improve the performance of dictionary attacks.

Access control mechanisms in the operating system restrict access to files and other resources to users holding the appropriate privileges. Only privileged users may have write access to the password file. Otherwise, an attacker could get access to the data of other users simply by changing their passwords, even if they are protected by cryptographic means. If read access is restricted to privileged users, then passwords in theory could be stored unencrypted. If the password file contains information that is also required by unprivileged users, then the password file must contain encrypted passwords. However, such a file can still be used in dictionary attacks. A typical example is /etc/passwd in Unix. Therefore, many versions of Unix store enciphered passwords in a file that is not publicly accessible. Such files are called *shadow password files*.

A weak form of read protection is provided by proprietary storage formats. For example, Windows NT did store encrypted passwords in a proprietary binary format. An unsophisticated user will be defeated but a determined attacker will obtain or deduce the information necessary to be able to detect the location of security relevant data. On its own, 'security by obscurity' is not very strong but it can add to other mechanisms like password encryption.

There is, however, the danger that a successful breach of such a peripheral defense may be blown out of all proportion. In early 1997, there was a flurry of claims that Windows NT password security had been broken. Sounds really serious, doesn't it? The fact behind these stories was the announcement of a program that converted encrypted passwords from binary format to a more readable presentation. Not a big deal after all the excitement.

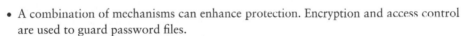 If you are worried about dictionary attacks but cannot hide the password file, you may consider *password salting*. When a password is encrypted for storage, additional information, the *salt*, is appended to the password before encryption. The salt is then stored with the encrypted password. If two users have the same password, they will therefore have different entries in the file of encrypted passwords. Salting slows down dictionary attacks as it is no longer possible to search for the passwords of several users simultaneously.

### Lesson

You have seen three security design principles.

- A combination of mechanisms can enhance protection. Encryption and access control are used to guard password files.
- Security by obscurity only protects against casual intruders. Do not place much trust in this strategy.
- If you can, separate security-relevant data from data that should be openly available. In Unix, /etc/passwd contains both types of data. Shadow password files achieve the desired separation.

## 3.6 SINGLE SIGN-ON

Passwords have separated friend from foe for centuries. In an IT environment, they control access to computers, networks, programs, files etc. As a user, you would not find it particularly convenient if you had to enter passwords over and over again when navigating through cyberspace to a bit of information. Sitting at your workstation and needing some information from a database held on a server on the network, would you be pleased if you had to:

- enter a first password at the workstation;
- enter a second password to get out onto the network;
- enter a third password to access the server;
- enter a fourth password to access the database management system;
- enter a fifth password to open a table in the database?

Forget about the problem of potentially having to remember five different passwords and picking the right one at each occasion. Having to re-enter the same password five times is bad enough.

A *single sign-on service* solves this problem. You enter your password once. The system stores this password and whenever you have to authenticate yourself again, the system will take the password and do the job for you. Such a single sign-on service adds to your convenience but it also raises new security concerns. How do you protect the stored password? Some of the cryptographic techniques will no longer work because the system now needs your password in clear.

### Lesson

System designers have to balance convenience and security. Ease-of-use is an important factor in making IT systems really useful. Unfortunately, many practices which are convenient also introduce new vulnerabilities. This is not the last time the *curse of convenience* will haunt you.

## 3.7  ALTERNATIVE APPROACHES

If you are dissatisfied with the level of security provided by passwords, what else can you do? From a general point of view, the following options are available. As a user, you can be authenticated on the basis of:

- something you know
- something you hold
- who you are
- what you do
- where you are.

### Something You Know

The user has to know some 'secret' to be authenticated. You have already seen a first example for this mode of authentication. A password is something you know. Another example is the personal identification number (PIN) used with bank cards and similar tokens. As a third example, consider the situation when you make a telephone query about your bank account. The clerk dealing with your call may ask you for further personal information like home address, date of birth or name of spouse before releasing any information.

In this mode of authentication, anybody who obtains your secret 'is you'. On the other hand, you leave no trace if you pass your secret to somebody else. When there is a case of computer misuse in your organization where somebody has logged in using your username and password, can you prove your innocence? Can you prove that you had not divulged your password?

## Something You Hold

The user has to present a physical token to be authenticated. A key that opens a lock is something you hold. A card or an identity tag used to control access to a company's premises are other examples of such a token. Driven by the cost of password management, large organizations have started to introduce *smart cards* for user authentication.

A physical token can be lost or stolen. Like before, anybody who is in possession of the token has the same rights as the legitimate owner. To increase security, physical tokens are often used in combination with something you know, e.g. bank cards come with a PIN, or they contain information identifying the legitimate user, e.g. a photo on a bank card. However, not even the combination of mechanisms can prevent a fraudster from obtaining the information necessary to impersonate a legitimate user nor does it stop a user from passing on that information voluntarily.

## Who You Are

Biometric schemes that use unique physical characteristics (traits, features) of a person such as face, fingerprints, iris patterns (Daugman, 1993), hand geometry, or possibly even DNA at some time in the future, may seem to offer the ultimate solution for authenticating a person. At the time of writing a lot of effort is going into the development of biometric schemes.

We will use the example of fingerprints to sketch how biometric authentication works. First, samples of the user's fingerprint, so-called *reference templates*, have to be collected. For higher accuracy, several templates may be recorded, possibly for more than one finger. These templates are stored in a secure database. This process is called *enrollment*. When the user logs on, a new reading of the fingerprint is taken and compared against the reference template. Biometric schemes are used for two purposes:

- Identification: $1:n$ comparison that tries to identify the user from a database of $n$ persons.

- Verification: 1:1 comparison that checks whether there is a match for a given user.

Authentication by password gives a clear reject or accept at each authentication attempt. In contrast, with biometrics the stored reference template will hardly ever match precisely the template derived from the current measurements. We need a *matching algorithm* that measures the similarity between reference template and current template and accepts the user if the similarity is above a predefined threshold. Thus, we have to face up to new problems, *false positives* and *false negatives*. Accepting the wrong user (false positive) is clearly a security problem. Rejecting a legitimate user (false negative) creates embarrassment and potential availability problems.

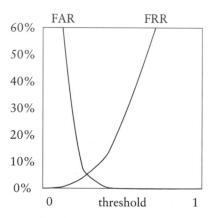

Figure 3.1:  Typical Values of FAR and FRR as a Function of the Matching Threshold

By setting the threshold for the matching algorithm, we can trade off a lower *false acceptance rate* (FAR) against a higher *false rejection rate* (FRR), or vice versa (Figure 3.1). Designers of biometric authentication systems have to find the right balance between those two errors. Where this balance will be found depends very much on the application. The *equal error rate* (EER) is given by the threshold value where the FAR and FRR are equal. Currently, the best state-of-the-art fingerprint recognition schemes have an EER of about 1–2%. Iris pattern recognition has a superior performance. Overall, the industry is just gaining experience with large-scale deployment of biometric schemes and it remains to be seen whether results from experiments conducted in controlled environments are a good indicator for practical performance.

Technical problems can actually already start at enrollment. The *failure to enrol rate* (FER) gives the frequency by which the system fails to enrol a user, e.g. because the skin on the fingers is so worn down that no good quality templates can be obtained. Then there is the problem of 'forged' fingers. Fingerprints, and biometric traits in general, may be unique but they are not secrets. You leave your fingerprints in many places and it has been demonstrated that it is not too difficult to construct rubber fingers that defeat most commercial fingerprint recognition systems (Van der Putte and Keuning, 2000; Matsumoto, 2002). If biometric authentication takes place in the presence of security personnel this would be a minor issue. However, when authenticating remote users additional precautions have to be taken to counteract this type of fraud.

There is a final issue. Will users accept such a mechanism? They may feel that they are treated like criminals if their fingerprints are taken. They may not like the idea of a laser beam scanning their retina.

### What You Do

People perform some mechanical tasks in a way that is both repeatable and specific to the individual. Handwritten signatures have long been used in banking to confirm the identity of users when signing cheques and credit card payment slips. Of course, forgeries are relatively easy to perpetrate. For greater security, users could sign on a special pad that measures attributes like writing speed and writing pressure. On a keyboard, typing speed and intervals between key strokes are being used to authenticate individual users. As before, the authentication system has to be set up so that false positives and false negatives are reduced to levels acceptable for the intended application.

### Where You Are

When you log on, the system may also take into account where you are. Some operating systems already do so and grant access only if you log on from a certain terminal. For example, a system manager may only log on from an operator console but not from an arbitrary user terminal. Similarly, as a user you may only be allowed to log on from the workstation in your office. Decisions of this kind will be even more frequent in mobile and distributed computing. If the precise geographical location has to be established during authentication, a system may use the services of the Global Positioning System (GPS). Identifying the location of a user when a login request is made may also help to resolve later disputes about the true identity of that user.

### Lesson

A password does not authenticate a person, successful authentication only implies that the user knows a particular secret. There is no way of telling the difference between the legitimate user and an intruder who has obtained that user's password.

## 3.8 FURTHER READING

The history of Unix password security is told by Morris and Thompson (1979), where quite interesting statistics on typical password choices can also be found, and taken on further by Feldmeier and Karn (1990). Practically every book on computer security contains extensive advice on the proper choice of passwords and on the importance of password security. You can find quite a number of password *crackers* on the Internet. Analyzing one of these programs will give you a good idea of the type of passwords crackers search for and on the size and sophistication of the dictionaries they are using. Running such a program without explicit authorization may bring you into conflict with the disciplinary rules of your organization and with the criminal law of many countries.

## 3.9 EXERCISES

**Exercise 3.1**   Check the password scheme on your own computer system. Are there any rules on password length, password format or password expiry? How are passwords stored in your system?

**Exercise 3.2**   Assume that you are only allowed to use the 26 characters from the alphabet to construct passwords.

- How many different passwords are possible if a password is at most $n$, $n = 4, 6, 8$, characters long and there is no distinction between upper-case and lower-case characters?

- How many different passwords are possible if a password is at most $n$, $n = 4, 6, 8$, characters long and passwords are case sensitive?

**Exercise 3.3**   Assume that passwords have length six and all alphanumerical characters, upper and lower case, can be used in their construction. How long will a brute force attack take on average if:

- it takes one-tenth of a second to check a password?
- it takes a microsecond to check a password?

**Exercise 3.4**   Assume that you are only allowed to use the 26 characters from the alphabet to construct passwords of length $n$. Assume further that you are using the same password in two systems where one accepts case-sensitive passwords but the other does not. Give an upper bound at the number of attempts required to guess the case-sensitive version of a password.

**Exercise 3.5**   Write a password generator that takes a random binary seed of length $s$ as input. Use the values $s = 8, 16, 32, 64$ in the following experiments.

- Ask different users to generate passwords with your scheme and monitor all instances when different users choose the same password.

- Generate a password and encrypt it. Try to discover the original password by trying out all values for the random seed. What is the expected number of guesses you have to make before finding the password?

**Exercise 3.6** Passwords are entered by users and checked by computers. Thus, there has to be some communications channel between user and computer. So far we have taken a very abstract view of this channel and assumed that it exists and that it is adequately secure. When is this assumption justified? When is it unjustified?

**Exercise 3.7** If you are required to use several passwords at a time, you may consider keeping them in a *password book*. A password book is a protected file containing your passwords. Access to the password book can again be controlled through a *master* password. Does such a scheme offer any real advantages?

**Exercise 3.8** There exists a time–memory trade-off in password guessing described in Hellman (1980). Let $N$ be the number of possible passwords. In a precomputation step using $N$ trial encryptions, a table with $N^{2/3}$ entries is constructed. If you later want to find a given encrypted password, you need $N^{2/3}$ trial encryptions.

How much memory space do you need when passwords of length six are chosen from a 5-bit character set? How quickly will you find the password if a trial encryption takes one millisecond?

**Exercise 3.9** Conduct a survey of commercially available biometric authentication systems. What are the false acceptance, false rejection and equal error rates for those systems?

# Chapter 4

## Access Control

You have now logged on to the system. You create new files and want to protect your files. Some of your files may be public, some only intended for a restricted audience and some may be private. You need a language for expressing your intended access control policy and you need mechanisms that enforce access control. This chapter introduces the vocabulary for talking about access control. Chapters 8 and 9 will look into specific access control policies.

### OBJECTIVES

- Introduce the fundamental model of access control.
- Look at a few sets of access operations and appreciate the danger of substituting your intuition for the actual definition of terms.
- Present essential access control structures, independent of specific security policies.
- Define partial orderings and lattices, mathematical concepts often used to express security policies.

## 4.1 BACKGROUND

Before immersing yourselves in the details of access control, consider the way computer systems – and the use of computer systems – have developed over the last few decades. Computer systems manipulate data and mediate access to shared resources like memory, printers etc. They have to provide access control to data and resources, although primarily for reasons of integrity and not so much for confidentiality. Traditional multiuser operating systems offer generic services to a considerable variety of users. By their very nature, these operating systems have simple and generic access operations and are not concerned with the meaning of the files they handle. Modern desktop operating systems support individual users in performing their job. In this scenario, you find quite complex access operations which are very much application specific. Users are not interested in the lower-level details of the execution of their programs. Not surprisingly, it may be quite difficult to map their high-level security requirements to low-level security controls. In a nutshell, you are witnessing the transition from *general purpose* computer systems to (flexible) *special purpose* computer systems. Keep this trend in mind when comparing the different access control models covered in this book.

## 4.2 AUTHENTICATION AND AUTHORIZATION

To discuss access control, we first have to develop a suitable terminology. The very nature of 'access' suggests that there is an active entity, a *subject* or a *principal*, accessing a passive *object* with some specific *access operation*, while a *reference monitor* (Chapter 5) grants or denies access. Figure 4.1 captures this view of access control.

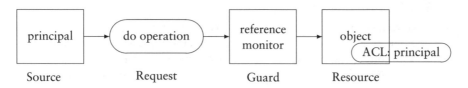

Figure 4.1: The Fundamental Model of Access Control

Access control then consists of two steps, *authentication* and *authorization*. We quote from Lampson *et al.* (1992).

> If *s* is a statement *authentication* answers the question "Who said *s*?" with a principal. Thus principals make statements; this is what they are for. Likewise, if *o* is an object *authorization* answers the question "Who is trusted to access *o*?" with a principal.

The security literature has two terms for the entity making an access request, *subject* and *principal*, but does not distinguish between those two concepts in a consistent way. The relationship between subjects and principals on the one side, and between subjects/principals and the human users of a computer system on the other, can further confuse the picture. To separate the meaning of these two terms we take our cue from earlier work on operating system security.

> Subjects operate on behalf of *human users* we call *principals*, and access is based on the principal's name bound to the subject in some unforgeable manner at authentication time. Because access control structures identify *principals*, it is important that principal names be globally unique, human-readable and memorable, *easily and reliably associated with known people* (Gasser, 1990).

This quote reflects traditional *identity-based access control* where security policies ultimately refer to human users. This is still the most common type of access control supported by commercial operating systems but, as discussed in Chapter 15, it is no longer the only paradigm in access control. In a general framework that is consistent with the traditions quoted above, we would refer to *principals* when discussing security policies and to *subjects* when discussing the operational systems that should enforce a security policy.

> **Principal** A principal is an entity that can be granted access to objects or can make statements affecting access control decisions (Gasser *et al.*, 1989).
>
> **Subject** A subject is an active entity within an IT system.

For the purpose of access decisions, subjects have to be bound to principals. When a subject requests access to a protected object the reference monitor checks whether the principal bound to the subject has the right to access the object. We might thus say that the subject 'speaks for' a principal. A typical example of a principal in an operating system is a *user identity*. The principals permitted to access a given object could be stored in an *access control list* (ACL) attached to the object (Figure 4.1). A typical example of a subject is a process running under a user identity (the principal). However, principals need not represent human users or attributes of human users. In Java a main parameter for access control is the *code source* (section 15.3) and the relation between principals and subjects is defined as follows (Gong, 1999).

> The term principal represents a *name* associated with a subject. Since subjects may have multiple names, a subject essentially consists of a collection of principals.

Typical objects are files or resources, like memory, printers, or nodes in a computer network. There is not meant to be a clear distinction between subjects and objects in the sense that every entity in the system has to be either a subject or an object. Depending on circumstances, an entity can be a subject in one access request and an object in another. The terms *subject* and *object* merely distinguish between the active and passive party in an access request. Subjects and objects present two options for focusing control. You can either specify:

- what a subject is allowed to do, or
- what may be done with an object.

This is an instance of the first design principle from section 2.4.1. Traditionally, the main task of an operating system was to manage files and resources, i.e. objects. In such a setting, you will encounter mostly access control mechanisms taking the second approach. However, we have just mentioned that application-oriented IT systems, like database management systems, offer services directed to the end user. Such a system may well incorporate mechanisms for controlling the actions of subjects.

In the following paragraphs, we will refer to:

- a set $S$ of subjects
- a set $O$ of objects, and
- a set $A$ of access operations.

There is no need yet to be more specific about any of these sets.

## 4.3 ACCESS OPERATIONS

Depending on how you look at a computer system, access operations vary from reading and writing to physical memory to method calls in an object-oriented system. Comparable systems may use different access operations and, even worse, attach different meanings to operations which appear to be the same. We will examine some typical sets of access operations taken from important early contributions in this area.

### 4.3.1 Access Modes

On the most elementary level, a subject may observe an object or alter an object. We therefore define the two *access modes*.

- Observe: look at the contents of an object.
- Alter: change the contents of an object.

Although most access control policies could be expressed in terms of observe and alter, such policy descriptions will often be too far removed from the application they are addressing, making it difficult to check whether the correct policy has been implemented. Hence, you usually find a richer set of access operations.

### 4.3.2 Access Rights of the Bell–LaPadula Model

At the next level of complexity, you find the *access rights* of the Bell–LaPadula security model discussed in section 8.2, and the *access attributes* of the Multics operating system (Organick, 1972), two of the milestones in the history of computer security.

The Bell–LaPadula model has four access rights, execute, read, append (sometimes also referred to as blind write) and write. Figure 4.2 gives the relation between these access rights and the two basic access modes observe and alter.

|         | execute | append | read | write |
|---------|---------|--------|------|-------|
| observe |         |        | X    | X     |
| alter   |         | X      |      | X     |

**Figure 4.2: Access Rights in the Bell–LaPadula Model**

To understand the rationale for this definition, consider how a multiuser operating system controls access to files. A user has to *open* a file before access is granted. Usually, files can be opened for read access or for write access. In this way, the operating system can avoid potential conflicts like two users simultaneously writing to the same file. For reasons of efficiency, write access usually includes read access. For example, a user editing a file should not be asked to open it twice, once for read and once for write. Hence, it is meaningful to define the write right so that it includes the observe and alter modes.

Few systems actually implement the append operation. Allowing users to alter an object without observing its content is not a useful operation in most applications. Audit logs, however, are one instance where the append right is useful. A process writing to the log file has no need to read the file, and probably should not read it at all.

Operating systems can use files, e.g. programs, without opening these files at all, hence the introduction of the execute right which includes neither observe nor alter mode. You may ask how a computer could execute a program without reading the program's instructions. You would of course be right and the Multics execute attribute indeed requires execute and read rights. However, there exist operations where the contents of an object are used in an execution without being read. Consider a cryptographic engine holding a master key in a special tamper-resistant register (Figure 4.3). There is physically no way the master key can be read out but access control rules may govern who is allowed to use this key for encryption. We can invoke this key without reading it and our execute right is just what we need to address such a situation.

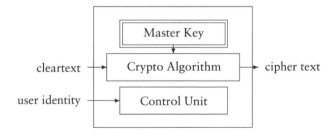

**Figure 4.3: A Cryptographic Engine.**

### Lesson

Beware of using your own intuition when interpreting access operations someone else has defined!

The Multics operating system distinguishes between access attributes for data segments and access attributes for directory segments. It is actually common practice to interpret a given set of access rights differently depending on the type of object. The terms 'read', 'write' and 'execute' are used again to name access attributes, but not in exactly the same meaning as in the Bell–LaPadula model. To maintain some clarity in our presentation, we will denote the Bell–LaPadula access rights by $\underline{e}, \underline{r}, \underline{a}, \underline{w}$. Figure 4.4 gives the mapping from Multics access attributes to Bell–LaPadula access rights.

| data segments: | | directory segments: | |
|---|---|---|---|
| read | $\underline{r}$ | status | $\underline{r}$ |
| execute | $\underline{e}, \underline{r}$ | status and modify | $\underline{w}$ |
| read and write | $\underline{w}$ | append | $\underline{a}$ |
| write | $\underline{a}$ | search | $\underline{e}$ |

◯ **Figure 4.4: Access Attributes in Multics**

### 4.3.3 Current Operating Systems

A current example is the Unix operating system in which access control policies are expressed in terms of three operations. There are:

- read: reading from a file
- write: writing to a file
- execute: executing a (program) file.

These operations differ from those of the Bell–LaPadula model. For example, in Unix write access does not imply read access. When applied to a directory, the access operations take the following meanings:

- read: list directory contents
- write: create or rename a file in the directory
- execute: search the directory.

As you can see, Unix controls who can create and delete files by controlling write access to the file's directory. The access rights specified for a file are changed by modifying the file's entry in its directory. Other operating systems include a special operation for deleting files.

This design decision has been made in our final example, the Windows 2000 operating system. The *standard permissions* listed in Brown (2000) are:

- read control
- delete
- write DACL (modify access control list)
- write owner (modify owner of a resource)
- synchronize (for synchronizing multithreaded programs).

Operations for modifying access rights, such as write DACL, are another ingredient you may want to use when setting security policies. Operations for manipulating a subject's access rights tend to be called grant and revoke when the subject's rights are modified by some other party, and assert and deny when the subject changes its own access rights. Operations of this nature are of interest in *delegation* policies, where one subject invokes another subject and the rights of the invoked subject have to be established.

Chapter 7 gives more information on the range of access permissions available in Windows 2000.

## 4.4 OWNERSHIP

When discussing access control, we also must state who is in charge of setting security policies. There are two fundamental options.

- We can define an *owner* for each resource and let the owner decree who is allowed to have access. Such a policy may be called *discretionary* because access control is at the discretion of the owner.

- A system-wide policy decrees who is allowed to have access. For obvious reasons, such a policy may be called *mandatory*.

Most operating systems support the concept of *ownership* of a resource and consider ownership when making access control decisions. They may include operations that redefine the ownership of a resource.

These intuitive explanations of discretionary and mandatory access control have been given just to make the point that they should not be confused with the definitions of discretionary and mandatory access control traditionally used in computer security. There, these terms refer to specific security policies stated in the Orange Book (US Department of Defense, 1985). Once more, you have to take care not to let your intuition mislead you.

## 4.5 ACCESS CONTROL STRUCTURES

Next, we have to state which access operations are permitted. We now have to decide on the structures to use for capturing security policies, while facing two competing requirements.

- The access control structure should help to express your desired access control policy.
- You should be able to check that your policy has been captured correctly.

### 4.5.1 Access Control Matrix

At a basic level, access rights can be defined individually for each combination of subject and object quite simply in the form of an *access control matrix (table)*:

$$M = (M_{so})_{s \in S, o \in O} \text{ with } M_{so} \subseteq A.$$

The entry $M_{so}$ specifies the set of access operations subject $s$ may perform on object $o$. This approach goes back to the early days of computer security (Lampson, 1974). Access control matrices are also referred to as *access permission matrices*. The Bell-LaPadula model employs an access control matrix to model the discretionary access control policies of the Orange Book (section 8.2). Figure 4.5 gives a simple example of an access control matrix for two users and three files.

- bill.doc may be read and written to by Bill while Alice has no access at all.
- edit.exe can be executed both by Alice and Bill but otherwise they have no access.
- fun.com can be executed and read by both users, but only Bill can write to the file.

The access control matrix is an abstract concept and not very suitable for direct implementation if the number of subjects and objects is large or if the sets of subjects and objects change frequently. In such scenarios, intermediate levels of control are preferable.

|       | bill.doc       | edit.exe    | fun.com                 |
|-------|----------------|-------------|-------------------------|
| Alice | –              | {execute}   | {execute, read}         |
| Bill  | {read, write}  | {execute}   | {execute, read, write}  |

○ **Figure 4.5: An Access Control Matrix**

### 4.5.2 Capabilities

You would hardly implement an access control matrix directly. There is a choice between two obvious options. Access rights can be kept with the subjects or with the objects. In the first case, every subject is given a *capability*, an unforgeable token that specifies this subject's access rights. This capability corresponds to the subject's row in the access control matrix. The access rights of our previous example given as capabilities are:

> Alice's capability: edit.exe: execute; fun.com: execute, read;
> Bill's capability: bill.doc: read, write; edit.exe: execute; fun.com: execute, read, write;

Typically, capabilities are associated with discretionary access control. When a subject creates a new object, it can give other subjects access to this object by granting them the appropriate capabilities. Also, when a subject (process) calls another subject, it can pass on its capability, or parts thereof, to the invoked subject.

Capabilities are by no means a new concept but up to now they have not become a widely used security mechanism. This is mainly due to the complexity of security management and to the traditional orientation of operating systems towards managing objects.

- It is difficult to get an overview of who has permission to access a given object.
- It is very difficult to revoke a capability; either the operating system has to be given the task or users have to keep track of all the capabilities they have passed on; this problem is particularly awkward when the rights in the capability include the transfer of the capability to third parties.

However, the advent of distributed systems has rekindled the interest in capability-based access control where security policies have to deal with users roaming physically or virtually between nodes in a computer network.

When you decide to employ capabilities, you also have to give some consideration to their protection. Where do you store the capabilities? If capabilities are only used within a single computer system, then it is feasible to rely only on integrity protection by the operating system (Chapter 5). When capabilities travel over a network, you also need cryptographic protection (Chapter 11).

### 4.5.3 Access Control Lists

An *access control list* (ACL) stores the access rights to an object with the object itself. An ACL therefore corresponds to a column of the access control matrix and states who may access a given object. ACLs are a typical security feature of commercial operating systems. The access rights of our previous example, given in the form of ACLs, are:

| | |
|---|---|
| ACL for bill.doc: | Bill: read, write; |
| ACL for edit.exe: | Alice: execute; Bill: execute; |
| ACL for fun.com: | Alice: execute, read; Bill: execute, read, write; |

Management of access rights based only on individual subjects can be rather cumbersome. It is therefore common to place users in *groups* and to derive access rights also from a user's group. The Unix access control model is based on simple ACLs each having three entries that assign access rights to the principals *user*, *group*, and *others* (section 6.5).

ACLs are a fitting concept for operating systems that are geared towards managing access to objects. If, however, you want to get an overview of the permissions given to an individual user, e.g. to revoke that user's permissions, you face a laborious search through all ACLs.

No matter how you implement the access control matrix, managing a security policy expressed by such a matrix is a complex task in large systems. In particular, it is tedious and error-prone to establish that all entries in such a matrix are as desired. Moreover, access control based only on subjects and objects supports a rather limited range of security policies. Further information, which may be appropriately included in an access control decision, may refer to the program the subject invokes to access the object. This is not a novel idea at all, as you can see from the following comment on access control in the Titan operating system, developed in Cambridge in the early 1960s (Needham, 1992).

> In particular, it was possible to use the identity of a program as a parameter for access-control decisions as well as, or instead of, the identity of the user, a feature which Cambridge people have ever since regarded as strange to omit.

### Lesson

Don't think that new technologies necessarily create new security problems. More often than not, the 'new' problems are reincarnations of old problems and the principles for their solution are already known.

## 4.6 INTERMEDIATE CONTROLS

In computer science, problems of complexity are solved by indirection (David Wheeler). The same can be done in access control. We introduce intermediate layers between users and objects to represent policies in a more manageable fashion.

### 4.6.1 Groups and Negative Permissions

The following discussions will be built around a simple example. Let Alice and Bill be students on a course. The lecturer wants to give students access to course material. Instead of putting all students individually into an ACL for each piece of course material, the lecturer could put all students into a *group* and put this group into the respective ACLs.

Groups are thus a means of simplifying the definition of access control policies. Users with similar access rights are collected in groups and groups are given permission to access objects. Some security policies demand that a user can be the member of one group only, others allow membership of more than one group.

Figure 4.6 shows an ideal world where all access permissions could be mediated through group membership. Often, security policies have special cases where it proves convenient to give some user a permission for an object directly, or to deny a user a permission that normally follows from membership of some group. A *negative permission* is an entry in an access control structure that specifies the access operations a user is not allowed to perform. In Figure 4.7, user $u_1$ is denied access to object $o_1$ and user $u_3$ is granted access to object $o_5$.

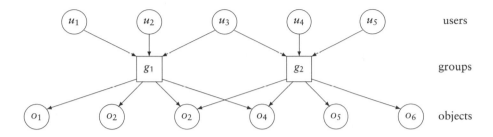

Figure 4.6: Groups Serve as an Intermediate ACL

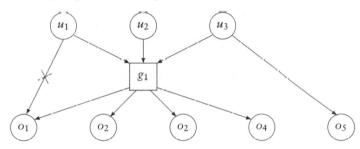

Figure 4.7: Access Control with a Negative Permission

The negative permission given to user $u_1$ that contradicts the positive permission given to group $g_1$ is an example of a *policy conflict*. When specifying a policy, you have to know how conflicts will be resolved by the reference monitor. If policies are defined by ACLs, a simple but widely used algorithm just processes the list until the first entry that corresponds to the principal given in the access request is found, and makes the decision based on this information only. Any conflicting entries later in the list are ignored.

### 4.6.2 Privileges

Turning your attention to operations, you could collect the right to execute certain operations in *privileges*. Typically, privileges are associated with operating system functions and relate to activities like system administration, backup, mail access or network access. You can view privileges as an intermediate layer between subjects and operations (Figure 4.8).

### 4.6.3 Role-based Access Control

Privileges usually come predefined with the operating system. A collection of application specific operations (procedures) is called a *role*. Subjects derive their access rights from

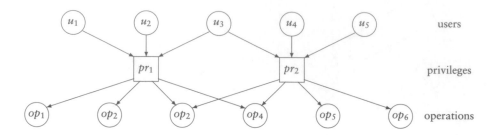

○ **Figure 4.8: Privileges as an Intermediate Layer between Subjects and Operations**

the role they are performing. Role-based access control (RBAC) has its focus on the users and on the jobs users perform.

Intermediate layers between subjects and objects help to reduce the complexities of managing access control. Intermediate layers can be inserted in more than one location, and you may use more than one layer to structure access control. Your choice of layers includes:

- *Roles*: a role is a collection of procedures. Roles are assigned to users. A user can have more than one role and more than one user can have the same role (Sandhu *et al.*, 1996).

- *Procedures*: procedures are 'high-level' access control methods with a more complex semantic than read or write. Procedures can only be applied to objects of certain datatypes. As an example, consider a funds transfer between bank accounts.

- *Datatypes*: each object is of a certain datatype and can be accessed only through the procedures defined for this datatype. Controlling access to an object by restricting the procedures that may access this object is a general programming practice. It is a fundamental concept in the theory of abstract datatypes.

In the example in section 4.6.1 the lecturer could create a role *Student* for the students on his course and assign the privilege to read course material to this role.

Although structured access control of this kind is highly desirable for many applications, it is not yet supported by many operating systems. Notable exceptions are the *user profiles* in IBM's AS/400 operating system (Park, 1995) and the *global groups* and *local groups* in Windows 2000 (Chapter 7). RBAC is more common in database management systems.

## 4.6.4 Protection Rings

Protection rings are a particularly simple example of an intermediate layer of hardware-based access control for subjects and objects. Each subject (process) and each object is assigned a number, depending on its 'importance'. In a typical example, processes are assigned one of the following numbers.

0 – operating system kernel
1 – operating system
2 – utilities
3 – user processes.

An access control decision is made by comparing the subject's and object's numbers. (The outcome of the decision depends on the security policy you try to enforce using protection rings.) These numbers correspond to concentric *protection rings*, with ring 0 in the center giving the highest degree of protection (Figure 4.9). If a process is assigned the number *i*, then we say the process 'runs in ring *i*'.

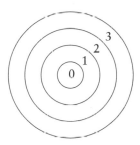

Figure 4.9: Protection Rings

Protection rings have been mainly used for integrity protection. Protection rings had already been used in the Multics operating system and special hardware was developed to support this security mechanism (Schroeder and Saltzer, 1972). Similar features are provided on the Intel 80x86 processors at the machine language level. Unix uses two levels with the root and operating system running in ring 0 and user processes running in ring 3. As another example, the QNX/Neutrino microkernel assigns software components to protection rings as follows.

• The Neutrino microkernel runs in ring 0.

• The Neutrino process manager runs in ring 1.

• All other programs run in ring 3.

Memory locations containing sensitive data, like the operating system code, can only be accessed by processes that run in rings 0 or 1. A typical policy based on protection rings is given in section 5.3.5. More examples can be found in Organick (1972, Chapter 4) and Pfleeger and Lawrence Pfleeger (2003, section 7.2).

## 4.7 PARTIAL ORDERINGS

With protection rings, we have introduced comparisons into the evaluation of security policies. Protection rings are a very simple example where we could decide for any two rings $i$ and $j$ which was the innermost. In general, this need not be the case. Consider an extension of the example in section 4.6.1. The department creates a group *Year_1* for first-year students to manage access for resources specifically dedicated to them. There is also a group *Year_2* for second-year students, *Year_3* for third-year students etc. The group of first-year students would be contained in the group of all students, but there is no such relation between groups *Year_1* and *Year_2*. The best we can aim for is a *partial ordering*.

> **Definition**   A partial ordering $\leq$ ("less or equal") on a set (of security levels) $L$ is a relation on $L \times L$ which is:
>
> - *reflexive*: for all $a \in L$, $a \leq a$ holds;
> - *transitive*: for all $a, b, c \in L$, if $a \leq b$ and $b \leq c$, then $a \leq c$;
> - *antisymmetric*: for all $a, b \in L$, if $a \leq b$ and $b \leq a$, then $a = b$.
>
> If two elements $a, b \in L$ are not comparable, we write $a \not\leq b$.

Typical examples of partial orderings are as follows.

- $(\mathcal{P}(X), \subseteq)$, the powerset of a set $X$ with the subset relation as partial ordering.

- $(N, |)$, the natural numbers with the 'divides' relation as partial ordering.

- The strings over an alphabet $\Sigma$ with the prefix relation as a partial ordering. A string $\beta$ is a prefix of a string $\alpha$ if there exists a string $\gamma$ so that we can write $\alpha = \beta\gamma$. In this case, we write $\beta \leq \alpha$.

*Hasse diagrams* are a graphical representation of partially ordered sets (posets). A Hasse diagram is a directed graph where the nodes are the elements of the set. The edges in the diagram give a 'skeleton' of the partial ordering. That is, for $a, b \in L$ we place an edge from $a$ to $b$ if and only if:

- $a \leq b$ and $a \neq b$, and
- there exists no $c \in L$, so that $a \leq c \leq b$ and $a \neq c$, $b \neq b$.

With this definition, $a \leq b$ holds if and only if there is a path from $a$ to $b$. Edges in the graph are all drawn to point upward. The Hasse diagram for the partially ordered set $(\mathcal{P}(\{a, b, c\}), \subseteq)$ is given in Figure 4.10.

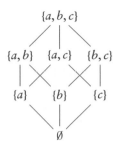

$\bigcirc$ **Figure 4.10: The Poset (Lattice)** $(\mathcal{P}(\{a, b, c\}), \subseteq)$

## 4.7.1 Abilities in the VSTa Microkernel

The capabilities of the VSTa microkernel nicely illustrate the use of partial orderings. As they are not quite capabilities as defined in section 4.5.2, let us use *abilities* instead. An ability is a finite string of positive integers. To indicate where a new integer begins a dot is placed in front of each integer. So, an ability is a string $.i_1.i_2.\cdots.i_n$ for some value $n$ where $i_1, \ldots, i_n$ are integers. There is no limit on the length $n$ of such a string. Indeed, $n$ may be equal to 0. Examples of abilities are .1.2.3, .4, or .10.0.0.5.

Abilities ordered through the prefix relation constitute a partial ordering. In our running example, the department might assign ability .3.1.101 to the group of students on course CS101. Course material for CS101 would again be labeled with ability .3.1.101, general material for first year students with .3.1, general second-year material with .3.2, and .3 would be used for general material for all students. These abilities are related by $.3 \leq .3.1 \leq .3.1.101$ but $.3.1 \nleq .3.2$.

For a policy that grants access if the object's label is a prefix of the subject's label, CS101 students will get access to their own course material, year one material and general information for students.

For a moment, consider the dual of the above policy. Access is granted if the subject's ability is a prefix of the object's ability. In this case, the ability '.', a dot followed by no integers, defines a superuser who has access to all objects as the empty string $\varepsilon$ is the prefix of any ability. Thus, by not assigning an ability to a subject you would grant that subject access to all objects.

**Lesson**

Access control algorithms compare attributes of subjects and objects. You always have to check what happens if one of those attributes is missing. Fail-safe behavior would suggest that access should be denied. Often this is not the case and you could be in for an unpleasant surprise.

### 4.7.2 The Lattice of Security Levels

Returning to the original policy in our example, if there is an object two groups of students should have access to, the department could use the longest common prefix of the abilities assigned to the two groups to label the document. For example, if *Year_1* and *Year_2* should get access to a document, ability .3 could be used as a label. On the other hand, if we have two objects labeled say with .3.1 and .3.2 and want to assign a label to a subject that has access to both, we could not do it in our current system.

In general, given the standard confidentiality policy where a subject may observe an object only if the subject's security level is higher than the object's security level, we wish to have unique answers to the following two questions.

- Given two objects at different security levels, what is the minimal security level a subject must have to be allowed to read both objects?
- Given two subjects at different security levels, what is the maximal security level an object can have so that it can still be read by both subjects?

The mathematical structure that allows us two answer these two questions exists. It is called a *lattice*. Formally, it can be defined as follows.

> **Definition**   A lattice $(L, \leq)$ consists of a set $L$ and a partial ordering $\leq$. For every two elements $a, b \in L$ there exists a *least upper bound* $u \in L$ and a *greatest lower bound* $l \in L$, i.e.:
>
> $$a \leq u, b \leq u, \quad \text{and} \quad \forall v \in L : (a \leq v \wedge b \leq v) \Rightarrow (u \leq v),$$
> $$l \leq a, l \leq b, \quad \text{and} \quad \forall k \in L : (k \leq a \wedge k \leq b) \Rightarrow (k \leq l).$$

In security, we say '$a$ is dominated by $b$' or '$b$ dominates $a$' if $a \leq b$. The security level dominated by all other levels is called *System Low*. The security level dominating all other levels is called *System High*. For example, the partially ordered set $(\mathcal{P}(\{a, b, c\}), \subseteq)$ of Figure 4.10 is a lattice with the empty set $\emptyset$ as *System Low* and the set $\{a, b, c\}$ as *System High*.

Whenever you meet a security system where security attributes are compared in some way, as in the case of our motivating example, you are likely to find that it is convenient if these attributes form a lattice. It is not necessary to understand lattices to grasp the essential facts of computer security. Nevertheless, it helps to understand lattices when reading many papers on this subject.

### 4.7.3 Multilevel Security

Much of security research in the 1970s and 1980s was driven by the demands of protecting classified information. In this domain, there already existed policies regulating physical access to classified documents. Documents were assigned *security levels*. A user's *clearance* dictated which documents the user could obtain. The *mandatory access control (MAC)* policies and *multilevel security* policies of the Orange Book make use of security levels and adapt these policies to IT systems. In their most elementary version,

top secret

|

secret

|

confidential

|

unclassified

 **Figure 4.11: Security Levels in Linear Order**

these policies refer to a linearly ordered hierarchy of four security levels, *unclassified,
confidential, secret, top secret* (Figure 4.11).

With a linear ordering of security levels you can only express a limited set of security
policies. You could not, for example, restrict access to documents relating to a secret
project $X$ just to the people working on $X$. Anyone at level *secret* would have access. To
be able to state such *need-to-know policies* that control access to the resources of specific
projects, the following lattice of security levels was introduced.

- Take $H$, a set of *classifications* with a hierarchical (linear) ordering $\leq_H$.
- Take a set $C$ of *categories*, e.g. project names, company divisions, academic depart-
  ments, etc. A *compartment* is a set of categories.
- A *security label (security level)* is a pair $(h, c)$, where $h \in H$ is a security level and $c \subseteq C$
  is a compartment.
- The partial ordering $\leq$ of security labels is defined by

$$(h_1, c_1) \leq (h_2, c_2) \text{ iff } h_1 \leq_H h_2 \text{ and } c_1 \subseteq c_2.$$

Figure 4.12 illustrates this construction. There are two hierarchical levels, *public* and
*private*, and two categories, *personnel* (PER) and *engineering* (ENG). In the ensuing
lattice, the following relations hold, for example:

$(public, \{PER\}) \leq (private, \{PER\}),$
$(public, \{PER\}) \leq (public, \{PER, ENG\}),$
$(public, \{PER\}) \not\leq (private, \{ENG\}).$

To see how this lattice of security labels can be used to implement mandatory *need-to-
know* (*least privilege*) policies, look at the lattice of Figure 4.12 in the light of the simple
confidentiality policy mentioned above. A subject with security label (*private*, {ENG})
will not be able to read any object that has the category PER in the compartment of its
label. Thus, even an object labeled (*public*,{PER, ENG}) will be out of bounds.

We started our discussion of security lattices with the simple hierarchical lattice of
Figure 4.11, typical for governmental multilevel security policies. We then added compartments to express a greater variety of policies. Systems have been built to enforce such
policies with very high levels of assurance. Today, we find applications that use multilevel
security systems because of their high assurance but have no hierarchical component in

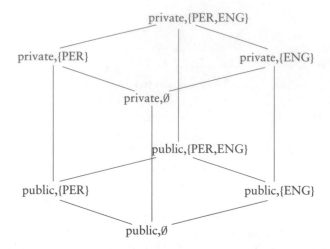

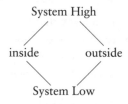

○  **Figure 4.12:  A Lattice of Security Labels**

○  **Figure 4.13:  A Lattice for a Firewall**

their security levels at all. For example, a firewall could use the lattice from Figure 4.13 to achieve a strict separation between the inside and the outside of a network.

## 4.8 FURTHER READING

The fundamental access control structures and security lattices are covered by Denning (1982), Amoroso (1994) and Pfleeger and Lawrence Pfleeger (2003). Influential early papers on access control (protection) are by Lampson (1974) and Saltzer (1974). Wilkes (1968) has more to say about access control in operating systems developed in the 1960s. More examples of security policies for protection rings are given by Nelson (1988) and Pfleeger and Lawrence Pfleeger (2003). A good survey on (RBAC) has been published by Sandhu *et al.* (1996). Further information about lattice-based access control models together with a description of how they are used to deal with confidentiality and integrity can be found in Sandhu (1993).

## 4.9 EXERCISES

**Exercise 4.1**    You are given two bits to capture access operations on a directory. How would you use the four operations available to you? How would you control the creation and deletion of files? How would you implement the concept of *hidden* files with these access operations? (Hidden files are only visible to authorized subjects.)

**Exercise 4.2**    Consider a system with the four access operations read, write, grant and revoke. You can use grant not only to give other subjects read and write access, you can also grant them the right to grant access to the objects you own. Which data structure and algorithm would you use to implement the grant and revoke operation so that you can revoke *all* access to an object you own?

**Exercise 4.3**    Discuss: what are the differences between groups and roles, if there are any differences at all?

**Exercise 4.4**    Explain why the partial ordering of abilities as defined in section 4.7.1 does not constitute a lattice. Try to convert the partial ordering into a lattice by adding any further elements you need to the set of abilities.

**Exercise 4.5**    You are given a security policy stating that a subject has access to an object if and only if the security level of the subject dominates the security level of the object. What is the effect of using the lattice:

with this policy?

**Exercise 4.6**    Let $(L, \leq)$ be a lattice of security levels where $L$ is a finite set. Show that unique elements *System Low* and *System High* must exist in such a lattice.

**Exercise 4.7**    Construct the lattice of security labels for the security levels *public*, *confidential* and *strictly confidential*, and for the categories ADMIN, LECTUR-ERS and STUDENTS. Which objects are visible to a subject with security label (*confidential*,{STUDENTS}) in a need-to-know policy? How many labels can be constructed from $n$ security levels and $m$ categories? For illustration, consider the values $n = 16$ and $m = 64$.

**Exercise 4.8**    You are given a security policy that uses the lattice of compartments as security labels. Access is granted only when the subject's label is a subset of the object's label. With the categories ADMIN, LECTURERS, and STUDENTS, which objects can be accessed by a subject with label {STUDENTS}? Why is a subject with label {ADMIN,STUDENTS} more constrained than a subject with label {STUDENTS}? Interpret the roles of the labels Ø and {ADMIN, LECTURERS, STUDENTS} in this policy.

**Exercise 4.9**  You are given a set of categories. Implement a lattice-based *need-to-withhold* policy where you selectively withdraw access rights from subjects.

# Chapter 5

## Reference Monitors

The previous chapter introduced some elementary concepts that are useful when writing access control policies. Now, we move to the basics of enforcing such policies. More refined policy descriptions and more refined access control systems are the subject of later chapters. We will present the core mechanisms for protecting the integrity of the operating system and for controlling access to memory, and focus on access control at the bottom levels of our layered system architecture. On our way, we will point out a few more general lessons for the design of secure systems.

### OBJECTIVES

- Introduce fundamental concepts of access control, such as *reference monitors* and *Trusted Computing Bases*.
- Discuss different options for the design of reference monitors.
- Introduce status and controlled invocation as two important security primitives.
- Understand the motivation for enforcing security at a low system layer, and get an overview of the security mechanisms available at the bottom system layers.

## 5.1 INTRODUCTION

There are three fundamental concepts in computer security which are sufficiently closely related to create confusion but deserve being kept apart. We refer to the Glossary of the Orange Book (US Department of Defense, 1985) for our definitions.

**Reference Monitor**   An access control concept that refers to an abstract machine that mediates all accesses to objects by subjects.

**Security Kernel**   The hardware, firmware, and software elements of a Trusted Computing Base that implement the reference monitor concept. It must mediate *all* accesses, be protected from modification, and be verifiable as correct.

**Trusted Computing Base (TCB)**   The totality of protection mechanisms within a computer system – including hardware, firmware, and software – the combination of which is responsible for enforcing a security policy. A TCB consists of one or more components that together enforce a unified security policy over a product or system. The ability of the TCB to correctly enforce a security policy depends solely on the mechanisms within the TCB and on the correct input by system administrative personnel of parameters (e.g., a user's clearance) related to the security policy.

So, the reference monitor is an abstract concept, the security kernel its implementation, and the TCB contains the security kernel among other protection mechanisms. Core requirements on the implementation of a reference monitor were formulated in the Anderson report (1972).

- The reference validation mechanism must be tamper proof[1].
- The reference validation mechanism must always be invoked[2].
- The reference validation mechanism must be small enough to be subject to analysis and tests to be sure that it is correct.

The common view of reference monitors and security kernels is very much colored by the original research agenda laid out by Anderson (1972). There, the security kernel includes the implementation of the reference validation mechanism, access control to the system itself, and components for managing the security attributes of users and programs. A strong case is made for implementing the security kernel in the bottom layers of the architecture from Figure 2.3. Conversely, you may find that the term security kernel is sometimes used to stand for the security mechanisms at those bottom layers.

---

[1]Today, *tamper resistant* has replaced *tamper proof* in the security literature, so as not to create the impression that a security component is unbreakable.
[2]This requirement is known as *complete mediation*.

### 5.1.1 Placing the Reference Monitor

In principle, reference monitors can be placed anywhere in our layered architecture. Indeed, examples of all possible design decisions can be found.

- In hardware: access control mechanisms in microprocessors will be discussed in section 5.3.

- In the operating system kernel: a *hypervisor* is a virtual machine that exactly emulates the host computer it is running on. It can be used to separate users, or applications for that matter, by providing each with a separate virtual machine. A Nexus operating system as considered for Microsoft's NGSCB architecture would be another example (England *et al.*, 2003).

- In the operating system: access control in Unix and Windows 2000 are covered in Chapters 6 and 7 respectively. The reference monitor of the Multics operating system is described in section 8.3.

- In the services layer: illustrated by access control in database management systems (Chapter 17), the Java Virtual machine, the .NET Common Language Runtime, or in the CORBA middleware architecture.

- In the application: developers of applications with very specific security requirements may decide to include security checks in the application code rather than invoking security services from a lower systems layer.

We can also ask where to place the reference monitor in respect to the 'application' it should control. The reference monitor can be provided by a lower systems layer, as depicted in Figure 5.1a. This is the typical pattern of access control in an operating system. Application programs request access to protect resources. The reference monitor is part of the operating system kernel and mediates all access requests. Access control in CORBA follows the same pattern.

Alternatively, the program could be run within an interpreter. The interpreter mediates all access requests by the program. An interpreted programming language like Java exemplifies this approach. The program is placed within the reference monitor, as shown in Figure 5.1b.

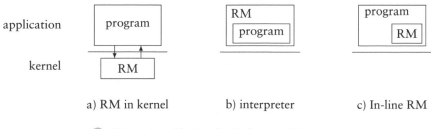

a) RM in kernel      b) interpreter      c) In-line RM

Figure 5.1: Placing the Reference Monitor

In the third approach, the program is rewritten to include the access control checks. The in-line reference monitors introduced by Erlingsson and Scheider (2000) are an example of this option. Now, the reference monitor is placed within the program, as in part (c) of Figure 5.1.

### 5.1.2 Execution Monitors

When deciding on an access request, the reference monitor has to work with information about the request and about the *target* the request refers to. We can differentiate between reference monitors on the basis of the information that is actually used to make access decisions (Schneider, 2000).

- An *execution monitor* (Schneider, 2000) only looks at the history of execution steps but does not try to predict the outcome of possible future executions. This variant is typically found in operating systems, which only keep a finite (and small) amount of information about the history of an execution.

- The reference monitor could consider all possible future executions of the target when making its decision. *Static type checking* is an example of this approach.

- The reference monitor could rewrite the target to ensure that granting the access request does not violate the security policy.

## 5.2 OPERATING SYSTEM INTEGRITY

Let us now identify in general terms the security mechanisms to be included in the security kernel. Assume you have an operating system that could enforce all your access control policies. Unauthorized access to resources is impossible, as long as the operating system works as intended. Of course, this is just the cue for an attacker. To circumvent your protection mechanisms, an attacker may try to disable the security controls by modifying the operating system. You now definitely face an integrity problem, even if you were originally concerned with confidentiality. The operating system is not only the arbitrator of access requests, it is itself an object of access control. The new security policy is:

> users must not be able to modify the operating system.

This is a generic security policy, deserving of strong and efficient support. To make your life more difficult, you have to address the following two competing requirements.

- Users should be able to use (invoke) the operating system.

- Users should not be able to misuse the operating system.

Two important concepts commonly used to achieve these goals are *status information* and *controlled invocation* (also called *restricted privilege*). These concepts can be used in any layer of a computing system, be it application software, operating system or hardware. However, to re-emphasize the point, these mechanisms can be disabled if the attacker gets access to a lower layer.

### 5.2.1 Modes of Operation

The first prerequisite for an operating system to be able to protect itself from the users is the ability to distinguish between computations 'on behalf of' the operating systems and computations 'on behalf of' a user. A *status flag* can be used to this effect, allowing the system to work in different *modes*. For example, the Intel 80x86 processors have two status bits thereby supporting four modes. The Unix operating system distinguished between *supervisor (root)* and *user* mode.

Why are such modes useful? For example, to stop users from writing directly to memory and corrupting the logical file structure, the operating system could grant write access to memory locations only if the processor is in supervisor mode.

### 5.2.2 Controlled Invocation

We continue our example. A user wants to execute an operation requiring supervisor mode, e.g. a write to a memory location. To deal with this request, the processor has to switch between modes, but how should this switch be performed? Simply changing the status bit to supervisor mode would give all privileges associated with this mode to the user without any control of what the user actually does. Therefore, it is desirable that the system only performs a predefined set of operations in supervisor mode and then returns to user mode before handing control back to the user. We refer to this process as *controlled invocation*.

## 5.3 HARDWARE SECURITY FEATURES

Hardware is the lowest layer in our model of an IT system. Hardware is also the place where computer security can link in with physical security. Security mechanisms at the hardware level are therefore a natural starting point for our investigations. This section looks at the security features of microprocessors, using the Motorola 68000 and the Intel 80386/486 as examples.

### 5.3.1 Security Rationale

There are two good reasons for placing security in one of the lower system layers (Figure 5.2). A security mechanism in any given layer can be compromised if an attacker gets in at a layer below. To evaluate the security of a system, you therefore have to check

○ **Figure 5.2: Protection in the Security Kernel**

that your security mechanisms cannot be bypassed. The more complex your system is, the more difficult this check becomes. At the core of your system, you can hope to find reasonably simple structures which are amenable to thorough analysis. This argument points to a first reason for placing security in the core.

> It may be possible to evaluate security to a higher level of assurance.

Microprocessor design is very much the science of establishing which set of operations is most useful to the majority of users. The right choice and the efficient implementation of generic operations determine overall performance. You can follow the same route when implementing security. Decide on the generic security mechanisms and put them in the core of your system. This is the second reason for placing security in the core.

> Putting security mechanisms into the core of the system reduces the performance overheads caused by security.

All the arguments we have put forward to bolster the case for putting security mechanisms into the core of the system have pushed us to the machine end on the man–machine scale (Figure 5.3). The consequences are predictable.

> Access control decisions made by reference monitors are far removed from access control decisions made by applications.

○ **Figure 5.3: The Place of the Security Kernel on the Man–Machine Scale**

## 5.3.2 A Brief Overview of Computer Architecture

We assume that the reader is familiar with the fundamental concepts of computer architecture. If necessary, this background can be acquired from any good textbook on this topic, e.g. Hennessy and Patterson (2002). For our purposes, the simple schematic description of a computer given in Figure 5.4 will do, consisting of a central processing unit (CPU), memory, a bus connecting the CPU and memory, and some input/output devices. In real life, all three entities can have a much more refined structure.

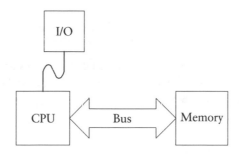

Figure 5.4: Schematic Picture of a Computer

### The Central Processing Unit

The core CPU components are as follows.

- *Registers*: there are general purpose registers and *dedicated* registers; important dedicated registers are:
    - (a) the *program counter*: points to the memory location that contains the next instruction to be executed;
    - (b) the *stack pointer*: points to the top of the system stack;
    - (c) the *status register*: allows the CPU to keep essential state information.
- *Arithmetic Logic Unit (ALU)*: executes instructions given in a machine-level language; executing an instruction may also set bits in the status register.

The *system stack* is a specially designated part of the memory. The stack can be accessed by *pushing* data on to its top or by *popping* data from its top. To switch between different programs, the CPU performs a *context switch* and saves the state of the current process, e.g. program counter, status register, etc., on the stack before giving control to the new process.

### Input/Output

Input devices such as keyboards and output devices such as monitors facilitate user interaction. For entering security-sensitive data like username and password, a *trusted path* from the I/O device to the TCB is required. An example is the secure attention sequence CTRL+ALT+DEL in Windows 2000. In applications where users sign documents, we would like to be sure that the document displayed is also the document that is actually being signed.

## Memory Structures

The following brief survey investigates the security characteristics of different memory structures.

- RAM (random access memory): this is read/write memory; you cannot rely on such memory to guarantee integrity or confidentiality.

- ROM (read-only memory): there is a built-in integrity guarantee so you would only have to add your own confidentiality mechanisms; ROM may be a good location for storing (parts of) the operating system.

- EPROM (erasable and programmable read-only memory): may be used for storing parts of the operating system or cryptographic keys; technologically more sophisticated attacks may pose a threat to security.

- WROM (write-once memory): this memory structure comes with a mechanism that allows you to freeze the memory contents once and for all; in hardware, this can be achieved by blowing a fuse that has been placed on the write line, but you may also come across 'logical fuses'; WROM may be a good location for storing cryptographic keys; write-only disks are being used for recording audit trails.

There exists a further distinction between *volatile* memory and *nonvolatile (permanent)* memory. Volatile memory loses its content if power is switched off. Physically, this process is neither instantaneous nor complete. If power is switched on immediately after having been switched off, the old data may still be held in memory. Even if power has been switched off for some time, it is possible that the old memory contents can be reconstructed by special electronic techniques. To counter those attacks, memory has to be overwritten repeatedly with suitable bit patterns that depend on the storage medium (US Department of Defense, 1987).

Permanent memory keeps its content if power is switched off. If sensitive data, like encryption keys, are stored in permanent memory and if attackers have direct access to memory bypassing the CPU, further measures like cryptographic or physical protection have to be implemented. For example, a light sensor is placed in a tamper-resistant module to detect an attempted manipulation and trigger the deletion of the data kept in the module. Physical protection is a topic of its own that falls outside the scope of this book. We restrict our attention to the situation where users get access to memory only through the CPU and we investigate how the CPU can enforce confidentiality and integrity. For example, what can be done to prevent a computer virus from overwriting a clean version of the operating system with an infected version?

It is important to remind yourself that 'memory' in Figure 5.4 is another abstraction. Logically, memory may consist of the main memory, caches for quick access, buffers, etc. Even backup media could be included in this list. Hence, a data object may exist simultaneously in more than one location in this memory hierarchy. Besides a persistent copy in secondary memory, there will be temporary copies. Usually, the location and lifetime of these temporary copies are not under the user's control. Security controls on a data object can be bypassed if one of the temporary copies is held in an unprotected memory area.

### 5.3.3 Processes and Threads

A process is a program in execution. As such, a process is an important unit of control for the operating system, and of course also for security. Roughly, a process consists of:

- executable code
- data
- the execution context, e.g. the contents of certain relevant CPU registers.

A process works in its own address space and can communicate with other processes only through primitives provided by the operating system. This logical separation between processes is a useful basis for security. On the other hand, a context switch between processes is an expensive operation as the operating system has to save the entire execution context on the stack.

*Threads* are strands of execution within a process. All threads share the process address space, thereby avoiding the overheads of a full context switch, but also avoiding control by a potential security mechanism.

### 5.3.4 Controlled Invocation – Interrupts

Processors are equipped to deal with interruptions in execution, created by errors in the program, user requests, hardware failure, etc. The mechanisms to do so are called varyingly *exceptions*, *interrupts* and *traps*. The different terms may refer to different types of events but as ever there are competing classifications, see e.g. Hennessy and Patterson (2002), for further reading.

We will use *trap* as the generic term and explain how traps can be used for security purposes. A trap is a special input to the CPU which includes an address, called an *interrupt vector*, in an *interrupt vector table*. The interrupt table gives the location of the program which deals with the *condition* specified in the trap (Figure 5.5). This program is called the *interrupt handler*. When a trap occurs, the system saves its current state on the stack and then executes the interrupt handler. In this way, control is taken away from the user program. The interrupt handler has to make sure that the system is restored to a proper state, e.g. by clearing the supervisor status bit, before returning control to the user program.

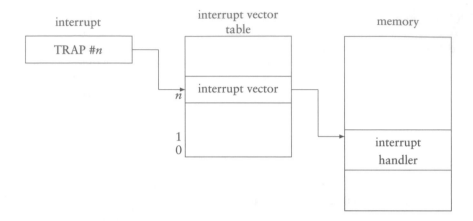

⃝ **Figure 5.5: Processing of an Interrupt**

It is possible for a further interrupt to arrive while the processor deals with a current interrupt. The processor may then have to interrupt the current interrupt handler. Improper handling of such a situation can lead to security flaws. A typical example would be a system where a user can interrupt the execution of a program by typing CTRL-C so that the processor returns to the operating system prompt with the status bit of the current process. A user could then enter supervisor mode by interrupting the execution of an operating system call. It is therefore important that before executing a program, the interrupt table is set up so that interrupts will be handled in an appropriate way.

From this discussion, it should be clear that the interrupt table is an interesting point of attack and has to be protected adequately. Changing an entry in the interrupt table so that it points to attack code, which is then executed before jumping to the proper interrupt handler, is one of the strategies used by virus writers (Figure 5.6). Using tables as a layer of indirection is a useful and frequently employed design technique. However, whenever such indirections are used, you should look out for attacks of the type just described.

### Lesson

Redirecting pointers is a very efficient attack method.

### 5.3.5 Protection on the Intel 80386/80486

The Intel 80386/486 are 32-bit microprocessors. Protection modes on the 80x86 support the integrity and confidentiality requirements of multitasking operating systems.

The Intel 80x86 has a 2-bit field in the status register defining four *privilege levels* (protection rings, section 4.6.4). The privilege level can only be changed by a single

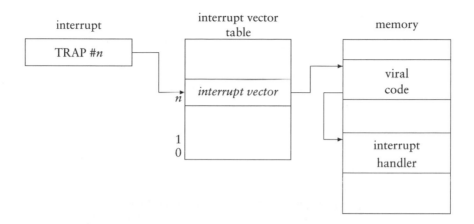

○ Figure 5.6: Inserting Viral Code by Redirecting an Interrupt Vector

instruction (POPF), which has to be executed at level 0. Software could be assigned to these levels as follows.

- 0 – operating system kernel
- 1 – rest of operating system
- 2 – I/O drivers etc.
- 3 – application software.

Not all operating systems make use of all four levels. For example, Unix only uses levels 0 and 3. The 80x86 implements the following security policy.

> Procedures can only access objects in their own ring or in outer rings. Procedures can invoke subroutines only within their own ring.

The 80x86 stores information about system objects like memory segments, access control tables or gates in *descriptors*. Descriptors are stored in the *descriptor table* and accessed via *selectors*. The privilege level of an object is stored in the DPL (descriptor privilege level) field of its descriptor. A selector is a 16-bit field containing an index pointing to the object's entry in the descriptor table and also a *requested privilege level* (RPL) field (Figure 5.7). The use of the RPL field will be explained in a moment. Only the operating system has access to selectors.

The system objects containing information about subjects, i.e. about processes, of course also have descriptors and selectors. When a subject requests access to an object, the relevant selectors are loaded into dedicated segment registers. For example, the privilege level of the current process, called the *current privilege level* (CPL), is the privilege level of the selector stored in the code segment (CS) register.

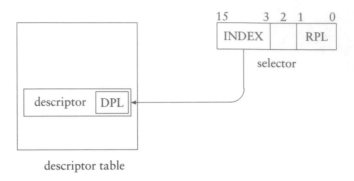

descriptor table

○ **Figure 5.7: Selectors and Descriptors**

Not surprisingly, we again face the problem of having to manage access to operations which require higher privileges. Assume that an application program in ring 3 needs a service from an operating system routine in ring 1. On the 80x86, this problem is solved by using *gates*. A gate is a system object that points to a procedure (in some code segment) where the gate has a privilege level different from that of the code it points to. Gates allow execute-only access to a procedure in an inner ring. Restrictions on outward calls are still enforced.

For a procedure to use a gate, the gate has to be in the same ring as the procedure. When invoking a subroutine through a gate, the current privilege level changes to the level of the code the gate is pointing to. When returning from the subroutine, the privilege level is restored to that of the calling procedure. A subroutine call also saves the information indicating the state of the calling procedure or the return address on a stack. To determine the appropriate privilege level of the stack, remember that the calling procedure cannot write to an inner ring. However, leaving the stack in the outer ring is unsatisfactory for security reasons as it leaves the return address rather unprotected. Therefore, part of the stack (how much is described in the gate's descriptor) is copied to a more privileged stack segment.

## The Confused Deputy Problem

By allowing outer-ring procedures to invoke inner-ring procedures, we create a potential security loophole. The outer-ring procedure may ask the inner-ring procedure to copy an object residing in the inner ring to the outer ring[3]. This will not be prevented by any of the mechanisms presented so far nor does it actually violate the security policy we have stated. We may therefore wish to extend the original security policy to be able to take into account not only the current privilege level but also the level of the calling process.

---

[3]Today, the term confused deputy problem is often used to describe situations where an unprivileged entity invokes an entity with higher privileges to perform actions that violate the security policy.

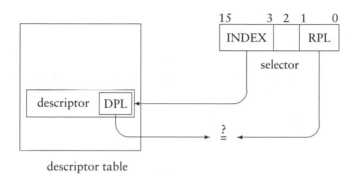

descriptor table

○ **Figure 5.8: Comparing RPL and DPL**

In the 80x86, such policies can be supported using the RPL field in the selector and the *adjust requested privilege level* (ARPL) instruction. The ARPL instruction changes the RPL fields of all selectors to the CPL of the calling procedure. The system can then compare the RPL (in the selector) and the DPL (in the descriptor) of an object and refuse to complete the requested operation if they differ (Figure 5.8).

### Lesson

For better precision in access control it may be beneficial to consider some aspect of the execution history when deciding on an access request.

## 5.4 PROTECTING MEMORY

Operating systems manage access to data and resources. They are usually not involved in the interpretation of user data. Multitasking operating systems interleave the execution of processes belonging to different users. Then, the operating system not only has to protect its own integrity but it also has to prevent users from accidentally or intentionally accessing other users' data. The integrity of the operating system itself is preserved by separating user space from operating system space. Logical separation of users prevents accidental and intentional interference between users. Separation can take place at two levels.

- File management deals with logical memory objects.
- Memory management deals with physical memory objects.

As far as security is concerned, this distinction is important. To see why, consider the two main ways of structuring memory, segmentation and paging. *Segmentation* divides data into logical units. Each segment has a unique name and items within a segment are addressed by giving the segment name and the appropriate offset within the segment. The operating system maintains a table of segment names with their true addresses in memory. The Multics operating system used segmentation for logical access control.

+ Segmentation is a division into logical units, which is a good basis for enforcing a security policy.

− Segments have variable length, which makes memory management more difficult.

*Paging* divides memory into pages of equal size. Addresses again consist of two parts, the page number and the offset within a page.

+ Paging is popular because it allows efficient memory management. Segments in Multics are actually paged.

− Paging is not a good basis for access control as pages are not logical units. Thus, one page may contain objects requiring different protection.

Even worse, paging may open a covert channel. Logical objects can be stored across page boundaries. When such an object is accessed, the operating system will at some stage require a new page and a *page fault* will occur. If page faults can be observed, as is the case in most operating systems, then a user is provided with information in excess of the proper result of the access request.

As an example, consider a password scheme. The user enters a password which is scanned character by character and compared with a reference password stored in memory. Access is denied the moment an incorrect match is found. If a password is stored across a page boundary, then an attacker can deduce from observing a page fault that the piece of the password on the first page had been guessed correctly. If the attacker can control where the password is stored on the page, password guessing becomes rather easy as sketched in Figure 5.9. In the first step, the password is placed in memory so that the first character is on a page separate from the rest of the password. The attacker now tries all values for the first character until a page fault occurs, indicating that the guess was correct. The password is then realigned in memory so that the first two password characters are on a page separate from the rest. The attacker already knows the first character and now tries all values for the second character until a page fault occurs. By continuing with this ploy, the attacker can search for each password character individually.

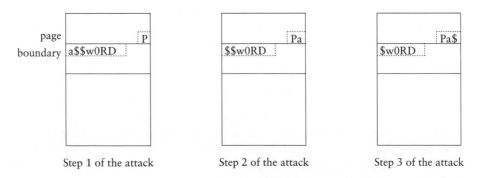

Figure 5.9: Using Page Faults as Covert Channels to Guess a Password

### 5.4.1 Secure Addressing

When you want the operating system to protect its own integrity and to confine each process to a separate address space, then one of your tasks is to control access to data objects in memory. Such a data object is physically represented as a collection of bits stored in certain memory locations. Access to a logical object is ultimately translated into access operations at machine language level. At this level, you can pursue three options for controlling access to memory locations.

- The operating system modifies the addresses it receives from user processes.

- The operating system constructs the effective addresses from relative addresses it receives from user processes.

- The operating system checks whether the addresses it receives from user processes are within given bounds.

Address sandboxing is an example of the first approach. An address consists of a *segment identifier* and an *offset*. When the operating system receives an address, it sets the correct segment identifier. Figure 5.10 shows how this can be done with two register operations. First, a bitwise AND of the address with mask_1 clears the segment identifier. Then a bitwise OR with mask_2 sets the segment identifier to the intended value, SEG_ID.

In the second approach, clever use of addressing modes keeps processes out of forbidden memory areas. If you need more background on addressing modes, consult Hennessy and Patterson (2002) or other books on operating systems or computer architecture. Of the various addressing modes, relative addressing is of particular interest for us.

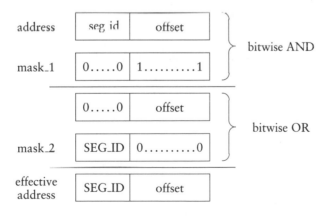

○ **Figure 5.10: Address Sandboxing**

**Relative Addressing**   The address is specified by an offset relative to a given base address.

Relative addressing allows position-independent coding. Thus a program can be stored anywhere in memory giving greater flexibility to the memory management utilities. It also facilitates the use of *fence registers*. The fence register contains the address of the end of the memory area allocated to the operating system. Addresses in a user program are interpreted as relative addresses (*offset, displacement*). The operating system then uses relative addressing with respect to the fence register (*base register addressing*) to calculate the effective addresses (Figure 5.11). In this way, only locations outside the operating system space can be accessed by user programs. Similar methods can be employed by the operating system to separate the memory areas allocated to different users.

This approach can be refined by defining the memory space allocated to a process through *base registers* and *bounds registers*. One can even go a step further and introduce base and bounds registers for a user's program space and data space respectively. To make proper use of such a facility, the processor must be able to detect whether a given memory location contains data or program code. The Motorola 68000 processor did support such a separation through *function codes* (Figure 5.12). Function codes signal the processor status to the address decoder, which may use this information to select between user memory and supervisor memory or between data and programs.

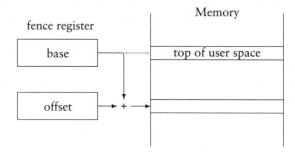

Figure 5.11: Base Register Addressing

| FC2 | FC1 | FC0 | |
|---|---|---|---|
| 0 | 0 | 0 | (undefined, reserved) |
| 0 | 0 | 1 | user data |
| 0 | 1 | 0 | user program |
| 0 | 1 | 1 | (undefined, reserved) |
| 1 | 0 | 0 | (undefined, reserved) |
| 1 | 0 | 1 | supervisor data |
| 1 | 1 | 0 | supervisor program |
| 1 | 1 | 1 | interrupt acknowledge |

Figure 5.12:  Motorola 68000 Function Codes

## Lesson

The ability to distinguish between data and programs is a very useful security feature. It provides a basis for protecting programs from modification.

From a more abstract point of view, memory has been divided into different regions. Access control can then refer to the *location* a data object or a program comes from.

## Lesson

You have now an example of location-based access control in a microcosm. In distributed systems or computer networks, you often require location-based access control in a macrocosm.

Most instruction sets have no means for instructions to check the type of their operands. In their absence, type information can be supplied in the program by specifying the address registers which have to be used in the different memory access operations. This solution requires proper programming discipline.

In contrast, in a *tagged architecture*, each data item has a tag specifying its type. Before execution, the CPU can detect any type violation directly from the value stored in memory. These tags could also be used to enforce security policies. Historically, tagged architectures have been popular in theoretical considerations rather than in actual implementations. The few examples of tagged architectures include the Burroughs B6500-7500 system and the IBM System/38 (Berstis *et al.*, 1978). (For the reader with an interest in the history of computing, von Neumann (1993) in his *First Draft of a Report on the EDVAC* in 1945 describes a tagged architecture.) Figure 5.13 shows a tagged architecture which indicates the type of memory objects, e.g. integer (INT), bit string (STR) or operand (OP). Tags can also be used to indicate which access operation may be performed on a memory location, e.g. read, write or execute.

| tag | data |
|-----|------|
| INT | . . . . . . . . . . . . . |
| OP | . . . . . . . . . . . . . |
| STR | . . . . . . . . . . . . . |
| . . . . . | . . . . . . . . . . . . . |
| . . . . . | . . . . . . . . . . . . . |
| . . . . . | . . . . . . . . . . . . . |

○ **Figure 5.13: A Tagged Architecture**

## 5.5 FURTHER READING

The fundamental access control paradigms are due to Lampson (1974). The original case for reference monitors is made in the Anderson report (1972). The outcome of computer security research aimed at the first multiuser operating systems is treated comprehensively by Denning (1982). A further survey of protection techniques is available in Landwehr (1983). An excellent account of the techniques used in the design of secure multiuser operating systems is available in Gasser (1988), which is out of print but available on the web at `http://www.acsac.org/secshelf/book002.html`. This book contains many useful pointers to technical reports in this area.

Building security kernels with Intel 80x86 processors is discussed by Sibert, Porras and Lindell (1996). Address sandboxing and related techniques are described by Wahbe *et al.*, (1993).

The early history of the development of secure computer systems has been collated by MacKenzie and Pottinger (1997). Opposing points in the discussion whether TCBs (security kernels) are still an appropriate paradigm in the construction of secure systems are taken in Blakely (1996, against) and Baker (1996, in favor). Theoretical foundations for the design of reference monitors are explored in Schneider (2000).

## 5.6 EXERCISES

**Exercise 5.1**   Microprocessors on smart cards used to have their entire card operating system in ROM. Currently, there are moves towards microprocessors where part of the operating system can be downloaded into EEPROM (electrically erasable programmable read-only memory). What are the advantages and disadvantages of keeping the operating system in ROM? What are the security implications of moving parts of the operating system into EEPROM?

**Exercise 5.2**   Can you have security without security kernels? Discuss the advantages and disadvantages of having a security kernel as the TCB.

**Exercise 5.3**   Look for examples that show how the following three principles are applied in building secure systems: separation of duties, abstract datatypes and atomic operations. (An atomic operation has to be executed in its entirety to preserve security. If it is interrupted, the system may end up in an insecure state.)

**Exercise 5.4**   So-called parasitic viruses infect executable programs. How can the ability to distinguish between programs and data help to construct a defense against such viruses?

**Exercise 5.5**   Some buffer overrun attacks put the code they want to be executed on the call stack. How can the ability to distinguish between programs and data help to construct a defense against this particular type of buffer overrun attack?

**Exercise 5.6**   Anti-virus software scans files for attack signatures. How could a virus intercept the read requests to memory and hide its existence?

**Exercise 5.7**   Consider a system that writes event numbers to its audit log and uses a table to translate these numbers into messages. What is the potential advantage of using this level of indirection in log file entries? What are the potential dangers?

**Exercise 5.8**   As a case study, examine how type enforcement is implemented in SE Linux.

# Chapter

# 6

## Unix Security

So far, we have looked at individual security mechanisms in isolation. In an actual implementation, they rely on each other. For example, access control and authentication have to work together, each would not be effective without the other. Hence, we now turn our attention to the security mechanisms provided by an operating system. Unix is our first example as it gives us the chance to inspect the mechanics of security at a fair level of detail. Security mechanisms in Linux are sufficiently similar to their counterparts in Unix for this chapter to serve as an introduction to Linux security.

### OBJECTIVES

- Understand the security features provided by a typical operating system.
- Introduce the basics of Unix security.
- See how general security principles are implemented in an actual system.
- Appreciate the task of managing security in a continuously changing environment.

## 6.1 INTRODUCTION

Operating systems combine building blocks like identification and authentication, access control and auditing to provide a coherent set of security controls. Once we decide to support flexible and 'feature-rich' security policies, security mechanisms become increasingly complex. In those circumstances, the TCB will be too large to fit into a small security kernel. In our layered model, we now look at the security controls provided at the operating system level. When assessing the security of an operating system, the following questions may guide your analysis.

- Which security features have been implemented?
- How can these security features be managed?
- What assurances are there that the security features will be effective?

There is a general pattern to the way security controls are organized in most commercial operating systems. Information about users (subjects) is stored in *user accounts*. Any *privileges* granted to a user can be stored in this account. *Identification* and *authentication* verify a user's identity, allowing the system to associate the user's privileges with any process started by the user. *Permissions* on resources (objects) can be set by the systems manager or the owner of a resource. When deciding whether to grant or deny an access request, the operating system may refer to the user's identity, the user's privileges and the permissions set for the object.

Security not only deals with the *prevention* of unauthorized actions but also with their *detection*. We have to face up to the fact that attackers may find their way round protection mechanisms. Provisions have to be made to keep track of the actions users have performed to be able to investigate security breaches or to trace attempted attacks. Therefore, operating systems will be required to keep and protect an *audit log (audit trail)* of security-relevant events.

Finally, the best security features of an operating system are worthless if they are not used properly. A system has to be started in a secure state, thus *installation* and *configuration* of the operating system are important issues. Inadequate default settings can be a major security weakness. Operating systems are highly complex and continually evolving software systems. Hence, there is always the chance that vulnerabilities are detected and removed or accidentally introduced in a new release. Alert systems managers have thus to stay in touch with current developments.

We have outlined a framework that structures operating system security along the lines of:

- principals, subjects and objects
- access control
- audit, configuration and management.

This chapter examines the security features of the Unix operating system. Because of its design history, Unix did not have a great reputation for reliability or security, see e.g. B.F. Miller, Frederiksen and So (1990), but it does offer a set of security features which can be quite effective if used properly, and attitudes towards Unix security have changed considerably. Different releases of Unix and Linux may differ in some technicalities and in the way some security controls are enforced. Commands and filenames used in this chapter are thus indicative of typical use but may be different on your particular system. In an attempt to standardize Unix security the POSIX 1003 series of standards defines a common interface to Unix systems. POSIX 1003.6 deals with security mechanisms.

This chapter is by no means intended to be a complete introduction to Unix security or an instruction on how to set up your Unix system securely. Rather, we will limit ourselves to presenting the basics of Unix security and to highlighting security features that illustrate points of general interest.

### 6.1.1 Unix Security Architecture

While most secure operating systems have a *security architecture* explaining how security is enforced and where security-relevant data is kept, Unix has a history of diverging and converging versions. This is a fair reflection of the fact that security features were added into Unix whenever the necessity arose, rather than being an original design objective.

Unix was originally designed for small multiuser computers in a networked environment and later scaled up to commercial servers, and scaled down to PCs. Like the Internet, Unix was developed for friendly environments such as research laboratories or universities, and security mechanisms were weak. As Unix developed, new security controls were added to the system and existing controls were strengthened. When deciding on how to implement a new feature, designers are guided very much by the desire to interfere as little as possible with the existing structures of Unix. The Unix design philosophy assumes that security is managed by a skilled administrator, not by the average computer user. Hence, support for security management often comes in the form of scripts and command line tools.

## 6.2 PRINCIPALS

The principals are so-called *user identities (UIDs)* and *group identities (GIDs)*. UIDs and GIDs are 16-bit numbers. Some UID values have special meanings, which may differ between systems but the superuser (root) UID is always 0. UID examples are listed in Table 6.1.

### 6.2.1 User Accounts

Information about principals is stored in *user accounts* and *home directories*. User accounts are stored in the /etc/passwd file. Entries in this file have the format

| −2 | nobody |
|------|----------|
| 0 | root |
| 1 | daemon |
| 2 | uucp |
| 3 | bin |
| 4 | games |
| 9 | audit |
| 567 | tuomaura |

○ **Table 6.1: Examples of User IDs**

user name:password:UID:GID:ID string:home directory:login shell

The *user name* is a string up to eight characters long. It identifies the user when logging in but is not used for access control. Unix does not distinguish between users with the same UID. The *password* is stored encrypted (section 6.3.1). The field *ID string* contains the user's full name. The last two fields specify the user's *home directory* and the Unix *shell* available to the user after successful login. Further user-specific settings are defined in the `.profile` file in the user's home directory. The actions taken by the system when a user logs in are specified in the file `/etc/profile`. Displaying the password file with `cat /etc/passwd` or `less /etc/passwd` will produce entries like

```
dieter:RT.QsZEEsxT92:10026:53:Dieter Gollmann:/home/staff
/dieter:/usr/local/bin/bash
```

## 6.2.2 Superuser (Root)

In every Unix system there is a user with special privileges. This *superuser* has UID 0 and usually the user name *root*. The root account is used by the operating system for essential tasks like login, recording the audit log, or access to I/O devices.

All security checks are turned off for the superuser who can do almost everything. For example, the superuser can become any other user. The superuser can change the system clock. The superuser can find a way round some of the few restrictions imposed on him. For example, a superuser cannot write to a filesystem mounted as read only but he can dismount the filesystem and remount it as writable. The superuser cannot decrypt passwords because `crypt` is a one-way function.

### 6.2.3 Groups

Users belong to one or more *groups*. Collecting users in groups is a convenient basis for access control decisions. For example, one could put all users allowed to access email in a group called `mail`, or all operators in a group `operator`. Every user belongs to a *primary group*. The GID of the primary group is stored in `/etc/passwd`. The file `/etc/group` contains a list of all groups. Entries in this file have the format

group name:group password:GID:list of users

For example, the entry

```
infosecwww:*:209:chez,af
```

tells us that group `infosecwww` has the password disabled, has GID 209, and has two members, `chez` and `af`. Table 6.2 lists group IDs with special meanings.

In System V Unix, a user can only be in one group at a time. The current group is changed with the `newgrp` command. Users are free to change into a group where they are already a member. If users attempt to change in to a group where they are not members, `newgrp` will prompt for a password and give temporary membership if the correct *group password* is entered. In Berkeley Unix, a user can reside in more than one group so there is no need for a `newgrp` command.

| | |
|---|---|
| 0 | system/wheel |
| 1 | daemon |
| 2 | uucp |
| 3 | mem |
| 4 | bin |
| 7 | terminal |

○ **Table 6.2: Special Group IDs**

## 6.3 SUBJECTS

The subjects are processes. Each process has a *process ID (PID)*. New processes are created using `exec` or `fork`. Each process is associated with a *real* UID/GID and an *effective* UID/GID. The real UID is inherited from the parent process. Typically it is the UID of the user who is logged in. The effective UID is inherited from the parent process or from the file being executed (section 6.5.1). POSIX-compliant versions also keep a *saved* UID/GID. The following example demonstrates both the use of real and effective UID/GID and the Unix logon process.

| Process | UID real | effective | GID real | effective |
|---|---|---|---|---|
| /bin/login | root | root | system | system |

User dieter logs on; the logon process verifies username and password and changes UID and GID:

| | | | | |
|---|---|---|---|---|
| /bin/login | dieter | dieter | staff | staff |

The logon process executes the user's login shell:

| | | | | |
|---|---|---|---|---|
| /bin/bash | dieter | dieter | staff | staff |

From the shell the user executes the command ls:

| | | | | |
|---|---|---|---|---|
| /bin/ls | dieter | dieter | staff | staff |

The user executes command su to start a new shell as root:

| | | | | |
|---|---|---|---|---|
| /bin/bash | dieter | root | staff | system |

## 6.3.1 Login and Passwords

In Unix, users are identified by *usernames* and authenticated by *passwords*. When the system is booted, the login process is started running as root. When a user logs in, this process verifies username and password. If the verification succeeds, UID/GID are changed to that of the user, and the user's login shell is executed. Root login can be restricted to terminals nominated in /etc/ttys. The last time a user has logged in is recorded in /usr/adm/lastlog and can be displayed e.g. with the finger command.

On many Unix systems, passwords are limited to eight characters. There exist tools that support good practice in choosing passwords by preventing the use of weak passwords. Passwords are enciphered (hashed, to be precise) with the crypt(3) algorithm, which repeats a slightly modified DES algorithm 25 times, using the all-zero block as start value and the password as key. The encrypted passwords are stored in the /etc/passwd file.

When the password field for a user is empty, the user does not have to provide a password on login. When the password field starts with an asterisk, the user cannot log in because such values can never be the result of applying the one-way function to a cleartext password. This is a common method of disabling a user's account.

Passwords are changed using the passwd(1) command. You are asked to supply your old password first to guard against someone else changing your password if you leave your screen unattended for a moment (regarded as bad practice anyway). Since characters are never displayed on the screen when a password is entered, you are asked to enter a new password twice, to ensure that what you think you typed and what you really typed are the same. After a change, you can confirm the effect of the change with a new login or with the su(1) (set user) command.

### 6.3.2 Shadow Password File

Security-conscious versions of Unix offer further provisions for password security. The file /etc/passwd is world-readable as it contains data from user accounts that are needed by many programs. Thus, an attacker can copy the password file and then search for passwords in an off-line dictionary attack. To remove this vulnerability, passwords are stored in a *shadow password file*, e.g. /.secure/etc/passwd, that can only be accessed by root. This file can also be used for password aging and automatic account locking. File entries have nine fields comprising:

- username;
- password;
- date of last change;
- minimum number of days between password changes;
- maximum number of days the password is valid;
- how many days in advance the user is warned that the password will expire;
- number of days the user may be in active;
- date when login may no longer be used;
- reserved.

Password salting is another method for slowing down dictionary attacks. The *salt* is a random 12-bit value that is added to the password proper, and stored in the clear.

## 6.4 OBJECTS

The objects of access control include files, directories, memory devices and I/O devices. For the purpose of access control, all are treated uniformly as *resources*. Resources are organized in a tree-structured file system.

### 6.4.1 The Inode

Each file entry in a directory is a pointer to a data structure called an *inode*. Table 6.3 gives fields in the inode that are relevant for access control. Each directory contains a pointer to itself, the file '.', and a pointer to its parent directory, the file '..'. Every file has an owner, usually the user who has created the file. Every file belongs to a group.

| mode | type of file and access rights |
|---|---|
| uid | user who owns the file |
| gid | group which owns the file |
| atime | access time |
| mtime | modification time |
| itime | inode alteration time |
| block count | size of file |
|  | physical location |

◯ **Table 6.3: Fields in the Inode Relevant for Access Control**

Depending on the version of Unix, a newly created file belongs either to its creator's group or to its directory's group.

Before discussing the field in the inode we inspect a directory with the command `ls -l` and get the listing

```
-rw-r--r-- 1 diego staff 1617 Oct 28 11:01 adcryp.tex

drwx------ 2 diego staff  512 Oct 25 17:44 ads/
```

which contains some of the information we are looking for.

- The first character gives the type of the file: '-' indicates a file, 'd' a directory, 'b' a block device file and 'c' a character device file.

- The next nine characters give the *file permissions*, to be discussed below.

- The following numerical field is the *link counter*, counting the number of links (pointers) to the file.

- The next two fields are the *name* of the owner and the *group* of the file.

- Then follows the size of the file in bytes.

- The time and date is mtime, the time of the last modification. `ls -lu` displays atime, the time of last access. `ls -lc` displays itime, the time of the last modification of the inode.

- The last entry is the name of the file. The '/' after `ads` indicates a directory. The filename is stored in the directory, not in the inode.

The *file permissions (permission bits)* are grouped in three triples that define read, write and execute access for *owner*, *group*, and *other* (also called *world*) respectively. A '-'

indicates that a right is not granted. Thus rw-r--r-- gives read and write access to the owner and read access to group and other, rwx------ gives read, write and execute access to the owner and no rights to group and other.

File permissions in Unix are also specified as octal numbers by splitting the nine permissions into three groups of three. Each access right is represented by a bit, which, if set, grants access. These numbers are shown in Table 6.4. A combination of rights is the sum of the corresponding numbers. For example, the permission rw-r--r-- is equivalent to 644. The permission 777 gives all access rights to owner, group and others.

| 400 | read by owner |
|-----|----------------|
| 200 | write by owner |
| 100 | execute by owner |
| 040 | read by group |
| 020 | write by group |
| 010 | execute by group |
| 004 | read by world |
| 002 | write by world |
| 001 | execute by world |

Table 6.4: Octal Representation of Access Permissions

## 6.4.2 Default Permissions

Unix utilities, like editors or compilers, typically use default permissions 666 when creating a new file and permissions 777 when creating a new program. These permissions can be further adjusted by the umask. The umask is three-digit octal number specifying the rights that should be withheld. Thus, umask 777 denies every access, umask 000 does not add any further restrictions. Sensible default settings are:

022 all permissions for the owner, read and execute permission for group and world;
037 all permissions for the owner, read permission for group, no permissions for world;
077 all permissions for the owner, no permissions for group and world.

The actual default permission is then derived by *masking* the default permissions of a Unix utility with the umask. A logical AND of the bits in the default permission and of the inverse of the bits in the umask is computed. For example, given default permission 666 and umask 077 we compute 666 AND NOT(077) which results in 600, giving the owner of the file read and write access while all other access is denied. The umask can be changed by the command

```
umask [-S] [mask]
```

where the flag -S indicates symbolic mode. When no mask is specified, the current umask is displayed.

The umask in /etc/profile defines a system-wide default setting. These default settings can be overruled for individual users by putting umask into the user's home directory in files like /etc/profile, .profile, .login, or .cshrc, depending on the way a particular Unix installation has been set up. Unlike in other operating systems, it is not possible to define individual default permissions for directories and let files inherit their permissions from their directory.

When a new file is created using the copy command cp, the permissions of the file are derived from the umask. When a new file is created by renaming an existing file using the command mv, the existing permissions are retained.

### 6.4.3 Permissions for Directories

Every user has a *home directory*, e.g. /home/staff/dieter. Subdirectories are created with the mkdir command. To put files and subdirectories into a directory, a user has to have the correct file permissions for the directory.

- Read permission allows a user to find which files are in the directory, e.g. by executing ls or similar commands.

- Write permission allows a user to add files to and remove files from the directory.

- Execute permission is required for making the directory the current directory and for opening files inside the directory. You can open a file in the directory if you know that it exists but you cannot use ls to see what is in the directory.

Thus, to get access to your own files, you need execute permission in the directory. To prevent other users from reading your files, you could either set the access permission accordingly or you could prevent access to the directory. To delete a file, you need write and execute access to the directory. You do not need any permission on the file itself. It can even belong to another user. To quote a systems manager on this feature:

> A real pain if you try and install a permanent file in someone's directory.

A remnant from earlier versions of Unix is the sticky bit. Its original purpose was to keep the text segment of a program in virtual memory after its first use. The system thus avoided having to transfer the program code of frequently accessed programs into the paging area. Today, the sticky bit is used to restrict the right to delete a file. For example, job queues are often world-writable so that anyone can add a file. However, in this case everyone would be able to delete files as well. When a directory has the sticky bit set, an entry can only be removed or renamed by a user if the user is the owner of the file, the owner of the directory, and has write permission for the directory, or by the superuser.

When ls -1 displays a directory with the sticky bit set, t appears instead of x as the execute permission for world.

## 6.5 ACCESS CONTROL

Access control is based on attributes of subjects (processes) and of objects (resources). Standard Unix systems associate three sets of access rights with each resource, corresponding to *owner, group, world*. *Superusers* are not subject to this kind of access control. Unix treats all resources in a uniform manner by making no distinction between files and devices. The permission bits are checked in the following order.

- If your uid indicates that you are the owner of the file, the permission bits for *owner* decide whether you can get access.
- If you are not the owner of the file but your gid indicates that your group owns the file, the permission bits for *group* decide whether you can get access.
- If you are neither the owner of the file nor a member of the group that owns the file, the permission bits for *other* decide whether you can get access.

It is therefore possible to set permission bits so that the owner of a file has less access than other users. This may come as a surprise but this fact is also a valuable general lesson. For any access control mechanism you have to know precisely in which order different access criteria are checked.

### 6.5.1 Set UserID and Set GroupID

We return to one of our favorite topics, controlled invocation. Unix requires superuser privilege to execute certain operating system functions, for example only root can listen at the *trusted ports* 0–123, but users should not be given superuser status. A way has to be found to meet both demands. The solutions adopted in Unix are *SUID (set userID) programs* and *SGID (set groupID) programs*. Such programs run with the effective user ID or group ID of their owner or group, giving temporary or restricted access to files not normally accessible to other users. When ls -1 displays an SUID program, then the execute permission of the owner is given as s instead of x:

```
-rws--x--x 3 root bin 16384 Nov 16 1996 passwd*
```

When ls -1 displays an SGID program, the execute permission of the group is given as s instead of x. In the octal representation of permissions a fourth octet placed in front of the permissions for owner, group and others is used to indicate SUID and SGID programs, and directories with the sticky bit set (Table 6.5).

| | |
|------|------------------------|
| 4000 | set user ID on execution |
| 2000 | set group ID on execution |
| 1000 | set sticky bit |

○ **Table 6.5: Octal Representation of SUID and SGID Programs**

If, as is often the case, root is the owner of an SUID program, a user who is executing this program will get superuser status *during execution*. Important SUID programs are:

| | |
|-------------|-----------------------|
| /bin/passwd | change password |
| /bin/login | login program |
| /bin/at | batch job submission |
| /bin/su | change UID program |

We have to add our customary warning. As the user has the program owner's privileges during execution of an SUID program, this program should only do what the owner intended. This is particularly true for SUID programs owned by root. An attacker who can change the behavior of an SUID program, e.g. by interrupting its execution, may embark on actions requiring superuser status not only during the attack but may also be able to change the system so that superuser status can be obtained on further occasions. In this respect, danger comes from SUID programs with user interaction. All user input, including command line arguments and environment variables, must be processed with extreme care. A particular pitfall is *shell escapes* which give a user access to shell commands while running as superuser. Programs should have SUID status only if it is really necessary. The systems manager should monitor the integrity of SUID programs with particular care. Two case studies where SUID programs were used for successful attacks are reported by Garfinkel, Spafford and Schwartz (2003).

## 6.5.2 Changing Permissions

The permission bits of a file are changed with the chmod command which can be run only by the owner of the file or by the superuser. This command has the following formats.

chmod [-fR] absolute_mode file          specifies the value for all
                                        permission bits

chmod [-fR] [who]+permission file       adds permissions

```
chmod [-fR] [who]-permission file          removes permissions

chmod [-fR] [who]=permission file          resets permissions as specified
```

In *absolute mode*, the file permissions are specified directly by an octal number. In *symbolic mode*, the current file permissions are modified. The *who* parameter can take the values:

u  ... changes the owner permissions;
g  ... changes the group permissions;
o  ... changes the other permissions;
a  ... changes all permissions.

The *permission* parameter can take the values:

r Read permission.
w Write permission.
x Execute permission for files, search permission for directories.
X Execute permission only if file is a directory or at least one execute bit is set.
s Set-user-ID or set-group-ID permission.
t Save text permission. (Set the sticky bit.)

The option -f suppresses error messages, the option -R applies the specified change recursively to all subdirectories of the current directory.

The SUID permission of a program can be set as follows.

```
chmod 4555 file      set suid flag
chmod u+s file       set suid flag
chmod 555 file       clear suid flag
chmod u-s file       clear suid flag
```

The GUID permission is set using g instead of the u option.

The command chown changes the owner of a file, chgrp changes the group of a file. The chown command could be a potential source of unwelcome SUID programs. A user could create an SUID program and then change the owner to root. To prevent such an attack, some versions of Unix only allow the superuser to run chown. Other versions allow users to apply chown to their own files and have chown turn off the SUID and SGID bit. Similar considerations apply to chgrp.

### 6.5.3 Limitations of Unix Access Control

Files have only one owner and one group. Permissions only control read, write and execute access. Thus, all other access rights, e.g. the right to shut down the system or the right to create a new user, have to be mapped to the basic file access permissions. Operations other than read, write, execute have to be left to the applications. In general, it is often impractical to implement more complex security policies with the Unix access control mechanisms. In this respect, Unix security lies more towards the machine end of the man–machine scale (Figure 6.1).

Figure 6.1: Unix Security on the Man–Machine Scale

# 6.6 INSTANCES OF GENERAL SECURITY PRINCIPLES

In this section, we will use Unix as a case study to demonstrate how some of our general security principles find their expression in practice.

## 6.6.1 Applying Controlled Invocation

A sensitive resource like a web server that potentially will be accessed by many users can be protected by controlled invocation schemes that combine the concepts of ownership, permission bits and SUID programs.

- Create a new UID 'web server' that owns the resource and all the programs that need access to the resource.
- Give access permission to the resource only to its owner.
- Define all the programs that access the resource as SUID programs.

**Lesson**

Beware of overprotection. If you deny users direct access to a file they need to perform their job, you have to provide indirect access through SUID programs. A flawed SUID program may give users more opportunities for access than wisely chosen permission bits. This is particularly true if the owner of the resource and the SUID program is a privileged user like root.

In this case we see an example of a technique that is often used in the design of secure systems. An abstract attribute is represented by a data structure in the system. This data structure is then reused by another security mechanism for a different purpose. The UID was introduced as the representation of real users in the system. Now, the UID is used for a new kind of access control where it no longer corresponds to real users.

### 6.6.2 Deleting Files

Favorite topic number two: logical versus physical memory structure. In particular, what happens if we remove (delete) a file from the filesystem? Does it still exist in some form?

Unix has two ways of copying files. The command cp creates an identical but independent copy owned by the user running cp. The commands link and ln only create a new filename with a pointer to the original file and increase the *link counter* of the original file. The new file shares its contents with the original. If the original file is deleted with rm or rmdir, it disappears from its parent directory but the contents of the file as well as its copy still exist. Hence, users may think that they have deleted a file whereas it still exists in another directory, and they still own it. If you want to be sure to get rid of a file, the superuser has to run ncheck to list all the links to that file and then delete those links. Also, if another process has opened a file which is then deleted by its owner, the file will remain in existence until that process closes the file.

Once a file has been deleted, the memory space allocated to this file becomes available again. However, until these memory locations have actually been used again they will still contain the file's contents. To avoid such *memory residues*, you should *wipe* the file by overwriting its contents with all-zeros or another pattern appropriate for the storage medium before deleting it. Even then your file may not have been deleted completely as advanced filesystems, e.g. a defragmenter, may move files around leaving more copies of the file on disk.

### 6.6.3 Protection of Devices

The next issue still relates to the distinction between logical and physical memory structures. Unix treats devices like files. Thus, access to memory or access to a printer can be controlled like access to a file through setting permission bits. Devices are created using the mknod command which should only be executable by root. A small sample of the devices commonly found in the directory /dev is:

| | |
|---|---|
| /dev/console | console terminal |
| /dev/mem | main memory map device (image of the physical memory) |
| /dev/kmem | kernel memory map device (image of the virtual memory) |
| /dev/tty | terminal |

Attackers can bypass the controls set on files and directories if they can get access to the memory devices holding these files. If the read or write permission bits for world are set on a memory device, an attacker can browse through memory or modify data in memory without being affected by the permissions defined for the files stored in this memory. Almost all devices should therefore be world-unreadable and world-unwritable.

Commands like the *process status* command `ps` display information about memory usage and therefore require access permissions for the memory devices. Defining `ps` as an SUID to root program allows `ps` to acquire the necessary permissions but a compromise of the `ps` command would leave an attacker with root privileges. A more elegant solution has `ps` as an SGID program and lets the group `mem` own the memory devices.

The `tty` terminal devices are another interesting example. When a user logs in, a terminal file is allocated to the user who becomes owner of the file for the session. (When a terminal file is not used, it is owned by root.) It is convenient to make this file world-readable and -writable so that the user can receive messages from other parties. However, this also introduces vulnerabilities. The other parties are now able to monitor the entire traffic to and from the terminal, potentially including the user's password. They can send commands to the user's terminal, for example reprogramming a function key, and have these commands executed by the unwitting user. In some systems, intelligent terminals execute some commands automatically. This gives an attacker the opportunity to submit commands using the privileges of another user.

### 6.6.4 Changing the Root of the Filesystem

Access control can be implemented by constraining suspect processes in a *sandbox*. Access to objects outside the sandbox is prevented. In Unix, the *change root* command `chroot` restricts the part of the filesystem available to an unauthorized user. This command can only be executed by root.

`chroot` &lt;directory&gt; &lt;command&gt;

changes the root directory from / to *directory* when *command* executes. Only files below the new root are thereafter accessible. If you employ this strategy, you have to make sure that user programs find all the system files they need. These files are 'expected' to be in directories like `/bin`, `/dev`, `/etc`, `/tmp`, or `/usr`. New directories of the same names have to be created under the new root and populated with the files the user will need by copying or linking to the respective files in the original directories.

### 6.6.5 Mounting Filesystems

When you have different security domains and introduce objects from another domain into your system, you may have to redefine the access control attributes of these objects.

The Unix filesystem is built by linking together filesystems held on different physical devices under a single root, denoted by '/'. This is achieved with the `mount` command. In a networked environment, remote filesystems (NFS) can be mounted from other network nodes. Similarly, users could be allowed to mount a filesystem from their own floppy disk (`automount`).

If you are security experts, warning bells should start to ring. The mounted filesystems could contain all sorts of unwelcome files, for example SUID to root programs sitting in an attacker's directory. Once the filesystem has been mounted, the attacker could obtain superuser status by running such a program. Danger also comes from device files which allow direct access to memory, where the permissions have been set so that an attacker has access to these files. Therefore, the command

$$\texttt{mount [-r] [-o options] device directory}$$

comes with a `-r` flag specifying read-only mount and options like

| | |
|---|---|
| nosuid | turns off the SUID and SGID bits on the mounted filesystem |
| noexec | no binaries can be executed from the mounted filesystem |
| nodev | no block or character special devices can be accessed from the filesystem. |

Again, different versions of Unix implement different options for `mount`.

### Lesson

UIDs and GIDs are *local* identifiers that need not be interpreted the same way on different Unix systems (from different vendors). When mounting remote filesystems, clients may misinterpret these identifiers. Hence, you ought to use *globally unique* identifiers across networks.

## 6.6.6 Environment Variables

Environment variables are kept by the shell and are normally used to configure the behavior of utility programs. Table 6.6 lists some environment variables for the *bash* shell. A process inherits the environment variables by default from its parent process and a program executing another program can set the environment variables for the program called to arbitrary values.

This is a problem as the invoker of SUID/SGID programs is in control of the environment variables these programs are given. An attacker could try to take control of execution by setting the environment variables to dangerous values. Furthermore, many libraries and programs are controlled by environment variables in obscure, subtle or undocumented ways. For example, an attacker may set IFS to unusual values to circumvent protection mechanisms that filter out dangerous inputs to SUID/SGID programs (more in Chapter 14). As a countermeasure, an SUID/SGID program could erase the entire environment and then reset a small set of necessary environment variables to safe values.

| PATH | search path for shell commands |
|------|-------------------------------|
| TERM | terminal type |
| DISPLAY | name of display |
| LD_LIBRARY_PATH | path to search for object and shared libraries |
| HOSTNAME | name of Unix host |
| PRINTER | default printer |
| HOME | path to home directory |
| PS1 | default prompt |
| IFS | characters separating command line arguments |

○ **Table 6.6: Environment Variables for the *Bash* Shell**

**Lesson**

Inheriting things you don't want or don't know about can become a security problem.

### 6.6.7 Searchpath

Our final favorite is the execution of programs taken from a 'wrong' location. Unix users interact with the operating system through a *shell* (a command line interpreter.) As a matter of convenience, a user can run a program simply by typing its name without specifying the full *pathname* that gives the location of the program within the filesystem. The shell will then look for the program following a *searchpath* specified by the PATH environment variable given in the .profile file in the user's home directory. (Use ls -a to see all files in your home directory and more.profile to see your profile.) When a directory is found which contains a program with the name specified, the search stops and that program will be executed. A typical searchpath looks like

```
PATH=.:$HOME/bin:/usr/ucb:/bin:/usr/bin:/usr/local:/usr/new:
    /usr/hosts
```

In this example, directories in the searchpath are separated by ':', the first entry '.' is the current directory. It is now possible to insert a Trojan horse by giving it the same name as an existing program and putting it in a directory which is searched earlier than the directory containing the original program.

To defend against such attacks, call programs by giving their full pathname, e.g. /bin/su instead of su. Also, make sure that the current directory is not in the searchpath of programs executed by root.

## 6.6.8 Wrappers

The access control and audit mechanisms presented so far are not very sophisticated. They adhere to the traditions of operating system security and concentrate on controlling access to resources. It is possible to implement controls at 'intermediate levels' by judicious use of the basic access control mechanisms. Alternatively, we can modify Unix itself to achieve this goal. The challenge here is to find a component of Unix which can be changed in such a way that useful security controls are added while the rest of the operating system remains unaffected. Given the complexities of Unix, this is a nontrivial task.

TCP wrappers very elegantly demonstrate this design approach. Unix network services like telnet or ftp are built upon the following principle. The inetd daemon listens to incoming network connections. When a connection is made, inetd starts the appropriate server program, and then returns to listening for further connections. This daemon is known as a *super-server* as it handles work for many server programs. The inetd daemon has a configuration file that maps services (port numbers) to programs. An entry in this configuration file has the format

> service type protocol waitflag userid executable command-line

For example, the entry for telnet could be

```
telnet stream tcp nowait root /usr/bin/in.telnetd in.telnet
```

When inetd receives a request for a service it handles, it consults the configuration file and creates a new process that runs the *executable* specified. The name of this new process is changed to the name given in the *command-line* field.

Usually, the name of the executable and the name given in *command-line* are the same. This redundancy opens the door for a nice trick. Point the inetd daemon to a *wrapper program* instead of the original executable and use the name of the process to remember the name of the original executable, which you want to run after the wrapper has performed its security controls. In our example, the configuration file entry for telnet could be replaced by

```
telnet stream tcp nowait root /usr/bin/tcpd in.telnet
```

The program executed is now /usr/bin/tcpd. This is the TCP wrapper executable. The process executing the wrapper will still be called in.telnet. Within this wrapper, you can perform all the access control or logging you want to do. In the original application, wrappers were used for IP address filtering (Chapter 13). Because the wrapper knows the directory it is in, i.e. /usr/bin, and its own name, i.e. in.telnet, it can then call the original server program, i.e. /usr/bin/in.telnet. The user will see no difference and receives exactly the same service as before.

**Lesson**

Adding another level of indirection is a powerful tool in computer science. In security, it can be used to attack systems and to protect systems. By inserting a TCP wrapper between the `inetd` daemon and the server program, you are able to add security controls without changing either the source code of the daemon or the source code of the server program.

The beauty of this example is its generality. The same principle can be used to protect a whole set of Unix network services.

**Lesson**

TCP wrappers combine a fundamental design principle, viz. controlled invocation, and an elegant trick that makes it possible to add security checks to services without having to change the programs that call these services. This is the ideal situation when you have to retrofit security into an existing system.

## 6.7  MANAGEMENT ISSUES

We will quickly run through some issues that are relevant for managing the operational security of Unix systems.

### 6.7.1  Managing the Superuser

The root account is used by the operating system to perform its own essential tasks but also for certain other system administration tasks. Because superusers are so powerful, they are also a major weakness of Unix. An attacker achieving superuser status can effectively take over the entire system. Thus, every precaution has to be taken to control access to superuser status.

An attacker who is able to edit `/etc/passwd` can become a superuser by changing its UID to 0 so the files `/etc/passwd` and `/etc/group` have to be write protected. To reduce the impact of a compromise, separate the duties of the systems manager, e.g. by having special users like `uucp` or `daemon` to deal with networking. If one of these special users is compromised, not all is lost. Systems managers should not use root as their personal account. When necessary, change to root can be requested by typing `/bin/su` (without specifying a user name). The operating system will not refer to a version of `su` that has been put in another directory. Record all `su` attempts in the audit log together with the user (account) who issued the command.

### 6.7.2  Trusted Hosts

In a friendly environment, it may be sufficient to authenticate a user only once although a number of different machines are being accessed. *Trusted hosts* in Unix support this mode of operation. Users from a trusted host can log on without password authentication. They only need to have the same username on both hosts. Trusted hosts of a machine are specified in /etc/hosts.equiv. Trusted hosts of a user are specified in the .rhosts file in the user's home directory.

User names must be synchronized across hosts, a task that becomes tedious as the number of hosts grows. (Vendor-specific configuration tools exist.) Once a host has been entered into /etc/hosts.equiv, all users on this host have access. Exceptions are difficult to configure.

### 6.7.3 Audit Logs and Intrusion Detection

Once the system has been installed and is operational, its security mechanisms should prevent illegal user actions. However, the protection mechanisms may not be adequate or flawed. Undesirable security settings may be mandatory to keep the system running. Therefore, further mechanisms are desirable to detect security violations or other suspicious events when they are happening or after they have happened. Some security-relevant events are recorded automatically in Unix log files.

- /usr/adm/lastlog – records the last time a user has logged in; this information can be displayed with the finger command.
- /var/adm/utmp – records accounting information used by the who command.
- /var/adm/wtmp – records every time a user logs in or logs out; this information can be displayed with the last command. To prevent this file from taking over all available memory, it may be pruned automatically at regular intervals.
- /var/adm/acct – records all executed commands; this information can be displayed with the lastcomm command.

The precise name and location of these files may be different on your Unix system. Accounting, turned on by the accton command, can also be used for auditing purposes. Further commands for observing a Unix system are find, grep, ps, users.

Examine the list of security-relevant events recorded in the log files just mentioned. Most of these events refer to a user so the log entry should include the UID of the process causing the event. How is auditing then affected by SUID programs? Such a program runs with the UID of its owner, not with the UID of the user running the program. Hence, the log entries should also include the real UID of the process.

### Lesson

User identifiers are a security attribute that is used for two purposes, access control and accountability. It is not always possible to employ the same attribute for both purposes at the same time. As long as UIDs correspond to 'real' users, access control based on permissions and auditing complement each other. Once you create special user identities to protect access to resources through SUID or SGID programs, you get an attribute that is of limited use in auditing.

### 6.7.4 Installation and Configuration

A crucial point in the life of an operating system is its installation. Operating systems will have many security features and features affecting security, all of which may not be well documented. Historically, default settings favored smooth installation and operation, giving too many privileges to the maintenance engineer or to the systems manager. It is appropriate to restrict the systems manager in the same way as every other user and to separate the roles of systems manager and security manager. Complex and badly documented features may render it very difficult to set up the system so that it effectively enforces the intended security policy. Unix by itself does little to ease the systems manager's job.

- Systems managers have to be knowledgeable about all security-relevant files and about dangerous default settings that have to be changed after installation.

- When a system is being set up, security-relevant parameters are defined with standard Unix editing commands. Permissions on resources are set at a level closer to the operating system than to an application. For example, users are installed by editing files like /etc/passwd. Protection of the passwd program is effected through commands like

```
chmod 4750 /bin/passwd chgrp staff /bin/passwd
```

- When auditing a system, Unix search commands are used. For example, the following instruction scans for accounts without a password.

```
awk -F: 'length($2) < 1 print $1' < /etc/passwd
```

SUID and SGID are found by

```
find  -type f ( -perm 2000 -o -perm 4000 ) -exec ls -ld {};
```

(Experienced Unix users take pride in crafting such commands but the average user would find it difficult to manage systems in such a fashion.)

- Access control policies are supported through simple discretionary access control. Structured protection can be implemented based on *group* membership and by using accounts with login disabled.

Thus, there is a place for add-on Unix security products, both for managing security features and for checking the current security status. Two popular checking tools are COPS (Framer and Spafford, 1990) and SATAN. They search for known flaws like weak passwords, bad permissions on files and directories, or malformed configuration files. These tools can be used by systems managers to detect vulnerabilities in the systems they manage but they are not universally popular as they can be used by an attacker for the very same purpose.

## 6.8 FURTHER READING

This chapter has taken snapshots of Unix security. If you want a fuller picture, there is an abundance of books on this topic, e.g., Curry (1992), Ferbrache and Shearer (1992) and Garfinkel, Spafford and Schwartz (2003). If you need specific information about a particular Unix version, consult the documentation provided by the manufacturers and the on-line documentation *(manual pages)* provided on your system. Multilevel secure Unix systems are discussed by Samalin (1997). Information about Security Enhanced (SE) Linux can be found on the Web. Security advisories from *Computer Emergency Response Teams (CERTs)* keep you up to date with new security vulnerabilities.

## 6.9 EXERCISES

**Exercise 6.1** Check the on-line documentation for security-relevant commands. Find your own entry in /etc/passwd and check the permission settings on your files and directories.

**Exercise 6.2** Create a subdirectory in your home directory and put a file welcome.txt with a short message in this subdirectory. Set the permission bits on the subdirectory so that the owner has execute access. Try to:

- make the subdirectory the current directory with cd;
- list the subdirectory;
- display the contents of welcome.txt;
- create a copy of welcome.txt in the subdirectory.

Repeat the same experiments first with read permission and then with write permission on the subdirectory.

**Exercise 6.3** Which Unix command will list all world-writable files in your directories?

**Exercise 6.4** How would you protect a tty device from other users?

**Exercise 6.5** Can you capture Unix access control through UID, GID and permissions within the framework of the VSTa abilities (section 4.7.1)?

**Exercise 6.6** Implement the Chinese Wall model and the Clark–Wilson model with the Unix security mechanisms.

**Exercise 6.7**    How would you set up the backup procedure to reduce security exposures?

**Exercise 6.8**    In your assessment, what are the strong and weak points of Unix security. Write a short report on this topic (1000 words).

# Chapter 7

## Windows 2000 Security

Unix access control treats all objects uniformly as resources. In contrast, access control in Windows 2000 can be tailored to individual object types. We will therefore use Windows 2000 as an example to show how a more fine-grained approach to access control might be structured. The emphasis is on 'might' as we do not use any particular version for reference but build on a description of possible extensions of Windows access control published by Swift *et al.* (2002). After all, like with any other operating system, Windows security is a moving target. Design principles are more stable.

### OBJECTIVES

- Introduce the basics of Windows 2000 security.
- Show how to use indirection to make access control more manageable.
- Show how inheritance of access rights in a directory can be managed.
- Move from identity-based access control to code-based access control.

## 7.1 INTRODUCTION

We will not try to give a complete overview of Windows 2000 security or guidance on how to make best use of all its security features. Our main goal is to contrast the security mechanisms of Unix and Windows 2000 and to highlight features of general interest which illustrate fundamental issues of computer security. Windows 2000 provides considerable support for managing security. We will focus on principles and mention other aspects such as graphical interfaces for managing the security features only in passing. The efforts to secure Windows are reflected in the fact that Windows 2000 (with Service Pack 3) received a Common Criteria EAL4 certificate (section 10.6) in October 2002.

### 7.1.1 Architecture

The Windows system architecture is given in Figure 7.1. There is a separation between *user mode* (typically protection ring 3) and *kernel mode* (protection ring 0), just as in Unix. The *Hardware Abstraction Layer (HAL)* provides the interfaces to the computer hardware. The core operating system services, comprising the *Windows executive*, run in kernel mode. The executive includes the *Security Reference Monitor (SRM)*, which is in charge of access control.

User programs make API (application program interface) calls to invoke operating system services. Context switch and transition from ring 3 to ring 0 are handled by the Local Procedure Call facility. Device drivers (often third-party products) are running in kernel mode and are thus also security relevant as vulnerabilities in their code, such as buffer overruns, can be exploited by an attacker to take over a Windows system. The components of the *security subsystem* running in user mode are as follows:

- *Log-on Process (winlogon)*: the process that authenticates a user when logging on.
- *Local Security Authority (LSA)*: involved at logon when it checks the user account and creates an *access token* (more of this later); it is also responsible for auditing functions.
- *Security Account Manager (SAM)*: maintains the user account database that is used by the LSA during user authentication for local logon.

Passwords are stored in the SAM in hashed form. The properties of hash functions imply that passwords cannot be retrieved from the values stored in the SAM. In addition, the database of password hashes is encrypted.

### 7.1.2 The Registry

The *registry* is the central database for Windows configuration data. Entries in the registry are called *keys* (not to be confused with cryptographic keys). The tool for modifying the registry is the *Registry Editor* (Regedit.exe or Regedt32.exe). You can also use the Registry Editor to display the registry. At the top level, the registry has five important predefined keys.

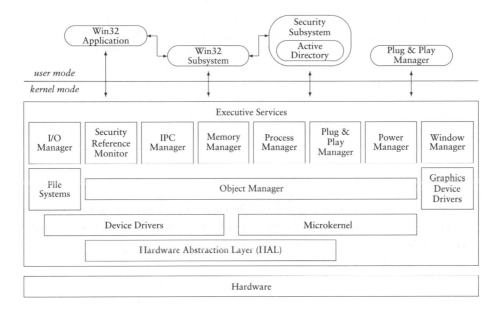

**Figure 7.1: Windows Systems Architecture (Microsoft product screen shot reprinted with permission from Microsoft Corporation)**

- HKEY_CLASSES_ROOT: contains file extension associations; e.g. you could specify that .doc files are handled by Word.

- HKEY_CURRENT_USER: configuration information for the user currently logged on.

- HKEY_LOCAL_MACHINE: configuration information about the local computer.

- HKEY_USERS: contains all actively loaded user profiles on the system.

- HKEY_CURRENT_CONFIG: information about the hardware profile used by the local computer at system startup.

A registry *hive* is a group of keys, subkeys, and values in the registry. Security-relevant hives are:

- HKEY_LOCAL_MACHINE\SAM

- HKEY_LOCAL_MACHINE\Security

- HKEY_LOCAL_MACHINE\Software

- HKEY_CURRENT_CONFIG

- HKEY_USERS\DEFAULT.

In the registry, the system can be tailored to user requirements and default protections are set. Of course, by modifying registry entries an attacker could modify the behavior of the operating system. For example, registry keys can point to locations where the operating system automatically looks for certain executable files. In Windows this is called a *path*. If the permissions set for such a key are weak, e.g. write permission for *Everyone*, then an attacker can insert malicious software by modifying the path. Protecting the integrity of registry data is therefore a necessity. Removing the Registry Editor from all machines not used for system management is a first line of defense. Some security-relevant keys should not even be changed via the Registry Editor but only through specific utilities.

When defining access control policies for registry keys you will face the customary dilemma that strong protection and ease of use cannot always be accommodated at the same time. A potential pitfall when setting policies is undefined keys. Consider, for example, the key that specifies which users and groups can access the register remotely.

HKEY_LOCAL_MACHINE\SYSTEM\CurrentControlSet\Control\
SecurePipeServers\Winreg.

If the key exists, it will be consulted when a user requests remote access to the registry. If the key does not exist, no checks specific to remote access will be performed. Remote access will be treated exactly like local access to the registry.

### 7.1.3 Domains

Stand-alone Windows computers are usually administered locally by their users. However, within organizations a more structured approach to system and security management is essential. As a user on a computer network, you would not like to log on over and over again when you need to access a resource or a service on another machine. As an administrator in charge of a computer network, you would not want to configure the security settings individually on each and every machine. Windows 2000 uses *domains* to facilitate single sign-on and centralized security administration.

A domain is a collection of machines sharing a common user accounts database and security policy. Domains can form a hierarchy. Users then do not require accounts with individual machines but with the domain.

In a domain, one server acts as the *domain controller* (DC). Other computers then join the domain. *Domain admins* create and manage domain users and groups on the DC. The domain controller authority has information about user passwords and can act as a trusted third party when a user (in general, a principal) authenticates itself to some other entity. Here, a design decision for a centralized authentication (password management) service has been made.

A domain can have more than one DC. Updates may be performed at any DC and are propagated using the *multimaster replication* model. Now, decentralization of services is used as a design principle to achieve better performance.

### 7.1.4 Active Directory

Objects are organized in the Active Directory, the directory service in Windows 2000. Active Directory can be viewed as a tree of *typed* objects (Figure 7.2). Containers are objects that may contain other objects. Active Directory can be dynamically extended by adding new object types or new properties to existing object types. Thus you can tailor the object types to your own requirements. Each *object type* has specific properties and a unique GUID (globally unique identifier). Moreover, each property has its own GUID. In Figure 7.2 an 'employee' object with properties **name, email, address** and **room** and a 'printer' object with properties **mode** and **room** are highlighted.

Logically related objects of different types can be placed in the same container. This is useful for managing resources in an organization because you do not need different structures for different types of objects, and because you can use the directory structure to define general access policies for containers and let the objects within the container inherit the policy (section 7.3.3).

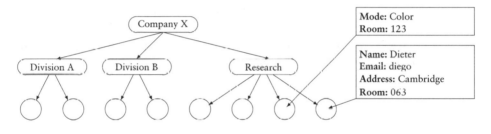

Figure 7.2: A Directory Tree

# 7.2 ACCESS CONTROL – COMPONENTS

Access control in Windows is more complex than access control in a typical filesystem. The objects it applies to can be files, registry keys, Active Directory objects, etc. Means for structuring policies in Windows 2000 are groups, roles and inheritance. The next sections will identify the principals, subjects and objects in Windows 2000 and explain where the access rules can be found, and how they are evaluated.

### 7.2.1 Principals

Principals are the active entities in a security policy. They are the entities that can be granted or denied access. In Windows 2000 principals may be local users, aliases, domain users, groups or machines. Principals have a human-readable name (username) and a machine-readable identifier, the SID (*security identifier*).

Users created by the Local Security Authority are local users. *Local principals* are administered locally and are visible only to the local computer. Examples are the local system, i.e. the operating system, and local users. The human-readable name of a local user or alias has the form

principal = MACHINE\principal,

for example 'TUHH-688432\Administrators'. Local users and aliases can be displayed from the command line[1] with the commands

> net user

> net localgroup

*Domain principals* are administered by domain admins on a domain controller. They are seen by all computers on the domain. Examples are domain users and the *Domain Admins* alias. The human-readable name of a domain user, group, alias or machine has the form

principal@domain = DOMAIN\principal,

for example 'diego@europe.microsoft.com = EUROPE\diego'. Domain users, groups and aliases can be displayed with the commands

> net user /domain

> net group /domain

> net localgroup /domain

There exist also *universal principals*, for example the *Everyone* alias. Information about principals is stored in accounts and user profiles. Local accounts are in the Registry (under HKEY_USERS). Domain accounts are at the DC but cached locally. The user profile is stored in the filesystem under '\Documents and Settings\'. Some predefined principals need not be stored anywhere.

## Groups and Aliases

A SID is an individual principal. A (global) *group* is a collection of SIDs managed by the DC. A group has its own group SID, so groups can be nested. The members of a group can make use of privileges and permissions given to the group. Groups constitute an intermediate layer of control. Permissions for an object are given to a group. Users are then given access to the object by becoming members of this group.

---

[1] Click on Start, then on Run, enter cmd, and type the command.

An *alias* (local group) is a collection of user and group SIDs managed by a DC or locally by the LSA. Aliases cannot be nested. Aliases are used to implement logical roles. An application developer can refer to an alias *Student*. At deployment time appropriate SIDs are assigned to this alias. Aliases are not 'roles' as defined earlier in section 4.6.3.

## Security Identifiers

The format of a SID is S-R-I-SA-SA-SA-N, with:

S: letter S,

R: revision number (currently 1),

I: identifier authority (48-bit),

SA: subauthority (32-bit),

N: relative identifier, unique in the authority's name space.

The following list gives a few typical principals together with their SIDs.

- Everyone (World): S-1-1-0.
- SYSTEM: S-1-5-18; the operating system on a machine runs locally as S-1-5-18; to other machines in the domain the machine is known under a separate domain-specific SID.
- Administrator: S-1-5-21-<local authority>-500; a user account created during operating system installation.
- Administrators: S-1-5-32-544; a built-in group with administrator privileges; it contains initially only the Administrator account.
- Domain Admins: S-1-5-21-<domain authority>-512; a global group that is a member of the Administrators alias on all machines in the domain.
- Guest: S-1-5-21-<authority>-501; the field <authority> is a 96-bit unique machine or domain identifier created when Windows or a DC is installed.

The SID is constructed when a user account is created and is fixed for the lifetime of the account. As a pseudo-random input (clock value) is used in its construction, you will not get the same SID if you delete an account and then recreate it with exactly the same parameters as before. Hence, the new account will not retain the access permissions given to the old account.

When a domain is created a unique SID is constructed for this domain. When a workstation or a server joins a domain, it receives a SID that includes the domain's SID. (Machines use their SIDs to check whether they are in the same domain.) As SIDs cannot be changed, moving a DC between domains is not a simple administrative process. The machine has to be completely re-installed and logically become a 'new' machine to receive a new SID and become a controller in a new domain.

## 7.2.2 Subjects

Subjects are the active entities in an operational system. In Windows 2000, the subjects are processes and threads. Security credentials for a process or a thread are stored in an *access token*.

| |
|:---:|
| User SID |
| Group and Alias SIDs |
| Privileges |
| Defaults for New Objects |
| Miscellaneous |

The SIDs serve as identity and authorization attributes. The token also contains the union of all privileges assigned to these SIDs. The defaults for new objects include parameters like owner SID, group SID and DACL (explained in section 7.2.3). The miscellaneous entries include the logon session ID and the token ID. Some of the fields in a token are read-only, others may be modified. A new process gets a copy of the parent's token, with possible restrictions. A token will not change even if a membership or a privilege is revoked. This makes for better performance and better reliability because a process can decide in advance whether it has sufficient access rights for a given task.

### Privileges

Privileges control access to system resources. A privilege is uniquely identified by its programmatic name, e.g. *SeTcbPrivilege*, and has also a display name, e.g. 'Act as part of the operating system'. Privileges are assigned to users, groups and aliases on a per machine basis. They are cached in tokens as locally unique identifiers (LUID). Privileges are different from access rights, which control access to *securable objects* (section 7.2.3). Typical privileges are:

- backup files and directories;
- generate security audits;
- manage and audit security log;
- take ownership of files and other objects;
- bypass traverse checking;
- enable computer and user accounts to be trusted for delegation;
- shut down the system.

### User Authentication – Interactive Logon

Windows users can be authenticated by username and password, but other options are supported too, e.g. authentication using a smart card. When a user logs on to a machine, authentication is initiated by pressing the *secure attention sequence* CTRL+ALT+DEL which invokes the Windows operating system logon screen and provides a *trusted path* from the keyboard to the logon process (winlogon.exe). The login dialog box is generated by the GINA DLL (Graphical Identification and Authentication dynamic-link library). The logon process is permanently running (under the principal *SYSTEM*).

To avoid spoofing attacks always press CTRL+ALT+DEL when starting a session, even when the logon screen is already displayed. The secure attention key generates calls to low-level Windows functions that cannot be duplicated by an application program. This trusted path is only present when a machine is actually running Windows. A machine running some other operating system could simulate the Windows logon screen and mount a spoofing attack (Hadfield, Hatter and Bixler, 1997).

Windows offers the option of displaying a *Legal Notice* as a warning message. Users have to acknowledge this warning message before logon can proceed. Users are then prompted for username and password. Username and password are gathered by the logon process and passed on to the LSA (lsass.exe). For local logon, the local LSA calls an *authentication package* that compares username and password against the values stored in the account database. When a match is found, the SAM returns to the LSA the user's SID and the SID of any group the user belongs to. Domain logon uses Kerberos and the user is authenticated by the LSA on a DC. The LSA then creates an access token containing the user's SIDs and privileges and passes the token to the logon process.

### Creating Subjects and Network Logon

In a next step, the logon process starts a shell (explorer.exe) in a new *logon session* under the user (principal) that has been authenticated and attaches the access token to this process. The shell spawns processes to the same logon session (Figure 7.3). These processes are the *subject* for access control purposes. Logging off destroys the logon session and all processes in it.

A process can spawn a new local process (subject) by calling *CreateProcess*. The new process gets a copy of the parent's token. Each process has its own token. Different processes within a logon session can have different credentials. Threads can be given different tokens.

The user's network credentials, e.g. the password, are cached in the *interactive logon session*. Processes can then create *network logon* sessions for that user at other machines. Network logon sessions do not normally cache credentials. In Windows 2000, machines are principals and can have a machine account with password in a domain. Thus, a DC can also authenticate machines.

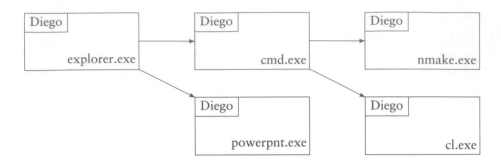

○ **Figure 7.3: Example: Processes in a User Session**

## 7.2.3 Objects

Objects are the passive entities in an access operation. In Windows 2000, there are *executive objects* like processes or threads, and *filesystem objects* like files or directories. Further objects are registry keys and devices such as printers. Securable objects have a *security descriptor*. Security descriptors for built-in objects are managed by the operating system. Security descriptors for private objects have to be managed by the application software. Creating securable objects can be a tedious task but enables highly granular access control.

### Security Descriptor

The security descriptor has the structure:

| Owner SID |
| --- |
| Primary Group |
| DACL |
| SACL |

The *Owner* SID field indicates the owner of the object. Objects get an owner when they are created. The owner is a principal that always has READ_CONTROL and WRITE_DAC permission. Ownership can also be obtained via the privilege 'Take ownership of files and other objects' (*SeTakeOwnershipPrivilege*). The *Primary Group* is included for POSIX compliance. The *Discretionary Access Control List (DACL)* determines who is granted or denied access to the object. The *System Access Control List (SACL)* defines the audit policy for the object.

### Permissions

A *permission* is an authorization to perform a particular operation on an object. To display permissions for a file, click on File, then on Properties, and finally on Security.

*Access rights* correspond to the operations that can be performed on an object. The *standard access rights* applying to most types of objects are:

- DELETE: delete the object;
- READ_CONTROL: read access (to security descriptor) for owner, group, DACL;
- WRITE_DAC: write access to DACL;
- WRITE_OWNER: write access to owner;
- SYNCHRONIZE: allows a process to wait for an object to enter the signaled state.

In Windows 2000, specific access rights can be tailored to each class of objects. In this way, access rights can be adapted to the requirements of applications, but developers would also potentially have to remember numerous specific rights. To address this issue, *generic access rights* are used as an intermediate description level. Each class of objects has a mapping from the generic access rights onto real access rights so there is no need to remember class-specific permissions. Table 7.1 shows the mapping of generic access rights for files and directories. The generic access rights are:

- GENERIC_READ
- GENERIC_WRITE
- GENERIC_EXECUTE
- GENERIC_ALL.

| GENERIC_EXECUTE | FILE_READ_ATTRIBUTES |
| --- | --- |
| | STANDARD_RIGHTS_EXECUTE |
| | SYNCHRONIZE |
| GENERIC_READ | FILE_READ_ATTRIBUTES |
| | FILE_READ_DATA |
| | FILE_READ_EA |
| | STANDARD_RIGHTS_READ |
| | SYNCHRONIZE |
| GENERIC_WRITE | FILE_APPEND_DATA |
| | FILE_WRITE_ATTRIBUTES |
| | FILE_WRITE_DATA |
| | FILE_WRITE_EA |
| | STANDARD_RIGHTS_WRITE |
| | SYNCHRONIZE |

○ **Table 7.1: Mapping of Generic Access Rights for Files and Directories**

## 7.2.4 Access Mask

Internally, the desired operation in an access request (requested rights) and the granted access rights are given as *access masks*. The access mask is a 32-bit value, with the bits assigned as follows.

| 0 –15 | specific rights defined for the object type the request refers to |
|---|---|
| 16 –23 | standard rights |
| 24 | Access system security, required to access a SACL |
| 25 | maximum allowed |
| 26 –27 | reserved |
| 28 | generic all |
| 29 | generic execute |
| 30 | generic write |
| 31 | generic read |

When the MAXIMUM_ALLOWED bit is set, the subject will be granted the maximum access rights allowed by the security descriptor. The granted rights are encoded in the *GrantedAccess*. The mapping of the standard rights is given as:

| 16 | DELETE |
|---|---|
| 17 | READ_CONTROL |
| 18 | WRITE_DAC |
| 19 | WRITE_OWNER |
| 20 | SYNCHRONIZE |

## 7.2.5 Extended Rights

In Active Directory, it is also possible to define access control on operations. Such access controls are called *extended rights*. Typical examples are *Send-As* and *Receive-As*, allowing to send mail or receive mail as a given mailbox. Extended rights are not defined by an access mask but by a GUID corresponding to a *controlAccessRight* object. The list of extended rights is not fixed. Developers can create new extended rights for custom operations.

# 7.3 ACCESS DECISIONS

Each object type has an *object manager* that handles the creation of objects and verifies that a process has the right to use an object. Active Directory, for example, is the object manager for directory objects. For access control, the object manager calls an access decision function implemented by the SRM. The SRM, the *policy decision point*, returns a yes/no answer to the object manager, the *policy enforcement point*.

In general, access control decisions consider the subject requesting access, the object to which access is requested and the desired access right. Not all three parameters need be considered in all circumstances. The credentials of the subject, including its principal, are stored in its token. The security attributes of an object are stored in its security descriptor. The desired access operation is given as an access mask.

The desired access is compared against the subject's token and the object's security descriptor when a handle to the object is being created, not at access time. Thus, changing a file DACL does not affect open file handles. This design decision leads to better performance and better reliability as all access control checks are made in advance, before the process starts a task.

Windows access control can be used in several ways, with varying levels of granularity and complexity. Access control based on the principal requesting access is known as *impersonation* because the process 'impersonates' the user SID of its token. This is a coarse method but simple to implement. Impersonation is a typical operating systems concept and does not work well at the application level. *Role-centric* access control uses groups and aliases to give a process suitable access rights for its task. In *object-centric* access control, application level objects get a security descriptor. This method allows for fine-grained access control, but matters can get complex at the same time.

## 7.3.1 The DACL

The following sections are not geared to a specific version of Windows but are based on proposals discussed by Swift *et al.* (2002). The DACL in the security descriptor is a list of *access control entries* (ACEs). The ACE format is:

| |
|---|
| Type: positive (grant) or negative (deny) |
| Flags |
| ObjectType |
| InheritedObjectType |
| Access rights |
| Principal SID: principal the ACE applies to |

The type determines how the ACE should be used by the access control mechanism. The type can take the values:

- ACCESS_ALLOWED_ACE;
- ACCESS_DENIED_ACE;
- ACCESS_ALLOWED_OBJECT_ACE (allows access to an object, property, property set or extended right);
- ACCESS_DENIED_OBJECT_ACE (denies access to an object, property, property set or extended right).

*ObjectType* is a GUID defining an object type. Applications can now include the *ObjectType* of objects in their access requests. For a given request, only ACEs with a matching *ObjectType* or without an *ObjectType* are evaluated. For example, to control read/write access on an object property, put the GUID of the property in *ObjectType*. To control create/delete access on objects, put the GUID of the object type in *ObjectType*.

The next example is an ACE for a web directory, granting users permission to set their own home page. This policy applies to all users so we use the PRINCIPAL_SELF SID as a placeholder. The application creating the home page will supply the current user's SID when making an access request.

| ACE1 | |
|---|---|
| Type: | ACCESS_ALLOWED_OBJECT_ACE |
| ObjectType: | GUID for web home page |
| InheritedObjectType: | GUID for User Account objects |
| Access rights: | write |
| Principal SID: | PRINCIPAL_SELF |

The next ACE allows Server Applications to create RPC endpoints in any container of type RPC Services. The ACE will be inherited into any container of type RPC Services.

| ACE2 | |
| --- | --- |
| Type: | ACCESS_ALLOWED_OBJECT_ACE |
| ObjectType: | GUID for RPC Endpoint |
| InheritedObjectType: | GUID for RPC Services |
| Access rights: | create child |
| Principal SID: | Server Applications |

**Property Sets**

To ease administration, it is possible to collect the properties of an object type in property sets. Instead of ACEs for all the properties of an object type, we need only one ACE that refers to the property set. A property set is identified by its GUID. In an access request, a list of properties can be passed to the reference monitor and a single check against the property set returns the result for each property. As a further advantage, changes to the properties of an object type do not force us to change the ACL.

### 7.3.2 The Decision Algorithm

When a subject requests access to an object, the SRM takes the subject's token and the object's ACL and the desired access mask to determine whether the requested access should be granted. It first checks if there exists a DACL. If there is no DACL, i.e. a so-called NULL DACL, no further checks are performed and access is granted.

Otherwise, the algorithm next checks whether the subject is the owner of the object. If the desired access mask contains a Read_Control or Write_DAC request, access is granted. If this is not the case, permissions are accumulated by building a granted access mask. For each ACE the subject's SIDs are compared with the SIDs in the ACE. The following three cases are possible.

1. The ACE does not contain a matching SID; the ACE will be skipped.

2. The ACE contains a matching SID specifying *AccessDenied* for a requested access right; access will be denied and no further checks take place.

3. The ACE contains a matching SID specifying *AccessAllowed*; if the access mask in the ACE, together with the access masks in all previously checked matching ACEs, contains all the permissions in the desired access mask, access is granted and no further checks take place; otherwise, the search goes on.

Access will be denied if the end of the DACL is reached and the granted mask is not equal to the requested mask. Thus, access will always be denied if there is an empty DACL and access will always be granted if there exists no DACL.

For negative ACEs to take precedence over positive ACEs, they must be placed at the top of the DACL. As you will see in the next section, to achieve a finer granularity of access control one might also place negative ACEs after positive ACEs.

### Lesson

Often, operating systems store access control information in different places. It is important to know in which order checks are performed. Sometimes, as in Unix, only the first matching access control entry is consulted. Other times, more specific entries coming later can overrule a previous entry. Finally, you have to know how the operating system reacts if it finds no entry matching an access request.

### 7.3.3  ACE Inheritance

When a new object is created its ACEs are usually inherited from the container (directory) the object is being placed in. In Active Directory a container may contain objects of different types, therefore a selective inheritance strategy is desirable.

The mechanisms proposed by Swift *et al*. (2002) control inheritance through inheritance flags that indicate whether an ACE has been inherited, and through the *InheritedObject-Type*. ACEs are inherited from the container at the time a new object is created. When a new object is created only ACEs with a matching *InheritedObjectType* or without an *InheritedObjectType* are copied into its ACL. This is illustrated in Figure 7.4.

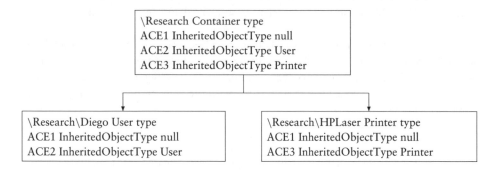

Figure 7.4:  Type-specific Inheritance within a Container

Changes to the container made later have no immediate effect on objects already in it. Such a strategy is known as *static inheritance*. If you change access permissions on a container and want to let the changes filter through to its content, you have to run a *propagation algorithm*. This algorithm should be *idempotent*. Re-applying the propagation algorithm a second time should cause no changes in access rights. Static inheritance has performance advantages and more predictable behavior compared to dynamic inheritance, where any changes to the container would automatically be applied to all its objects.

When setting permissions on a container we usually do not know yet which objects will eventually be placed in it. In particular, we might not know the owners of these objects but many access policies give the owner of an object specific rights. Hence, we have to be able to specify the rights an owner would inherit without already naming the owner. For this purpose, Windows 2000 uses a special placeholder SID, CREATOR_OWNER. This SID is replaced in an inherited ACE by the owner's SID when a new object is created.

### Inheritance Flags

The inheritance flags further specify how ACEs are inherited. The following flags have been defined.

- INHERITED_ONLY_ACE: ACE is only used for inheritance, and is ignored by the access-checking mechanism.

- NO_PROPAGATE_INHERIT is inherited only by the next generation but not propagated further.

- OBJECT_INHERIT_ACE is inherited by all sub-objects that are not containers.

- CONTAINER_INHERIT_ACE is inherited by sub-objects that are containers.

### Exceptions to Rules

In practice, there will be exceptions even for the best-thought-out general rules. So, we want a scheme where it is both easy to define and apply general rules, and to define exceptions from those rules. As ACEs are evaluated in the order they appear in the DACL, placing locally added ACEs in front of inherited ACEs implements a policy where specific entries take precedence over more generic entries. In consequence, ACEs from closer containers are placed in front of more distant containers. Thus, it is possible for a positive ACE to appear before a matching negative ACE, as shown in Figure 7.5. There, ACE2 is defined directly for *Letter_A* in the container *Documents* and therefore appears before the inherited ACE. Because ACE1 is only inherited to objects of type *Letter*, it is not inherited by *Invoice_A*.

Placing more specific entries in front of more general entries is one way of implementing exceptions from general rules. Windows 2000 has a further mechanism for creating exceptions. Setting the flag SE_DACL_PROTECTED in the security descriptor of an object blocks inheritance of ACEs altogether, and you are starting with a clean slate when setting permissions on an object. In Figure 7.6, this flag is set in the descriptor of *Letter_A* and its DACL only contains a locally defined ACE2.

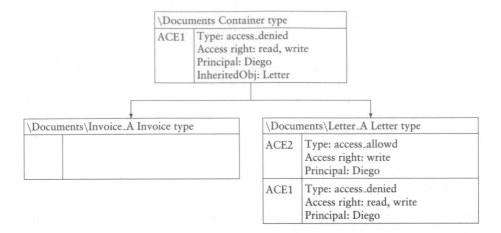

○ **Figure 7.5:  Locally Added ACEs are Placed in Front of Inherited ACEs**

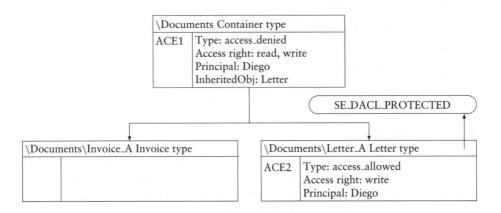

○ **Figure 7.6:  SE_DACL_PROTECTED Blocks Inheritance of ACEs**

## 7.4 RESTRICTED CONTEXT

So far access control has (implicitly) referred to users. The SIDs in the security token of a process are initially set when a user logs in and then passed on to other processes within the session. We may want to take a complementary approach and also control what certain programs can do. It is today quite usual but not particularly helpful to refer to such programs as 'untrusted code'. This misses the point. We are just adhering to good security engineering practices and follow the principle of *least privilege*. Code is only running with the permissions it needs to do its job.

In Windows, a flavor of *code-based access control* can be implemented using *restricted tokens*. A process running with a restricted token is a *restricted context*. Restricted tokens remove privileges from a given access token. Group SIDs can be disabled by being marked as USE_FOR_DENY_ONLY. This feature can be useful when a server thread *impersonates* a client, i.e. runs in the context of the client's access token. The client's token may grant too many rights for comfort[2] and deny-only SIDs provide a means of disabling access rights granted to the client.

By adding a *restricted* SID to the token, a process with a restricted token gets access only if both the SID and the restricted SID are granted access. In the example in Figure 7.7 a process with the restricted token:

| User SID | Diego |
|---|---|
| Group SIDs | Administrators |
| | *use for deny only* |
| | Users |
| Restricted SIDs | MyApp |
| Privileges | (none) |
| . . . | |

| ACE1: | ACE3: | |
|---|---|---|
| Access Rights: read, write | Access Rights: read | |
| Principal SID: Diego | Principal SID: Admin | |

| ACE2: | ACE2: | ACE1: |
|---|---|---|
| Access Rights: read | Access Rights: read | Access Rights: read, write |
| Principal SID: MyApp | Principal SID: MyApp | Principal SID: Diego |

    (a) access granted          (b) access denied          (c) access denied

○ **Figure 7.7: Access with Restricted Tokens**

requests read access to objects with three different DACLs. In case (a) both the principal SID *Diego* and the restricted SID *MyApp* have read permission so access is granted. In case (b) the *Admin* group SID has been marked for deny only so ACE3 will be skipped

---

[2]Presented with client-defined inputs and access rights, the server might perform dangerous operations (confused deputy problem).

and access will be denied because the principal does not have the required right. In case (c), the restricted SID *MyApp* has no read permission so access is denied although the principal would have the required right.

To restrict the access rights of a program we create a restricted SID representing this program. In our example, we have a restricted SID for *MyApp*. This SID has to be entered into the DACLs of all objects the program should have access to. Restricted SIDs may be created per program and added to the ACLs of required resources (object types), or per object type and be added to the restricted tokens of subjects that should have access.

## 7.5 ADMINISTRATION

We conclude this chapter with a few further remarks on managing Windows security.

### 7.5.1 User Accounts

Security relevant information about users is kept by the SAM in the user account database. User accounts are edited using the *User Manager for Domains* utility and can also be displayed from the command line with net user *username*. Among others, the following fields can be defined.

- *Username:* the unique name used for logon.
- *Full name:* the name of the user owning the account.
- *Expiration date:* by default accounts do not have an expiration date.
- *Password dates:* time password was last changed, time password expires (you can force users to change their password at the next logon by expiring the current password), time from when password can be changed; you can also indicate whether users may change their passwords.
- *Logon hours* and *workstations:* you can specify when the user is allowed to log in and from which machines the user is allowed to log in. The *forcibly disconnect remote users from server when logon hours expire* setting determines whether a user is thrown out outside hours or allowed to continue with an existing session. In the latter case, only new logons are prevented.
- *User profile path* and *logon script name:* the profile defines the user's desktop environment, i.e. program groups, network connections, screen colours, etc. The logon script is a batch file or executable file that runs automatically when a user logs on.
- *Home directory:* you can also specify whether the home directory is on the local machine or on a network server.
- *Local and global groups:* groups the user is a member of.

## 7.5.2 Default User Accounts

Windows supports security management through default accounts. You have seen first examplesin section 7.2.1. There exist three types of default user and group accounts.

- *Predefined accounts* are installed with the operating system.

- *Built-in accounts* are installed with the operating system, application and services.

- *Implicit accounts* are created implicitly when accessing network resources.

Default users and groups created by the operating system can be modified, but not deleted. *LocalSystem* is a built-in account used for running system processes and handling system-level tasks. Users cannot login to this account, but certain processes can do so.

*Administrator* and *Guest* are predefined accounts installed locally. The *Administrator* account cannot be removed or disabled. It has complete access to files, directories, services and other facilities. Although access permissions on files and directories can be set so that *Administrator* does not have access, the *Administrator* would still be able to change the access permissions and then get access after all. By default, the *Administrator* account for a domain is a member of the groups *Administrators*, *Domain Admins*, *Domain Users*, *Enterprise Admins*, *Schema Admins* and *Group Policy Creator Owners*.

In a domain, the local Administrator account is primarily used when the system is first installed. Once installation is completed, the actual administrators can be made members of the *Administrators group*. Thus, individual administrator privileges can be revoked more easily.

The *Guest* account is intended for users who only need occasional access. Permissions can be given to this account like to any other user account. When Windows 2000 is installed, the *Guest* account is disabled.

*Built-in groups* have predefined user rights and permissions and provide another level of indirection when assigning access rights to users. Users obtain standard access rights by becoming members of such a built-in group. Typical examples of built-in groups are *Administrators*, *Backup Operators*, *User* or *Guests*. System managers are advised to stick to the built-in groups when implementing their security policies and to define groups with different permission patterns only if there are strong reasons for doing so.

A number of *predefined groups* are installed with Active Directory domains. Furthermore, there exist *implicit groups* that can also be used for efficient definition of access permissions.

- *Everyone:* contains all local and remote users, including *Guest*; this group can be used to grant or deny permissions to all users.

- *Interactive:* contains all users logged on locally.

- *Network:* contains all users logged on over the network.

- *System:* is the operating system.

- *Creator Owner:* is the creator or owner of a file or a resource.

### 7.5.3 Audit

Windows 2000 records security-relevant events in the security log. Security-relevant events to be logged when access to an object is requested can be defined in the SACL of the object. Entries in the log file are generated by the SRM. Security-relevant events typically include valid and invalid logon attempts, privilege use and events like creating, deleting or opening a resource (file). The events to be logged can be selected and displayed using the *Event Viewer*.

A maximum size of the audit log can be set. There are three *wrapping options* for defining the course of action when the log reaches its maximal size.

- *Overwrite events as needed:* any record can be overwritten to make room for new entries.

- *Overwrite events older than [x] days:* entries older than a specified number of days may be overwritten.

- *Do not overwrite events:* old records are never overwritten; the log must be cleared manually before new events can be logged.

With the last two options, the system manager can set up the system so that it shuts down automatically when the log is full. The CrashOnAuditFail entry in the registry is set as follows.

```
HKEY_LOCAL_MACHINE\System\CurrentControlSet\Control\Lsa
Name: CrashOnAuditFail
Type: REG_DWORD
Value: 1
```

This somewhat disruptive setting would be necessary to meet the Orange Book C2 requirements.

### 7.5.4 Summary

With its range of conceptual tools that support security administration, and in particular for managing security policies at the application level, Windows can be placed closer to the man–oriented end of the man-machine scale than Unix (Figure 7.8).

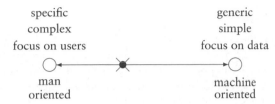

specific              generic
complex             simple
focus on users     focus on data

man            machine
oriented        oriented

**Figure 7.8: Windows Security on the Man–Machine Scale**

## 7.6 FURTHER READING

Most security handbooks devoted to a specific operating system do not go beyond the surface of the security system and concentrate on existing features and their management. For this type of reference, you have to check the latest publication lists, and the material on Microsoft's http://www.msdn.microsoft.com web site. An explanation of Windows access control that goes into greater depth is given by Brown (2000).

If you are interested in operating systems security case studies beyond Unix and Windows, you will find a good description of AS/400 security that does delve into reasonable technical details in Park (1995). AS/400 (Applications System 400) is an IBM operating system for mid-range computers. It is an object-oriented operating system popular in the financial sector and is regarded to be reasonably secure. Access control at the middleware layer (CORBA) is the subject of Lang and Schreiner (2002).

## 7.7 EXERCISES

**Exercise 7.1** Create a container for a lecture course. The container should contain objects of different types: course description, lecture notes, exercise solutions, student projects. Define groups and DACLs on the container and on objects so that:

- the course leader has access to all resources;
- students enrolled on the course have read access to lecture notes and read/write access to their own project;
- all students have read access to the course description;
- a student is nominated as tutor and gets read access to exercise solutions as well;
- one given exercise solution is made available to all students on the course.

**Exercise 7.2**   In Unix and Windows 2000, access rights are defined for users and groups. To facilitate better security management, users are placed into groups. How do the two operating systems decide on an access request when users have fewer privileges than their group? How are access rights that have been given to a group withheld from individual members?

**Exercise 7.3**   Discuss how 'controls at an intermediate layer' are used in Windows 2000.

**Exercise 7.4**   Unix UIDs can be set by the administrator. Windows creates randomized SIDs. Discuss the design rationale for taking control from the administrator and having randomized identifiers defined by the system.

**Exercise 7.5**   Default Windows accounts cannot be deleted. Examine the design rationale for this design decision.

**Exercise 7.6**   Application software may enforce its own security control. The developer then has to implement these controls, but does not know yet how parameters such as users or groups will be instantiated when the software is deployed. Examine how Windows 2000 provides interfaces between the development and deployment of security policies.

**Exercise 7.7**   How would you use default accounts to manage machines in an environment where workstations are all managed individually?

**Exercise 7.8**   Explain the main issues in configuring and auditing a secure operating system (500–1000 words).

# Chapter 8

## Bell–LaPadula Model

What is your security policy? Which rules decide who gets access to your data? To formulate a security policy, you have to describe the entities governed by the policy and you have to state the rules that constitute your policy. This could be done informally in a natural language document. In practice, such documents too often suffer from ambiguities, inconsistencies and omissions. To avoid these problems, you might prefer to have a formal statement of your security policy. A security model does just that.

Security models play an important role in the design and evaluation of high assurance security systems. Their importance was already noted in the Anderson report (1972). The design process starts from a formal specification of the policy the system should enforce, i.e. the security model, and a high-level specification of the system itself. By adding more details to this high-level specification you can arrive at a series of lower-level specifications. Then, you have to show that the high-level specification implements the desired policy. For high assurance, a formal proof may be required. You also have to show that the lower-level specifications are consistent with our policy but at these levels it becomes increasingly difficult to conduct formal proofs.

This chapter is intended as a case study that demonstrates this approach. The Bell–LaPadula model was developed to capture multilevel security policies for classified data. We will describe this model and use the Multics operating system as our example to show how the model can be used when analyzing a system designed to enforce these policies. The next chapter will give a survey of other important security models.

### OBJECTIVES

- Demonstrate how security policies can be formalized.
- Introduce the Bell–LaPadula model, and discuss its scope and limitations.
- Show how a formal model can be used when analyzing a security system.
- Present some important milestones in the history of computer security.

## 8.1 STATE MACHINE MODELS

State machines (automata) are a popular tool for modeling many aspects of computing systems and we assume that the readers of this book are already familiar with this topic. Not surprisingly, state machines are also the basis for some important security models. The essential features of a state machine model are the concept of a *state* and of state changes occurring at discrete points in time. A state is a representation of the system under investigation at one moment in time, which should capture exactly those aspects of the system relevant to our problem. The possible *state transitions* can be specified by a state transition function which defines the next state depending on the present state and input. An output may also be produced.

A simple example of a state machine is a light switch. It has two states, *on* and *off*, and one input, *press*, that moves the system from state *on* into state *off*, and from state *off* into state *on*. A more sophisticated example would be a ticket vending machine. Its state has to record the ticket requested and the money still to be paid. The inputs are ticket requests and coins. The outputs are the tickets and any change returned. An example from computer science is microprocessors. The state of the machine is given by its register contents and the inputs are the machine instructions.

If we want to talk about a specific property of a system, like security, using a state machine model, we first have to identify all the states that fulfill this property. We then have to check, whether all state transitions *preserve* this property. If this is the case and if the system starts in an *initial state* having this property, then we can prove by induction that the property will always hold.

## 8.2 THE BELL–LAPADULA MODEL

The *Bell–LaPadula (BLP) model* is probably the most famous of the security models. It was developed by Bell and LaPadula at the time of the first concerted efforts to design secure multiuser operating systems. If those systems were to process classified information at different security levels, they had to enforce the multilevel security (MLS) policy described in section 4.7.3. Users should only get information they are entitled to according to their clearance.

BLP is a state machine model capturing the confidentiality aspects of access control (Bell and LaPadula, 1996). Access permissions are defined both through an access control matrix and through security levels. Security policies prevent information flowing downwards from a high security level to a low security level. BLP only considers the information flow that occurs when a subject observes or alters an object.

## 8.2.1 The State Set

Our description of the BLP model uses the notation introduced in Chapter 4. We have:

- a set of *subjects* $S$;
- a set of *objects* $O$;
- the set of *access operations* $A = \{\text{execute}, \text{read}, \text{append}, \text{write}\}$ that directly mirror the access rights of section 4.3.2;
- a set of *security levels* $L$, with a partial ordering $\leq$.

We want to use the state of the system for checking its security, so the state set of our model has to capture all current instances of subjects accessing objects and all current permissions.

We can use a table to record which subject has access to which object at the given point in time. The rows in the table are indexed by subjects, the columns by objects, and an entry in the table gives the access operations the subject currently performs on the object. In mathematical notation, such a table corresponds to a collection of tuples $(s, o, a)$, indicating that subject $s$ currently performs operation $a$ on object $o$. Tuples are elements of the set $S \times O \times A$ (Cartesian product of the sets $S$, $O$, $A$) so a table corresponds to an element of the power set $\mathcal{P}(S \times O \times A)$. It is customary to use the symbol $b$ to denote the table of current access operations in the BLP model, and $B$ to denote the set of all such tables.

The current access permission matrix is written as $M = (M_{so})_{s \in S, o \in O}$. We use $\mathcal{M}$ to denote the set of all access permission matrices.

The BLP model uses three functions to assign security levels to subjects or objects respectively.

- $f_S : S \to L$ gives the maximal security level each subject can have.
- $f_C : S \to L$ gives the current security level of each subject.
- $f_O : O \to L$ gives the *classification* of all objects.

The current level of a subject cannot be higher than its maximal level, hence $f_C \leq f_S$, in words '$f_S$ dominates $f_C$'. You will see the reason for introducing $f_C$ in a moment. The maximal security level is sometimes called the subject's *clearance*. Other sources use clearance only to denote the security levels of users.

For convenience, we write $f$ for the triple $(f_S, f_C, f_O)$ and use $F \subset L^S \times L^S \times L^O$ to denote the set of all possible security-level assignments. All of this has left us with a

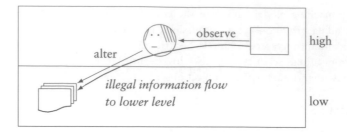

Figure 8.1: Declassification of an Object Using a Subject as Channel

rather complicated state set $B \times M \times F$. An individual state will be given by the three components $(b, M, f)$. Defining the state set is indeed the major issue in BLP. We do not have to describe inputs, outputs or the precise structure of state transitions, to give the BLP security properties.

### 8.2.2 Security Policies

BLP defines security as the property of states. MLS policies allow a subject to read an object only if the subject's security level dominates the object's classification. These MLS policies are also called *mandatory security policies*.

### The Simple Security Property

A first obvious property is the *simple security property (ss-property)*.

> A state $(b, M, f)$ satisfies the *ss-property*, if for each element $(s, o, a) \in b$ where the access operation $a$ is `read` or `write`, the security level of the subject $s$ dominates the classification of the object $o$, i.e. $f_O(o) \le f_S(s)$.

In the ss-property subjects act as observers. This policy captures the traditional *no read-up* security policy that applies when a person requests access to a classified document. However, we are now in a computer system where subjects are processes. Thus, subjects have no 'memory' like a person would, but they have access to memory objects. Subjects can thus act as channels by reading one memory object and transferring information to another memory object. In this way, data may be declassified improperly (Figure 8.1). For example, an attacker might insert a high-level Trojan horse that copies the content of higher-level objects into low-level objects.

### The ∗-Property

Transferring a policy of the pen-and-paper world into IT systems we have struck on an issue that did not exist before. We also need a policy to control write access. Simply preventing subjects from altering objects at lower levels would create a new problem. Such a policy would imply that a high-level subject is not able to send any message to a low-level subject. There are two ways to escape from this restriction.

- Temporarily downgrade a high-level subject. This is the reason for introducing the current security level $f_C$.

- Identify a set of subjects which are permitted to violate the *-property. These subjects are called *trusted subjects*.

The first approach assumes that a subject forgets all it knew at a higher security level the moment it is downgraded. This looks implausible if you view subjects as human beings but BLP is about modeling computers. There, subjects (processes) have no memory of their own. The only thing they 'know' is the contents of the objects (files) they are allowed to observe. In this situation, a temporary downgrade indeed solves the problem. In an alternative interpretation, $f_S$ specifies a user's clearance. Users are allowed to log in below their clearance and $f_C$ indicates at which level a user actually has logged in.

BLP includes a *no write-down* policy that refers to the current security level $f_C$, the so-called *-property (star-property[1]).

> A state $(b, M, f)$ satisfies the *-property, if for each element $(s, o, a) \in b$ where the access operation $a$ is append or write, the current level of the subject $s$ is dominated by the classification of the object $o$, i.e. $f_C(s) \le f_O(o)$.
>
> Furthermore, if there exists an element $(s, o, a) \in b$ where the access operation $a$ is append or write, then we must have $f_O(o') \le f_O(o)$ for all objects $o'$ with $(s, o', a') \in b$ and $a'$ is read or write.

The illegal information flow downwards in Figure 8.1 is blocked by the *-property.

When adopting the second approach, the no write-down policy only applies to subjects that are not trusted. By definition, a *trusted subject* may violate the security policy. Indeed, to focus your mind you may well use the adjective *trusted* precisely as an indicator for system components that can hurt you. In contrast, if you have convinced yourself that a subject will not hurt you, then call it *trustworthy*.

### The Discretionary Security Property

The Orange Book uses *discretionary access control (DAC)* for policies that control access based on named users and named objects. Subjects holding an access permission may pass that permission on to other subjects. In BLP, such policies are expressed by an access control matrix and captured by the *discretionary security property (ds-property)*.

> A state $(b, M, f)$ satisfies the *ds-property*, if for each element of $(s, o, a) \in b$ we have $a \in M_{so}$.

---

[1] The first version of the model did not included this property, and the symbol * was reputedly used as a placeholder until a proper name for the policy could be found.

### 8.2.3 The Basic Security Theorem

A state $(b, M, f)$ is called *secure*, if the ss-, $*$-, and ds-properties are satisfied. A transition from state $v_1 = (b_1, M_1, f_1)$ to state $v_2 = (b_2, M_2, f_2)$ is called secure, if both $v_1$ and $v_2$ are secure. To see which checks have to be performed to determine whether the new state is secure, consider, for example, the ss-property. The state transition *preserves* the ss-property iff:

1. each $(s, o, a) \in b_2 \setminus b_1$ satisfies the ss-property with respect to $f_2$; ($b_2 \setminus b_1$ denotes the set difference between $b_2$ and $b_1$);

2. if $(s, o, a) \in b_1$ does not satisfy the ss-property with respect to $f_2$, then $(s, o, a) \notin b_2$.

Preservation of the $*$-property and of the ds-property can be described in a similar way. We are now in a position to state an important property of the BLP model.

> **Basic Security Theorem**  If all state transitions in a system are secure and if the initial state of the system is secure, then every subsequent state will also be secure, no matter which inputs occur.

A formal proof of this theorem would proceed by induction over the length of input sequences. The proof would build on the fact that each state transition preserves security but would not refer to the specific BLP security properties.

**Lesson**

The Basic Security Theorem is an artifact of state machine modeling, not a consequence of the specific security properties chosen in the BLP model.

In practice, the Basic Security Theorem limits the effort needed to verify the security of a system. You are allowed to check each state transition individually to show that it preserves security and you have to identify a secure initial state. As long as you start your system in this secure initial state, it will remain secure.

### 8.2.4 Tranquility

McLean (1987) triggered a heated discussion about the value of the BLP model by putting forward a system that contained a state transition, which:

- downgraded all subjects to the lowest security level;
- downgraded all objects to the lowest security level;
- entered all access rights in all positions of the access control matrix $M$.

The state reached by this transition is secure according to the definitions of BLP. Should such a state be regarded as secure? As BLP says that this is the case, does BLP capture security correctly? There are two opinions.

- The case against BLP (McLean): intuitively, a system that can be brought into a state where everyone is allowed to read everything is not secure. Therefore, BLP has to be improved.

- The case for BLP (Bell): if the user requirements call for such a state transition, then it should be allowed in the security model. If it is not required, then it should not be implemented. This is not a problem of BLP but a problem of correctly capturing the security requirements.

At the root of this disagreement is a state transition that changes access rights. Such changes are certainly possible within the general framework of BLP but the originators of the model were really contemplating systems where access rights are fixed. The property that security levels and access rights never change is called *tranquility*. Operations that do not change access rights are called *tranquil*.

## 8.2.5 Aspects and Limitations of BLP

BLP is a very significant security model. It has played an important role in the design of secure operating systems and almost any new model has been compared to BLP. In this context it is helpful to separate several features of BLP.

1. The descriptive capabilities of the model: the BLP state set describes all current access operations and all current access permissions.

2. The security policies are based on security levels and an access control matrix. It is easy to introduce other structures in their place. For example, to model access control in a situation where a subject is allowed to access objects only through certain programs, an $S \times S \times O$ access control structure is more appropriate.

3. The actual security properties: in BLP we have the ss-property, *-property and ds-property. The Biba model (section 9.1) differs from BLP mainly in its security properties.

4. The specific solution: e.g. the state transitions in the Multics interpretation (section 8.3).

The fact that BLP defines security in terms of access control is a major reason for its popularity. Therefore, it is not too difficult to express the actions of an operating system or a database management system in terms of BLP. However, although it is an important security model, BLP does not cover all aspects of security. It has been criticized for:

- only dealing with confidentiality, not with integrity;
- not addressing the management of access control;
- containing covert channels.

The absence of integrity policies is a feature of BLP, rather than a flaw. As you will see in the next chapter, it is quite reasonable for a security model to limit its ambitions. BLP has no policies regulating the modification of access rights. As a matter of fact, BLP was originally intended for systems where there is no change of security levels.

A *covert channel* is an information flow that is not controlled by a security mechanism (Canadian System Security Centre, 1993) . Object names are a blatant covert channel if low-level subjects may see high-level object names and are only denied access to the contents of the objects. In BLP, you could use the access control mechanism itself to construct a covert channel. Information could flow from a high security level to a low security level as follows.

- A low-level subject creates an object, dummy.obj, at its own level.

- Its high-level accomplice (a Trojan horse?) either upgrades the security level of dummy.obj to high or leaves it unchanged.

- Later, the low-level subject tries to read dummy.obj. Success or failure of this request discloses the action of the high-level subject. One bit of information has been transmitted from high to low.

Telling a subject that a certain operation is not permitted constitutes information flow. This leads to interesting solutions in database security (*polyinstantiation*), where an object may have different values at different security levels to avoid this kind of problem (Denning *et al.*, 1988; Lunt *et al.*, 1990).

**Lesson**

Sometimes, it is not sufficient to hide only the contents of objects. Their existence may also have to be hidden.

## 8.3 THE MULTICS INTERPRETATION OF BLP

The Multics (Multiplexed Information and Computing Service) operating system was the object of an ambitious research project aiming to develop a secure, reliable, etc. multiuser operating system (Organick, 1972; Bell and LaPadula, 1975). Much research on security, like BLP, was triggered by the Multics project. An overview of the protection mechanisms in Multics is given by (Organick, 1972, Chapter 4). Because of its wide-ranging goals and its security requirements, Multics became too cumbersome for some project members, who then created something much simpler, viz. Unix. The history of the two systems highlights the balance between usability and security as far as commercial success is concerned. The last system running Multics was decommissioned in 2000.

Studying Multics gives us a chance to see how a security model, the BLP model in this case, is used in the design of a secure operating system. As a formal model for access control, BLP is very well suited for capturing the security requirements of operating systems. As a matter of fact, it was developed just for that purpose. The inductive definition of security in BLP makes it relatively easy to build a secure system. We only need to define state transitions properly to guarantee security. To prove that Multics is secure, we have to find a description of Multics which is consistent with BLP. We will follow by and large the presentation given by Bell and LaPadula (1975) to show how the BLP concepts are mapped into Multics.

### 8.3.1 Subjects and Objects in Multics

The *subjects* in Multics are processes. Each subject has a *descriptor segment* that contains information about the process, including information about the objects the process currently has access to. For each of these objects, there is a *segment descriptor word* (SDW) in the subject's descriptor segment. The format of the SDW is given in Figure 8.2. The SDW contains the name of the object, a pointer to the object, and *indicator* flags for read, execute and write access. These indicators refer to the access attributes specified in section 4.3.2. The security levels of subjects are kept in a *process level table* and a *current-level table*. The *active segment table* keeps track of all active processes. Only active processes have access to an object.

| segment-id | | ptr | |
|---|---|---|---|
| r: on | e: off | w: on | |

○ **Figure 8.2: Multics SDW**

Objects in Multics are memory segments, I/O devices, etc. Objects are organized hierarchically in a directory tree. Directories are again segments. Information about an object, like its security level or its access control list (ACL), are kept in the object's parent directory. To change an object's access control parameters and to create or delete an object therefore requires write or append access right to the parent directory.

To access an object, a process has to traverse the directory tree from the *root* directory to the target object. If there is any directory in this path that is not accessible to the process, the target object is not accessible either. In other words, an unclassified object in a secret directory cannot be read by an unclassified user. Hence, it makes little sense to place objects into directories with a higher security level and we always require that the security level of an object dominates the security level of its parent directory. This property is called *compatibility*. You have to deal with the same issue in modern operating systems like Unix. If you want to make your files accessible to other users, you also have to get the access control settings on the directory path right.

We now have all the necessary information to identify the components of the BLP state set with data in the Multics systems tables and descriptor segments.

- The current access $b$: stored in the SDWs in the descriptor segments of the active processes; the active processes are found in the *active segment table*.
- The access control matrix $M$: represented by the ACLs; for each object, the ACL is stored in the object's parent directory; each ACL entry specifies a process and the access rights the process has on that object.
- The level function $f$: the security levels of the subjects are stored in special process security level tables, the *process level table* and the *current-level table*; the security level of an object is stored in its parent directory.

### 8.3.2 Translating the BLP Policies

Section 4.3.2 already introduced the Multics access attributes for data segments and directory segments. We also explained how these access attributes correspond to the access rights of the BLP model. As a reminder, we restate the access attributes for data segments.

| access attribute | access right |
|------------------|--------------|
| read | $\underline{r}$ |
| execute | $\underline{e}$, $\underline{r}$ |
| read and write | $\underline{w}$ |
| write | $\underline{a}$ |

The BLP security properties have now to be rephrased in terms of the security levels of processes and data segments and of the indicators stored in the SDWs. For example, the *-property is written as follows.

> For any SDW in the descriptor segment of an active process, the current level of the process:
> - dominates the level of the segment if the read or execute indicator is on and the write indicator is off;
> - is dominated by the level of the segment if the read indicator is off and the write indicator is on;
> - is equal to the level of the segment if the read indicator is on and the write indicator is on.

Figure 8.3 indicates how compliance with the *-property can be verified. The security level $L_c$ of the current process is held in the *current-level table*. The contents of the *descriptor segment base register* (DSBR) point to the head of the descriptor segment of the current process. This descriptor segment happens to contain the SDW for an object where the access attribute is write only. Hence, the write indicator is on and the read indicator is off. The object's security level $L_o$ is taken from its parent directory and compared with $L_s$ to check that $L_s \geq L_o$ holds.

### 8.3.3 Checking the Kernel Primitives

Finally, a set of *kernel primitives* has to be specified. These kernel primitives are the state transitions in an abstract model of the Multics kernel and we would have to show that

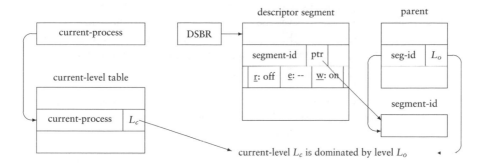

current-level $L_c$ is dominated by level $L_o$

○ Figure 8.3. The *-Property for Access Attribute Write Only

they preserve the BLP security policies. Then, the preconditions of the Basic Security Theorem hold and we have a proof for the 'security' of Multics. Of course, this is not a complete proof of security. You still would have to show that the implementation of the kernel primitives, and in the end their execution on a given hardware platform, complies with their specification.

We choose get-read to look at a kernel primitive in detail. The get-read primitive takes as its parameters a process-id and a segment-id. The operating system has to check whether:

- the ACL of segment-id, stored in the segment's parent directory, lists process-id with read permission;
- the security level of process-id dominates the security level of segment-id;
- process-id is a trusted subject or the current security level of process-id dominates the security level of segment-id.

If all three conditions are met, access is permitted. If no SDW for segment-id exists, a corresponding SDW is added to the descriptor segment of process-id with the read indicator turned on. If a SDW for segment-id already exists in the descriptor segment of process-id, the read indicator in this SDW is turned on. If any of the three conditions is not met, access is denied.

The following are some further primitives that have been proposed for implementation in the Multics kernel.

- release-read: a process releases an object; the read flag in the corresponding SDW is turned off; if thereafter no indicator is on, the SDW is removed from the descriptor segment.
- give-read: a process grants read access to another process (DAC).
- rescind-read: a process withdraws a read permission given to another process.
- create-object: a process creates an object; the operating system has to check that write access on the object's directory segment is permitted and that the security level of the segment dominates the security level of the process.

- delete-object: when deleting an object, the same checks are performed as in create-object.
- change-subject-current-security-level: the operating system has to check that no security violations are created by the change; this kernel primitive as well as the primitive change-object-security-level were not intended for implementation (tranquility).

Ideally, processors are developed so that their instruction sets dovetail with the kernel primitives of the operating system. Conversely, kernel primitives can be designed to match the support provided by existing processors.

## 8.4 FURTHER READING

The original reports on the BLP model have been republished in the *Journal of Computer Security* (Bell and LaPadula, 1996). A framework for policies on changing access rights in the BLP model is discussed by McLean (1990). The research literature is full of contributions extending the scope of the BLP model while still enforcing its MLS policies.

The outcome of computer security research aimed at the first multiuser operating systems is treated comprehensively by Denning (1982). A further survey of protection techniques is compiled by Landwehr (1983). Comments on Multics security and in particular on the complexity of security management and the complexity of assessing the correctness of the design can be found in Saltzer (1974). Lessons learned during the work on Multics security are discussed by Karger and Schell (2002).

## 8.5 EXERCISES

**Exercise 8.1**    Describe the *-property in terms of the basic access modes alter and observe.

**Exercise 8.2**    Identify further covert channels in the BLP model.

**Exercise 8.3**    Write a short essay stating your position in the Bell vs McLean debate.

**Exercise 8.4**    BLP does not specify policies for changing access rights. Which policies would you suggest?

**Exercise 8.5**    Rewrite the ss-property for the Multics operating system.

**Exercise 8.6**   Specify the checks that have to be made for get-write and release-write kernel primitives.

**Exercise 8.7**   Specify the checks that have to be made for the create-object and delete-object kernel primitives.

**Exercise 8.8**   Specify the checks that have to be made for the change-subject-current-security-level kernel primitive.

# Chapter 9

# Security Models

The BLP model was designed to capture one specific security policy. It was so successful, however, that there was a time when it was treated as 'the model of security' in general. Not surprisingly it was found lacking in this respect, but this should not be taken as a criticism of the model itself. Rather, security requirements are application dependent and there exist applications that are substantially different from the military environment multilevel security comes from.

This chapter will take a wider look at security models. We will add models for integrity policies (Biba, Clark–Wilson) and for policies that, in contrast to the tranquility assumption of BLP, dynamically change access rights (Chinese Wall). We will also use the term 'security model' in a wider sense. The Clark–Wilson model, for example, does not formalize a single specific policy but provides a descriptive framework that can serve as a blueprint for formalizing a wider class of security policies. Furthermore, we will discuss models that are of interest primarily from a theoretical point of view as they provide a basis for proving some fundamental facts about access control.

## OBJECTIVES

- Present a wider range of modeling techniques for access control.
- Introduce basic concepts relevant for commercial security policies.
- Provide theoretical foundations for analyzing access control problems.
- Appreciate that some decision problems in security are inherently undecidable.

# 9.1 THE BIBA MODEL

Consider integrity policies that label subjects and objects with elements from a lattice $(L, \leq)$ of integrity levels, and that prohibit the corruption of 'clean' high-level entities by 'dirty' low-level entities. Information may only flow downwards in the integrity lattice. As in BLP, we will only concern ourselves with information flows caused directly by access operations. We are using 'clean' and 'dirty' as shorthand for high integrity and low integrity. The concrete meaning of integrity levels would depend on the given application.

The Biba model (1977) formalizes this type of integrity policy. It is a state machine model similar to BLP, and we will use the mathematical notations introduced in the previous chapter. The assignment of integrity levels to subjects and objects is given by the functions $f_S : S \to L$ and $f_O : O \to L$. Unlike BLP, there is no single high-level integrity policy. Instead, there are a variety of approaches. Some even yield mutually incompatible policies.

## 9.1.1 Static Integrity Levels

Mirroring the tranquility property of BLP, we can state policies where integrity levels never change. The following two policies *prevent* clean subjects and objects from being contaminated by dirty information.

> **Simple Integrity Property**    if subject $s$ can modify (alter) object $o$, then $f_S(s) \geq f_O(o)$. (No write-up).

> **Integrity \*-Property**    if subject $s$ can read (observe) object $o$, then $s$ can have write access to some other object $p$ only if $f_O(p) \leq f_O(o)$.

These two integrity properties are the dual of the mandatory BLP policies and are the basis for claims that integrity is the dual of confidentiality.

## 9.1.2 Dynamic Integrity Levels

The next two integrity properties automatically *adjust* the integrity level of an entity if it comes into contact with low-level information. The integrity level $\inf(f_S(s), f_O(o))$ is the greatest lower bound of $f_S(s)$ and $f_O(o)$. It is well defined as we are dealing with a lattice of integrity levels.

> **Subject Low Watermark Property**    subject $s$ can read (observe) an object $o$ at any integrity level. The new integrity level of the subject is $\inf(f_S(s), f_O(o))$, where $f_S(s)$ and $f_O(o)$ are the integrity levels before the operation.

> **Object Low Watermark Property**    subject $s$ can modify (alter) an object $o$ at any integrity level. The new integrity level of the object is $\inf(f_S(s), f_O(o))$, where $f_S(s)$ and $f_O(o)$ are the integrity levels before the operation.

These are examples of policies with dynamically changing access rights. As integrity levels can only be lowered, there is a danger that all subjects and objects eventually end up at the lowest integrity level.

### 9.1.3 Policies for Invocation

The Biba model can be extended to include an access operation invoke. A subject can *invoke* another subject, e.g. a software tool, to access an object. This is a step towards formulating access control at intermediate layers. What kind of policy should govern invocation? If we want to make sure that invocation does not bypass the *mandatory integrity policies* we could add the:

**Invoke Property**   subject $s_1$ can invoke subject $s_2$ only if $f_S(s_2) \leq f_S(s_1)$.

Subjects are only allowed to invoke tools at a lower level. Otherwise, a dirty subject could use a clean tool to access, and contaminate, a clean object.

Alternatively, we may want to use tools exactly for this purpose. Dirty subjects should have access to a clean object, but only if they use a clean tool to do so (controlled invocation). This tool may perform a number of consistency checks to ensure that the object remains clean. Integrity protection mechanisms in operating systems that use *protection rings* (section 4.6.4) fall into this category. In this scenario, we would not want a more privileged subject to use less privileged tools and we get the:

**Ring Property**   a subject $s_1$ can read objects at all integrity levels. It can only modify objects $o$ with $f_O(o) \leq f_S(s)$ and it can invoke a subject $s_2$ only if $f_S(s_1) \leq f_S(s_2)$.

Quite obviously, the last two properties are inconsistent and it will depend on the application which property is more appropriate.

# 9.2 THE CHINESE WALL MODEL

The Chinese Wall model proposed by Brewer and Nash (1989) models access rules in a consultancy business where analysts have to make sure that no conflicts of interest arise when they are dealing with different clients. Informally, conflicts arise because clients are direct competitors in the same market or because of the ownerships of companies. Analysts have to adhere to the following security policy.

> There must be no information flow that causes a conflict of interest.

The state set of the BLP model needs some slight adaptations to address this policy.

- The set of companies is denoted by $C$.

- The analysts are the *subjects* and $S$ is the set of subjects. The *objects* are items of information. Each object refers to a single company. The set of objects is denoted by $O$.

- All objects concerning the same company are collected in a *company dataset*. The function $y : O \rightarrow C$ gives the company dataset of each object.

- *Conflict of interest classes* indicate which companies are in competition. The function $x : O \to \mathcal{P}(\mathcal{C})$ gives the conflict of interest class for each object, i.e. the set of all companies that should not learn about the contents of the object.

- The *security label* of an object $o$ is the pair $(x(o), y(o))$.

- *Sanitized information* has been purged of sensitive details and is not subject to access restrictions. The security label of a sanitized object is $(\emptyset, y(o))$.

Conflict of interests do not only arise from objects currently accessed but also from objects that have been accessed in the past. We therefore need a data structure to record the history of the subjects' actions. This purpose is served by a Boolean $S \times O$ matrix $N$, with

$$N_{s,o} = \begin{cases} \text{true, if the subject } s \text{ has had access to object } o, \\ \text{false, if the subject } s \text{ never had access to object } o. \end{cases}$$

Setting $N_{s,o}$ = false for all $s \in S$ and all $o \in O$ gives an initial state that fulfills the following security properties.

The first security policy deals with direct information flow. We want to prevent a subject from being exposed to a conflict of interest. Therefore, access is granted only if the object requested belongs to:

- a company dataset already held by the user;
- an entirely different conflict of interest class.

Formally, we can express this as the *ss-property*.

> A subject $s$ will be permitted access to an object $o$ only if for all objects $o'$ with $N_{s,o'}$ = true, $y(o) = y(o')$ or $y(o) \notin x(o')$.

On its own, this property does not fully implement the stated security policy. Indirect information flow is still possible. Consider the following example (Figure 9.1). Two competitors, Company_A and Company_B, have their accounts with the same Bank. Analyst_A, dealing with Company_A and the Bank, updates the Bank portfolio with sensitive information about Company_A. Analyst_B, dealing with Company_B and the Bank, now has access to information about a competitor's business. We therefore introduce a ∗-*property* to regulate write access.

> A subject $s$ is granted write access to an object $o$, only if $s$ has no read access to an object $o'$ with $y(o) \neq y(o')$ and $x(o') \neq \emptyset$.

Write access to an object is only granted if no other object can be read which is in a different company dataset and contains unsanitized information. In the example of Figure 9.1 both write operations will be blocked by the ∗-property. The ∗-property stops unsanitized information from flowing out of a company dataset.

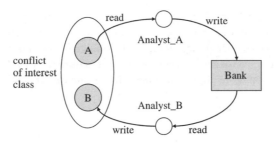

○ **Figure 9.1: Indirect Information Flow within a Conflict of Interest Class**

In contrast to BLP, where the assignment of access rights is usually assumed to be static, you have now seen a model where access rights have to be reassigned in every state transition.

## 9.3 THE CLARK–WILSON MODEL

Clark and Wilson (1987) address the security requirements of commercial applications. They argue that these requirements are predominantly about (data) integrity, i.e. about preventing unauthorized modification of data, fraud and errors. This is a rather wide definition of integrity. As a matter of fact, the authors even include issues of concurrency control, which are beyond our scope of security. Integrity requirements are divided into two parts.

- *Internal consistency* refers to properties of the internal state of a system and can be enforced by the computing system.
- *External consistency* refers to the relation of the internal state of a system to the real world and has to be enforced by means outside the computing system, e.g. by auditing.

The general mechanisms for enforcing integrity are:

- *well-formed transactions*: data items can be manipulated only by a specific set of programs; users have access to programs rather than to data items;
- *separation of duties*: users have to collaborate to manipulate data and to collude to circumvent the security system.

Separation of duties appears repeatedly in the operation of a secure system. It is reasonable to require that different persons develop, test, certify and operate a system. In turn, it may be required that during operation different persons have to collaborate to enable a transaction.

The Clark–Wilson model uses programs as an intermediate control level between subjects and objects (data items). Subjects are authorized to execute certain programs. Data items can be accessed through specific programs (Figure 9.2). Defining the set of programs that may access data of a certain type is a general mechanism in software engineering (see *abstract data types* – Denning, 1982; *object-oriented programming*), which can be gainfully employed in constructing secure systems. It is testimony to the influence of BLP that Clark and Wilson write about 'labelling subjects and objects with programs instead of security levels'.

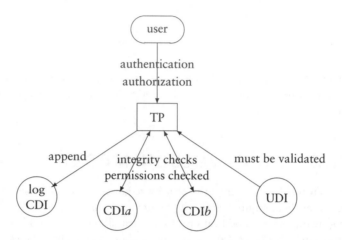

○ **Figure 9.2:  Basic Principles of Access Control in the Clark–Wilson Model**

In the Clark–Wilson model, integrity means 'being authorized to apply a program to a data item that may be accessed through this program'. Clark and Wilson stress the difference between military and commercial security requirements. There is some truth in the observation that the relative importance of confidentiality and integrity is not the same in these two worlds but there will be military applications with integrity requirements and commercial applications with confidentiality requirements. For our purpose, there is a much more relevant distinction. The access operations in the Clark–Wilson model are programs performing complex application – specific manipulations. Access operations in BLP are simple and generic as befits an operating system. We thus look at the difference between a general purpose operating system (BLP) and an application – oriented IT system (Clark–Wilson).

Overall, the following points are considered in the Clark–Wilson model.

1. Subjects have to be identified and authenticated.
2. Objects can be manipulated only by a restricted set of programs.
3. Subjects can execute only a restricted set of programs.
4. A proper audit log has to be maintained.
5. The system has to be certified to work properly.

In a formalization of this model, the data items governed by the security policy are called constrained data items (CDIs). Inputs to the system are captured as unconstrained data items (UDIs). Conversion of UDIs to CDIs is a critical part of the system which cannot be controlled solely by the security mechanisms in the system. CDIs can be manipulated only by transformation procedures (TPs). The integrity of a state is checked by integrity verification procedures (IVPs).

Security properties are on one side defined through five *certification rules*; suggesting the checks that should be conducted so that the security policy is consistent with the application requirements.

CR1 IVPs must ensure that all CDIs are in a valid state at the time the IVP is run (integrity check on CDIs).

CR2 TPs must be certified to be valid, i.e. valid CDIs must always be transformed into valid CDIs. Each TP is certified to access a specific set of CDIs.

CR3 The access rules must satisfy any separation of duties requirements.

CR4 All TPs must write to an append-only log.

CR5 Any TP that takes a UDI as input must either convert the UDI into a CDI or reject the UDI and perform no transformation at all.

Four *enforcement rules* describe the security mechanisms within the computer system that should enforce the security policy. These rules have some similarity to discretionary access control in BLP.

ER1 For each TP, the system must maintain and protect the list of entries (CDI$a$, CDI$b$, ...) giving the CDIs that TP is certified to access.

ER2 For each user the system must maintain and protect the list of entries (TP1, TP2, ...) specifying the TPs that user can execute.

ER3 The system must authenticate each user requesting to execute a TP.

ER4 Only a subject that may certify an access rule for a TP may modify the respective entry in the list. This subject must not have execute rights on that TP.

As a final remark, the Clark–Wilson model is a framework and guideline ('model') for formalizing security policies rather than a model of a specific security policy.

# 9.4 THE HARRISON–RUZZO–ULLMAN MODEL

The BLP model does not state policies for changing access rights or for the creation and deletion of subjects and objects. The Harrison–Ruzzo–Ullman (HRU) model defines *authorization systems* that address these issues (1976). To describe the HRU model, we need:

- a set of *subjects S*;
- a set of *objects O*;
- a set of *access rights R*;
- an access matrix $M = (M_{so})_{s \in S, o \in O}$; the entry $M_{so}$ is the subset of $R$ specifying the rights subject $s$ has on object $o$.

There exist six *primitive operations* for manipulating the set of subjects, the set of objects and the access matrix.

- **enter** $r$ into $M_{so}$
- **delete** $r$ from $M_{so}$
- **create subject** $s$
- **delete subject** $s$
- **create object** $o$
- **delete object** $o$

Commands in the HRU model have the format:

**command** $c(x_1, \ldots, x_k)$
  **if** $r_1$ in $M_{s_1, o_1}$ **and**
  **if** $r_2$ in $M_{s_2, o_2}$ **and**
    $\vdots$
  **if** $r_m$ in $M_{s_m, o_m}$
  **then**
    $op_1$
    $op_2$
    $\vdots$
    $op_n$
**end**

The indices $s_1, \ldots s_m$ and $o_1, \ldots o_m$ are subjects and objects that appear in the parameter list $(x_1, \ldots x_k)$. The conditions check whether particular access rights are present. The list of conditions may be empty. If all conditions hold, the sequence of basic operations is executed. Each command contains at least one operation. For example, the command

**command** *create_file*$(s, f)$
    **create** $f$
    **enter** $\underline{o}$ into $M_{s,f}$
    **enter** $\underline{r}$ into $M_{s,f}$
    **enter** $\underline{w}$ into $M_{s,f}$
**end**

is used by subject $s$ to create a new file $f$ so that $s$ is the owner of the file (access right o) and has read and write permission to the file (access rights r and w). The owner $s$ of file $f$ grants read access to another subject $p$ with

command *grant_read*$(s, p, f)$
  if o in $M_{s,f}$
  then enter r in $M_{p,f}$
end

The access matrix describes the state of the system. The effect of a command is recorded as a change to the access matrix. It is customary to denote the modified access control matrix by $M'$. The HRU model can capture security policies regulating the allocation of access rights. To verify that a system complies with such a policy, you have to check that there exists no way for undesirable access rights to be granted.

> A state, i.e. an access matrix $M$, is said to *leak* the right $r$ if there exists a command $c$ that adds the right $r$ into a position of the access matrix that previously did not contain $r$. More formally, there exist $s$ and $o$ so that $r \notin M_{s,o}$ but $r \in M'_{s,o}$.

> A state, i.e. an access matrix $M$, is said to be *safe* with respect to the right $r$ if no sequence of commands can transform $M$ into a state that leaks $r$.

Verifying compliance with a security policy in the HRU model thus comes down to verifying safety properties (section 9.6). However, you find yourself now in a rather unenviable position.

> **Theorem**   Given an access matrix $M$ and a right $r$, verifying the safety of $M$ with respect to the right $r$ is an undecidable problem (Harrison, Ruzzo and Ullman, 1976).

You thus cannot tackle the safety problem in its full generality but have to restrict the model to have a better chance of success. For example, you could only allow *mono-operational* systems in which each command contains a single operation.

> **Theorem**   Given a mono-operational authorization system, an access matrix $M$, and a right $r$, verifying the safety of $M$ with respect to the right $r$ is decidable (Harrison, Ruzzo and Ullman, 1976).

Limiting the size of the authorization system is another way of making the safety problem tractable.

> **Theorem**   The safety problem for arbitrary authorization systems is decidable if the number of subjects is finite (Lipton and Snyder, 1978).

These results on the decidability of the safety problem reveal glimpses of the 3$^{rd}$ design principle (section 2.4.3). If you design complex systems that can only be described by complex models, it becomes difficult to find proofs of security. In the worst case (undecidability), there does not exist an universal algorithm that verifies security for all problem instances. If you want verifiable security properties, you are better off when you limit the complexity of the security model. Such a model may not describe all desirable security properties, but you may gain efficient methods for verifying 'security'. In turn, you would be advised to design simple systems that can be adequately described in the simple model. If there is too wide a gap between system and model, proofs of security in the model will not carry much weight.

### Lesson

The more expressive a security model is, both with respect to the security properties and the systems it can describe, the more difficult it is usually to verify security properties.

## 9.5 INFORMATION FLOW MODELS

In the BLP model, information can flow from a high security level to a low security level through a covert channel. *Information flow models* consider any kind of information flow, not only the direct information flow through access operations as modeled by BLP. Informally, a state transition causes an information flow from an object $x$ to an object $y$, if we may learn more about $x$ by observing $y$. If we already knew $x$, no information can flow from $x$. You may distinguish between:

- explicit information flow: observing $y$ after the assignment `y := x;` tells you the value of $x$;
- implicit information flow: observing $y$ after the conditional statement `IF x=0 THEN y:=1;` may tell you something about $x$ even if the assignment `y := 1;` had not been executed. For example if $y = 2$, you know that $x \neq 0$.

### 9.5.1 Entropy and Equivocation

A precise and quantitative definition of information flow can be given in terms of information theory. The amount of information that can be derived from an observation is formally defined by the entropy of the object (variable) we are observing. Let $\{x_1, \ldots, x_n\}$ be the values a variable $x$ can take, and let $p(x_i)$ be the probability for $x$ to take the value $x_i$, $1 \leq i \leq n$. The *entropy* $H(x)$ of $x$ is defined as

$$H(x) = -\sum_{i=1}^{n} p(x_i) \log_2 p(x_i).$$

For example, let $x$ take all values between 0 and $2^w - 1$ with equal probability. Then

$$H(x) = -\sum_{i=1}^{2^w} \frac{1}{2^w} \log_2 \left( \frac{1}{2^w} \right) = w.$$

That is, a binary word of length $w$ carries $w$ bits of information if all words of length $w$ are equally likely.

The information flow from $x$ to $y$ is measured by the change in the equivocation (conditional entropy) of $x$ given the value of $y$. Let $x$ and $y$ be two variables that can take the values $\{x_1, \ldots, x_n\}$ and $\{y_1, \ldots, y_m\}$ with probabilities $p(x_i)$ and $q(y_j)$. Let $p(x_i, y_j)$ be the joint probability for $x$ and $y$ to take the values $x_i$ and $y_j$, and let $p(x_i \mid y_j)$ be the conditional probability for $x$ to take the value $x_i$ if $y$ takes the value $y_j$. The *equivocation* $H_y(x)$ of $x$ given the value of $y$ is defined as

$$H_y(x) = - \sum_{i=1}^{n} \sum_{j=1}^{m} p(x_i, y_j) \log_2 p(x_i|y_j)$$

Rewriting $p(x_i, y_j)$ as $p(x_i|y_j)q(y_j)$ we get

$$H_y(x) = - \sum_{j=1}^{m} q(y_j) \sum_{i=n}^{m} p(x_i|y_j) \log_2 p(x_i|y_j).$$

As an example, consider the assignment IF x=0 THEN y:=1; from above. Let $x$ and $y$ be binary variables, with $y$ initially set to 0 and both values of $x$ equally likely. We get

$$p(0|0) = p(1|1) = 0, p(1|0) = p(0|1) = 1, \text{ hence } H_y(x) = 0.$$

Indeed, after performing the assignment and observing $y$, we know the exact value of $x$. All information in $x$ has flowed to $y$. If $x$ could take the values 0, 1, 2 with equal probability, we get $q(0) = \frac{2}{3}, q(1) = \frac{2}{3}$,

$$p(0|0) = p(1|1) = p(2|1) = 0, \; p(1|0) = p(2|0) = \frac{1}{2}, \; p(0|1) = 1, \text{ and } H_y(x) = \frac{2}{3}.$$

## 9.5.2 A Lattice–based Model

The components of the information flow model are:

- a lattice $(L, \leq)$ of *security labels*;
- a set of labeled *objects*;
- the security policy: information flow from an object with label $c_1$ to an object with label $c_2$ is permitted only if $c_1 \leq c_2$; any information flow that violates this rule is illegal.

A system is called *secure* if there is no illegal information flow. The advantage of such a model is that it covers all kinds of information flow. The disadvantage is that it becomes more difficult to design secure systems. For example, it has been shown that checking whether a given system is secure in the information flow model is an *undecidable* problem.

Furthermore, we have to distinguish between *static* and *dynamic* enforcement of information flow policies. In the first case, the system (program) is considered as a static object. The second case considers the system under execution. We may find that some information flow may be possible in theory (and therefore should be detected in the static analysis) but will never occur during execution. Therefore, static analysis tends to produce too restrictive systems.

*Noninterference* models are an alternative to information flow models. They provide a different formalism to describe what a subject knows about the state of the system. Subject $s_1$ does not interfere with subject $s_2$ if the actions of $s_1$ have no influence on $s_2$'s view of the system. Currently, information flow and noninterference models are areas of research rather than the basis of a practical methodology for the design of secure systems.

## 9.6  EXECUTION MONITORS

The previous two sections have shown that certain security problems are undecidable. There cannot be a general algorithm that solves all instances of these problems. Now, our theoretical investigations will follow a different route. We will start from the typical access control mechanisms in use today and characterize the policies these mechanisms can enforce. After all, a policy is useful in practice only if it can be enforced reasonably efficiently. We consider three classes of security policies (Schneider, 2000).

- Access control policies define restrictions on the operations principals can perform on objects.
- Information flow policies restrict what principals can infer about objects from observing system behavior (section 9.5).
- Availability policies restrict principals from denying others the use of a resource.

Access control mechanisms deployed today in firewalls, operating systems, middleware architectures like CORBA, or in web services have in common that they observe (monitor) the execution of the system and step in if an execution step is prohibited by the given security policy. The term *Execution Monitoring* (EM) was introduced by Schneider (2000) for enforcement mechanisms that monitor execution steps of a target system and terminate the target's execution if a violation of the security policy is about to occur.

Execution monitors have two important limitations. First, they do not have a model of the target system so they cannot predict the outcomes of possible continuations of the execution they are observing, and they cannot modify the target system. Compilers and theorem-provers, for example, work by analyzing a static representation of the target and can deduce information about all of its possible executions. These methods are therefore not EM mechanisms. Second, EM mechanisms cannot modify a target before executing it. In-line reference monitors and reflection in object-oriented systems thus do not fall into the EM category.

### 9.6.1 Properties of Executions

Executions of the target system are sequences of steps. The precise nature of these steps will depend on the actual target. Typical examples would be memory access operations or file access operations. In our general discussion let $\Psi$ denote the set of all finite and infinite sequences of steps, and $\Sigma_S$ the sequences representing executions of the target system $S$. A security policy $p$ is defined as a predicate on the set of executions. A target $S$ satisfies the security policy $p$ if $p(\Sigma_S)$ equals *true*. The safety property of the HRU model and also the BLP, Biba and Chinese Wall policies are all examples of security policies.

Let $\Sigma$ denote a set of executions. A security policy $p$ that can be enforced by an execution monitor must be specified by a predicate of the form

$$p(\Sigma) : (\forall \sigma \in \Sigma : \hat{p}(\sigma))$$

where $\hat{p}$ is a predicate on individual executions. This observation provides a link to the literature on linear-time concurrent program verification (Alpern and Schneider, 1985). There, a set $\Gamma \subset \Psi$ of executions is called a *property* if membership of an element is determined by the element alone, not by other members of the set. A security policy must therefore be a property to have an enforcement mechanism in EM.

However, not every security policy is a property. Some security policies cannot be defined as a predicate on individual executions. For example, information flow policies demand that a low user cannot distinguish an execution where a high user is active from some other execution where the high user is inactive.

Furthermore, not every property is EM enforceable. Enforcement mechanisms in EM cannot look into the future when making decisions on an execution. Consider an execution $\sigma$ that complies with the security policy but has a prefix $\sigma'$ that does not. Informally, the execution goes through an 'insecure' state but would be permissible in the end. As a simple example, consider a policy that requires a matching 'close file' for every 'open file' command. An execution monitor has to prohibit an insecure prefix and stop executions that would be secure. For such policies, EM would be a *conservative* approach that stops more executions than necessary.

### 9.6.2 Safety and Liveness

Among the properties of executions there are two broad classes of particular significance.

- Safety properties: nothing bad can happen. (The 'safety' property of access matrices in the HRU model meets indeed this description.)

- Liveness properties: something good will happen eventually.

There exists a close relationship between safety and the type of policies that can be enforced by execution monitors. We will formally define safety properties by characterizing their complements. In the definition, the first $i$ steps of a sequence $\sigma \in \Psi$ will be denoted by $\sigma[..i]$. A property $\Gamma$ is called a safety property if for every finite or infinite execution $\sigma$

$$\sigma \notin \Gamma \Rightarrow \exists i (\forall \tau \in \Psi : \sigma[..i]\tau \notin \Gamma)$$

holds (Lamport, 1985). If an execution $\sigma$ is unsafe, there has to be some point $i$ in the execution after which it is no longer possible to revert to a safe continuation of the execution.

If the set of executions for a security policy is not a safety property, then there exists an unsafe execution that could be extended by future steps into a safe execution. As we have discussed above, such properties (policies) do not have an enforcement mechanism from EM. So, if a policy is not a safety property, it is not EM enforceable. Put the other way round, execution monitors enforce security policies that are safety properties. However, not all safety properties have EM enforcement mechanisms.

To summarize our findings we return to the three classes of security policies we set out from.

- Access control policies define safety properties; partial executions ending with an unacceptable operation being attempted will be prohibited.

- Information flow policies do not define sets of executions that are properties; thus, information flow cannot be a safety property and in turn cannot be enforced by EM.

- Availability policies do not define safety properties; any partial execution could be extended so that the principal would get access to the resource in the end.

Availability policies that refer to a Maximum Waiting Time (MWT; Gligor, 1984) are safety properties. Once an execution has waited beyond the MWT, any extension will naturally also be in violation of the availability policy.

## 9.7 FURTHER READING

Surveys of research on security models are given by Landwehr (1983) and McLean (1994). The original paper by Clark and Wilson (1987) is highly recommended reading. An implementation of the Clark–Wilson model using capabilities is described in Karger (1991). A slight extension of the Biba model providing mandatory integrity controls that can be used to implement Clark–Wilson is proposed by T.M.P. Lee (1991). A detailed treatment of the decidability properties of the HRU model and of information flow models, with definitions, proofs and more theorems, is given by Denning (1982). For noninterference models, refer to Goguen and Meseguer's paper (1982). Applications of security models in the security evaluation of smart cards are described by Bieber *et al.* (2000) and Schellhorn *et al.* (2000).

# 9.8 EXERCISES

**Exercise 9.1**　The Biba model can capture a variety of integrity policies. Give examples for application areas where:

- a policy with static integrity labels;
- a policy with dynamically changing integrity labels;
- the ring-property;

is appropriate.

**Exercise 9.2**　Can you use BLP and Biba to model confidentiality and integrity simultaneously? Can you use the same security labels for both policies?

**Exercise 9.3**　Can you fit the Chinese Wall model into the BLP framework?

**Exercise 9.4**　Should the ∗-property in the Chinese Wall model refer to current read access only or to any past read access?

**Exercise 9.5**　Give a formal model that describes the Clark–Wilson enforcement rules.

**Exercise 9.6**　Let $x$ be a 4-bit variable that can take all values between 0 and 15 with equal probability. Given the assignment IF $x>7$ THEN y:=1; and the initial value $y = 0$, compute the conditional entropy $H_y(x)$.

**Exercise 9.7**　Develop a security model for documents which are declassified after 30 years.

**Exercise 9.8**　In a medical information system that controls access to patient records and prescriptions:

- doctors may read and write patient records and prescriptions;
- nurses may read and write prescriptions only but should learn nothing about the contents of patient records.

How can you capture this policy in a lattice model that prevents information flow from patient records to prescriptions? In your opinion, which security model is most appropriate for this policy?

# Chapter 10

## Security Evaluation

Users of secure systems need some kind of assurance that the products they use provide adequate security. They could:

1. rely on the word of the manufacturer/service provider;
2. test the system themselves;
3. or rely on an impartial assessment by an independent body (*evaluation*).

Users have to be security experts to be able to take the second option. Most users are not in this position. So some kind of security evaluation is the only alternative to taking a security product on trust. This chapter will explore security evaluation and discuss whether current evaluation schemes have any benefits to offer.

### OBJECTIVES

- Appreciate the fundamental problems any security evaluation process has to address.
- Propose a method for comparing evaluation criteria.
- Give an overview of the major evaluation criteria.
- Assess the merits of evaluated products and systems.

## 10.1 INTRODUCTION

The *Trusted Computer System Evaluation Criteria* (TCSEC, the Orange Book; US Department of Defense, 1985) were the first evaluation criteria to gain wide acceptance. Several criteria have since been developed to address perceived shortcomings of the Orange Book. The wish to unify the different criteria which had arisen has today resulted in the Common Criteria (CCIB, 2004a). Important milestones in the development of security evaluation criteria are the:

- Information Technology Security Evaluation Criteria (ITSEC; Commission of the European Communities, 1991);

- Canadian Trusted Computer Product Evaluation Criteria (CTCPEC; Canadian System Security Centre, 1993);

- Federal Criteria (National Institute of Standards and Technology & National Security Agency, 1992).

We will structure our discussion of evaluation criteria by asking the following questions.

### What is the *Target* of the Evaluation?

Evaluation criteria refer to *products*: i.e. off-the-shelf components that will be used in a variety of applications and have to meet generic security requirements, e.g. an operating system; or to *systems*, i.e. a collection of products assembled to meet the specific requirements of a given application. In the first case, one has to agree on a set of generic requirements. The *security classes* of the Orange Book and the *protection profiles* of the Federal and Common Criteria try to achieve just that. In the second case, requirements capture and analysis become part of each individual evaluation. ITSEC was suited to the evaluation of systems.

The distinction between products and systems highlights a fundamental dilemma in security evaluation: users are not security experts but have specific security requirements. Evaluation of off-the-shelf products with respect to generic criteria, which capture typical requirements, can be a useful decision criteria for a nonexpert, but the products may not address the actual security requirements. Evaluation of customized systems will address the perceived requirements, but we now ask the nonexpert user to confirm that the security requirements have been properly captured. If further help is provided at this stage, we start to cross the borderline between a security evaluation intended for the general public and the task of a security consultant who advises a particular client.

### What is the *Purpose* of the Evaluation?

The Orange Book distinguishes between:

- *evaluation*: assessing whether a product has the security properties claimed for it;

- *certification*: assessing whether a(n) (evaluated) product is suitable for a given application;
- *accreditation*: deciding that a (certified) product will be used in a given application.

This is the terminology of the Orange Book. Of course, other sources will use different terms or use the same terms differently. The names given to the various activities are therefore less important than the fundamental differences in their respective goals.

### What is the *Method* of the Evaluation?

The credibility of evaluation very much hinges on the methods used in evaluation. There are two situations an evaluation method should prevent from arising.

1. An evaluated product is later found to contain a serious flaw.

2. Different evaluations of the same product disagree in their assessment of the product. *Repeatability* and *reproducibility* are therefore often included among the requirements an evaluation methodology should meet.

Security evaluation can be product oriented or process oriented. *Product oriented (investigational)* methods examine and test the product. They may tell more about the product than process-oriented methods but different evaluations may well give different results. Is this a problem for credibility?

*Process- (audit-) oriented* methods look at documentation and the process of product development. They are cheaper and it is much easier to achieve repeatable results but the results themselves may not be very valuable. The first version of the European *Information Technology Security Evaluation Manual* (Commission of the European Communities, 1993) was a prime example of repeatability overpowering content. Is this a problem for credibility?

### What is the *Organizational Framework* of the Evaluation Process?

Security evaluations should arrive at an independent, commonly accepted verdict on the properties of products. An independent *evaluation facility* can either be a government agency (the approach taken originally in the US) or a properly accredited private enterprise (e.g. in Europe; UK ITSEC Scheme, 1991). In both schemes, a government body backs the evaluation process and issues the certificates. Accredited evaluation facilities might issue certificates themselves (as in Germany) and we could imagine schemes where empirical evidence of the expertise of the evaluators replaces a formal accreditation.

If all evaluations are conducted by a single government agency, then it will hardly be necessary to create further organizational overheads to ensure the consistency of evaluations. However, there is still the danger of *interpretation drift (criteria creep)* over time. Evaluations may be slow due to lack of competition and limitation in resources at the evaluation facility. There may also be a problem of staff mobility when experienced evaluators leave for higher salaries in the private sector. A government body may charge for an evaluation or, as in the US, conduct evaluations as a free public service.

In an environment with private evaluation facilities, *certification agencies* have to enforce the consistency of evaluations (repeatability, reproducibility) between different facilities and may, as in Europe, confirm the verdict of the evaluation facility. The precise formulation of the criteria becomes more important to avoid differing interpretations. Evaluations are being paid for and commercial pressures should lead to faster evaluations and the resources required from the sponsor of an evaluation may be more predictable. On the other hand, precautions have to be taken so that commercial pressures do not lead to incorrect results.

Further organizational aspects concern the contractual relationship between the sponsor of an evaluation, the product manufacturers and the evaluation facility. Moreover, there have to be appropriate procedures for the start of an evaluation, for the issuing of evaluation certificates and for the reevaluation of modifications to evaluated products.

## What is the *Structure* of the Evaluation Criteria?

Security evaluation aims to give assurance that a product/system is secure. Security and assurance may be related to:

- *functionality*: the security features of a system, e.g. DAC, MAC, authentication, auditing;
- *effectiveness*: are the mechanisms used appropriate for the given security requirements? For example, is user authentication by passwords sufficient or does the application require a cryptographic challenge-response protocol?
- *assurance*: the thoroughness of the evaluation.

The Orange Book defines evaluation classes for a given set of typical Department of Defense requirements. Therefore, all three aspects are considered simultaneously in the definition of its evaluation classes. ITSEC provides a flexible evaluation framework that can deal with new security requirements. Therefore, the three aspects are addressed independently.

## What are the *Costs* and *Benefits* of Evaluation?

In addition to the fee paid for an evaluation, you also have to consider indirect costs like the time devoted to producing the evidence required for evaluation, training the evaluators and liaising with the evaluation team. When considering the cost of evaluation, you may again distinguish between the evaluation of off-the-shelf products and of customized systems. In the first case, the evaluation sponsor can potentially spread the cost between a larger number of customers. In the second case, the sponsor, or a single customer, may have to bear all the costs on their own.

Evaluations may be required by government procurement guidelines or be mandated by law or some industry standards. Evaluations may also improve a product in the users' perception.

## 10.2 THE ORANGE BOOK

Work towards security evaluation guidelines started in the US in 1967. It led to the *Trusted Computer System Evaluation Criteria* (Orange Book), the first guideline for evaluating security products (operating systems). Although these efforts were concentrated in the 'national security' sector, the authors of the Orange Book intended to create a more generally applicable document that provides:

- a yardstick for users to assess the degree of trust that can be placed in a computer security system;
- guidance for manufacturers of computer security systems;
- a basis for specifying security requirements when acquiring a computer security system.

Security evaluation examines the security-relevant part of a system, i.e. the Trusted Computing Base (TCB) (section 5.1). The access control policies of the Orange Book are already familiar from the Bell–LaPadula model (section 8.2), discretionary access control and mandatory access control based on a lattice of security labels. A *reference monitor* verifies that subjects are authorized to access the objects they request.

High assurance is linked to formal methods, simple TCBs and structured design methodologies. Bell–LaPadula is an obvious candidate for a formal model capturing the Orange Book security policies but other models have also been used in TCSEC evaluations. It is assumed that greater simplicity in the TCB will allow more comprehensive analysis. Complex systems will generally therefore fall into the lower evaluation classes.

The *evaluation classes* of the Orange Book are designed to address typical patterns of security requirements. For this reason, *specific security feature requirements* and *assurance requirements* are combined in the definition of these evaluation classes. The main headings in the description of an evaluation class are:

1. *Security policy*: mandatory and discretionary access control policies expressed in terms of subjects and objects;

2. *Marking of objects*: labels specify the sensitivity of objects;

3. *Identification of subjects*: individual subjects must be identified and authenticated;

4. *Accountability*: audit logs of security-relevant events have to be kept;

5. *Assurance*: operational assurance refers mainly to the security architecture, life cycle assurance refers to issues like design methodology, testing and configuration management;

6. *Documentation*: system managers and users of a secure system require guidance to install and use its security features properly; evaluators need test and design documentation;

7. *Continuous protection*: security mechanisms cannot be tampered with.

The Orange Book uses these criteria to define four security divisions and seven security classes. Products in higher security classes provide more security mechanisms and higher assurance through more rigorous analysis. The four divisions are:

**D** Minimal Protection
**C** Discretionary Protection ('need to know')
**B** Mandatory Protection (based on 'labels')
**A** Verified Protection

The security classes of the Orange Book are defined incrementally. All requirements of one class are automatically included in the requirements of all higher classes. The Orange Book was the basis for application-independent security evaluations, performed by a national security organization.

## D – Minimal Protection

In this class, you find products that were submitted for evaluation but did not meet the requirements of any Orange Book class.

## C1 – Discretionary Security Protection

C1 systems are intended for an environment where *cooperating users process data at the same level of integrity*. Discretionary access control (DAC) based on individual users and/or groups enables users to share access to objects in a controlled fashion. Users have to identify themselves and their identity has to be authenticated.

For operational assurance, the TCB has to have its own execution domain and there must exist features for periodically validating the correct operation of the TCB. Life cycle assurance only refers to security testing for 'obvious flaws'. A User's Guide (one chapter in the documentation), a Trusted Facility Manual (for the system administrator), test documentation and design documentation have to be provided. In summary, C1 systems are suitable for a friendly environment and do not pretend to offer strong security.

## C2 – Controlled Access Protection

C2 systems make *users individually accountable for their actions*. DAC is enforced at the granularity of single users. The propagation of access rights now has to be controlled. Subjects must not get access to objects managed by the TCB that contain information produced by a prior subject *(object reuse)*. Audit trails of security-relevant events, as specified explicitly in the definition of class C2, have to be kept.

Testing and documentation have to cover the newly added security features but assurance is still rather modest. Tests continue to look for obvious flaws only.

C2 was regarded as the most reasonable class for commercial applications (European Computer Manufacturers Association, 1993) although C2 systems are intrinsically rather weak. Most of the major vendors offered C2-evaluated versions of their operating systems or database management systems. Sometimes, they provided special utilities that help to install their systems in a C2-compliant configuration (Park, 1995).

## B1 – Labeled Security Protection

Division B is intended for products that handle classified data and enforce the mandatory Bell–LaPadula policies. There are *labels* for each subject and object, constructed from hierarchical classification levels and nonhierarchical categories as explained in section 4.7.3. The integrity of these labels has to be protected. Identification and authentication contribute to determining the security label of a subject.

Once protection is based on labels, you have to consider what happens to labeled objects when they are *exported* to another system, or to a printer. The solutions depend on the nature of the export channel. Communications and I/O channels can be single level or multi level. In multilevel channels, objects are exported with their labels. In single-level channels, the TCB and an authorized user designate the sensitivity level of exported information. Human-readable output has to be labeled too, e.g. by printing the classification on each page of a sensitive document.

To achieve higher assurance, an informal or formal model of the security policy is required. Testing and documentation now have to be much more thorough. Design documentation, source code and object code have to be analyzed. All flaws uncovered in testing must be removed.

However, class B1 is not very demanding with respect to the structure of the TCB. Hence, complex software systems like multilevel secure Unix systems or database management systems have received B1 certificates. Class B1 is intended for system high environments with compartments (section 4.7.3).

System V/MLS (from AT&T) and a number of other operating systems from vendors like Hewlett-Packard, DEC and Unisys, and database management systems like Trusted

Oracle 7, INFORMIX-Online/Secure, and Secure SQL Server (from Sybase) have been rated B1.

## B2 – Structured Protection

Class B2 increases assurance, mainly by adding requirements to the design of the system. MAC also governs access to physical devices. Users have to be notified about changes to their security levels. There has to be a *Trusted Path* for login and initial authentication.

A formal model of the security policy and a Descriptive Top Level Specification (DTLS) of the system are required. Modularization is an important design feature of the system architecture. The TCB provides distinct address spaces to isolate processes. Hardware support, e.g. for segmentation, supports memory management. A *covert channel analysis* has to be conducted and events potentially creating a covert channel have to be audited. Security testing establishes that the TCB is *relatively resistant to penetration*. The Trusted XENIX operating system from Trusted Information Systems has been rated B2.

## B3 – Security Domains

B3 systems are *highly resistant to penetration*. Many of the new elements in class B3 have to do with security management. A security administrator is supported. Auditing mechanisms *monitor the occurrence or accumulation* of security-relevant events and issue automatic warnings in suspicious situations. *Trusted recovery* after a system failure has to be facilitated. More system engineering efforts are called for to minimize the complexity of the TCB and exclude modules that are not security relevant. A *convincing argument* establishes the consistency between the formal model of the security policy and the informal DTLS.

Various versions of XTS-300 (and XTS-200) from Wang Government Services have been rated B3. XTS-300 is a multilevel secure operating system (STOP) running on a Wang proprietary x86 hardware base.

## A1 – Verified Design

Class A1 is functionally equivalent to B3 and achieves the highest assurance level through the use of formal methods. Formal specification of policy and system, and consistency proofs show with a high degree of assurance that the TCB is correctly implemented. Evaluation for class A1 requires:

- a formal model of the security policy;
- a Formal Top Level Specification (FTLS), including abstract definitions of the functions of the TCB;
- consistency proofs between model and FTLS (formal, where possible);

- that the TCB implementation has informally been shown to be consistent with the FTLS;
- a formal analysis of covert channels (informal for timing channels); continued existence of covert channels has to be justified and bandwidth may have to be limited.

In addition, more stringent configuration management and distribution control (site security acceptance testing) shall ensure that the version installed at a customer site is the same as the (evaluated) master copy.

Typical A1-rated products are network components like MLS LAN (from Boeing) and the Gemini Trusted Network Processor. The SCOMP operating system had also been evaluated to level A1. When the Orange Book was written, there were considerations to define even higher assurance classes *beyond A1*, with more requirements on system architecture, testing, formal specification and verification, and trusted design environment. Given the difficulties of evaluating complex software products even to lower assurance levels, there was little incentive to progress work in this direction.

## 10.3 THE RAINBOW SERIES

The Orange Book is part of a collection of documents on security requirements, security management and security evaluation published by NSA and NCSC[1]. Each document in this series is known by the colour of its cover, and as there are plenty of them, they became known collectively as the Rainbow Series. The concepts and terminology introduced in the Orange Book are adapted to the specific aspects of database management systems and of computer networks in the *Trusted Database Management System Interpretation* (Lavender/Purple Book; NCSC, 1991) and in the *Trusted Network Interpretation* (Red Book; NCSC, 1987). These criteria were originally developed for the evaluation of systems that process classified data in government (military) applications.

## 10.4 INFORMATION TECHNOLOGY SECURITY EVALUATION CRITERIA

The harmonized European Information Technology Security Evaluation Criteria (Commission of the European Communities, 1991) were the result of Dutch, English, French and German activities in defining national security evaluation criteria. A first draft was published in 1990 and the Information Technology Security Evaluation Criteria (ITSEC) were formally endorsed as a Recommendation by the Council of the European Union on 7 April 1995. As a European document, ITSEC exists in a number of translations, which adds to the difficulties of interpreting the criteria uniformly.

---

[1] The US National Security Agency and National Computer Security Center.

ITSEC is a logical progression from the lessons learned in various Orange Book inter-pretations. The Orange Book was found to be too rigid and ITSEC strives to provide a framework for security evaluation that can deal with new sets of security requirements when they arise. The link between functionality and assurance is broken. The criteria apply to *security products* as well as to *security systems*. The term *Target of Evaluation (TOE)* was introduced in ITSEC.

The *sponsor* of the evaluation determines the operational requirements and threats. The *security objectives* for the TOE further depend on legal and other regulations. They establish the required security functionality and evaluation level. The *security target* specifies all aspects of the TOE that are relevant for evaluation. It describes the security functionality of the TOE, possibly also envisaged threats, objectives and details of security mechanisms to be used. The security functions of a TOE may be specified individually or by reference to a predefined *functionality class*.

The seven *evaluation levels* E0 to E6 express the level of confidence in the correctness of the implementation of security functions. E0 stands for inadequate confidence. For each evaluation level, the criteria enumerate items to be delivered by the sponsor to the evaluator. *The evaluator shall ensure that these items are provided, taking care that any requirements for content and presentation are satisfied, and that the items clearly provide, or support the production of, the evidence that is called for.* Close cooperation between the sponsor/developer and the evaluator is recommended.

European security evaluation criteria responded to the problems exposed by the Red Book, and also the Trusted Database Interpretation, by separating function and assurance requirements and considering the evaluation of entire security systems. The flexibility offered by ITSEC may sometimes be an advantage but it also has its drawbacks. Remember the fundamental dilemma highlighted in section 2.4.3. How can users, who are not security experts, decide whether a given security target is right for them?

## 10.5 THE FEDERAL CRITERIA

The next link in the evolutionary chain of evaluation criteria is the US Federal Criteria (National Institute of Standards and Technology & National Security Agency, 1992). They took the next logical step, giving more guidance in the definition of evaluation classes but retaining some degree of flexibility. The Federal Criteria stick to the evaluation of products and to the linkage between function and assurance in the definition of evaluation classes and try to overcome the rigid structure of the Orange Book through the introduction of product-independent *protection profiles*. A protection profile has five sections.

- *Descriptive elements*: the 'name' of the protection profile, including a description of the information protection problem to be solved.

- *Rationale*: fundamental justification of the protection profile, including threat, environment and usage assumptions, a more detailed description of the information protection problem to be solved, and some guidance on the security policies that can be supported by products conforming to the profile.

- *Functional requirements*: establish the protection boundary that must be provided by the product, such that expected threats within this boundary can be countered.

- *Development assurance requirements*: for all development phases from the initial design through to implementation, including the development process, the development environment, operational support and development evidence.

- *Evaluation assurance requirements*: specify the type and intensity of the evaluation.

## 10.6 THE COMMON CRITERIA

For security evaluation to be commercially attractive, evaluation certificates should be recognized as widely as possible. A first step in this direction is agreement on a common set of evaluation criteria. Therefore, various organizations in charge of national security evaluations came together in the Common Criteria Editing Board (CCEB) and produced the Common Criteria (CCIB, 2004a) in an effort to *align* existing and emerging evaluation criteria like TCSEC, ITSEC, CTCPEC and the Federal Criteria. In 1999, the Common Criteria (CC) also became the international standard ISO 15048. The CCEB has been succeeded by the CC Implementation Board (CCIB).

The CC merge ideas from their various predecessors. (As an unfortunate consequence of this merger, the reader is faced with an extremely voluminous document.) The CC have been developed for the security evaluation of products or systems. The generic term Target of Evaluation (TOE) is used again. The CC abandon the strict separation of functionality classes and assurance levels adopted in ITSEC and follow the Federal Criteria in using Protection Profiles like predefined security classes. The Security Target (ST) expresses security requirements for a specific TOE, e.g. by reference to a Protection Profile. The ST is the basis for any evaluation. The Evaluation Assurance Level (EAL) defines what has to be done in an evaluation.

### 10.6.1 Protection Profiles

To guide the users, information about security objectives, rationale, threats and threat environment, and further application notes are collected in a Protection Profile (PP). A PP is a (reusable) set of security requirements that meets specific user needs. Figure 10.1 gives the structure of a PP. It is intended that user communities should develop their own PPs to capture their typical security requirements. Some PPs resembling those of the Orange Book were given for illustration but anybody can write their own PP and there exists a process for adding and vetting new profiles. Today, you can find PPs for single-level and multilevel operating systems, database management systems, firewalls,

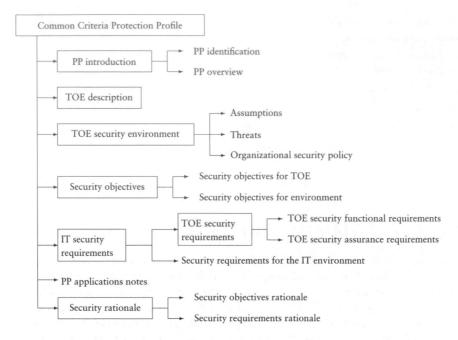

○ **Figure 10.1: Common Criteria Protection Profile**

trusted platform modules, postage meters, automatic cash dispensers, electronic mallets, secure signature-creation devices and for several aspects of smart card security.

## 10.6.2 Evaluation Assurance Levels

EALs specify the duties both of the developer of a TOE and of the evaluator. There are seven incrementally defined EALs.

**EAL1 – functionally tested**    The tester receives the TOE, examines the documentation and performs some tests to confirm the documented functionality. Evaluation should not require any assistance from the developer and the outlay for evaluation should be minimal.

**EAL2 – structurally tested**    The developer provides test documentation and test results from a vulnerability analysis. The evaluator reviews the documentation and repeats some of these tests. The effort required from the developer is small and a complete development record need not be available.

**EAL3 – methodically tested and checked**    The developer uses configuration management, documents security arrangements for development and provides high-level design documentation and documentation on test coverage for review. This level is intended for developers who already follow good development practices but do not want to implement further changes to their practices.

**EAL4 – methodically designed, tested and reviewed**   The developer provides low-level design and a subset of security functions (TCB) source code for evaluation. There have to be secure delivery procedures. The evaluator performs an independent vulnerability analysis. Usually EAL4 is the highest level that is economically feasible for an existing product line. Developers have to be ready to incur additional security-specific engineering costs.

**EAL5 – semiformally designed and tested**   The developer provides a formal model of the security policy, a semiformal high-level design and functional specification as well as the full source code of the security functions. A covert channel analysis has to be conducted. The evaluator performs independent penetration testing. For evaluation at this level, it helps if the TOE has been designed and developed with the intent of achieving EAL5 assurance. The additional costs of evaluation beyond the costs of the development process itself ought not to be large.

**EAL6 – semiformally verified design and tested**   The source code must be well structured and the access control implementation (reference monitor) must have low complexity. The evaluator has to conduct more intensive penetration testing and the cost of evaluation should be expected to increase.

**EAL7 – formally verified design and tested**   The developer provides a formal functional specification and a high-level design. The developer has to demonstrate or prove correspondence between all representations of the security functions. The security functions must be simple enough for formal analysis. This level can typically only be achieved with a TOE that has a tightly focused security functionality and is amenable to extensive formal analysis.

## 10.6.3 Evaluation Methodology

The Common Evaluation Methodology (CEM) specifies all the steps that have to be followed when validating the assurance requirements in an ST (CCIB, 2004b). The Common Criteria Recognition Agreement (CCRA) provides recognition of evaluations performed in another country. The CEM addresses assurance levels EAL1 to EAL4. Only these assurance levels are mutually recognized. Higher assurance levels are only accepted within a single country. In the US, the Common Criteria Evaluation and Validation Scheme (CCEVS) is the national program for performing security evaluations according to the CC. There is a validation body that approves participating security testing laboratories, provides technical guidance and validates the results of security evaluations.

## 10.7 QUALITY STANDARDS

The ultimate step towards audit-based evaluation would be to assess how a product is developed without any reference to the product itself. A company then becomes a 'certified producer of secure systems'. Such an approach has proven popular in the area of quality control. Standards like ISO 9000 advise organizations how to put into place internal quality management and external quality assurance to vouch for the quality of their products. Some vendors claim that being registered under an ISO 9000 quality seal is a better selling argument than a security certificate for a particular product and that security evaluation should move in this direction.

The attractions such a proposal has for companies developing secure systems are evident. The costs of evaluation are much reduced. If the developers of secure systems win in this proposal, will the users of secure systems lose out? This is not a foregone conclusion. After all, a certificate is no guarantee that a system cannot be broken. Therefore, you have to assess each evaluation scheme on its own merits to decide whether individually evaluated products offer more security than products from accredited developers.

## 10.8 AN EFFORT WELL SPENT?

Security evaluation according to the CC is now required in some countries by public sector customers. Major operating system and database management system vendors offer evaluated products. However, outside the government sector there has been little enthusiasm for evaluated products. Still, there are exceptions and in certain markets CC evaluations are pursued by most vendors. At the time of writing, the smart card sector is such an example. A decade earlier, one could have pointed to the vendors of PC security software.

Security evaluation has been criticized as an expensive process driven by government requirements. Such opinions were voiced, for example, in a report published by the European Computer Manufacturers Association (ECMA; 1993). This report appreciates the role Orange Book class C2 had played in establishing a baseline for operating system security but insists on a balance between cost, productivity and security, noting that any two of these factors will pull against the third. The ECMA warns against treating IT security as a mere technological issue and observes an investment imbalance with more effort (mis)directed towards security evaluation while the importance of the operational management of security systems is neglected. The report recommends looking into quality standards like ISO 9000 as an alternative to security evaluation.

In their critique of the current evaluation process, the cost of evaluation (10% – 40% of development costs) and the time delay until an evaluation is completed are of course areas of concern. Further issues mentioned are:

- ambiguities in the interpretation of the criteria and *criteria creep*, i.e. change in the interpretation of the criteria over time;
- the cost of reevaluating new versions of an evaluated product;
- the secrecy of the evaluation process.

Finally, you should note that certificates apply to a particular version and a particular configuration of a product. In an actual installation, it is quite likely that a different configuration and probably already a different version are used so that the certificate strictly speaking does not offer direct security guarantees. Hence, there have been several attempts to develop evaluation methodologies that make it easy to reevaluate a new version of a previously evaluated product with reduced cost and effort. The RAMP scheme in the Rainbow Series is one such example.

## 10.9 FURTHER READING

The early history of security evaluation and of formal security modeling is told by MacKenzie and Pottinger (1997). Practical aspects of security evaluation with an overview of the Orange Book classes are covered by Chokhani (1992). The developments in IT that led to the Orange Book and beyond are narrated by Schaefer (2004). A brief description of the A1-evaluated BLACKER system can be found in Weissman (1992). A prototype that was developed to meet A1 requirements but did not become a commercial product is described in Karger *et al.* (1990). For a case study on assurance and covert channel aspects of multilevel secure systems, see Kang, Moore and Moskowitz (1998).

The CTCPEC have the reputation of being the most concise and readable of the evaluation criteria. Web sites containing evaluation criteria, ancillary documents and lists of evaluated products are:

- http://www.radium.ncsc.mil/tpep/library/rainbow/ for the Rainbow Series,
- http://www.csrc.nist.gov/cc and http://www.commoncriteriaportal.org/ for the CC.

## 10.10 EXERCISES

**Exercise 10.1** Security evaluation has to deal with moving targets. Product development does not stand still while one particular version is being evaluated. How could evaluation certificates be kept up to date? Consult schemes like RAMP when drafting your proposal.

**Exercise 10.2**    Security products have to hit moving targets. The threat environment will change during the lifetime of a fielded product. How would you set up a scheme for the evaluation of anti-virus products that keeps certificates up to date in a changing threat environment? Are there any components of your scheme that should be included in the evaluation of operating systems?

**Exercise 10.3**    It is sometimes claimed that evaluated products are mainly used as an insurance against the accusation of not following established best practice, and not because they offer better security. What do you expect from a security evaluation scheme that does provide added value?

**Exercise 10.4**    Evaluation criteria exist to help security-unaware users meet specific security requirements. Are PPs the right solution for this problem?

**Exercise 10.5**    ITSEC covers the security evaluation of systems. Consultants advise clients on solutions to their security problems. Where would you draw the boundary between consultancy and evaluation? Has evaluation any advantage over contracting consultants?

**Exercise 10.6**    Write a PP for firewalls.

**Exercise 10.7**    Examine the options for blocking and monitoring covert channels. How is the usability of a system affected by blocking covert channels?

# Chapter 11

# Cryptography

Once upon a time – in the 1980s, at the high tide of research on multilevel security – you could hear claims that there was nothing cryptography had to offer computer security. Computer security was about TCBs, reference monitors, discretionary and mandatory access control, and formal verification of system specifications. The contributions of cryptography appeared to be peripheral indeed. One-way functions to store passwords were the only obvious instance of a cryptographic mechanism used in secure operating systems.

By the mid 1990s, the mood had swung round to the other extreme. Cryptography was seen as the miraculous cure that would solve all computer security problems. Secure operating systems were dismissed as a thing of the past, too expensive, too restrictive, too far away from user demand, doomed to extinction like the dinosaurs. Export restrictions on strong cryptographic algorithms were seen as the main obstacle that needed to be overcome to make computers secure. A further decade on, a more sober assessment has been reached of the contributions cryptography can offer to computer security. Still, cryptographic techniques are an essential component in securing distributed systems.

## OBJECTIVES

- Appreciate that there is a variety of applications that use cryptography with quite different intentions.
- Introduce the basic concepts of cryptography.

- Understand the type of problems cryptography can address, and the type of problems that need to be addressed when using cryptography.
- Indicate the computer security features that are required to support cryptography.

## 11.1 INTRODUCTION

In the traditional definition, cryptography is the science of secret writing. Cryptanalysis is the science of analyzing and breaking ciphers. Cryptology encompasses both subjects. Once they were the domain of spies and secret agents. These origins still endow cryptography with a certain mystique.

Modern cryptography is very much a mathematical discipline. It is outside the scope of this book to present the mathematical background that is necessary to understand the finer points of cryptography. Instead, we will try to explain how cryptography can be used in computer security and point out that very often computer security is a prerequisite to making cryptography work.

### 11.1.1 The Old Paradigm

Cryptography has its roots in communications security. Communications security addresses the situation described in Figure 11.1. Two entities *A* and *B* communicate over an insecure channel. The antagonist is an *intruder* who has full control over this channel, being able to read their messages, delete messages and insert messages. The two entities *A* and *B* trust each other. They want protection from the intruder. Cryptography gives them the means to construct a secure logical channel over an insecure physical connection. In this respect, cryptography is fundamentally different from the computer security mechanisms discussed so far. All of them are vulnerable to compromise from the 'layer below'. However, access to the physical communications link does not compromise cryptographic protection.

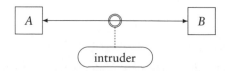

○  **Figure 11.1: Communications Security**

In distributed systems, the traffic between clients and servers is a new point of attack for would-be intruders. Vulnerabilities introduced by insecure communications links can naturally be counteracted by services and mechanisms from communications security. Such services include:

- data confidentiality: encryption algorithms hide the content of messages;
- data integrity: integrity check functions provide the means to detect whether a document has been changed;
- data origin authentication: Message Authentication Codes or Digital Signature Algorithms provide the means to verify the source and integrity of a message.

Data origin authentication includes data integrity. You cannot claim to have verified the source of a message that has been modified in transit. Conversely, if the sender's address is part of the message, you also have to verify the source of a message when verifying its integrity. In such a setting, data integrity and data origin authentication are equivalent concepts. A separate notion of data integrity makes sense in other applications, e.g. for file protection in anti-virus software.

The traditional view of who is friend and who is foe has its place in computer security but it is no longer the major force driving applications of cryptography in computing. Unfortunately, it still dominates the public perception of cryptography. This view is also reflected in those verification tools for cryptographic protocols, whose axioms assume that $A$ and $B$ will behave according to the rules of the protocol and only consider the effects of the intruder's actions.

## 11.1.2 New Paradigms

Take a fresh look. In electronic commerce, a customer enters a business transaction with a merchant. Both parties do not expect the other to cheat, but disputes are possible and it is always better to have rules agreed in advance than to solve problems in an *ad hoc* fashion. Customer and merchant will therefore have reasons to run a protocol that does not assume that the other party can be trusted in all circumstances. The antagonist is now a misbehaving *insider*, rather than an intruder, and the third party in Figure 11.2 is no longer the intruder but a *trusted third party (TTP)*, e.g. an arbitrator. *Nonrepudiation* services generate the evidence the arbitrator will consider when resolving a dispute.

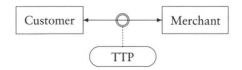

Figure 11.2: Electronic Commerce Security

Many countries have laws specifying when and how a *law enforcement agency (LEA)* can get an interception warrant that obliges a telecommunications service provider to give access to communications between particular users. The third party in Figure 11.3 is now a client of the telecommunications operator who has to be provided with a *legal intercept* service. In this context, *key escrow* services that reveal the key used to encrypt the traffic were once a topic discussed with great emotion.

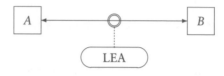

Figure 11.3: **Communications Security and Law Enforcement**

### 11.1.3 Cryptographic Keys

Cryptographers have adopted the lock as their favorite icon to signal the services they render to the public. A quick look at the user interfaces of current 'security-enabled' web browsers or email products will confirm this observation. Analogies are fraught with danger, and you should not take them too far, but there are some important concepts that carry over from locksmiths to cryptographers. To lock and unlock a door, you need a key. Locks differ in strength. Some are easy to pick while others are so strong that intruders resort to brute force attacks to break through a door or choose a different path altogether and break into a house through a window instead.

Cryptographic algorithms use keys to protect data. There are again variations in strength, ranging from schemes that can be broken with simple statistical methods to those that are far beyond the current grasp of mathematical analysis and computational abilities. *Brute force attacks* exhaustively search the entire key space and give an upper bound for the strength of an algorithm.

Modern cryptography does not rely on the secrecy of its algorithms. The key used in a cryptographic transformation should be the only item that needs protection. This principle was postulated by Kerckhoffs as early as the nineteenth century. It is particularly appropriate in the setting of our new security paradigms where a large user community with competing interests has to be supported. *De facto* standardization and open evaluation of public algorithms is a natural process in such a situation, giving each party the chance to conduct its own security assessment and making it easier for new participants to join in.

*Key management*, in the most general meaning of the phrase, is thus of paramount importance for the security of cryptographic schemes. You have to address questions like:

- where are keys generated?

- how are keys generated?
- where are keys stored?
- how do they get there?
- where are the keys actually used?
- how are keys revoked and replaced?

At this point, the circle closes and we return to computer security. Cryptographic keys are sensitive data stored in a computer system. Access control mechanisms in the computer system have to protect these keys. When access control fails, cryptographic protection is compromised. In most security systems currently fielded, the cryptographic algorithms are the strongest part and wily attackers will look for other vulnerabilities rather than wasting their time on cryptanalysis.

### Lesson

Cryptography is rarely ever the solution to a security problem. Cryptography is a translation mechanism, usually converting a communications security problem into a key management problem and ultimately into a computer security problem. Hopefully, the resulting problem is easier to solve than the original problem. In summary, cryptography can enhance computer security, but it is not a substitute for computer security.

### 11.1.4 Cryptographic Mechanisms

Cryptographic mechanisms are the basic building blocks of cryptographic schemes. They are used in cryptographic protocols and rely on good key management to offer effective protection. The cryptographic mechanisms most frequently applied in computer security are:

- encryption algorithms
- digital signature schemes and
- integrity check functions (cryptographic hash functions).

Breaking with the traditions of cryptography, these concepts will be introduced in reverse order. First, we state a few basic facts about modular arithmetic to prepare the ground.

## 11.2 MODULAR ARITHMETIC

Many modern cryptographic algorithms build on algebraic principles. They can be defined over exciting algebraic structures like elliptic curves or Galois fields. However, we will stay more down to earth and only use integers in our description.

Let $m$ be an integer. In the following, we will call $m$ the modulus. We then define an equivalence relation $\equiv$ on the set of integers by

$$a \equiv b \bmod m \text{ if and only if } a - b = \lambda \cdot m \text{ for some integer } \lambda.$$

We say '$a$ is equivalent to $b$ modulo $m$'. You can check that $\equiv$ is indeed an equivalence relation that divides the set of integers into $m$ equivalence classes

$$(a)_m = \{b \mid a \equiv b \bmod m\}, \quad 0 \le a < m.$$

It is more customary to designate the equivalence class by $a \bmod m$ and we will follow this convention. You can verify the following useful properties.

- $(a \bmod m) + (b \bmod m) \equiv (a + b) \bmod m$.
- $(a \bmod m) \cdot (b \bmod m) \equiv (a \cdot b) \bmod m$.
- for every $a \not\equiv 0 \bmod p$, $p$ prime, there exists an integer $a^{-1}$ so that $a \cdot a^{-1} \equiv 1 \bmod p$.

For a prime modulus $p$, the multiplicative order modulo $p$ is defined by:

Let $p$ be a prime and $a$ an arbitrary integer. The *multiplicative order* of $a$ modulo $p$ is the smallest integer $n$ so that $a^n \equiv 1 \bmod p$.

*Fermat's Little Theorem* states that the multiplicative order modulo $p$ of any nonzero element must be a factor of $p - 1$.

**Theorem**   For every $a \not\equiv 0 \bmod p$, $p$ prime, we have $a^{p-1} \equiv 1 \bmod p$.

This fact is used in the construction of quite a few cryptographic algorithms. The security of these algorithms is often related, and on a few occasions equivalent, to the difficulty of one of the following problems from number theory.

- Discrete Logarithm Problem (DLP): given a prime modulus $p$, a basis $a$, and a value $y$, find the *discrete logarithm* of $y$, i.e. an integer $x$ so that $y = a^x \bmod p$.

- $n$-th Root Problem: given integers $m$, $n$ and $a$, find an integer $b$ so that $b = a^n \bmod m$. The solution $b$ is the $n$-th root of $a$ modulo $n$.

- Factorization: given an integer $n$, find its prime factors.

With the right choice of parameters, these problems are a suitable basis for many cryptographic algorithms. However, not all instances of these problems are difficult to solve. Obviously, if $p$ or $n$ are small integers these problems can be solved by exhaustive search within reasonable time. Today, 512-bit integers are regarded as too short, 1024-bit integers are a more common recommendation, and of course you could use longer integers if you can tolerate the decrease in performance as arithmetic operations will take longer. Length is not the only aspect you have to consider. The difficulty of these problems also depends on the structure of $p$ and $n$. (To pursue this topic further, you have to leave this book and turn to more specialized mathematical sources.)

# 11.3 INTEGRITY CHECK FUNCTIONS

A cryptographic hash function $h$ maps inputs $x$ of arbitrary bit length to outputs $h(x)$ of a fixed bit length $n$. This is known as the *compression* property. Hash functions tend to be faster and less resource consuming than the other cryptographic mechanisms mentioned; the *ease of computation* property demands that given $x$, it is easy to compute $h(x)$.

To see how integrity check functions can be employed, we show how you might protect a program $x$ that must not be tampered with. This strategy is used, for example, by some anti-virus products. Compute the hash value $h(x)$ in a clean environment and store it in a place where it cannot be modified, e.g. on a CD-ROM. To check the status of the program, recompute the hash value and compare it with the value stored. Protection of the hash value is important. Computing the hash value does not require any secret information, hence anybody can create a valid hash value for a given file.

## 11.3.1 Collisions and the Birthday Paradox

In our example, it is important that it is infeasible to find collisions. We have a *collision* if there are two inputs $x, x'$, $x \neq x'$, with $h(x) = h(x')$. In this case, an attacker might modify the program in a way that leaves the hash value unchanged and the changes to the program would not be detected.

The probability of finding a collision by brute force search depends on the bit-length of the hash. If we are given an $n$-bit hash $y$, the expected number of tries before an $x$ with $h(x) = y$ is found is $2^{n-1}$. However, if we are just looking for arbitrary collisions, a set of about $2^{\frac{n}{2}}$ inputs is likely to contain a pair causing a collision. This result is based on the *birthday paradox*. Put $m$ balls numbered 1 to $m$ into an urn, draw a ball, list its number and put it back. Repeat this experiment. For $m \to \infty$, the expected number of draws before a previously drawn number appears converges to $\sqrt{\frac{1}{2}m\pi}$.

## 11.3.2 Manipulation Detection Codes

Manipulation Detection Codes *(MDCs)*, also called *modification detection codes* or *message integrity codes*, are used to detect changes to a document. Depending on the given application, the requirements put on MDCs may differ. The security properties one might demand from a hash functions $h$ include:

- *Preimage resistance (one-way)*: given a value $y$, it is in general computationally infeasible to find a value $x$ so that $h(x) = y$;

- *Second preimage resistance (weak collision resistance)*: given an input $x$ and $h(x)$, it is computationally infeasible to find another input $x'$, $x \neq x'$, with $h(x) = h(x')$;

- *Collision resistance (strong collision resistance)*: it is computationally infeasible to find any two inputs $x$ and $x'$, $x \neq x'$, with $h(x) = h(x')$.

MDCs come in two flavors (Menezes, van Oorschot and Vanstone, 1997).

- A *one-way hash function (OWHF)* has the compression, ease-of-computation, preimage resistance, and second preimage resistance properties.
- A *collision-resistant hash function (CRHF)* has the compression, ease-of-computation, second preimage resistance, and collision resistance properties.

The result of applying a hash function is varyingly called:

- *hash value*
- *message digest*
- *checksum.*

The last term leaves ample room for confusion. In communications security, checksums refer to error correcting codes, typically a cyclic redundancy check (CRC). A CRC is a linear function, so creating collisions is easy. Checksums used by anti-virus products, on the other hand, must not be computed with a CRC but with a cryptographic hash function (MDC).

The function $f(x) := g^x \bmod p$ is a one-way function when the parameters $p$ and $g$ are chosen judiciously. This function is called *discrete exponentiation*. To invert discrete exponentiation, you have to solve the DLP introduced in section 11.2. Discrete exponentiation is indeed a useful primitive in the construction of cryptographic schemes as you will see later in this chapter. However, discrete exponentiation is not a particularly fast operation so you have to turn to other algorithms when processing large quantities of data at high speed.

Fast hash functions tend to be constructed along similar design patterns. At the core of the hash function is a *compression function f* that works on inputs of fixed length. An input $x$ of arbitrary length is broken up into blocks $x_1, \ldots x_m$ of a given block size, where padding must be added to the last block. The hash of $x$ is then obtained by repeated application of the compression function. Let $h_0$ be a (fixed) *initial value*. Compute

$$h_i = f(x_i||h_{i-1}) \quad \text{for } i = 1, \ldots, m$$

and take $h_m$ as the hash value of $x$ (Figure 11.4). (The symbol $||$ denotes concatenation.)

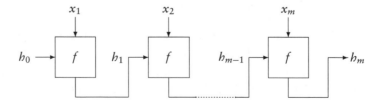

🔵  **Figure 11.4: Construction of a Hash Function**

### 11.3.3 Message Authentication Codes

Message Authentication Codes (MACs) provide assurance about the source and integrity of a message (data origin authentication). A MAC is computed from two inputs, the message and a secret cryptographic key. Therefore, MACs are sometimes called keyed hash functions. Formally, a MAC is a family of functions $h_k$ parameterized by the secret key $k$. Each member of the family has the compression and the ease-of-computation property. An additional *computation resistance* property must hold.

> For any fixed value of $k$ unknown to the adversary, given a set of values $(x_i, h_k(x_i))$, it is computationally infeasible to compute $h_k(x)$ for any new input $x$.

To authenticate a message, the receiver has to share the secret key used to compute the MAC with the sender. A third party that does not know the key cannot validate the MAC. A MAC algorithm can be derived from an MDC algorithm $h$ using the following HMAC construction (Bellare, Canetti and Krawczyk, 1996; Krawczyk, Bellare and Canetti, 1997). For a given key $k$ and message $x$, compute

$$HMAC(x) = h(k||p_1||h(k||p_2||x))$$

where $p_1$ and $p_2$ are bit strings (padding) that extend $k$ to a full block length of the compression function used in $h$.

### 11.3.4 Secure Hash Algorithm

We pick the Secure Hash Algorithm (SHA-1) to demonstrate how a hash function is designed in practice[1]. This algorithm was designed to operate with the US Digital Signature Standard (DSS). Other hash functions are MD4 (not strongly collision-resistant, see Dobbertin, 1996), MD5 (standard choice in Internet protocols, not strongly collision-resistant[2]) and RIPE-MD. SHA-1 processes 512-bit blocks and generates a 160-bit hash value. Arguments are interpreted both as integers and as bit strings. The algorithms for converting between bit strings and integers are omitted from our description.

The input is padded by appending a one, then a string of zeros so that the last input block has length 448, and finally a 64-bit field indicating the length of the input before padding. The initial value is defined by five 32-bit values, given in hexadecimal representation.

```
A = 67452301
B = efcdab89
C = 98badcfe
D = 10325476
E = c3d2e1f0
```

---

[1] At the time of writing (February 2005) a collision attack on SHA-1 was reported. Such an attack limits the applications where SHA-1 can be used and is likely to lead to the standardization of new hash algorithms.
[2] At the rump session of Eurocrypt 2005 M. Daum and S. Lucks presented a generic attack for constructing pairs of postscript documents that have the same MD5 hash.

The compression function of SHA-1 processes a 512-bit input in a loop of 80 steps, changing internal functions and constants every 20 steps and yielding a 160-bit output. The functions are:

$$f_t(X, Y, Z) = (X \wedge Y) \vee ((\neg X) \wedge Z) \quad \text{for } t = 0, \ldots, 19,$$
$$f_t(X, Y, Z) = X \oplus Y \oplus Z \quad \text{for } t = 20, \ldots, 39,$$
$$f_t(X, Y, Z) = (X \wedge Y) \vee (X \wedge Z) \vee (Y \wedge Z) \quad \text{for } t = 40, \ldots, 59,$$
$$f_t(X, Y, Z) = X \oplus Y \oplus Z \quad \text{for } t = 60, \ldots, 79.$$

The operators are bitwise AND, OR, and exclusive OR, applied to 32-bit words. The constants, given in hexadecimal representation, are:

$$K_t = \texttt{5a827999} \quad \text{for } t = 0, \ldots, 19,$$
$$K_t = \texttt{6ed9eba1} \quad \text{for } t = 20, \ldots, 39,$$
$$K_t = \texttt{8f1bbcdc} \quad \text{for } t = 40, \ldots, 59,$$
$$K_t = \texttt{ca62c1d6} \quad \text{for } t = 60, \ldots, 79.$$

At the start of the compression function, five 32-bit variables $a, b, c, d, e$ are initialized with the intermediate hash value. For the first input block, the initial values $A, B, C, D, E$ are used. The 512-bit input block is subdivided into 16 32-bit words $m_t$ and expanded to 80 32-bit words $w_t$ according to the following algorithm

$$w_t = m_t \quad \text{for } t = 0, \ldots, 15,$$
$$w_t = (w_{t-3} \oplus w_{t-8} \oplus w_{t-14} \oplus w_{t-16}) <<< 1 \quad \text{for } t = 16, \ldots, 79,$$

where $<<< s$ indicates a cyclic shift to the left by $s$ bits. The compression function now executes the following loop where addition is performed modulo $2^{32}$:

```
for t = 0 to 79 do
    begin
            temp = (a <<< 5) + f_t(b, c, d) + e + w_t + K_t;
            e = d;
            c = b <<< 30;
            b = a;
            a = temp;
    end;
```

Finally, the variables $a, b, c, d, e$ are added to the previous intermediate hash value. The result serves as the initial hash value when processing the next input block.

## 11.4 DIGITAL SIGNATURES

In Figure 11.1, MACs help the parties $A$ and $B$ to detect fraudulent messages inserted by the intruder on the communications channel. However, MACs do not constitute evidence a third party could use to decide whether *A* or *B* sent a particular message. They are therefore of little use in the electronic commerce scenario of Figure 11.2 when customers need assurance that merchants cannot fake orders and merchants need assurance that customers have to honor the orders they made. In those situations, a *digital signature* is required.

A digital signature scheme consists of a key generation algorithm, a signature algorithm and a verification algorithm. A digital signature of a document is a value depending on the contents of the document and on some secret only known to the signer, i.e. a private signature key. The signature associates the document with a public verification key. The verification algorithm usually takes the document and the public verification key as input, but in exceptional cases the document – or parts of the document – can be recovered from the signature and the document does not have to be provided for signature verification. Figure 11.5 gives a schematic representation of a typical digital signature scheme where the private signature key is applied to a hash of the document. The following *verifiability* property characterizes digital signature schemes.

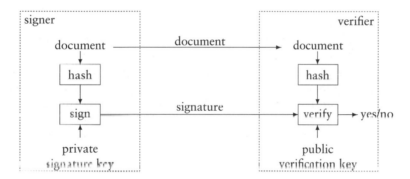

Figure 11.5: Schematic Representation of a Generic Digital Signature Scheme

A third party can resolve disputes about the validity of a digital signature without having to know the signer's private key.

Digital signatures support nonrepudiation. Public key cryptography (section 11.5) is a natural source for digital signature schemes. In such a scheme, the connection between the private signature key and the public verification key has the property that it is computationally infeasible to derive the signature key from the verification key. Despite the similarities in the underlying mathematical techniques, you should draw a clear distinction between digital signatures and public key encryption algorithms. These two schemes meet fundamentally different purposes. Encryption protects the confidentiality of a message and has to be invertible. Digital signatures provide data origin authentication and nonrepudiation. A digital signature algorithm need not be invertible. As a matter of fact, invertibility causes some additional security concerns.

### 11.4.1 One-time Signatures

You do not need fancy mathematics to construct a signature scheme. To obtain *one-time signatures* you only need a cryptographic hash function $h$ (Lamport, 1979). To sign an $n$-bit document, you pick your private key by choosing at random $2n$ values $x_{i,0}, x_{i,1}$ and publish the values (commitments) $y_{i,0} = h(x_{i,0}), y_{i,1} = h(x_{i,1})$, $1 \le i \le n$, as your public key. The $i$-th bit of the signature $s$ for a document $m$ is then given by

$$s_i = \begin{cases} x_{i,0} & \text{if } m_i = 0 \\ x_{i,1} & \text{if } m_i = 1 \end{cases}.$$

Evidently, you cannot use your private key again, hence the name one-time signatures. The verifier has your public key and checks

$$y_{i,0} = h(s_i) \quad \text{if } m_i = 0,$$
$$y_{i,1} = h(s_i) \quad \text{if } m_i = 1.$$

You will have spotted that the verifier needs additional evidence to confirm that the values $y_{i,0}, y_{i,1}$ are indeed your public key. We will return to this topic in section 12.5.1.

Moreover, instead of relying on the difficulty of a mathematical problem or on the strength of some other cryptographic primitive, you could rely on the difficulty of compromising a *tamper-resistant* hardware device. The device contains a secret signature key and/or *secret* verification keys. The device is constructed so that it cannot use the signature key for verification or a verification key for signing. To sign a document, the device uses its signature key to construct a MAC, which it then attaches to the document. To verify this signature, the verifier's device has to hold the signer's signature key as a verification key and uses this key to construct a MAC and compare it with the signature received.

### 11.4.2 ElGamal Signatures and DSA

The ElGamal signature scheme (1985) shows that signing is not 'encryption with a private key'. Let $p$ be a large and appropriately chosen prime number. Let $g$ be an integer of order $p - 1$ modulo $p$. Let $a$ be the private signature key of user $A$ and $y = g^a \bmod p$ the corresponding public verification key.

Assume that the document to be signed is an integer $m$, $0 \le m < p$. Otherwise, you can apply a suitable hash function and sign the digest of the document. To sign $m$, user $A$ picks a random number $k$, $0 \le k < p$, such that $\gcd(k, p - 1) = 1$, computes $r = g^k \bmod p$, and solves the equation

$$a \cdot r + k \cdot s \equiv m \bmod p - 1$$

in the unknown $s$. The pair $(r, s)$ constitutes $A$'s signature on $m$. The verifier needs $A$'s verification key $y$ and checks

$$y^r \cdot r^s \stackrel{?}{=} g^m \bmod p.$$

For a correct signature, the equation

$$y^r \cdot r^s = g^{ar+ks} = g^m \bmod p$$

holds. The security of this scheme is closely related but not equivalent to the DLP. A number of more secure and more efficient signature schemes have been derived from the ElGamal signature scheme. One such signature algorithm is the Digital Signature Algorithm (DSA; US Department of Commerce, National Institute of Standards and Technology, 2000). In this scheme, the private and public keys of a user $A$ are generated as follows.

1. Select a prime $q$ such that $2^{159} < q < 2^{160}$.

2. Choose an integer $t$, $0 \leq t \leq 8$, and a prime $p$, $2^{511+64t} < p < 2^{512+64t}$, so that $q$ divides $p - 1$.

3. Select $\alpha$, $1 < \alpha < p - 1$, and compute $g = \alpha^{(p-1)/q} \bmod p$. If $g = 1$, try again with a new $\alpha$. (This step computes a generator $g$ of order $q$ modulo $p$.)

4. Select $a$ such that $1 \leq a \leq q - 1$.

5. Compute $y = g^a \bmod p$.

6. $A$'s private key is the value $a$, the public key is $(p, q, g, y)$.

For $A$ to sign a document $m$, the hash value $h(m)$ is computed with SHA-1 and converted into an integer. Then:

1. randomly select an integer $k$, $1 \leq k \leq q - 1$;
2. compute $r = (g^k \bmod p) \bmod q$;
3. compute $k^{-1} \bmod q$;
4. compute $s = k^{-1}(h(m) + ar) \bmod q$.

$A$'s signature on $m$ is the pair $(r, s)$. The signature is checked with $A$'s public key $(p, q, g, y)$ by:

1. verifying $1 \leq r \leq q$ and $1 \leq s \leq q$;
2. computing $w = s^{-1} \bmod q$;
3. computing $u_1 = w \cdot h(m) \bmod q$ and $u_1 = r \cdot w \bmod q$;
4. computing $v = (g^{u_1} y^{u_2} \bmod p) \bmod q$.

and accepted if and only if $v = r$. The ECDSA (elliptic curve digital signature algorithm) is similar to the DSA but works with points of an elliptic curve instead of integers modulo the prime $p$. ECDSA has been specified in the standard ANSI X9.62.

## 11.4.3 RSA Signatures

The RSA algorithm, named after its inventors Rivest, Shamir and Adleman (1978), can be equally used for signing and for encryption. This very specific property of RSA can be blamed for many of the prevailing misconceptions about digital signatures and public key cryptography. In the RSA signature scheme, a user $A$ picks two prime numbers $p$ and $q$, and a private signature key $e$ with $\gcd(e, p - 1) = 1$ and $\gcd(e, q - 1) = 1$. The public verification key consists of the product $n = p \cdot q$ and an exponent $d$ with

$$e \cdot d \equiv 1 \bmod \operatorname{lcm}(p - 1, q - 1).$$

The document to be signed is an integer $m$. If the original document is too long, you can apply a hash function and padding to obtain a digest for signing. Take a suitable hash function $h$ and compute $h(m)$ so that $1 \leq h(m) < n$. In terms of security, the hash value is redundant information the verifier can use to identify genuine documents. To sign $m$, $A$ forms the signature

$$s = h(m)^e \bmod n.$$

The verifier needs $A$'s verification key $(n, d)$ and checks

$$s^d \overset{?}{=} h(m) \bmod n.$$

For a correct signature, this equation holds because of

$$s^d = h(m)^{e \cdot d} = h(m) \bmod n.$$

The security of RSA is closely related but not equivalent to the difficulty of factoring. The security of any given implementation of RSA depends on further factors. For example, the high-level description given above does not explain how $h(m)$ is encoded as an integer modulo $n$. Bad choices of the encoding function can introduce vulnerabilities. Padding a 160-bit SHA-1 hash with leading zeros to get a 1024-bit integer would be a bad choice. The currently recommended way of implementing RSA is known as RSA-PSS (probabilistic signature scheme).

## 11.5 ENCRYPTION

We reserve the term *encryption* for algorithms that protect the confidentiality of data. An encryption algorithm, also called a *cipher*, enciphers *plaintext (cleartext)* under the control of a cryptographic key. We write $eK(X)$ to denote that plaintext $X$ is encrypted under key $K$. *Decryption* with the appropriate decryption key retrieves the plaintext from the ciphertext. We write $dK(X)$ to denote that ciphertext $X$ is decrypted under key $K$. A *deterministic* encryption algorithm maps a plaintext always to the same ciphertext for a fixed key. A *probabilistic* encryption algorithm gives different results for different encryptions of the same plaintext under the same key.

Some encryption algorithms provide the means for detecting integrity violations but this is not always the case. You may even see signature algorithms described as 'encryption with a private key' but this is often wrong and always misleading.

Encryption algorithms come in two flavors. In *symmetric algorithms*, the same key is used for encryption and decryption. This key has to be kept secret. All parties sharing the same key can read data encrypted under that key. To set up private channels with different parties, you need a new key for each channel. Maintaining a large number of shared secret keys can become a quite onerous management task.

In *asymmetric encryption algorithms*, also called *public key algorithms*, different keys are used for encryption and decryption. The encryption key can be made public, the decryption key has to remain private. Obviously, the two keys are algorithmically related, but it should not be feasible to derive the private key from its public counterpart. To differentiate between symmetric and public key cryptosystems, we will use *secret key* only in the context of symmetric systems and *private key* only in the context of asymmetric systems.

With secret key cryptosystems, the security management task of getting the right key into the right place is evident. Public key cryptography seems to make management a lot easier. After all, public keys are public and need no protection. Or do they? When you use public key encryption to encipher a document, you probably will need to know who will be able to read the enciphered document. More generally, private keys authenticate a principal or serve as capabilities carrying access rights, e.g. to read a document. Now, it becomes a major task to guarantee the link between a public key and the access rights or principals associated with the corresponding private key. We will return to this topic in section 12.5.1.

Encryption algorithms can also be divided into *block ciphers* and *stream ciphers*. There exist two criteria to make this distinction.

- Block size: a block cipher encrypts larger blocks of data, typically 64-bit blocks, with a complex encryption function. Security of block ciphers depends on the design of the encryption function. A stream cipher encrypts smaller blocks of data, typically bits or bytes, with a simple encryption function, for example bitwise exclusive OR. As you can imagine, this distinction becomes blurred at the edges. Is a 16-bit block still a large block? When is an encryption algorithm simple?

- Key stream: a block cipher encrypts blocks belonging to the same document all under the same key. A stream cipher encrypts under a constantly changing key stream. Security of stream ciphers relies on the design of the key stream generator. With this definition, DES in a feedback mode (see below) is classified as a stream cipher.

## 11.5.1 Data Encryption Standard

The Data Encryption Standard (DES) is an important milestone in the histories of computer security and cryptography. DES was developed in the 1970s as a US government standard for protecting nonclassified data and was published as a Federal Information Processing Standard (US Department of Commerce, National Bureau of Standards, 1977). DES encrypts 64-bit plaintext blocks under the control of 56-bit keys. Each key is extended by a parity byte to give a 64-bit working key. Like many block cipher algorithms, DES is based on the Feistel principle. Feistel ciphers iterate the same basic step in a number of rounds. The input to round $i$ is divided into two halves, $L_i$ and $R_i$, and the output is computed as

$$L_{i+1} = R_i$$
$$R_{i+1} = L_i \oplus F(K_i, R_i)$$

where $F$ is some nonlinear function and $K_i$ is the subkey for that round (Figure 11.6). The inverse of this operation can be computed by the same circuit,

$$R_i = L_{i+1}$$
$$L_i = R_{i+1} \oplus F(K_i, L_{i+1})$$

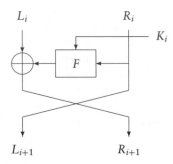

○  **Figure 11.6: The Feistel Principle**

The nonlinear function $F$ in DES expands the 32-bit input $R_i$ into a 48-bit block and computes the bitwise exclusive OR with the 48-bit subkey $K_i$. This intermediate result is divided into eight 6-bit blocks, which serve as input to eight *S-boxes (substitution boxes)*. Each S-box converts its 6-bit input into a 4-bit output. The output of the S-boxes is put through a *P-box (permutation box)* that performs a bit permutation on its 32-bit input to give the result of $F$.

DES has 16 such *rounds*. Each round uses a different 48-bit subkey $K_i$, derived from the 56-bit DES key. The input to the first round is processed by an *initial permutation IP*, the output of the last round by the inverse permutation $IP^{-1}$. A sketch of DES is given in Figure 11.7. We omit all details of the key scheduling algorithm, the expansion scheme, the S-boxes and the permutations.

When DES became a standard in the 1970s, it was given a 'shelf life' of 15 years. DES has aged remarkably well and is still in wide use, particularly in the commercial and financial sectors, despite having been superseded by the Advanced Encryption Standard (AES; US Department of Commerce, National Institute of Standards and Technology , 2001). The major challenge to the security of DES did not come from new cryptanalytic techniques but from its key size. Today, exhaustive search through a 56-bit key space is feasible

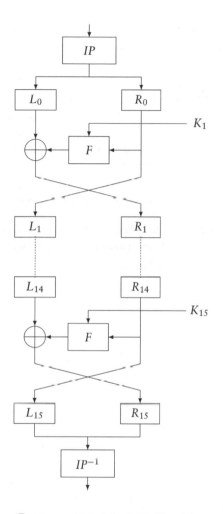

Figure 11.7: The DES Algorithm

without dedicated equipment. The performance of workstations has kept increasing over the years and networking lets the amateur cryptanalyst harness even more resources. With such opposition, you would expect a 56-bit key to survive for weeks or months, rather than for decades or centuries. Multiple encryption extends the key size without changing the algorithm. The favored option is *triple DES* using three 56-bit keys. A variation popular because of its backwards compatibility with single DES uses two 56-bit DES keys, $K_1$ and $K_2$, to encipher a plaintext $P$ by $C = eK_1(dK_2(eK_1(P)))$.

The Rijndael algorithm (Daemen and Rijmen, 1999) was adopted as the AES, a US Federal Standard, in 2001. The algorithm can be used with key sizes of 128 bits, 192 bits and 256 bits. AES works with 128-bit data blocks. Rijndael is specified to work also with 192-bit and 256-bit data blocks, where the block length can be chosen independently of the key length.

## 11.5.2 Block Cipher Modes

Block ciphers can be used in a variety of encryption modes. In *electronic code book (ECB) mode*, each plaintext block is enciphered independently under the same key. This mode may leak information about the plaintext. If a plaintext block is repeated, this will show up in the ciphertext. Furthermore, there is very limited integrity protection. Decryption will not detect whether the sequence of ciphertext blocks has been changed, whether some blocks are missing or whether blocks have been duplicated.

In *cipherblock chaining (CBC) mode* (Figure 11.8), the previous ciphertext block $C_{i-1}$ is added (bitwise exclusive OR) to the next plaintext block $P_i$ before encryption, i.e.

$$C_i = eK(P_i \oplus C_{i-1}).$$

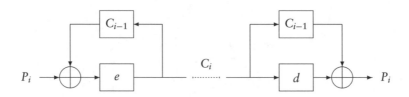

Figure 11.8: Cipherblock Chaining Mode

Hence, repeated plaintext blocks will not show up as repeated ciphertext blocks. For the first plaintext block $P_1$, an initialization vector is used as $C_0$. The initialization vector is usually kept secret, although in many applications this would not be a necessary security condition. The initialization vector should be changed for every message to make sure that an observer cannot detect that two plaintexts start with the same blocks. The initialization vector is required for decryption of the first ciphertext block. Ciphertext block $C_i$ is decrypted by

$$P_i = C_{i-1} \oplus dK(C_i).$$

If a ciphertext block is corrupted, the 'damage' is restricted to only two plaintext blocks. Assume that $\tilde{C}_i$ is used instead of $C_i$. After

$$\tilde{P}_i = C_{i-1} \oplus dK(\tilde{C}_i)$$
$$P_{i+1} = \tilde{C}_i \oplus dK(C_{i+1})$$

normal decryption service is resumed.

*Output feedback (OFB) mode* (Figure 11.9) uses the block cipher as the key stream generator for a stream cipher. In this mode, the plaintext can be processed in chunks that

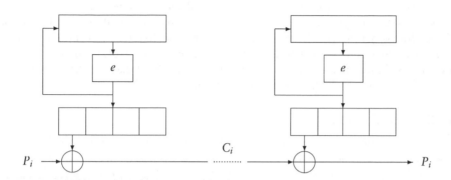

Figure 11.9: Output Feedback Mode

are smaller than the block size of the cipher algorithm. A register stores the input to the encryption function. The initial contents of this register are defined by an initialization vector. To encrypt a plaintext chunk, add it to a subblock from the output of the encryption function (bitwise exclusive OR). The output of the encryption function is fed back to the shift register. Decryption is exactly the same process as encryption. The initialization vector must change for every message but need not be kept secret. An error in the transmission of a ciphertext block $C_i$ only affects the corresponding plaintext block $P_i$. An attacker can therefore selectively modify plaintext bits by changing the ciphertext in the corresponding positions.

*Cipher feedback (CFB) mode* (Figure 11.10) uses the block cipher to generate a data-dependent key stream. Again, the plaintext can be processed in chunks that are smaller than the block size of the cipher algorithm. In this mode, previous ciphertext blocks are fed back into a shift register. The contents of the register are encrypted and a subblock of

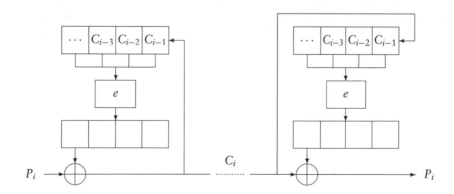

Figure 11.10: Cipher Feedback Mode

this ciphertext is added (bitwise exclusive OR) to the next plaintext chunk. Decryption is exactly the same process as encryption. In this mode, the initialization vector must change for every message. The initialization vector is required for decryption of the first ciphertext block and need not be kept secret. A transmission error, or modification, of a ciphertext block affects decryption until the modified block has left the shift register feeding the encryption function at the receiver's end.

### 11.5.3 RSA Encryption

The set-up is already familiar from the RSA signature scheme. When RSA is used as a public key encryption algorithm, user $A$ picks two prime numbers $p$ and $q$, and a private decryption exponent $d$ with $\gcd(d, p - 1) = 1$ and $\gcd(d, q - 1) = 1$. The public encryption key consists of the product $n = p \cdot q$ and an exponent $e$ with

$$e \cdot d \equiv 1 \bmod \mathrm{lcm}(p - 1, q - 1).$$

Messages have to be divided into blocks so that each block is an integer less than $n$. To send a message block $m$ to $A$, the sender computes

$$c = m^e \bmod n.$$

The receiver $A$ uses the private decryption key $d$ to obtain

$$c^d = m^{e \cdot d} = m \bmod n.$$

Do not be deceived by the simplicity of this algorithm. Proper implementation can be quite tricky and simplistic implementations of 'textbook RSA' are likely to be insecure.

### Padding

RSA is a block cipher. According to the key length, messages are broken into blocks of 1024 (or 2048, 4096, ...) bits. When encrypting a message, padding may have to be added to make the message length a multiple of the block length. Padding can defeat some attacks. When decrypting a message, the receiver can check the padding data and discard plaintexts with syntactically incorrect padding. On the other hand, padding might be exploited for an attack. Once, the standard PKCS # 1 v1.5 recommended to pad a data value $D$ as follows.

| 00 | 02 | PS | 00 | D |
|----|----|----|----|---|

The first two bytes of the padding have the values 0 and 2 respectively. $PS$ is a string of pseudo-randomly generated nonzero bytes of length $|n| - |D| - 3$ ($|.|$ gives length in bytes). Then there is another byte of value 0 before the data $D$.

Bleichenbacher (1998) found an attack against RSA with this padding scheme that requires approximately $2^{20}$ chosen ciphertexts to get the plaintext if the receiver signals whether decryption fails or succeeds. A typical setting for this attack would be the SSL protocol (section 13.4). The data value to be retrieved is a session key, the receiver is a server. The attacker intercepts an encrypted session key. The attacker then sends a chosen ciphertext to the server. The server replies with an error message when decryption fails. No error signals success and narrows the interval containing the session key. The attacker keeps repeating this game and after about $2^{20}$ attempts the key is uniquely defined (in crypto, one million can be a small number).

Because of this attack, Optimal Asymmetric Encryption Padding (OAEP) was adopted as the new standard for padding RSA messages. OAEP was attractive because it came with a formal proof of its security (Bellare and Rogaway, 1995). The proof, however, was found to be flawed but could be fixed (Shoup, 2001). In the meantime, new attacks are appearing (Manger, 2001) and at the time of writing research on secure padding schemes is still ongoing.

**Lesson**

Even if cryptographic algorithms are secure at an abstract mathematical level, it may be possible to find attacks against concrete implementations. Thus, additional security analysis at lower levels of abstraction is being called for.

### 11.5.4 ElGamal Encryption

In the ElGamal public key algorithm, $p$ is again a large and appropriately chosen prime number and let $g$ be an integer of large order modulo $p$. Let $a$ be the private decryption key of user $A$ and $y_a = g^a \bmod p$ the corresponding public encryption key. Messages have to be divided into blocks so that each block is an integer less than $p$. To send a message block $m$ to $A$, the sender picks a random number $k$, computes $r = g^k \bmod p$, and sends the ciphertext

$$(c_1, c_2) = (r, my_a^k)$$

to $A$. With its private decryption key $a$, $A$ obtains

$$\frac{c_2}{c_1^a} = \frac{my_a^k}{r^a} = \frac{mg^{ak}}{g^{ak}} = m.$$

In this scheme, a ciphertext block is twice as long as a plaintext block. On the other hand, if two plaintext blocks are equal, the corresponding ciphertext blocks will still be different. The random number $k$ must be used for one encryption only. Reuse of random numbers seriously weakens the cipher.

## 11.6 STRENGTH OF MECHANISMS

Measuring the strength of cryptographic algorithms is an imprecise art, sometimes resting on firm mathematical foundations, other times relying on intuition and experience. A cryptographic algorithm can be:

- empirically secure

- provably secure
- unconditionally secure.

An algorithm is *empirically secure* if it has withstood the test of time. Prolonged analysis has found no serious weakness and although there is no proof that the algorithm may not eventually fall to a new and ingenious attack, the algorithm has found acceptance within the cryptographic community. Taking aside its key length, DES was the prime example of an empirically secure algorithm. New analytical methods like differential cryptanalysis have strengthened rather than weakened the perceived security of DES.

*Provably secure* algorithms seem to offer what computer security has been longing for, i.e. provable security. Provable security is expressed within the framework of complexity theory. An algorithm is secure if breaking the algorithm is at least as difficult as solving another problem that is known to be hard. This sounds wonderful but it pays to read the small print.

Being 'at least as difficult' is an asymptotic concept. It holds for problem instances that are 'sufficiently large'. The theory will not tell you what is sufficiently large. Instead, you have to assess the current power of computing equipment and the progress in algorithm design. For example, the size of numbers we can factor has constantly increased over the years. You would agree, this is an empirical argument. Even worse is to come. Cryptography's favorite hard problems are factoring and the DLP. There is actually no proof that these problems are necessarily difficult to solve. Again, cryptography relies on empirical arguments that no fast algorithms have been found so far and that a major breakthrough looks extremely unlikely. To be more positive, this theory has also led to constructive results that give lower bounds on the effort required to break a cryptographic scheme in relation to the difficulty of breaking some other cryptographic primitive.

Provably secure algorithms can be broken by an attacker with sufficient computing resources. Of course, you would hope that the resources necessary are beyond the capacity of any attacker. *Unconditionally secure* algorithms cannot be broken even by attackers with unlimited computing power. Unconditional security is expressed in terms of information theory. An algorithm is secure if an attacker does not gain additional information about the plaintext from observing the ciphertext.

The standard example of an unconditionally secure algorithm is the *one-time pad*. Sender and receiver share a truly random key stream which they use only once. The ciphertext is the bitwise exclusive OR of plaintext and key stream. The receiver exclusive ORs the same key stream to the ciphertext to retrieve the plaintext:

$$\text{ciphertext} \oplus \text{key stream} = \text{plaintext} \oplus \text{key stream} \oplus \text{key stream} = \text{plaintext}.$$

Because every key is equally probable, the attacker cannot guess anything about the plaintext that could not have been guessed before seeing the ciphertext.

Be wary! Even unconditionally secure ciphers have been broken. When operators cut corners and use the same key stream twice, an attacker overlaying the two ciphertexts will see the combination of two plaintexts:

$$\text{ciphertext}_1 \oplus \text{ciphertext}_2 = \text{plaintext}_1 \oplus \text{key stream} \oplus \text{plaintext}_2 \oplus \text{key stream}$$
$$= \text{plaintext}_1 \oplus \text{plaintext}_2.$$

Making sense out of two overlaying plaintext messages is not exactly a hard cryptanalytic problem. The Venona project documents that such incidents happened even at the height of the Cold War.

The last remark highlights a crucial fact. More often than not, cipher systems are broken because of bad key management rather than because of an inherent weakness in the algorithm. The Enigma machine of World War II is the most famous illustration of this point. The security of key management protocols is therefore of utmost importance. Key management protocols are covered in Chapter 12.

## 11.7 PERFORMANCE

To give an indication of the execution times for cryptographic algorithms, we summarize some of the performance data reported by Preneel *et al.* (2003), where very detailed studies for many algorithms and platforms can be found. The measurements we quote refer to (not optimized) software implementations of the algorithms, running on a Pentium III processor under Linux. Execution times vary between different compilers. Table 11.1 gives performance measurements for hash functions, stream ciphers and block ciphers as the number of instruction cycles per byte. Table 11.2 compares RSA and two ECDSA variants. Measurements are given as the number of cycles (in millions)

| algorithm | cycles/byte |
|---|---|
| RC4 | 7–8 |
| MD5 | 7–8 |
| SHA-1 | 15 |
| SHA2-512 | 83 |
| Rijndael-128 | 25–30 |
| DES | 60 |

○ **Table 11.1: Performance Measurements for Hash Functions and Symmetric Key Algorithms**

per invocation. RSA encryption and RSA signatures use the public exponent $e = 3$ to demonstrate the maximum gain achievable using short public exponents. The key length of the algorithms is given for reference.

| algorithm | operation | cycles per invocation | key setup (cycles) | key length (bits) |
|---|---|---|---|---|
| RSA-OAEP | encrypt | 2.026 M | 1.654 M | 1024 |
| | decrypt | 42.000 M | | |
| RSA-PSS | sign | 42.000 M | 1.334 M | 1024 |
| | verify | 2.029 M | | |
| ECDSA-GF($p$) | sign | 4.775 M | 4.669 M | 160 |
| | verify | 6.085 M | | |
| ECDSA-GF($2^m$) | sign | 5.061 M | 4.825 M | 163 |
| | verify | 6.809 M | | |

Table 11.2:  **Performance Measurements for Asymmetric Encryption and Digital Signature Algorithms**

## 11.8 FURTHER READING

If you are interested in the history of secret communications, Kahn (1967) is the book for you. For an up-to-date professional reference on cryptography, use Menezes, van Oorschot and Vanstone (1997). Schneier (1996) gives a nice and nonmathematical introduction to modern cryptography, together with an extensive bibliography and collection of cryptographic algorithms. In these books, you will find all the details of and further information on the algorithms presented in this chapter. New cryptologic results are posted to the eprint server of the International Association for Cryptologic Research eprint.iacr.org.

The founding paper of public key cryptography is by Diffie and Hellman (1976). Only recently the wraps have been removed from even earlier classified research by CESG on public key systems (Ellis, 1970). Prime numbers are an important ingredient in many public key algorithms. An excellent explanation of primality testing can be found in Granville (2005). For developments on new block cipher modes, consult the NIST special publications 800-38A, 800-38B, and 800-38C. The Venona documents can be found at http://www.nsa.gov/venona/.

# 11.9 EXERCISES

**Exercise 11.1** Cryptographic protocols are intended to let agents communicate securely over an insecure network. Is this statement correct?

**Exercise 11.2** Cryptography needs physical security. To what extent is this statement correct?

**Exercise 11.3** Assuming that it is computationally infeasible to launch attacks that require $2^{80}$ computations of hash values, how long should the hash values be to achieve weak and strong collision resistance respectively?

**Exercise 11.4** For DSA, show that the condition $v = r$ holds for valid signatures.

**Exercise 11.5** Given a modular exponentiation algorithm for $n$-bit integers that needs about $n^3$ operations, how much does performance deteriorate by moving from 1024-bit to 2048-bit RSA?

**Exercise 11.6** Consider the RSA signature algorithm without a hash function, i.e. $s = m^e \bmod n$. Explain how, and to what extent, an attacker could forge signatures if there are no format checks on the message $m$.

**Exercise 11.7** When a document is too long to be processed directly by a DSA, a hash of the document is computed and then signed. Which properties do you require from this hash function to prevent an attacker from forging signatures?

- Distinguish between situations where the attacker only knows messages signed by the victim and situations where the attacker can choose messages the victim will sign.

- Distinguish between *selective* forgeries, where the attacker has control over the content of the forged message, and *existential* forgeries, where the attacker has no control over the content of the forged message.

- Consider the specific requirements of hash functions used with an invertible signature algorithm like RSA.

**Exercise 11.8** Can you use RSA securely with any pair of primes? Investigate the reasons for using strong primes and the properties usually required from a strong prime. Do your reasons remain valid when the primes get ever longer?

**Exercise 11.9** In the ElGamal signature scheme, show how the private signature key can be compromised if the random value $k$ is used in signing two different documents.

**Exercise 11.10** Are NP-complete problems a suitable basis for constructing cryptographic algorithms?

# Chapter 12

# Authentication in Distributed Systems

Cryptography transforms (communications) security problems into key management problems. To use encryption, digital signatures, or MACs, the parties involved have to hold the 'right' cryptographic keys. With public key algorithms, parties need authentic public keys. With symmetric key algorithms, parties need shared secret keys. This could be achieved by sending letters through the mail – a common method of distributing PINs for credit cards – or by couriers traveling between sites and delivering keys. These proposals are either not very secure or not very cheap. Ideally, we would like to conduct key management over the existing communications infrastructure.

When two parties negotiate a new key, be it because they are communicating for the first time or because they are starting a new session, they may also have to prove who they are. Proving identity and establishing keys were once both called authentication. This chapter will discuss and separate these two issues.

## OBJECTIVES

- Clarify the possible meanings of authentication.
- Present some major key establishment protocols.
- Discuss how public keys can be linked to user identities.
- Show how cryptographic protocols are being applied in computer security.

## 12.1 INTRODUCTION

Public key algorithms tend to be computationally more expensive than symmetric key algorithms. Cost factors include computation time and bandwidth. Both depend on key length. It is furthermore desirable to use long-term keys only sparingly to reduce the 'attack surface'. This is a precaution against attacks that need to collect large amounts of encrypted material. As a solution for both problems, long-term keys are used to establish short-term *session keys*.

It is good cryptographic practice to restrict the use of keys to a specific purpose. In key management, we may use key encrypting keys and data encrypting keys. Examples of *key usage* are encryption, decryption, digital signature (for authentication) and nonrepudiation in communications security. In public key cryptography, you are strongly advised not to use a single key pair both for encryption and for digital signatures. Other examples of key usage are master keys and transaction keys in hierarchical key management schemes.

## 12.2 KEY ESTABLISHMENT AND AUTHENTICATION

Once upon a time, protocols establishing a session key were called authentication protocols. After all, it is their purpose to let you know 'whom you are talking to'. In the literature, in particular in older sources, you may still find this convention. Today the terminology used in cryptology distinguishes between authentication and key establishment. The separation of key establishment from authentication can be traced in the development of international standards. In the 1980s, the ISO/OSI framework (ISO 7498-2; International Organization for Standardization, 1989), still had a session-oriented view of entity authentication.

> **Peer Entity Authentication**    The corroboration that a peer entity in an association is the one claimed. This service is provided for use at the establishment of, or at times during, the data transfer phase of a connection to confirm the identities of one or more of the entities connected to one or more of the other entities.

By the early 1990s, the International Standard ISO/IEC 9798-1 (International Organization for Standardization, 1991) defined entity authentication in a way that no longer included the establishment of a secure session.

> **Entity Authentication**    Entity authentication mechanisms allow the verification, of an entity's claimed identity, by another entity. The authenticity of the entity can be ascertained only for the instance of the authentication exchange.

In this interpretation, entity authentication checks whether an entity is alive. This property is related to *dead peer detection* in communications networks.

In *unilateral* authentication only one of the entities is authenticated. In *mutual* authentication, the identities of both entities are verified.

### 12.2.1 Remote Authentication

Whenever you change your environment, you have to reappraise the suitability of established security mechanisms. Moving from a centralized system to a distributed system definitely has an impact on security. To see how change can affect you, have another look at authentication by password (Chapter 3). Passwords are useful when a user works on a terminal that has a fixed link to a host. Here, you may have valid reasons to believe that the connection between terminal and host is secure and that it is not possible to eavesdrop on passwords, change or insert messages, or to take over a session. In a distributed setting, this fundamental assumption on the security of the communications link is unlikely to be justified.

Unprotected passwords transmitted over networks are an obvious vulnerability. Exploitation of this vulnerability can easily be automated. *Password sniffers* are programs that listen to network traffic and extract packets containing passwords and other security-relevant information. Still, passwords are a popular authentication mechanism in distributed systems. Take the *http* protocol as an example. It is run between a client and a server. The client sends *http* requests to the server. To authenticate the client, *http* has built-in authentication mechanisms based on a shared secret (the password) known by client and server. There are two types of authentication, Basic Access Authentication and Digest Access Authentication.

In Basic Access Authentication, the client just has to provide the password. When the client asks for a protected resource, the server replies with the 401 Unauthorized response code. The client then sends authentication information (the base64 encoded password) to the server, and the server checks whether the client is authorized to access the resource. All authentication data is sent in the clear. A protocol run looks like this.

- Client: `GET /index.html HTTP/1.0`
- Server: `HTTP/1.1 401 Unauthorized`
  `WWW-authenticate Basic realm="SecureArea"`
- Client: `GET /index.html HTTP/1.0`
  `Authorization: Basic am91dXN1cjphLmIuQy5E`
- Server: `HTTP/1.1 200 Ok` (and the requested document)

In contrast, Digest Access Authentication does not send passwords in the clear. A cryptographic hash function $h$ (typically MD5) is used in a *challenge-response* protocol. The WWW-authenticate parameters sent by the server include a unique challenge, called a *nonce*. It is the server's responsibility to make sure that every 401 response comes with a unique, previously unused nonce value. The client replies with an authorization response containing the plaintext username, the nonce value it just received and the so-called request-digest, computed as request-digest = $h(h(\text{username}||\text{realm}||\text{password})\ ||\text{nonce}||h(\text{method}||\text{digest-uri}))$

where 'digest-uri' relates to the requested URI and 'method' gives the *http* request method. A detailed description of this protocol with all its options is given in RFC 2617.

The term nonce was proposed by Needham and Schroeder (1978) to denote a unique value that is used only once. Nonces play an important role in protocol design. A nonce can be a counter value, a time stamp or a random number. A nonce is not necessarily unpredictable but some protocols require unpredictable nonces. It depends on the particular security goals which type of nonce should be used.

A further example of remote user authentication by password is the RADIUS protocol (Remote Authentication Dial-In User Service, RFC 2865). Like *http* Digest Access Authentication, RADIUS includes a challenge-response option where the password is not transmitted in the clear.

## 12.2.2 Key Establishment

The process whereby a shared secret becomes available to two or more parties for later cryptographic use is today called *key establishment*. This process involves the parties wishing to establish the shared keys, often called the *principals*, and possibly third parties like authentication servers. Principals in key establishment protocols are not necessarily the same as principals in access control (Chapter 4). When the third party could violate the security goals of the protocol, it is called a *trusted third party* (TTP). The principals have to trust the TTP when they invoke its services.

Sometimes, an analysis of the mathematical details of a cryptographic protocol reveals the existence of a subset of *weak keys* that would allow an insider to cheat. When designing a key exchange protocol you therefore should answer two questions.

- Which party will suffer if a weak key is established?

- Which parties can control the choice of key?

If a misbehaving insider can influence key generation so that a weak key is chosen, then there may be scope for insider attacks. This issue is known as *key control*. Key establishment services can thus be further distinguished according to the contributions each principal makes to the new key, and to the actual security guarantees provided (Menezes, van Oorschot and Vanstone, 1997).

- Key transport: one party creates the secret value and securely transfers it to the other(s).

- Key agreement: both parties contribute to the generation of the secret value so that no party can predict the outcome.

- Key authentication: one party is assured that no other party aside from a specifically identified second party may gain access to a particular secret key.

- Key confirmation: one party is assured that a second (possibly unidentified) party has possession of a particular secret key.

- Explicit key authentication: both key authentication and key confirmation hold.

Figure 12.1 shows how the meaning of entity authentication has evolved over time. Other factors to consider when assessing a protocol are third party requirements. Is a TTP involved? Would it be off-line or on-line?

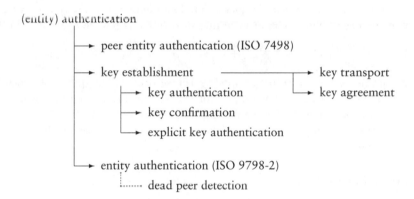

Figure 12.1: Terminology of Authentication and Key Establishment

# 12.3 KEY ESTABLISHMENT PROTOCOLS

Cryptographic protocols that establish keys for use by other protocols are known as key establishment protocols. Today, the research literature offers an extensive choice of such protocols. The following protocols have been selected to illustrate important design techniques.

## 12.3.1 Authenticated Key Exchange Protocol

Our first protocol, AKEP2 (Authenticated Key Exchange Protocol 2; Bellare and Rogaway, 1994), uses 'cheap' hash functions instead of encryption and does not rely on a TTP. The two principals $A$ and $B$ share two long-term symmetric keys $K$ and $K'$ and in each protocol run generate fresh random numbers (nonces), $n_a$ and $n_b$ respectively. The protocol uses a keyed hash function (MAC) $h_K$ and a keyed one-way function $h'_{K'}$. AKEP2 is a three-pass protocol.

$$
\begin{aligned}
&1.\ A \to B: \quad n_a \\
&2.\ B \to A: \quad B, A, n_a, n_b, h_K(B, A, n_a, n_b) \\
&3.\ A \to B: \quad A, n_b, h_K(A, n_b)
\end{aligned}
$$

In the first step, $A$ sends a challenge $n_a$. In the second step, $B$ responds with $h_K(B, A, n_a, n_b)$ and sends its own challenge $n_b$. The shared key is $k = h'_{K'}(n_b)$. In the third step, $A$ responds to this challenge with $h_K(A, n_b)$. AKEP2 provides mutual entity authentication and (implicit) key authentication.

## 12.3.2 The Diffie–Hellman Protocol

The Diffie and Hellman (1976) protocol is a key agreement protocol. Principals $A$ and $B$ do not share a secret in advance. They use a large and appropriately chosen prime number $p$ and an element $g$ of large order modulo $p$. Principal $A$ picks a random number $a$ and sends $y_a = g^a \bmod p$ to $B$. Principal $B$ picks a random number $b$, sends $y_b = g^b \bmod p$ to $A$, and computes $y_a^b$. On receipt of $y_b$, $A$ uses its own secret $a$ to compute $y_b^a$. This is because

$$y_a^b = g^{ab} = g^{ba} = y_b^a.$$

Then both parties share the secret $g^{ab} \bmod p$. The security of this protocol depends on the difficulty of the Discrete Logarithm Problem (section 11.2). An attacker able to compute discrete logarithms could obtain $a$ and $b$ from $g^a \bmod p$ and $g^b \bmod p$. It is not known whether the security of the Diffie–Hellman protocol is equivalent to the Discrete Logarithm Problem.

### Man-in-the-middle Attack

There is one slight problem left. Neither party knows with whom it shares the secret. This can be exploited by an attacker $M$ in a man-in-the-middle attack. The attacker inserts itself on the communications path between $A$ and $B$, replies to $A$ when $A$ initiates a protocol run and at the same time starts a protocol run with $B$ where $M$ pretends to be $A$ (Figure 12.2). Principals $A$ and $B$ might believe they have established a shared key but in actual fact $M$ shares key $g^{ax} \bmod p$ with $A$ and key $g^{bz} \bmod p$ with $B$, and can read all traffic between $A$ and $B$ while acting as a relay.

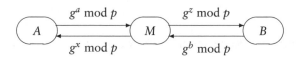

Figure 12.2: Man-in-the-middle Attack against the Diffie–Hellman protocol

### Station-to-station Protocol

To secure the Diffie–Hellman protocol, authentication has to be added. The station-to-station (STS) protocol (Diffie, van Oorschot and Wiener, 1992) does this as follows. In addition to a Diffie–Hellman exchange that establishes a shared session key $K := g^{ab} \bmod p$, the protocol uses an encryption algorithm and a signature algorithm. No specific algorithms are prescribed. In the following, $S_a$ and $S_b$ are the signature keys of $A$ and $B$, $sS_a$ and $sS_b$ denote signatures generated under these keys. The steps in the protocol are:

1. $A \rightarrow B$: $g^a$
2. $B \rightarrow A$: $g^b, eK(sS_b(g^b, g^a))$
3. $A \rightarrow B$: $eK(sS_a(g^a, g^b))$

In step 1, $A$ initiates a Diffie–Hellman key exchange as before. After, receiving $g^a$, $B$ picks a random number $b$ and computes the session key $K := g^{ab}$ mod $p$. After step 2, $A$ can complete its part of the Diffie–Hellman key exchange and derive $K$, and then decrypt the second part of $B$'s message and verify $B$'s signature. After the last message, $B$ can decrypt and verify $A$'s signature. STS is a key agreement protocol that provides mutual entity authentication and explicit key authentication.

### 12.3.3 The Needham–Schroeder Protocol

The Needham and Schroeder (1978) protocol is a key transport protocol. Two parties $A$ and $B$ obtain their session key from a server $S$. Both principals share a secret key with the server in advance. A symmetric cipher is used for encryption. Nonces (random challenges) are included in the messages to prevent replay attacks. The conventions are used in the description of the protocol are:

- $K_{as}$: a secret key shared by $A$ and $S$;
- $K_{bs}$: a secret key shared by $B$ and $S$;
- $K_{ab}$: a session key created by $S$ for use between $A$ and $B$;
- $n_a, n_b$: nonces generated by $A$ and $B$ respectively;

Figure 12.3 shows the steps that take place when entity $A$ requests from the server $S$ a session key $K_{ab}$ that is intended for communication with $B$. In the first three steps of the protocol, $A$ obtains the session key from $S$ and forwards it to $B$. By checking the nonce $n_a$ returned in the server's message, $A$ can verify that the session key has been issued in response to its recent request and is not a replay from a former protocol run. In the last two steps, $B$ verifies that $A$ is currently using the same session key. In steps 4 and 5, $A$ performs a unilateral entity authentication of $B$.

1. $A \rightarrow S$: $A, B, n_a$
2. $S \rightarrow A$: $eK_{as}(n_a, B, K_{ab}, eK_{bs}(K_{ab}, A))$
3. $A \rightarrow B$: $eK_{bs}(K_{ab}, A)$
4. $B \rightarrow A$: $eK_{ab}(n_b)$
5. $A \rightarrow B$: $eK_{ab}(n_b - 1)$

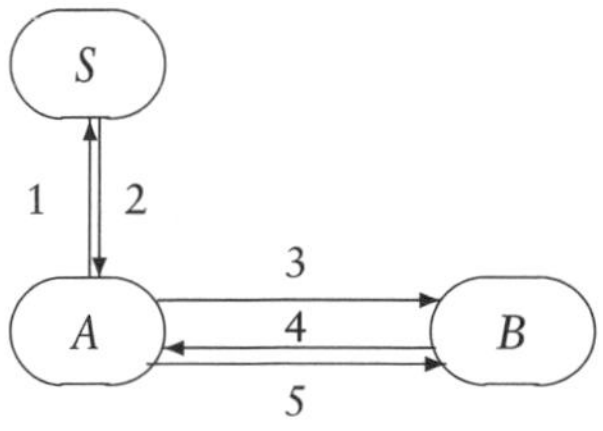

**Figure 12.3: The Message Flow in the Needham–Schroeder Protocol**

### The Denning–Sacco Attack

The Needham–Schroeder protocol achieves its goals under the standard assumption that the long term keys $K_{as}$ and $K_{bs}$ are not compromised, and if just a single protocol run is considered. Denning and Sacco (1981) discovered a *replay attack* where the adversary $M$ impersonates $A$ reusing a compromised session key $K_{ab}$. The adversary starts at step 3 of the protocol and replays to $B$ the third message from the protocol run when the compromised session key was established. $B$ decrypts the message and reuses the compromised session key.

$$3.\ M \rightarrow B:\quad eK_{bs}(K_{ab}, A)$$
$$4.\ B \rightarrow M:\quad eK_{ab}(n'_b)$$
$$5.\ M \rightarrow B:\quad eK_{ab}(n'_b - 1)$$

This is a *known key attack*, using a compromised old session key to compromise a future session. As far as $B$ is concerned, the Needham–Schroeder protocol does not provide *key freshness*.

> A key is *fresh* (from the viewpoint of one party) if it can be guaranteed to be new (Menezes, van Oorschot and Vanstone, 1997).

Key freshness helps to protect against replay attacks.

### Perfect Forward Secrecy

When analyzing protocols, it makes sense to treat the compromise of past session keys differently from the compromise of long-term secret keys. When a long-term key is compromised, we can no longer protect future sessions. However, we would still like past sessions to remain secure. A protocol achieves *perfect forward secrecy* if the compromise of session keys or long-term keys does not compromise past session keys. The term forward secrecy indicates that the secrecy of old session keys is carried forward into the future.

### 12.3.4 Password-based Protocols

In the Needham–Schroeder protocol, client and server already share secret keys when they start a protocol run. Thus, both systems must be equipped to store keys securely. If the client is a person accessing the server via an 'untrusted' device we can only rely on shared secrets the users can memorize, i.e. we are back to something like passwords. We could then use a password $P$ to encrypt a randomly generated session key $K_s$, and then use the session key to encrypt further data.

$$1.\ A \rightarrow B:\quad eP(K_s)$$
$$2.\ B \rightarrow A:\quad eK_s(\text{data})$$

This naïve protocol has a problem. It is vulnerable to an *off-line dictionary attack*. The attacker guesses the password $P$, decrypts the first message and gets a candidate session key $K'_s$, which is then used to decrypt the second message. When meaningful text emerges it is likely that the password has been guessed correctly.

The Encrypted Key Exchange (EKE) protocol avoids this problem (Bellovin and Merritt, 1992). It uses a symmetric encryption algorithm to encrypt data with the password $P$ as the key, and also a public key encryption system. In a protocol run, principal $A$ generates a random public key/private key pair $K_a, K_a^{-1}$. In the first message $A$ sends the public key $K_a$ to $B$, encrypted under $P$ (symmetric encryption). In the second message $B$ sends the randomly generated session key $K_s$ to $A$, encrypted first under $K_a$ (public key encryption) and then under $P$ (symmetric encryption).

$$1.\ A \rightarrow B: \quad eP(K_a)$$
$$2.\ B \rightarrow A: \quad eP(eK_a(K_s))$$

It is left as an exercise to show that this protocol is not vulnerable to an off-line dictionary attack. Generating fresh key pairs for each protocol run is not exactly a trivial exercise. There has been further work on the design of more efficient password-based key establishment protocols, and on their formal analysis; see e.g. Halevi and Krawczyk (1999).

## 12.4 KERBEROS

The Kerberos system was developed at MIT within the project Athena in the 1980s. Athena provided computing resources to students across and beyond MIT's campus and included additional administrative functionalities like accounting. The risks and threats addressed by Kerberos, as stated by Miller *et al.* (1987), are:

> The environment is not appropriate for sensitive data or high risk operations, such as bank transactions, classified government data, student grades, controlling dangerous experiments, and such. The risks are primarily uncontrolled use of resources by unauthorized parties, violations of integrity of either system's or user's resources, and wholesale violations of privacy such as casual browsing through personal files.

Kerberos has since found wide acceptance. Several industry standards have adopted Kerberos for distributed systems authentication, notably the Internet RFC 1510. Kerberos authenticates clients to services in a distributed system. Authentication is built around the concepts of *tickets* and central security servers.

Kerberos has its origin in the Needham–Schroeder key exchange protocol (section 12.3.3). A symmetric cipher system, like DES, is used for encryption. Users are authenticated by username and password, but passwords are not transmitted over the network. RFC 1510 gives a detailed specification of Kerberos Version 5, including the error messages that are issued when a protocol run cannot proceed. Our simplified description omits some of the data fields in the Kerberos messages and deals only with the case where a protocol run is successfully completed.

Kerberos involves a user $A$ at a client machine $C$, a server $B$, and an authentication server $S$. User $A$ shares a secret key $K_{as}$ with the authentication server $S$. This key is derived from the user's password with a one-way function. $K_{bs}$ is a secret key shared by $B$ and $S$, $K_{ab}$ is the session key created by $S$ for use between $A$ and $B$, $n_a$ is a nonce generated by $A$, and $T_a$ is a time stamp referring to $A$'s clock. The ticket for $B$ is $ticket_B = eK_{bs}(K_{ab}, A, L)$ where $L$ is the lifetime of the ticket. The core protocol works as follows.

1. $A \rightarrow S$ :    $A, B, n_a$
2. $S \rightarrow A$ :    $eK_{as}(K_{ab}, n_a, L, B), ticket_B$
3. $A \rightarrow B$ :    $ticket_B, eK_{ab}(A, T_a)$
4. $B \rightarrow A$ :    $eK_{ab}(T_a)$

To start a session, user $A$ logs on at client $C$ entering username and password. The client sends $A$'s request for authentication to $B$ to $S$. The first message contains $A$'s identity, the name of the server, and a nonce, all sent in the clear. In the second step, $S$ looks up $A$'s key $K_{as}$ in its database (the protocol stops if $A$ is unknown to $S$), generates the session key $K_{ab}$ and $ticket_B$. $S$ sends the session key, in a data structure encrypted under $K_{as}$, and the ticket to $A$. At the client, the key $K_{as}$ is derived from $A$'s password and used to decrypt the first part of the reply. $A$ gets the session key $K_{ab}$ and verifies the nonce. In the third step, $A$ sends ticket and *authenticator* $eK_{ab}(A, T_a)$ to $B$. $B$ decrypts the ticket with $K_b$ and obtains the session key $K_{ab}$. $B$ checks that the identifiers in the ticket and authenticator match, that the ticket has not expired and that the time stamp is valid. The validity period for time stamps has to consider the skew between the local clocks of $A$ and $B$. In the fourth step, $B$ returns the time stamp $T_A$ encrypted under the session key $K_{ab}$ to $A$.

Kerberos is traditionally deployed using several ticket-granting servers (TGSs) in conjunction with an authentication server. The Kerberos Authentication Server (KAS) authenticates principals at logon and issues tickets, which in general are valid for one login session and enable principals to obtain other tickets from TGSs. The authentication server is sometimes called the Key Distribution Center (KDC). A TGS issues tickets that give principals access to network services demanding authentication. Figure 12.4 shows the steps that take place in a protocol run involving a KAS and a TGS. Here, $K_{a,tgs}$ is a session key created by the KAS for use between $A$ and the TGS. There is a second nonce

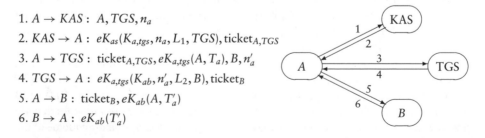

1. $A \rightarrow KAS$ :   $A, TGS, n_a$
2. $KAS \rightarrow A$ :   $eK_{as}(K_{a,tgs}, n_a, L_1, TGS), ticket_{A,TGS}$
3. $A \rightarrow TGS$ :   $ticket_{A,TGS}, eK_{a,tgs}(A, T_a), B, n'_a$
4. $TGS \rightarrow A$ :   $eK_{a,tgs}(K_{ab}, n'_a, L_2, B), ticket_B$
5. $A \rightarrow B$ :   $ticket_B, eK_{ab}(A, T'_a)$
6. $B \rightarrow A$ :   $eK_{ab}(T'_a)$

**Figure 12.4: The Message Flow in the Kerberos Authentication Protocol**

$n'_a$ and time stamp $T'_a$. $L_1$ and $L_2$ are the lifetimes of the two tickets. The *ticket-granting ticket* (TGT) ticket$_{A,TGS}$ is constructed as

$$\text{ticket}_{A,TGS} = eK_{tgs}(K_{a,tgs}, A, L_2)$$

where $eK_{tgs}$ is a key shared by the KAS and TGS.

## 12.4.1 Realms

A KAS is at the heart of a Kerberos realm. A Kerberos realm is a single administrative domain that controls access to a collection of servers. To get Kerberos up and running, principals have to be registered with the KAS, the TGSs have to receive access control information, and all the necessary keys have to be put in place by the security administrator.

Kerberos has all the advantages of a centralized security system. A single security policy is enforced by a limited number of security servers. Thus, it is relatively easy to check that the system set-up complies with the security policy and to implement changes if so desired.

A realm often corresponds to a single organization. To facilitate access to services in other organizations, we need inter-realm authentication. This requires a 'trust relationship' between the authentication servers in different realms. In this case, 'trust' is a shared secret key. Between organizations, key sharing is often underpinned by contractual agreements. Is trust transitive? If there is trust between realms $R_1$ and $R_2$, and between realms $R_2$ and $R_3$, can a client in $R_1$ get access to a server in $R_3$? There is no universal answer. The outcome depends on prior agreements between the realms.

As an example, consider a user $A$ in realm $R_1$ who requests from its authentication server KAS$_1$ a ticket for a server $B$ in realm $R_3$. The user, or some discovery service, has found out that KAS$_1$ has a trust relationship with KAS$_2$ and that KAS$_2$ has a trust relationship with KAS$_3$, and that these trust relationships are transitive. On $A$'s request, KAS$_1$ generates a TGT for realm $R_2$ and forwards this TGT together with $A$'s request to KAS$_2$. In turn, KAS$_2$ generates a TGT for realm $R_3$, and forwards this TGT together with $A$'s request to KAS$_3$. KAS$_3$ creates the ticket for $B$ and sends it to $A$. The client where $A$ has logged on presents this ticket when requesting a service from $B$.

## 12.4.2 Kerberos and Windows

Kerberos has become the authentication protocol of choice in Windows. Windows domains correspond to Kerberos realms. Domain controllers act as KDCs. The principals that may run Kerberos are users but also machines. In Windows, authentication is the basis for later access control decisions. The principals in Windows access control are the SIDs. (Here, we finally have a clash between the two definitions of principal.) Therefore, a principal's SIDs have to be stored in the ticket. A Kerberos ticket, as defined in

RFC 1510, contains among others a mandatory field cname for the client name and an optional authorization-data field. In Windows, cname holds the principal's name and realm, e.g. diego@tuhh.de, authorization-data holds the group SIDs. Details of Microsoft's implementation of Kerberos can be found in Brown (2000).

### 12.4.3 Delegation

In distributed systems, controlled invocation literally takes on a new dimension. A user may log on at a local node and then execute a program on a remote node. To obtain access to resources at the remote node, the process executing the program will need the relevant access rights. Typically, the program would be endowed with the access rights of the user and then run with these access rights on the remote node. This process is called *delegation*.

The process on the remote node is now running with all the access rights delegated by the user. In a distributed system, users may not feel too comfortable about releasing all their rights to a node they have little control over. If there is weak protection on the remote node, an attacker may grab the user's access rights and use them for illicit purposes. It may be desirable for users to be able to control which rights they delegate, to have accountability mechanisms that monitor the use of delegated access rights.

The Kerberos implementation in Windows supports different modes of delegation. When explaining these modes, we briefly follow the popular convention of calling the parties involved Alice and Bob. So, when Alice needs a service from Bob, where Bob has to access servers on her behalf, and when she knows in advance what Bob is going to need, she applies for *proxy tickets* for the relevant servers and gives the tickets and the corresponding session keys to Bob. These server tickets are marked as proxy tickets and must contain special authorizations that limit how Bob can use Alice's credentials, e.g. state the name of a file Bob is allowed to print. If she does not know in advance what Bob is going to need, Alice applies for a *forwarded* TGT for Bob and transfers this ticket and corresponding session key to Bob. In this way, Alice delegates her identity to Bob. Bob can now apply for tickets on her behalf. Bob can impersonate Alice. Brown (2000), aptly calls this 'the fast and loose way to delegate credentials'. Principals can be nominated as OK-AS-DELEGATE to have some control over the delegation of credentials (identities).

Is delegating identities a good idea at all? At the level of subjects this is quite reasonable. SIDs give access rights and a process running on behalf of a user cannot constantly go back to that user and ask whether it is alright to pass on a SID to another process. However, when a user Alice delegates her identity to another user, she is doing the equivalent of giving her password away (for the time the forwarded ticket is valid). Sharing of passwords is usually frowned upon and may violate Alice's corporate security policy.

Concepts from operating system security may not always be appropriate at the application layer. Calling both users and processes Alice and Bob does not add to clarity either. In general, anthropomorphic metaphors like 'Alice talks to Bob' or 'Bob verifies Alice's identity' can be very misleading. In computer security, the entities are computers, not human beings, they send messages over a network, they do not talk, and you have to decide what you mean by verifying $A$'s identity. There is definitely no visual contact between computers.

### Lesson

Alice and Bob are semantic sugar. They allow you to tell nice stories but they also invite you to think at the wrong level of abstraction.

### 12.4.4 Revocation

How can access rights be revoked from a principal? The system administrator of the KAS and the TGS have to update their databases so that these access rights are no longer available to the principal. The access rights have thus been revoked for the next session, i.e. the next time the principal logs on or requests a ticket from the TGS. The tickets the principal already has in possession are, however, valid until they expire. For example, KAS tickets usually have a lifetime of about one day. This is another instance of the TOCTTOU problem.

You now face a trade-off between convenience and security. If the TGS issues tickets with a distant expiry date, the principal has no need to access the TGS that often and the TGS may occasionally be off-line without too much impact on the users. However, revocation of an access right will take effect with a longer delay. If the TGS issues tickets with short lifetimes, principals have to update their tickets more regularly and the availability of the security servers becomes more important for system performance.

### 12.4.5 Summary

For a full assessment of Kerberos, you have to go beyond analyzing the authentication protocol and the strength of the underlying cryptographic algorithms. You also have to examine its non-cryptographic security features. The following points are part of such an investigation.

- Timeliness of messages is confirmed by checking time stamps. Therefore, reasonably synchronous clocks are required throughout the whole system and the clocks themselves have to be protected against attacks. Secure clock synchronization in itself may require authentication.

- Checking of time stamps allows for some clock skew. The typical acceptance window of five minutes is rather large and can be exploited easily by replay attacks.

- Servers have to be on-line. The KAS is needed on-line at login, the TGS is needed when a ticket is requested. Requirements on the availability of a TGS may be relaxed as discussed above.

- Session keys (for a symmetric cipher) are generated by Kerberos servers (authentication and ticket-granting servers). As the session keys are used in subsequent communications between principals, trust in the servers has to encompass trust that servers will not misuse their ability to eavesdrop.

- Password guessing and password spoofing attacks are possible (Wu, 1999).

- Keys and tickets are held on the client's machine. Therefore, you rely on the protection mechanisms on that node for the security of Kerberos. As long as Kerberos users worked from simple terminals, this was not much of an issue. The situation changed once users ran Kerberos on a PC or a multiuser workstation.

- The initial client request is not authenticated. An attacker sending spoofed authentication requests would get tickets in return. This could constitute a denial-of-service attack against the authentication server or be an attempt to collect material for a cryptanalytic attack. As a countermeasure, the server could ask the user for authentication in a *preauthentication* phase before generating any tickets.

Furthermore, it is important to distinguish the security of the protocol itself from the security of implementations of Kerberos. For example, one implementation of Kerberos Version 4 reportedly used a weak random-number generator for key generation, so that keys could be found easily by exhaustive search.

# 12.5 PUBLIC KEY INFRASTRUCTURES

The description of the STS protocol omitted one important detail. How do $A$ and $B$ know that the verification keys they are using to check signatures indeed correspond to the right party? This is a crucial problem in public key cryptography. We rarely want to run protocols between cryptographic keys but between principals that have meaningful names (identities) at a higher protocol layer, e.g. usernames of clients or Domain Name System (DNS) names of servers. There has to be a reliable source that links those identities with cryptographic keys. Note that with symmetric ciphers, the parties $A$ and $B$ often trust a server to create this connection.

## 12.5.1 Certificates

Diffie and Hellman (1976) envisaged a public directory where one could look up the public keys of users, just as in a phone directory. In a student project in 1978, Kohnfelder implemented this directory as a set of digitally signed data records containing a name and a public key. He coined the term *certificate* for these records. Certificates originally had a single function, binding between names and keys. Today, the term is used somewhat more widely and you can find explanations like this:

> Certificate: A signed instrument that empowers the Subject. It contains at least an Issuer and a Subject. It can contain validity conditions, authorization and delegation information (Ellison *et al.*, 1999).

In this spirit, we can define a certificate as a digitally signed document that binds a subject to some other information. Subjects can be people, keys, names, etc. Identity (ID) certificates bind names to keys. Sometimes this is still the default interpretation of the term certificate. Attribute certificates bind names to authorizations. Authorization certificates bind keys to authorizations.

## 12.5.2 Certification Authorities

The binding between subject and key, or some other information, is established by the party that issues (signs) the certificate. This party is known as the Issuer. Certification Authority (CA) is just another name for Issuer. When you issue certificates for your own use, you are a CA. Sometimes CA is used more narrowly for organizations issuing ID certificates. The application determines the technical and procedural trust requirements a CA has to meet. The CA has to protect its own private key. It may have to check that the subject is who he/she claims to be and that the attributes in the certificate are correct. Checks may be performed at various levels of thoroughness. The VeriSign certificate classes may serve as an example. At the most elementary level, the CA just checks that subject names are unique. At the highest level, the subject has to appear in person with government-approved identity documents. Some of these checks can be performed by a Registration Authority (RA) and the CA's main task is the issuing of certificates.

Public Key Infrastructure (PKI) is the somewhat imprecise term used to describe the system for issuing and managing certificates. Depending on your source, a PKI may be:

- software for managing digital certificates;
- a system of hardware, software, policies and people providing security assurances;
- the technology for securing the Internet;
- a worldwide system of digital ID cards.

There is no 'correct' definition. Whenever you encounter a so-called PKI, you have to establish which interpretation is intended at that particular moment before drawing any further conclusions.

## 12.5.3 X.509/PKIX Certificates

Today, X.509 version 3 is the most commonly used PKI standard. The original ITU-T Recommendation X.509 (International Organization for Standardization, 1997) was part of the X.500 Directory (CCITT, 1988), which has since also been adopted as IS

9594-1. X.500 was intended as a global, distributed database of named entities such as people, computers, printers, etc., i.e. a global, on-line telephone book. X.509 certificates would bind public keys (originally passwords) to X.500 pathnames (Distinguished Names) to note who has permission to modify X.500 directory nodes. X.500 was geared towards identity-based access control.

> Virtually all security services are dependent upon the identities of communicating parties being reliably known, i.e. authentication (International Organization for Standardization, 1997).

This view of the world predates applets and many new e-commerce scenarios, where a different kind of access control is more appropriate.

Compared to previous versions, the X.509 v3 certificate format (Figure 12.5) includes extensions to increase flexibility. Extensions can be marked as *critical*. If a critical extension cannot be processed by an implementation, the certificate must be rejected. Noncritical extensions may be ignored. Critical extensions can be used to standardize policy with respect to the use of certificates.

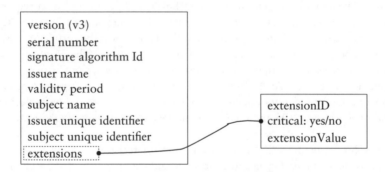

◯  **Figure 12.5: X.509 v3 Certificate Format**

PKIX is the Internet X.509 PKI (Housley *et al.*, 2002). It adapts X.509 v3 to the Internet by specifying appropriate extensions. A *public key certificate* (PKC) contains a subject's public key and some further information. An *attribute certificate* (AC) contains a set of attributes for a subject. Attribute certificates are issued by Attribute Authorities. A PKI is the set of hardware, software, people, policies and procedures needed to create, manage, store, distribute and revoke PKCs. A Privilege Management Infrastructure (PMI) is a collection of ACs, with their issuing Attribute Authorities, subjects, relying parties and repositories.

X.509 and PKIX are name-centric PKIs. To associate a key with access rights, you have to know the subject the key belongs to. Authorization attributes are linked to a cryptographic key via a common name in a public key certificate and an attribute certificate. An alternative is SPKI, the Simple Public Key Infrastructure (Ellison *et al.*, 1999). SPKI is a key-centric PKI. SPKI certificates bind keys directly to attributes (access rights).

### Lesson

Like user identities, certificates are used for two purposes. They can identify an entity associated with a cryptographic key or they can specify the access rights to be given to the holder of a cryptographic key (without revealing the holder's identity).

### 12.5.4 Certificate Chains

Technically, it is wrong to claim that a certificate is needed to verify a digital signature. An authentic copy of the verification key is needed. Verification keys may be stored in certificates but can also be stored in protected memory. However, there are systems that require all verification keys to be stored in certificates. The Java 2 security model is an example.

To check a certificate, another verification key is needed, which might be vouched for by a certificate. This creates a certificate chain. Ultimately, you need a *root verification key* whose authenticity cannot be guaranteed by a certificate. Typically a set of root verification keys is installed in browsers/mail programs. When you get messages like 'You do not trust this certificate' then there is no chain rooted in one of those root verification keys. In a system that requires certificates for signature verification you can use self-signed certificates to store root keys. A self-signed certificate can be verified with the public key contained in it.

Certificates have expiry dates. It is wrong to believe that a certificate cannot be used after it has expired. Deciding what should be done with expired certificates is a policy decision. In the world of passports, for example, an EU passport is valid for travel within the EU for a year after it has expired. There are two main policies for considering expiry date (and revocation) status when evaluating a certificate chain.

In the *shell model* all certificates have to be valid at the time of evaluation. If a top-level certificate expires or is revoked, all certificates signed by the corresponding private key have to be reissued under a new key. This conservative approach has been implemented in SPKI. When the shell model is applied, a CA should only issue certificates that expire before its own certificate.

In the *chain model* the issuer's certificate has to be valid at the time the certificate was issued. If a top-level certificate expires or is revoked, certificates signed by the corresponding private key remain valid. This model requires a time-stamping service that reliably establishes when a certificate was issued. A Time Stamp Authority (TSA) is a TTP that provides a proof-of-existence for a particular data at an instant in time. A TSA does not check the documents it certifies. TSP, the PKIX Time Stamp Protocol, is described in RFC 3161.

### 12.5.5 Revocation

A certificate may have to be revoked if a corresponding private key has been compromised or if a fact the certificate vouches for is no longer valid. Certification Revocation Lists (CRLs) distributed at regular intervals or on demand are the solution proposed in X.509. CRLs make sense if on-line checks are not possible or are too expensive. When on-line checks are feasible, CRLs can be queried on-line. But when on-line checks are feasible, certificate status can be queried on-line and CRLs may become superfluous. Instead, the current status of a certificate could be queried with a protocol like the Online Certificate Status Protocol (OCSP, RFC 2560). The German signature infrastructure, for example, requires checks against positive lists of valid certificates. Short-lived certificates are an alternative to revocation.

### 12.5.6 Electronic Signatures

Handwritten signatures play an important part in commercial and legal transactions. (Not because they are difficult to forge, but because they signal intent.) When such transactions are executed electronically, an equivalent of handwritten signatures is required. Digital signatures have been proposed as the solution. However, a digital signature is just a cryptographic mechanism for associating documents with verification keys. Security services that associate documents with persons are usually called *electronic signatures*. Electronic signature services often use digital signatures as a building block but could be implemented without them.

There have been numerous efforts to integrate electronic signatures into legal systems. A prominent example is the EU Electronic Signature Directive (Directive 1999/93/EC of 13 December 1999 on a Community framework for electronic signatures). The Directive uses electronic signatures as a technology-neutral term, but so-called *advanced electronic signatures* have *de facto* to be implemented with digital signatures. Advanced electronic signatures are vouched for by *qualified certificates*. Further requirements on certification-service providers (CAs and the like) and signature-creation devices (for example smart cards) apply. Figure 12.6 gives a schematic overview of all the components of a secure electronic signature service, and of the basis of their security.

### Lesson

In the end, cryptographic protection has to be anchored in a non-cryptographic base.

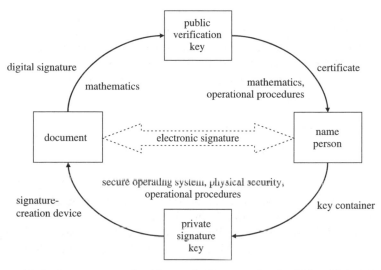

○ **Figure 12.6: Components of an Electronic Signature Service Using Digital Signatures**

# 12.6 TRUSTED COMPUTING – ATTESTATION

Let us switch the focus back from people to machines. There may be situations where we might only engage in a transaction with a remote platform if we know exactly which hardware and software configuration has been installed on that machine. We might request this information from the remote platform, but how can we be sure that the information we get is correct? This is one of the problems addressed by the Trusted Computing Group (TCG). The process of vouching for the accuracy of information is called *attestation*.

The so-called Trusted Platform Module (TPM) is the hardware component at the core of the security architecture specified in the TCG. In a TPM, integrity check values for hardware and software components are stored in Platform Configuration Registers (PCRs). The TPM furthermore contains an embedded Endorsement Key (EK) that cannot be removed. The EK is a 2048-bit RSA key pair, where the public key identifies the TPM and the private key is used for decrypting messages sent to the TPM. It must be possible to determine whether an EK belongs to a genuine TPM. Generally, this is achieved by a certificate from the TPM manufacturer.

The TPM could sign the contents of the PCR with a trusted key but if attestations issued by the TPM are always signed by the same key, an observer could link them all. To make attestations unlinkable, the TPM can therefore create Attestation Identity Keys (AIKs). An AIK is an RSA signature key pair generated by the TPM. The TPM needs the services of a TTP, a so-called privacy CA (pCA), to get a certificate that confirms that the AIK belongs to a genuine TPM. The following protocol was once considered for obtaining such a certificate. The TPM sends its public EK and the public part of the attestation identity key $AIK_i$ to the pCA. The CA checks that the EK belongs to a genuine TPM, stores the mapping between the EK and the AIK, and returns the certificate $Cert_{pCA}$ to the TPM. When the TPM uses the private part of $AIK_i$ to sign the PCR contents in an attestation, it includes $Cert_{pCA}$ in the message sent to the verifier.

1. TPM→ pCA:          EK, $AIK_i$
2. pCA→ TPM:          $Cert_{pCA}$
3. TPM→ Verifier:     $AIK_i$, $sAIK_i(PCR)$, $Cert_{pCA}$

You might have noted that the attempt to make attestations unlinkable has failed. In the first message all attestation keys are linked to EK, and thus all attestations can still be linked. There has been further work on this problem, e.g. on Direct Anonymous Attestation. Complete anonymity, however, is not desirable because there is also the requirement that it should be possible to recognize attestations coming from TPMs known to have been compromised. Protocols that show how these competing goals might be achieved have been proposed, e.g. in Brickell, Camenisch and Chen (2004) and Camenisch (2004).

## 12.7 FURTHER READING

A detailed specification of Kerberos is contained in the Internet RFC 1510 (Kohl and Neumann, 1993). An analysis of Kerberos security, in the context of the environment it was developed for, is given by Bellovin and Merritt (1990). Extensions to Kerberos refine its access control features, e.g. through *Privilege Attribute Certificates (PACs)* in SESAME (Ashley and Vandenwauver, 1999), OSF DCE or PERMIS. KryptoKnight is a protocol suite developed by IBM as an alternative to Kerberos (Bird *et al.*, 1995). Like Kerberos, KryptoKnight is a centralized system where security servers provide authentication and key distribution. Integrity check functions are used instead of encryption to bypass the export problems faced in the 1990s.

Despite their ephemeral nature, the PKIX roadmap (Aresenault and Turner, 2000) and the Internet Draft of the SPKI (Ellison *et al.*, 1999) should be mentioned for their discussion of the theory of certificates. Lessons learned while deploying a PKI in an international company are reported by El-Asa *et al.*, (2002).

## 12.8 EXERCISES

**Exercise 12.1**   In the *http* basic authentication protocol, analyze the security gains (if any) when the client sends a hash of the password instead of a base64 encoding of the password.

**Exercise 12.2** Show that the AKEP2 protocol provides mutual entity authentication and implicit key authentication.

**Exercise 12.3** Show that the STS protocol provides mutual entity authentication and explicit key authentication.

**Exercise 12.4** Consider this simple password-based challenge-response protocol run between a user $A$ and a server $S$. $P_A$ denotes $A$'s password, $n$ is a random nonce generated by the server and $h$ is a known cryptographic hash function.

$$1.\, S \rightarrow A : \quad eP_A(n)$$
$$2.\, A \rightarrow S : \quad eP_A(h(n))$$

Show that this protocol is vulnerable to an off-line password guessing attack.

**Exercise 12.5** Justify the claim that the EKE protocol is not vulnerable to an off-line password guessing attack.

**Exercise 12.6** Justify the claim that the STS protocol is not vulnerable to the same man-in-the-middle-attack as the Diffie–Hellman protocol.

**Exercise 12.7** Modify the Needham–Schroeder key exchange protocol so that both parties $A$ and $B$ can contribute input to the generation of the session key.

**Exercise 12.8** Give a short description of the KryptoKnight protocol and discuss its advantages, or disadvantages, compared to Kerberos.

**Exercise 12.9** Design an extension of Kerberos that allows access between domains. Which administrative arrangements have to be in place to make such a scheme feasible? Which additional steps would you introduce in the protocol?

**Exercise 12.10** A company keeps an archive of signed electronic records, together with the relevant certificates. Should the shell model or the chain model be used when checking the validity of documents in the archive?

**Exercise 12.11** Consider a scheme where certificates are used to delegate access rights. Should the shell model or the chain model be used when deciding on access requests?

**Exercise 12.12** Consider a scheme where certificates are used to delegate access rights. Should a subject be able to delegate rights it cannot exercise itself? In your answer, distinguish between name-centric and key-centric PKIs.

# Chapter 13

## Network Security

Networks connect computers. Being connected is a mixed blessing. More interactions are possible, but so are more unwelcome interactions. You may therefore wish to control how users on the network are able to access your system, how users on your system are able to access the network and how your data is protected when it travels through the network. Network security is more than just applied cryptography. It also includes access control at the network level and intrusion detection.

### OBJECTIVES

- Obtain an overview of the security challenges specific to networks and understand how network security contributes to and depends on computer security.
- Get an introduction to the design of network security protocols, using the basic Internet security protocols IPsec and SSL/TLS as examples.
- See how network boundaries can serve as security perimeters.
- Understand the principles and limitations of firewalls and Intrusion Detection Systems.

## 13.1  INTRODUCTION

Computer networks are the communications infrastructure for transmitting data between nodes in a distributed system. Data to be sent by an application in one node has to be prepared for transport, transmitted as a sequence of electronic or optical signals and reassembled and presented to an application program at the receiver's end. Network protocols have to find a route from sender to receiver, deal with the loss or corruption of data and also with the loss of connections, e.g. when builders cut through a telephone cable. It is good engineering practice to address these concerns one at a time and use a layered architecture, with application protocols at the top and protocols that physically transmit encoded information at the bottom.

The ISO/OSI security architecture (International Organization for Standardization, 1989) defines *security services* to combat network security threats. Security services are implemented by *security mechanisms*. The mechanisms providing these services mostly come from cryptography. Typical examples are encryption, digital signatures and integrity check functions. Cryptographic protection has a nice property: a secure protocol in layer $N$ will not be compromised when it is run on top of insecure protocols at the layers below. There is one exception to this rule. When your goal is anonymity and you take precautions to hide the identities of participants in one layer, then the data added by lower layer protocols may still reveal information about the source and destination of messages.

However, not all network security problems can be solved using cryptography. Further defenses are access control mechanisms (firewalls) and intrusion detection systems. The design of protocols that are resilient to denial-of-service attacks or do not amplify such attacks is yet another concern in network security.

### 13.1.1  Threat Models

Attackers on a network can be *passive* or *active*. A passive attacker just listens to traffic. When the attacker is interested in the content of messages, we talk about *eavesdropping*, *wiretapping* or *sniffing*. *Traffic analysis* tries to identify communications patterns and may be possible even when the attacker cannot read individual messages. An attacker might try to identify messages coming from the same source (linkability) or find out who is talking to whom, and how often. In mobile services, the attacker might also be interested in a user's location.

An active attacker may modify messages, insert new messages or corrupt network management information like the mapping between Domain Name System (DNS) names and Internet Protocol (IP) addresses. In *spoofing attacks* messages come with forged sender addresses. In *flooding* (*bombing*) attacks a large number of messages is directed at the victim. In *squatting* attacks, the attacker claims to be at the victim's location. Active attacks are not necessarily more difficult to mount than passive attacks. For example, in actual practice it is much easier to send an email with a forged sender address than to intercept an email intended for someone else.

An attacker may try to learn about the internal structure of your network and use this information to launch attacks. Information gleaned from network management protocols that collect diagnostics about the load and availability of nodes can become security sensitive. At the same time, these protocols are needed to use the network efficiently. By being overprotective, you can easily diminish the quality of services provided by the network.

### 13.1.2 Communication Models

The security protocols in Chapter 12 were described at an abstract level. Messages traveled directly between principals and we did not consider the precise nature of this exchange. The analysis of security protocols is often conducted in such a model. The Internet is represented as a cloud. Messages can be seen and modified by anyone bent on doing so. This view of the world is captured in formal models for protocol analysis that put the attacker in charge of all communications. To use a metaphor from the world of pen and paper, the sender writes a note on a piece of paper and drops it on the floor. Later, the receiver goes through his/her garbage bin to see what has arrived.

Such an abstract model is not necessarily the best model for addressing all security issues. In security analysis, we might assume a less powerful and potentially more realistic adversary. For example, we might take the view that the adversary is not in charge of the entire Internet and can only read those messages directly addressed to him/her, but can spoof arbitrary sender addresses. Section 13.1.3 gives an example of such a security analysis. In protocol design, we might find that entities in the network, like firewalls or Network Address Translators, get in the way of Alice and Bob running their protocol, and need special attention.

### 13.1.3 TCP Session Hijacking

To open a Transmission Control Protocol (TCP) session with a server $B$, a client machine $A$ initiates the following three-way handshake protocol.

$$
\begin{array}{lll}
1. & A \rightarrow B: & \text{SYN, ISSa} \\
2. & B \rightarrow A: & \text{SYN|ACK, ISSb, ACK(ISSa)} \\
3. & A \rightarrow B: & \text{ACK, ACK(ISSb)}
\end{array}
$$

SYN and ACK indicate that respective bits have been set. ISSa and ISSb are 32-bit sequence numbers. The acknowledgements are computed as ACK(ISSa) = ISSa + 1 and ACK(ISSb) = ISSb + 1.

Assume that messages are always delivered to the intended recipients and cannot be observed in transit. The only action an attacker can take is to insert bogus source addresses in its own messages. This protocol is then secure as long as the sequence numbers are reasonably random. To impersonate another party, the attacker has to guess the sequence number sent to that party. Hence, RFC 793 specifies that the 32-bit counter be incremented by one in the low-order position about every four microseconds. However, Berkeley-derived Unix kernels increment it by 128 every second, and by 64 for each new connection. There is not too much randomness left to confound an attacker.

The attack made possible by this implementation decision was described as early as 1985 (Morris, 1985) and was later generalized (Bellovin, 1989). The attacker $C$ first opens a genuine connection to its target $B$ and receives a sequence number ISSb. The attacker then impersonates $A$, sending a packet with $A$'s address in the source field,

$$C(A) \rightarrow B: \text{SYN, ISSc.}$$

$B$ replies with

$$B \rightarrow A: \text{SYN|ACK, ISSb', ACK(ISSc)}$$

to the legitimate $A$. $C$ does not see this message but uses ISSb to predict the current value ISSb' and sends

$$C(A) \rightarrow B: \text{ACK, ACK(ISSb').}$$

If the guess is right $B$ assumes that it has a connection with $A$, when in fact $C$ is sending the packets. $C$ cannot see the output from this session, but it may be able to execute commands with $A$'s privileges on the server $B$. This attack could be run in a Unix environment where the attacker spoofs messages from a trusted host $A$ (section 6.7.2). Protocols such as *rsh* are vulnerable as they employ address-based authentication, assuming that users logging in from a trusted host have already been authenticated.

To defend against this attack, a firewall could block all TCP packets arriving from the Internet with a local source address. This scheme works if all your trusted hosts are on the local network. If trusted hosts also exist in the Internet, the firewall has to block all protocols that use TCP and address-based authentication. As a better solution, you could avoid address-based authentication entirely. Cryptographic authentication is much more preferable.

### 13.1.4 TCP SYN Flooding Attacks

After responding to the first SYN packet, the server $B$ stores the sequence number ISSb so that it can verify the ACK from the client. In a TCP SYN flooding attack, the attacker initiates a large number of TCP open requests (SYN packets) to $B$ without completing the protocol runs, until $B$ reaches its half-open-connection limit and cannot respond to any new incoming requests. Modifications of the TCP handshake protocol that allow the server to remain stateless are left as an exercise. As part of a TCP session hijacking attack, $C$ could launch a SYN flooding attack against $A$ so that $A$ does not process the SYN-ACK packet from $B$ and would not tear down the connection the attacker wants to open.

# 13.2 PROTOCOL DESIGN PRINCIPLES

The seven layer model of the ISO/OSI architecture (Figure 13.1) is a familiar framework for layering network protocols. Layered models provide a useful abstraction for discussing network security. Layered models also return us to a topic familiar from section 2.4.2. Security services at the top can be tailored to a specific application. However, different applications each need their own security protocols. Security services at the bottom can protect traffic from all higher layers, relieving application protocol designers from security concerns. However, some applications may find that this protection does not meet their requirements too well.

| application |
| --- |
| presentation |
| session |
| transport |
| network |
| link |
| physical |

○ **Figure 13.1: The ISO/OSI Seven Layer Model**

In a layered model, *peer entities* in a layer $N$ communicate using an $(N)$-protocol. Protocols at layer $N + 1$ see a virtual connection at layer $N$ and need not consider aspects of any lower layer (Figure 13.2). Of course, the $(N)$-protocol builds on protocols from lower layers. There exists a general pattern for passing data to the lower layers. Messages in the $(N)$-protocol are called $(N)$-*protocol data units (PDUs)*. The $(N)$-protocol transmits an $(N)$-PDU by invoking *facilities* at layer $N - 1$. At this stage, the $(N)$-PDU may be fragmented and otherwise processed. The results are then equipped with headers and trailers to become $(N - 1)$-PDUs. The recipient of these $(N - 1)$-PDUs uses information

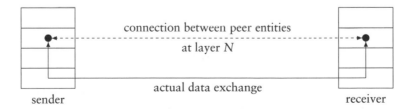

○ **Figure 13.2: Virtual Connection at Layer $N$**

○ **Figure 13.3: Processing an** $(N)$**-PDU**

from the headers and trailers to reassemble the $(N)$-PDU. Figure 13.3 gives a simplified view of this process.

There are two principal options for implementing security services at layer $N - 1$ that are called by an $(N)$-protocol. The upper-layer protocol can be *aware* of the security services at the lower layer or the security services could be *transparent*. In the first case, the upper-layer protocol has to change its calls so that they refer to the security facilities provided. In the second case, the upper-layer protocol does not have to change at all. In both cases, the headers in the $(N - 1)$-PDU are a convenient location for storing security-relevant data.

The Internet protocol stack has four layers (Figure 13.4). Protocols at the application layer are *telnet, ftp, http, smtp* (Simple Mail Transfer Protocol) or SET (Secure Electronic Transaction). The protocols at the transport layer are TCP (Transmission Control Protocol) and UDP (User Datagram Protocol). At the Internet layer, there is the Internet Protocol (IP). TCP and UDP use *port numbers* to indicate the application protocol a PDU belongs to. Common port numbers are 21 (*ftp*), 23 (*telnet*), 25 (*smtp*, sending email), 110 (*pop3*, collecting email), 143 (*imap*, collecting email), 80 (*http*), 443 (*https*, secure web pages) or 53 (DNS, name lookups). The protocols at the link (and physical) layer are specific to the network technology.

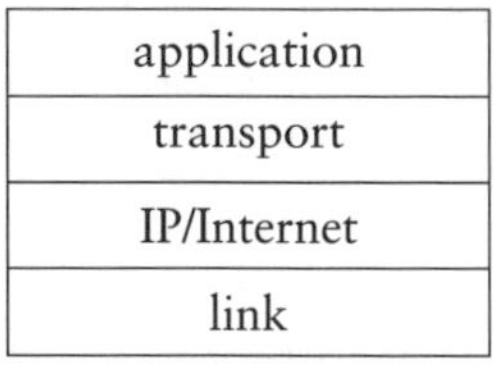

| application |
| --- |
| transport |
| IP/Internet |
| link |

○ **Figure 13.4: The Internet Layers**

TCP and IP are at the heart of the Internet, together with UDP and the management protocol ICMP. Originally, these protocols were designed for friendly and cooperating users linked by an unreliable network, so security was no concern at all. Today, the use of TCP/IP is widespread and a strong demand for security has emerged. The Internet

Engineering Task Force (IETF) has standardized security protocols at the Internet and transport layers in RFCs (Requests for Comment). Within the IETF there are numerous ongoing activities regarding the revision of the existing security protocols and the development of new security protocols.

# 13.3 IP SECURITY

IP is a connectionless and stateless protocol that transmits IP packets (datagrams). These are the PDUs at the Internet layer. The core IP specification provides a best-effort service. IP is connectionless and stateless, so each datagram is treated as an independent entity, unrelated to any other IP datagram. There is no guaranteed delivery of packets, no mechanism for maintaining the order of packets and no security protection. IP version 4 was published as RFC 791 in 1981. Since then, the Internet has kept growing and, in consequence, IP had to be adapted to cope with new demands. IP version 6 (IPv6) is specified in RFC 1883. We will refer to this version when discussing IP security mechanisms.

The security architecture for IP (IPsec) is introduced in RFC 2401. IPsec is optional for IPv4 and mandatory for IPv6. IPsec includes two major security mechanisms, the IP Authentication Header (AH) described in RFC 2402 and the IP Encapsulating Security Payload (ESP), covered in RFC 2406. The IP security architecture does not include mechanisms to prevent traffic analysis.

## 13.3.1 Authentication Header

The IP AH protects the integrity and authenticity of IP packets but does not protect confidentiality. It was introduced primarily for political reasons. In the 1990s, export restrictions on encryption algorithms created the case for an authentication-only mechanism. These export restrictions have been lifted by and large and it is now recommended to use ESP only, to simplify implementations of IPsec.

## 13.3.2 Encapsulating Security Payloads

ESP can be used to provide confidentiality, data origin authentication, data integrity, some replay protection and limited traffic flow confidentiality. An ESP packet (Figure 13.5) contains the following fields.

- Security Parameters Index (SPI) is a 32-bit field, uniquely identifying the *security association* for the datagram together with the destination IP address and the security protocol (ESP).

- Sequence Number is an unsigned 32-bit field containing a monotonically increasing counter value; this value must be included by the sender but is processed at the receiver's discretion.

- Payload Data is a variable-length field containing the transport layer PDU.

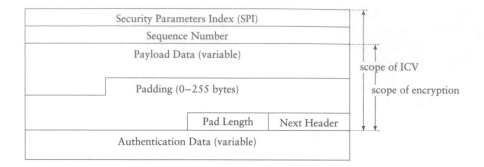

Figure 13.5: ESP Packet

- Padding is an optional field containing padding data for the encryption algorithm; the length of the data to be encrypted has to be a multiple of the algorithm's block size.

- Pad Length.

- Next Header is the type of the transport layer PDU.

- Authentication Data is a variable number of 32-bit words containing an Integrity Check Value (ICV) computed over the ESP packet minus the Authentication Data.

SPI and the sequence number constitute the ESP header. The fields after the payload are the ESP trailer. ESP can be used in two modes. In *transport mode* (Figure 13.6), an upper-layer protocol frame, e.g., from TCP or UDP, is encapsulated within the ESP. The IP header is not encrypted. Transport mode provides end-to-end protection of packets exchanged between two end hosts. Both nodes have to be IPsec aware.

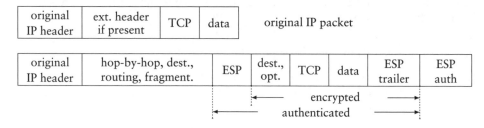

Figure 13.6: Applying ESP to IPv6 Packet, Transport Mode

In *tunnel mode* (Figure 13.7) an entire datagram plus security fields is treated as a new payload of an outer IP datagram. The original inner IP datagram is encapsulated within the outer IP datagram. IP tunneling can therefore be described as IP within IP. This mode can be used when IPsec processing is performed at security gateways on behalf of end hosts. The end hosts need not be IPsec aware. The gateway could be a perimeter firewall

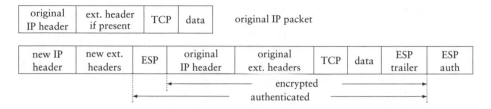

| original IP header | ext. header if present | TCP | data | original IP packet |
|---|---|---|---|---|

| new IP header | new ext. headers | ESP | original IP header | original ext. headers | TCP | data | ESP trailer | ESP auth |
|---|---|---|---|---|---|---|---|---|

encrypted

authenticated

○ **Figure 13.7: Applying ESP to IPv6 Packet, Tunnel Mode**

or a router. This mode provides gateway-to-gateway security rather than end-to-end security. On the other hand, we get traffic flow confidentiality as the inner IP datagram is not visible to intermediate routers and the original source and destination addresses are hidden.

### 13.3.3 Security Associations

To generate, decrypt or verify an ESP packet a system has to know which algorithm and which key (plus initialization vector) to use. This information is stored in a Security Association (SA; RFC 2401). The SA is the common state between two hosts for communication in one direction. Bidirectional communication between two hosts requires two security associations, one in each direction. Therefore, SAs are usually created in pairs.

An SA is uniquely identified by an SPI (carried in AH and ESP headers), an IP Destination Address, and a security protocol (AH or ESP) identifier. It contains the relevant cryptographic data like algorithm identifiers, keys, key lifetimes and possibly IVs. There can be a sequence number counter and an anti-replay window. The SA also tells whether tunnel mode or transport mode is employed. The list of active SAs is held in the SA database (SAD). SAs can be combined, e.g. for multiple levels of nesting of IPsec tunnels. Each tunnel can begin and end at different IPsec gateways along the route. Figure 13.8 shows a typical configuration where a remote host has security associations with a gateway and with an internal host.

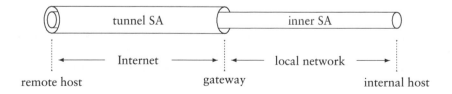

○ **Figure 13.8: Combining SAs**

### 13.3.4 Internet Key Exchange Protocol

SAs could be created manually. This works if the number of nodes is small but does not scale to reasonably sized networks of IPsec-aware hosts. The alternative to manual keying is IKE, the Internet Key Exchange protocol (RFC 2409). A new version, IKEv2, is under development. The security goals are entity authentication and the establishment of a fresh, shared secret. The shared secret is used to derive further keys. The goals further include the secure negotiation of all cryptographic algorithms, e.g. authentication method, key exchange method, algorithms for encryption and MAC, or hash algorithms. A so-called cookie mechanism (not to be confused with *http* cookies) is used to raise resistance to denial-of-service attacks. There are options for perfect forward secrecy, deniable authentication and identity protection.

IPsec provides a flexible set of key establishment methods with many options and parameters. Some might say, too many. IPsec needs large numbers of symmetric keys. There is one key for each SA and there are different SAs for each combination from

$$\{ESP, AH\} \times \{tunnel, transport\} \times \{sender, receiver\}.$$

IKE operates in two phases. Phase 1 sets up an SA as a secure channel to carry further SA negotiation, as well as error and management traffic. This phase involves heavy-duty entity authentication and key exchange. The phase 1 protocol has two variants, a slow *main mode* (six messages) with more security guarantees, and a faster *aggressive mode* (four messages). Main mode and aggressive mode each give the choice of multiple authentication mechanisms. Authentication based on signatures and preshared (symmetric) keys is deployed in practice. Authentication based on public key encryption and revised public key encryption is part of the specification but not of practical relevance. In phase 2, SAs for general use are negotiated. Fast negotiations take place over the secure channel established in phase 1. Many phase 2 runs are allowed for each run of phase 1, and multiple pairs of SAs can be negotiated per run.

IPsec specifies authentication and encryption services independently of the key management protocols that set up the SAs and session keys. Thus, IPsec security services are not tied to any particular key management protocol. If a key management protocol were found to be flawed, this protocol could be replaced without further repercussions on IPsec implementations.

### 13.3.5 IPsec Policies

IPsec policies determine the security processing that should be applied to an IP datagram. IPsec-aware hosts have a Security Policy Database (SPD). The SPD is consulted for each outbound and inbound datagram. The fields in the IP datagram are matched against fields in SPD entries. Matches can be based on source and destination addresses (and ranges of addresses), transport layer protocol, port numbers, etc. A match identifies an SA or a group of SAs (or the need for a new SA). Managing IPsec policy and deployments is complex and an ongoing area of research.

### 13.3.6 Summary

IPsec provides transparent security for everyone using IP, without changing the interface to IP. Upper-layer protocols need not be re-engineered to invoke security and need not even be aware that their traffic is protected at the IP layer (Figure 13.9). However, there is not much scope for tuning the level of protection to the requirements of the application. IP has to be concerned about its performance as a communications protocol and cannot spend much time on checking application-specific data to pick an SA. IPsec provides host-to-host security, but not user-to-user or application-to-application security.

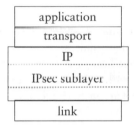

○ **Figure 13.9: IP Security**

IPsec increases protocol processing costs and communications latency as sender and receiver perform cryptographic operations. IPsec may provide security for all upper-layer protocols, but it also creates overheads for all. IPsec does not prescribe a particular key management protocol. This allows different nodes to pick their favorite scheme, but different nodes have to agree on a scheme before they can use IPsec to protect the traffic between them.

## 13.4 SSL/TLS

The TCP protocol provides a reliable byte stream between two nodes. TCP is a stateful connection-oriented protocol that detects when packets are lost, when packets arrive out of order, and discards repeated data. TCP performs address-based entity authentication when establishing a session between two nodes, but has chosen a rather vulnerable implementation of this protocol as highlighted in section 13.1.3. TCP lacks strong cryptographic entity authentication, data integrity or confidentiality. These services were introduced in the *Secure Socket Layer (SSL)* protocol developed by Netscape, mainly to protect World Wide Web traffic. RFC 2246 on the *Transport Layer Security Protocol* (TLS v1.0) is by and large identical with SSL version 3 (SSLv3) so the protocol has become known as SSL/TLS. RFC 3268 defines AES-based cipher suites for TLS.

Within the Internet protocol stack, SSL sits between the application layer and TCP (Figure 13.10). Hence, SSL can rely on the properties guaranteed by TCP and, for example, need not concern itself with the reliable delivery of data. Like TCP, SSL is

| application |
|:---:|
| SSL |
| TCP |
| IP |
| link |

Figure 13.10: The SSL Security Layer

stateful and connection oriented. The SSL *session state* contains information required for the execution of cryptographic algorithms, such as a session identifier, the specification of the cipher suite, shared secret keys, certificates, random values used by protocols such as Diffie–Hellman (section 12.3.2) etc. To contain the overheads caused by key management, one SSL session can include multiple connections. The characteristic example is an *http* 1.0 session between a client and a server, where a new connection is made to transfer each part of a composite document. Only a subset of the state information has to change for each connection.

SSL has two components, the *SSL Record Layer* and the *SSL Handshake Layer*. The SSL Record Layer takes blocks from an upper-layer protocol, fragments these blocks into *SSL Plaintext records*, and then applies the cryptographic transformation defined by the *cipher spec* in the current session state. Essentially, the SSL Record Layer provides a service similar to IPsec, and the parallels between the IPsec SAs and the SSL state are by no means accidental.

The *SSL Handshake Protocol* sets up the cryptographic parameters of the session state. Figure 13.11 shows the messages exchanged between client and server. Components in brackets are optional. To illustrate this protocol, we will step through a run where the client authenticates the server. The client initiates the protocol run with a *ClientHello* message, containing a random number, a list of suggested ciphers, ordered according to the client's preference, and a suggested compression algorithm.

| M1: | ClientHello: | ClientRandom[28] |
|---|---|---|
| | | Suggested Cipher Suites: |
| | | TLS_RSA_WITH_IDEA_CBC_SHA |
| | | TLS_RSA_WITH_3DES_EDE_CBC_SHA |
| | | TLS_DH_DSS_WITH_AES_128_CBC_SHA |
| | | Suggested Compression Algorithm: NONE |

The server selects the cipher TLS_RSA_WITH_3DES_EDE_CBC_SHA from the suggested suite. RSA will be used for key exchange, triple DES in CBC mode for encryption, and SHA as the hash function. The server replies with a *ServerHello* message and a certificate chain.

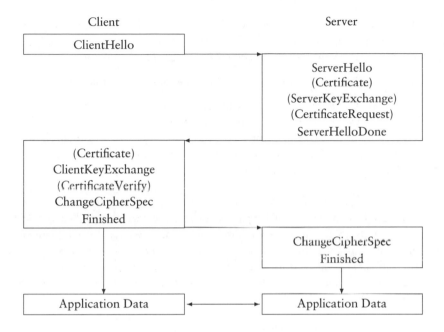

◯  **Figure 13.11: The SSL Handshake Protocol**

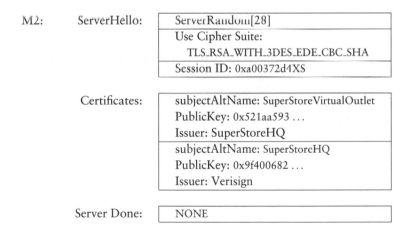

In our example, no certificate is requested from the client. The client verifies the certificate chain referring to the *subject alternative name* extensions in the certificates and then locally creates a random 48-byte *PreMasterSecret*. The *MasterSecret* is the first 48 bytes of

PRF(PreMasterSecret, "master secret", ClientRandom || ServerRandom).

Here, PRF is shorthand for a more complex function based on MD5 and SHA that takes as inputs a secret, a label and a seed. (The symbol || denotes concatenation). The *MasterSecret* serves as input to the construction of a *key block* of the form

PRF(MasterSecret, "key expansion", ClientRandom || ServerRandom).

All required MAC and encryption keys for client and server are extracted from the key block. The keys protecting traffic from client to server are different from the keys protecting traffic from server to client. Thus, the parties can easily distinguish between messages they send and messages they receive and they are not subject to *reflection attacks* where a message is replayed to its sender.

The client now transmits the *PreMasterSecret* to the server, using the key management algorithm specified in the selected cipher suite and the server's certified public key. (The client should then immediately destroy the *PreMasterSecret*. In our example, the algorithm is RSA and the public key is 0x521aa593 ... . The ChangeCipherSpec message indicates that subsequent records will be protected under the newly negotiated cipher suite and keys. The client then ties the third message to the first two through two hashes constructed with MD5 and SHA.

| M3: | A: ClientKeyExchange: | RSA_Encrypt( ServerPublicKey,PreMasterSecret) |
| | B: ChangeCipherSpec: | NONE |
| | C: Finished | MD5(M1 \|\| M2 \|\| M3A) SHA(M1 \|\| M2 \|\| M3A) |

The server decrypts the *PremasterSecret* and computes from it the *MasterSecret*, the *key block*, and all derived secret keys valid for this session with the client. The server verifies the hash appended to the client's message and replies with:

| M4: | A: ChangeCipherSpec: | NONE |
| | B: Finished | MD5(M1 \|\| M2 \|\| M3A \|\| M3C) SHA(M1 \|\| M2 \|\| M3A \|\| M3C) |

The client verifies the hash in the server's message. Both parties have now established shared secret keys which they can use to protect application traffic.

### 13.4.1 Summary

SSL/TLS includes a handshake protocol whereby client and server agree on a cipher suite, establish the necessary keying material, and authenticate each other. Today, SSL is the most widely used Internet security protocol, supported by all the major web browsers. SSL adds a security layer between application protocols and TCP, so applications explicitly have to ask for security. Thus, application code has to be changed, but the required changes are not much more than edit operations, for example replacing a TCP connect call in the pre-SSL application with an SSL-connect call. The SSL-connect call will initialize the cryptographic state parameters and make the original TCP connect call.

Client and server have to protect the parameters of the security contexts (or IPsec SAs) they have established. Otherwise, the security provided by SSL (or IPsec) will be compromised. We are once more turned back to computer security.

**Lesson**

Cryptographic protection cannot be compromised from the layer below in the communications network. It can very much be compromised from the layer below in the operating system of a network node.

## 13.5 DNS

Applications often know entities by their DNS (Domain Name System) names. For communications, we need the IP address currently corresponding to the DNS name. This information is maintained by DNS name servers. A DNS lookup gives the IP address for a DNS name. A reverse lookup gives the DNS name corresponding to an IP address. An attacker managing to corrupt this information could then misdirect other users to fake sites, make some sites appear to be unavailable and create more mayhem. The problems are exacerbated if other name servers update their caches with corrupted entries.

The original DNS lookup protocol uses quite a simple method for spoofing prevention. Work on a secure DNS service (DNSSEC) is underway. The security issues surrounding DNS are an instance of problems encountered in general whenever different types of identifiers have to be linked.

## 13.6 FIREWALLS

Cryptographic mechanisms protect the confidentiality and integrity of data in transit. Authentication protocols verify the source of data. To control which traffic is allowed to enter our system (ingress filtering) or to leave our system (egress filtering) we may deploy a *firewall*.

   **Firewall**   A network security device controlling traffic flow between two parts of a network.

Firewalls are often installed between the network of an entire organization and the Internet, but they could also be installed in an intranet to protect individual departments. For example, a company could put a firewall between the subnet of its R&D department and the main company network.

Firewalls should control network traffic to and from the protected network, but all traffic has to go through the firewall for protection to be effective. Dial-in lines and wireless

LANs are notorious examples of alternative (unprotected) entry points into the network behind the firewall. A firewall can allow or block access to services, authenticate users or machines before allowing access to services, and monitor the traffic in and out of the network. Firewalls became popular in the early 1990s, a time when end hosts were often PCs that could not defend themselves at all. Then, it made sense to centralize security enforcement at the network boundary.

Firewalls defend a protected network against parties who try to access services that should only be available internally from outside the network. They can also restrict access from inside to external services that are deemed dangerous or unnecessary for the work of an organization. A firewall can decide to route sensitive traffic via a *Virtual Private Network* (VPN). A VPN establishes a secure connection between the gateways of subnets of an organization that are not directly connected. All traffic between the subnets has to go through these gateways where cryptographic protection is added to extend the security perimeter. A firewall can also perform Network Address Translation (NAT; RFC 3022), hiding internal machines with private addresses behind public IP addresses, and translating public addresses to private addresses for internal servers.

At each network layer we can find parameters that could be used for access control decisions. At OSI layer 3 we have source and destination IP addresses. At OSI layer 4 we have TCP and UDP port numbers. Most firewalls assume that the port number defines the service but this is not always true. At OSI layer 7 there is information related to various applications: email addresses, email contents, web requests, executable files, viruses and worms, images, usernames and passwords, to name just a few. In general, machines on the boundary of a network can be used to control access to the network, add cryptographic protection to data leaving the network, or hide the internal structure of the network.

### 13.6.1 Packet Filters

Packet filters work at OSI layers 3 and 4. Rules specifying which packets are allowed through the firewall and which are dropped are applied to packets individually. Typical rules specify source and destination IP addresses, and source/destination TCP and UDP port numbers. Rules for traffic in both directions can be defined. Such a firewall can be implemented by a TCP/IP packet filtering router which examines the TCP/IP headers of every packet going through and can drop packets.

Only crude rules can be enforced and certain common protocols are difficult to handle. For example, when a client sends an *ftp* request to an *ftp* server, the firewall cannot link the data packets coming back from the server to this request. We can have blanket rules for all packets coming in on port 20, or all packets on port 20 from IP addresses nominated in advance, but we cannot have dynamically defined rules.

## 13.6.2 Stateful Packet Filters

Stateful (dynamic) packet filters understand requests and replies. For example, they would know about the (SYN, SYN-ACK, ACK)-pattern of a TCP open sequence. Rules are usually only specified for the first packet in one direction and state is created after the first outbound packet. Further packets in the communication are then processed automatically. Stateful firewalls can support policies for a wider range of protocols than simple packet filters, e.g. *ftp*, IRC or H323.

Packet filtering can be done by routers, giving high performance at lower cost. Moreover, it is easier to configure securely platforms that offer only limited functionality. Linux systems use *iptables* as the data structure for defining packet filtering rulesets. The filtering policies that can be enforced are limited by the parameters that can be observed in the TCP and IP headers, but can be specified more easily.

## 13.6.3 Circuit-level Proxies

Circuit-level proxies have rules similar to packet filters but do not route packets. Rules determine which connections are allowed and which will be blocked. Allowed connections generate a new connection from firewall to destination. This type of firewall is mentioned here for completeness, as it is rarely used in practice anymore. The functionality is similar to that of stateful packet filters but the performance is lower.

## 13.6.4 Application-level Proxies

For each application protocol the firewall can police, a proxy implements the server and client parts of the protocol on the firewall. When a client connects to the firewall, the proxy at the firewall acts as the server and validates the request. Proxies are another instance of *controlled invocation*. A mail proxy, for example, could filter out viruses, worms and spam. If the client request is allowed, the proxy acts as a client and connects to the destination server. Responses come back through the firewall and are again processed and checked by the proxy. The proxy server is the only entity seen by the outside world and it appears transparent to the internal users except for filtering, e.g. removing email attachments.

Application-level proxies would typically run on a hardened PC. Application proxies can provide close control over the content of incoming and outgoing traffic. In this respect, application-level proxies are offering a high level of security, provided the configuration is appropriate. On the downside, the amount of processing per connection is large and configuration is more complicated. In this respect, application-level proxies are less secure, and security vulnerabilities in firewall products have been reported. Performance is lower and cost is higher compared to packet filters. Moreover, you need a proxy server for each service you want to protect. Therefore, this approach does not scale too easily with the growing number of Internet services on offer.

The actions of packet filters have been compared to telephone call barring by number. They block calls to certain numbers, e.g. to premium rate numbers. In contrast, application-level proxies are like telephone call monitoring by listening to the conversations.

### 13.6.5  Firewall Policies

*Permissive* policies allow all traffic but block certain dangerous services, like *telnet* or *snmp*, or port numbers known to be used by an attack. It is easy to make mistakes. If you forget to block something you should, it is allowed, and might be exploited for some time without you realizing it. *Restrictive* policies block all traffic and allow only traffic known to meet a useful purpose, such as *http*, *pop3*, *smtp*, or SSH. This is the more secure option. If you block something that is needed, someone will complain and you can then allow the protocol. A policy is usually represented as an ACL with positive and negative entries. A typical firewall ruleset could look like this.

- Allow from internal network to Internet: *http*, *ftp*, SSH, DNS
- Allow from anywhere to Mail server: *smtp* only
- Allow from Mail server to Internet: *smtp*, DNS
- Allow from inside to Mail server: *smtp*, *pop3*
- Allow reply packets
- **Block everything else.**

Defining and managing rulesets is an important issue when deploying firewalls in practice.

### 13.6.6  Perimeter Networks

Where should a mail server be placed in relation to the firewall? A mail server requires external access to receive mail from outside, so it should be on the inside of the firewall. Only then can the firewall protect access to the mail server from outside. A mail server also requires internal access to receive mail from the internal network, so it should be outside of the firewall. You might want to stop worms and viruses spreading from your network or prevent confidential documents leaving your network. As a solution, you could create a perimeter network, also known as Demilitarized Zone (DMZ) for servers which require (selective) access from both inside and outside of the firewall (Figure 13.12). Besides mail servers, this would also be the place to put web servers and name servers.

### 13.6.7  Limitations and Problems

Firewalls do not protect against insider threats. Blocking services may create inconveniences for users. Network diagnostics may be harder. Some protocols are hard to support. Packet filtering firewalls do not provide any content-based filtering. If email is allowed through, then emails containing viruses are allowed through. Even application-proxy firewalls may not perform thorough checks on content. Firewalls do not know

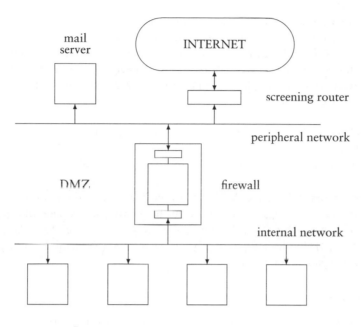

○ **Figure 13.12: Demilitarized Zone**

about operating system or application vulnerabilities. A lot of services are today using *http* at port 80 so it becomes increasingly difficult to decide which traffic on this port is legitimate.

Protocol tunneling, i.e. sending data for one protocol through another protocol, negates the purpose of a firewall. As more and more careful administrators block almost all ports but have to leave port 80 open, more and more protocols are tunneled through *http* to get through the firewall. Another candidate for tunneling is the SSH protocol.

Encrypted traffic cannot be examined and filtered, so protocols like *https* and SSH that provide end-to-end cryptographic protection cannot be monitored by the firewall. The alternative is to have proxies for this protocol in the firewall, but then we lose end-to-end security. These developments have led some to announce the near demise of firewalls as a component of security architectures and to predict that security services will move back from the network into the end hosts. *Personal firewalls* are moving access control on network traffic back to the end systems.

## 13.7 INTRUSION DETECTION

Cryptographic mechanisms and protocols are fielded to prevent attacks. Although it would be nice to prevent all attacks, in reality this is rarely possible. New types of attack occur, like denial-of-service attacks (where cryptography may make the problem worse). Perimeter security devices like firewalls mainly *prevent* attacks by outsiders. They may fail to do so. A firewall may be misconfigured, a password may be sniffed off the network, a new attack type may emerge. Moreover, these devices do not *detect* when an attack is underway or has taken place. For detecting network attacks, an Intrusion Detection System (IDS) can be fielded.

An IDS consists of a set of sensors gathering data, either located on the hosts or on the network. The sensor network is managed from a central console. There, data is analyzed, intrusions reported and, possibly, reactions triggered. There are two approaches for detecting intrusions, misuse detection and anomaly detection. The communications between sensors and console should be protected, as well as the storage of the signature database and of the logs generated. There should also be a secure scheme for getting signature updates from the IDS vendor. Otherwise, the IDS itself could be attacked and manipulated. There have already been incidents where vulnerabilities in IDS systems have been exploited for attacks.

### 13.7.1 Vulnerability Assessment

Vulnerability assessment examines the security state of a network. Information about open ports, software packages running (which version? patched?), network topology etc. is collected, and a prioritized list of vulnerabilities is compiled. Vulnerability assessment is only as good as the knowledge base being used, which has to be updated constantly to handle new threats. Several organizations track security vulnerabilities and lists of available patches. Good sources for this information are the Computer Emergency Response Teams (CERTs), e.g. the CERT at CMU (`http://www.cert.org/`), SANS (`http://www.sans.org/`) and Security Focus (`http://www.securityfocus.com/`) where the BugTraq archive is maintained, and the web sites of major software and hardware manufacturers.

### 13.7.2 Misuse Detection

Misuse detection looks for *attack signatures*. Attack signatures are patterns of network traffic or activities in log files that indicate suspicious behavior. Example signatures might include the number of recent failed login attempts on a sensitive host, a pattern of bits in an IP packet indicating a buffer overflow attack, or certain types of TCP SYN packets that indicate a SYN flooding attack. The IDS may also consult the security policy and a database of known vulnerabilities and attacks for the system monitored.

Again, these systems are only as good as the information in the database of attack signatures. New vulnerabilities are constantly being discovered and exploited. Vendors need to keep up to date with the latest attacks and issue database updates. The customers need to install the updates. The database of known vulnerabilities and exploitation methods can become large and unwieldy and may slow down the IDS. At the time of writing (2005), all commercial IDS products were based on misuse detection. These systems are also known as knowledge-based IDS.

### 13.7.3 Anomaly Detection

Statistical anomaly detection (or behavior-based detection) uses statistical techniques to detect potential intrusions. First, the 'normal' behavior is established as a baseline. During operation, a statistical analysis of the data monitored is performed and the deviation from the baseline is measured. If a threshold is exceeded, an alarm is issued. Such an IDS does not need to know about security vulnerabilities in a particular system. The baseline defines normality. So, there is a chance to detect novel attacks without having to update a knowledge base.

On the other hand, anomaly detection detects just anomalies. Suspicious behavior does not necessarily constitute an intrusion. A burst of failed login attempts at a sensitive host could be due to an attack or to the administrator having forgotten the password. Some interesting insights into this problem can be gleaned from Bejtlich (2000). Attacks are not necessarily anomalies. A careful attacker might just 'fly under the radar' of the IDS and remain undetected. This is particularly true when the baseline is adjusted dynamically and automatically. A patient attacker may be able to gradually shift 'normality' over time until his planned attack no longer generates an alarm. Thus, we have to be concerned about *false positives* (false alarms) when an attack is flagged although none is taking place, and *false negatives* when an attack is missed because it falls within the bounds of normal behavior.

### 13.7.4 Network-based IDS

A network-based IDS (NIDS) looks for attack signatures in network traffic. Typically, a network adapter running in promiscuous mode monitors and analyzes all traffic in real-time as it travels across the network. The attack recognition module uses network packets as the data source. There are three common techniques for recognizing attack signatures: pattern, expression or bytecode matching, frequency or threshold crossing (e.g. to detect port scanning activity), and correlation of lesser events (not much yet in commercial products). *Snort* is a popular NIDS developed in the open-source community.

### 13.7.5 Host-based IDS

A host-based IDS (HIDS) looks for attack signatures in log files of hosts. It can also verify the checksums of key system files and executables at regular intervals. Some products can use regular-expressions to refine attack signatures (e.g. passwd program executed AND .rhosts file changed). Some products listen to port activity and generate alerts when specific ports are accessed, providing limited NIDS capability. There is a trend towards host-based intrusion detection. The most effective IDSs combine NIDS and HIDS.

Due to the near real-time nature of IDS alerts, an IDS can be used as a response tool, but automated responses are not without dangers. An attacker might trick the IDS to respond, with the response aimed at an innocent target (say, by spoofing the source IP address). Users can be locked out of their accounts because of false positives. Repeated email notifications become a denial-of-service attack on the administrator's email account.

### 13.7.6 Honeypots

Honeypots are resources used to track attackers and to learn and gather evidence about hacker activities. They are designed to mimic real systems, but do not contain, and therefore reveal, real production data. By definition, every activity monitored on the honeypot is an attack.

> **Honeypot**   A honeypot is an information system resource whose value lies in unauthorized or illicit use of that resource (Spitzner, 2003).

Honeypots can engage in a session with an attacker at different levels of interaction. Low-interaction honeypots offer basic emulations of some services and of the operating system. There is not much an attacker can do on such a honeypot so there is a limit to the adversarial behavior the honeypot can log. Moreover, an attacker might quickly recognize the honeypot for what it is and walk away. There already exist tools for detecting honeypots. The more sophisticated the emulations become, the more types of behavior can be observed. High-interaction honeypots offer real services, with fake data. The more interactions are possible, the greater is the danger that an attacker can misuse the honeypot as a staging post for launching attacks against other machines.

## 13.8 FURTHER READING

This chapter could only give a brief sketch of the issues and techniques in network security. Network security is covered comprehensively by Ford (1994) and Stallings (2003), Internet security by Atkins *et al.* (1997). Good books on firewalls are by Cheswick, Bellovin and Rubin (2003) and Zwicky, Cooper and Chapman (1995). Technical issues that arise in network intrusion detection are discussed by Ptacek and Newsham (1998).

The best source for material on Internet security is of course the Internet. The web site of the Internet Engineering Task Force is `http://www.ietf.org`. Documents on IPsec can be found at `http://www.ietf.org/html.charters/ipsec-charter.html`. The IETF specifications are, like networking technology, continuously changing. This is very much the case for work on Internet security so you should not be disappointed if some aspects of IPsec or SSL/TLS have changed by the time you read this book.

# 13.9 EXERCISES

**Exercise 13.1** The ARP (Address Resolution Protocol) associates hardware addresses with IP addresses. This association may change over time. Each network node keeps an ARP cache of corresponding IP and hardware addresses. Cache entries expire after a few minutes. A node trying to find the hardware address for an IP address that is not in its cache broadcasts an ARP request that also contains its own IP and hardware address. The node with the requested IP address replies with its hardware address. All other nodes may ignore the request. How could ARP spoofing be performed? Which defences can be used against spoofing?

**Exercise 13.2** Develop a stateless implementation of the TCP handshake protocol that is not vulnerable to TCP SYN flooding attacks.

**Exercise 13.3** A client $A$ (`a.example.org`) wants to access a server $B$ known by its DNS name `b.example.com`. The client asks its local name server for $B$'s IP address. If the name server has not cached this information it queries the authoritative name server for $B$. The query includes a 16-bit sequence number. The local name server updates its cache if a reply with the correct sequence number is received. Other replies are discarded. Consider an attacker that simultaneously sends to $A$'s name server spoofed queries for $B$'s IP address and spoofed replies from $B$'s name server with a wrong address for $B$. How quickly will this attack succeed in tricking $A$'s name server into accepting a spoofed binding of $B$'s IP address? (Name servers can deal with many lookups in parallel.)

**Exercise 13.4** For IPsec and SSL, the nodes running the protocol are assumed to be secure. Which additional security mechanisms do you need at these nodes to make this assumption true?

**Exercise 13.5** Which security features do you expect from a secure email system, and from the machines running a secure email system? Which protocol layer is most appropriate for such a security service? In your answer, distinguish between services that want to offer anonymity and those that do not.

**Exercise 13.6** Examine the implications of tunneling IP through IP on the design of a packet filtering firewall.

**Exercise 13.7** The Internet is a source of virus infections. Firewalls protect the internal network from the outside. Can firewalls protect against virus infections? Consider the different types of firewall in your answer. How does cryptographic protection at the TCP/IP layer or at the application layer affect a firewall's ability to protect against viruses?

**Exercise 13.8** A company allows its employees to use laptops at home and when traveling. Propose a security architecture to protect the laptops, and the company's intranet.

# Chapter 14

## Software Security

Computer security makes the headlines when the latest *computer worm* causes havoc on the Internet or when a critical vulnerability in some widely used software product is discovered. Some attacks fool the user into clicking on an email attachment and thereby executing the attack code. Others target memory management flaws using a *buffer overrun* to manipulate the control flow at a layer below the programming abstractions used by the software developer. In both cases, the attacker is then able to run code with elevated privileges. The programming errors exploited are sometimes quite simple and it might seem a trivial task to eradicate these problems. In some instances, this assessment is true but implementing a complex system is a challenging task and there is a long history of security bugs in software systems.

In this chapter we will analyze the general causes of software vulnerabilities. Detailed instructions for developers on how to write secure code are beyond our scope. Books covering software security at that level are listed at the end of the chapter.

## OBJECTIVES

- Present the basic causes that lead to many software security failures.
- Discuss the dangers of broken abstractions.
- Convey a better understanding of the defenses available when designing software systems.
- Provide a taxonomy of malware.

## 14.1 INTRODUCTION

On a stand-alone machine, a personal computer in the true sense of the word, you are in control of the software components sending inputs to each other. On a machine connected to the Internet, hostile parties can provide input. Networking software is a popular target for attacks as it is built to receive external input and involves low-level manipulations of memory buffers. Software is secure if it can handle intentionally malformed input so that the integrity of the runtime system remains protected. Secure software is not the same as software with added security features.

### 14.1.1 Security and Reliability

Software security is related to software quality and software reliability, but there are important differences in focus. Reliability deals with accidental failures. Failures are assumed to occur according to some given probability distribution. Improvements in reliability can be calculated based on this distribution. To make software more reliable, it is tested against typical usage patterns: 'It does not matter how many bugs there are, it matters how often they are triggered'. In security the attacker picks the distribution of the inputs. Hence, traditional testing methods are not geared towards finding security bugs. To make software more secure, it has to be tested against atypical usage patterns (but there are typical attack patterns).

### 14.1.2 Malware Taxonomy

Software that has a malicious purpose is called malware. There are different types of malware and computer security has adopted anthropomorphic metaphors for their classification. A *computer virus* is a piece of self-replicating code attached to some other piece of code, with a *payload*. The payload can range from the nonexistent via the harmless, e.g. displaying a message or playing a tune, to the harmful like deleting and modifying files. A computer virus *infects* a program by inserting itself into the program code. A *worm* is a replicating but not infecting program. When the mass media report computer security incidents this distinction between worms and viruses is not always made and you might read about a virus attack when the code spreading around would be better described as a worm.

A *Trojan horse* is a program with hidden side effects that are not specified in the program documentation and are not intended by the user executing the program. A *logic bomb* is a program that is only executed when a specific trigger condition is met.

### 14.1.3 Hackers

Originally, a hacker was someone familiar with the intricate details of a computer system, able to use the system in a way beyond the grasp of ordinary users. Over time, the term hacker has acquired a negative connotation, describing a person who illicitly breaks into computer systems. There is still a distinction between *white hats* who use their skills to help software developers, and *black hats* who break into systems intent on creating mischief and damage. Observers of the Internet report an increased amount of plain criminal activity.

Many attacks exploit well-known security weaknesses (or design features) in an automated and efficient manner, rather than needing ingenuity and deep technical knowledge. Attackers that run attacks with tools acquired from someone else are known as *anklebiters* or *script kiddies*.

Experimenting with dangerous code at home may be an intellectual challenge but is fraught with danger. Anti-virus researchers have learned the importance of (physically) separating experimental from operational systems. Otherwise, there is the danger that code escapes out of the laboratory into the wild. Distributing code that performs actions on other people's machines is likely to bring you into conflict with the law. So, the usual warning applies: don't try this at home.

### 14.1.4 Change in Environment

Change is one of the biggest enemies of security. You may have a system that offers perfectly adequate security. You change a part of the system. You may be aware of the security implications of this change and still get it wrong. Even worse, you may feel that the change has nothing do with security only to wake up to an unpleasant surprise. There is a lot of folklore about the respective security of even and odd numbered versions of operating systems, observing a regular interchange between versions containing new features and versions patching the problems found in those new features.

## 14.2 CHARACTERS AND NUMBERS

Many software flaws are due to broken abstractions. Security-relevant problems of this kind can already be found with elementary concepts like characters and integers. The descriptions of these problems will refer to the way characters and integers are actually represented in memory. Hexadecimal values will be indicated by a prefix 0x or a prefix % (typically in a URL), reflecting the different conventions currently in use.

### 14.2.1 Characters (UTF-8 Encoding)

A software developer writes an application that should give users access to a specific subdirectory A/B/C only. Users enter a filename as input. The pathname to the file is constructed by the application as A/B/C/input. This attempt to constrain the users can be bypassed easily. An adversary could step up in the directory tree using ../ and access the password file by entering

../../../../../etc/passwd.

As a countermeasure, the developer performs some *input validation* and filters out the offending character combination '. . / '. However, this is not the end of the story.

The UTF-8 encoding of the Unicode character set (RFC 2259) was defined to use Unicode on systems that were designed for ASCII. ASCII characters (U0000-U007F) are represented by ASCII bytes (0x00-0x7F). All non-ASCII characters are represented by sequences of non-ASCII bytes (0x80-0xF7). The encoding rules are defined as follows:

```
U000000 - U00007F:  0xxxxxxx

U000080 - U0007FF:  110xxxxx 10xxxxxx

U000800 - U00FFFF:  1110xxxx 10xxxxxx 10xxxxxx

U010000 - U10FFFF:  11110xxx 10xxxxxx 10xxxxxx 10xxxxxx
```

The xxx bits are the least significant bits of the binary representation of the Unicode number. For example, the copyright sign U00A9 = 1010 1001 is encoded in UTF-8 as 11000010 10101001 = 0xC2 0xA9. Only the shortest possible UTF-8 sequence is valid for any Unicode character, but many UTF-8 decoders also accept the longer variants. When multibyte UTF-8 formats are accepted, a character gets more than one representation. Here are three ways of writing '/'.

|        | format    | binary    | hex |
|--------|-----------|-----------|-----|
| 1 byte | 0xxx xxxx | 0010 1111 | 2F  |
| 2 byte | 110x xxxx | 1100 0000 | C0  |
|        | 10xx xxxx | 1010 1111 | AF  |
| 3 byte | 1110 xxxx | 1110 0000 | E0  |
|        | 10xx xxxx | 1000 0000 | 80  |
|        | 10xx xxxx | 1010 1111 | AF  |

Once, there was a vulnerability in Microsoft's IIS, caused by the fact that illegal Unicode representations for single-byte characters were accepted but not checked for during input validation. A URL starting with

{IPaddress}/scripts/..%c0%af../winnt/system32/

got translated into the directory C:\winnt\system32 because %c0%af is the 2-byte UTF-8 encoding of /. Hence, ..%c0%af../ becomes ../../. There is a further twist to this story. Consider now the URL

{IPaddress}/scripts/..%25%32%66../winnt/system32/.

To see what happens when this URL is processed, write the sequence %25%32%66 in binary. You get 00100101 00110010 01100110, i.e. the ASCII characters %2f. The URL is thus decoded to IPaddress/scripts/..%2f../winnt/system32/. No problem yet, but if the URL is decoded a second time, %2f is read as / and the URL gets translated to the directory `C:\winnt\system32`. In a way, the act of observation changes the meaning of characters.

## 14.2.2 Integer Overflows

In mathematics, integers form an infinite set. On a computer system, integers are represented as binary strings of fixed length (*precision*), so there is only a finite number of 'integers'. Programming languages have signed and unsigned integers, short and long (and long long) integers. If the result of a computation gets too large for the chosen representation, a *carry overflow* occurs. In this case, the familiar rules for integer arithmetic no longer apply. For example, with unsigned 8-bit integers arithmetic operations are performed modulo 256 and we have $255 + 1 = 0$, $16 \times 17 = 16$, and $0 - 1 = 255$.

Signed integers are represented as 2's complement numbers. The most significant (leftmost) bit indicates the sign of the integer. If the sign bit is zero, the number is positive and is given in normal binary representation. If the sign bit is one, the number is negative. To calculate the 2's complement representation of $-n$:

- invert the binary representation of $n$ by changing all ones to zeros and all zeros to ones. For 8-bit integers, this step computes $255\text{-}n$;
- then add one to the intermediate result. For 8-bit integers, this step computes $255 - n + 1 = 256 - n$. The number 256 corresponds to the carry bit.

Thus, adding a negative 2's complement number to the positive number of the same magnitude gives indeed zero as the result. Computation with signed integers can again give unexpected results. For example, for signed 8-bit integers we have $127 + 1 = -128$ and $-128/-1 = -1$. When switching between signed and unsigned integers, a large positive value may become a negative value: $0\text{xFF} = 2^8 - 1$ (unsigned) $= -1$ (signed).

Conversion between integer representations can cause security problems. The following guard command compares a signed integer variable `size` to the result of `sizeof(buf)` that returns a result of data type `size_t`, i.e. an unsigned integer,

$$\text{if(size} < \text{sizeof(buf)).}$$

If `size` is negative and if the compiler casts the result of `sizeof(buf)` to a signed integer, the buffer can overflow. Integer truncation is another potential source of problems. Once, a Unix version had the following vulnerability. A program receiving a UID as input (given as a signed integer) first checked that UID≠0 to prevent root access. The UID was later truncated to an unsigned short integer. Input `0x10000` became `0x0000` (root!).

In mathematics, the axioms that define the integers imply results like $a + b \geq a$ if $b \geq 0$. With computer integers, such obvious 'facts' are no longer true. Such discrepancies between the abstract model and the actual implementation can lead to buffer overruns (section 14.4.1). Consider the following code snippet that copies two character strings into a buffer and checks that the combined length of the two strings (plus a terminating symbol) fit into the buffer.

```
char buf[128];
combine(char *s1, size_t len1, char *s2, size_t len2)
{
        if (len1 + len2 + 1 <= sizeof(buf)) {
        strncpy(buf, s1, len1);
        strncat(buf, s2, len2);
        }
}
```

On a 32-bit system, an attacker could construct s1 in such a way that len1 < sizeof(buf) and set len2 = 0xFFFFFFFF. Then strncat will be executed and the buffer will overrun as

$$len1 + 0xFFFFFFFF + 1 == len1 < sizeof(buf).$$

Computer integers do not implement the mathematical abstraction 'integers', but integers modulo $2^w$, where $w$ is the number of bits chosen for their representation. This break in abstraction can lead to programmers making mistakes of the kind just discussed.

> Many programmers appear to view integers as having arbitrary precision, rather than being fixed-sized quantities operated on with modulo arithmetic (Ashcraft and Engler, 2002).

### Lesson

Declare all integers as unsigned integers unless you really need negative numbers. If you are measuring the size of objects in memory, you don't need negative numbers. If your compiler flags a signed–unsigned mismatch, check whether you really need two different representations. If you do, pay attention to the checks you are implementing.

### 14.2.3 Arrays

Computing array indices uses integer arithmetic. If there is no check that the result of such a calculation does not exceed the length of the array, a memory location above the array will be accessed. (A typical beginner's mistake in introductory programming courses.) Wrap-around to lower addresses can occur when arithmetic operations give negative results or when the effects of modular addition are not considered by the programmer. When computing array indices, you therefore should check upper and lower bounds.

In the following example we assume an array of 4-byte elements and 32-bit addresses. The memory location of array elements is computed as

$$address\_element[index] = base\ of\ array + index \times size\ of\ element.$$

Let the array start at address `0x01720314` and let `0x0010FF08` be a memory location we want to overwrite. We first compute the difference between target address and base of array,

```
      0x10010FF08
-     0x001720314
      0x0FE9EFBF4
```

and divide the result by four to get the index `0x3FA7BEFD`, which is 1067958013 in decimal representation. If there are no checks on bounds for array indices, we could overwrite the target address by writing to the array in position 1067958013.

## 14.3 CANONICAL REPRESENTATIONS

Names (identities, identifiers) are a widely used abstraction. We give names to files and directories so that we can find them later. Network nodes have identifiers at the different levels of the protocol stack (DNS names, IP addresses, ... ). Names are also used in security decisions. A firewall may let traffic pass to and from certain nodes only. Security policies define which files a user may access. When an entity has more than one name or when names have equivalent representations, an attacker may try to bypass security controls by giving an alternative name that had not been considered when setting the security policy. Problems of this nature are encountered frequently. Filenames, URLs or IP addresses can all be written in more than one way.

- File name: `c:\x\data = c:\y\z\..\..\x\data = c:\y\z\%2e%2e\`
  `%2e%2e\x\data`
- Dotless IP: $a.b.c.d = a \cdot 2^{24} + b \cdot 2^{16} + c \cdot 2^{8} + d$
- Symbolic links: file name pointing to another file.

The problem this causes for security enforcement can be illustrated already at the level of colloquial English. The file-sharing service Napster had been ordered by court to block access to certain songs. Napster implemented a filter that blocked downloads based on the name of the song. Napster users bypassed this control by using variations of the name of songs. This is a particularly awkward problem because the users decide which names are equivalent.

Next, consider case-insensitive filenames. In this case, myfile and MyFile are equivalent names for the same file. Combine a filesystem with case-insensitive filenames with a security mechanism that uses case-sensitive filenames. (Something like this happened once involving the Apache web server and the HFS+ filesystem.) Assume that permissions are defined for one version of the name only, e.g. for MyFile. The attacker requests access to myfile, no restrictions are set, so the security mechanism grants the request and the filesystem gives access to the resource that should have been protected.

To address this problem, perform *canonicalization* before making access control decisions. Canonicalization is the process that resolves the various equivalent forms of a name to a single standard name. The single standard name is known as the *canonical name*. Canonicalization is relevant whenever an object has different but equivalent representations.

### Lesson

Do not rely on the names received as user input, convert them–correctly–to your standard representation. 'Do not trust your inputs' is the battle cry of Howard and LeBlanc (2002). Use regular expressions to define and validate names and input values. Use full pathnames rather than systems that generate the full filename automatically. Preferably, do not make decisions based on names at the application level but use the operating system access controls.

## 14.4 MEMORY MANAGEMENT

Ancient cities and medieval castles had rings of protective walls to keep attackers out. To defeat these defenses, attackers tunneled under walls to make them collapse. Similarly, software developers may have designed impressive logical defenses. If the attacker can tunnel through to memory, the logical defenses are undermined from below. Flaws in memory management can open the cracks that let the attacker penetrate the system.

The programming languages C and C++ were designed to let the programmers perform their own memory management. There are situations where this feature is called for but it is now up to the developers to get memory management right. Languages like Java or C# take these tasks away from the developer, and thus remove a possible source of errors.

Figure 14.1 shows a typical memory configuration. The runtime *stack* using the highest memory addresses contains the stack frames of the processes currently on the call stack. A stack frame contains information like return address, local variables and function arguments. The stack grows downwards in memory. The *heap* starting from the lowest memory addresses (in user space) contains dynamically allocated buffers. The heap grows upwards in memory.

### 14.4.1 Buffer Overruns

In code written in a typical programming language values are stored in variables, arrays, etc. To execute a program, memory sections (buffers) are allocated to variables. If the value assigned to a variable exceeds the size of the buffer allocated, a *buffer overrun* (overflow) occurs and memory locations not allocated to this variable are overwritten. If the memory location overwritten had been allocated to some other variable, the value of

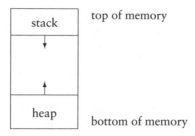

top of memory

bottom of memory

○ **Figure 14.1: Memory Configuration**

that other variable is changed. Unintentional buffer overruns can make software crash. Intentional buffer overruns are a concern if an attacker can modify security-relevant data by assigning a deliberately malformed value to some other variable. Attractive targets are return address (specifies the next piece of code to be executed) and security settings. Buffer overruns have been the source of security vulnerabilities for some time. We give two historic examples to make our case.

### 14.4.2 VMS Login

One version of Digital's VMS operating system had a bug in the login procedure. Users could specify the device they wanted to log in to by giving their username as

username/DEVICE =<machine>

In one version of the operating system the length of the argument *machine* was not checked. A device name of more than 132 bytes overwrote the privilege mask of the process started by login. Users thus could set their own privileges by giving an appropriate 'machine name'.

### 14.4.3 A Finger Bug

The second example is the Internet worm of 1988. Amongst other vulnerabilities, the worm exploited a buffer overrun in the *fingerd* daemon to break into VAX systems running Unix 4BSD. A special 536-bit long message to the *fingerd* was used to overwrite the system stack:

```
pushl   $68732f         push '/sh,<NUL>'
pushl   $6e69622f       push '/bin'
movl    sp, r10         save address of start of string
pushl   $0              push 0 (arg 3 to execve)
pushl   $0              push 0 (arg 2 to execve)
pushl   r10             push string addr (arg 1 to execve)
pushl   $3              push argument count
movl    sp, ap          set argument pointer
chmk    $3b             do "execve" kernel call
```

The stack has now been set up so that the command `execve("/bin/sh",0,0)` will be executed on return to the *main* routine, opening a connection to a remote shell via TCP (Spafford, 1989).

### 14.4.4 Stack Overruns

Buffer overrun attacks on the call stack are known as stack overruns. To demonstrate the basic principle of such an attack, Figure 14.2 (left) gives an outline of the frame that would be pushed on the stack when the function `void function(int a, int b, int c)` with local variables $x$ and $y$ has been called. First come the input values in reverse order, followed by the return address and the saved frame pointer, pointing to the top of the previous stack frame. Finally, buffers for any local variables defined within the function are allocated. (The precise layout of a stack frame is operating system specific.)

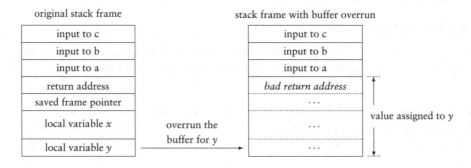

Figure 14.2: Stack Smashing Attack

Assume that there are no checks within the function on the size of the value assigned to $y$. An attacker could then assign a value to $y$ that overruns the buffer allocated to $y$, overwriting memory locations above $y$. Specifically, an attacker can overwrite the return address with the start address of the attacker's code (Figure 14.2). The attacker's code would then run with the privileges of the current process. Note that this attack would not be possible if the stack grew upwards from the bottom of memory.

The final task for the attacker is to find a way of getting the attack code into the system. A simple method is to send the code to one of the input variables so that it gets stored on the stack. When the attacker cannot predict precisely where the input variable and thus the attack code will be placed, a *landing pad* of NOP (no operation) instructions at the start of the code can compensate for variations in the location the code will be found in.

### 14.4.5 Nonexecutable Stacks and Canaries

Generic defenses against buffer overruns will be discussed in section 14.7. Here, we mention only two stack-specific defenses. Architectures with a *nonexecutable stack* stop attack code from being placed on the stack. Code does not have to be recompiled, but existing software that requires an executable stack will work no longer.

Attempts at changing the return address might be detected by placing a (random) check value as a *canary*[1] in the memory position just below the return address (Cowan *et al.*, 1998). Before returning, the system checks that the canary still has the correct value (Figure 14.3). To make use of this technique, code has to be recompiled so that the insertion and subsequent check of the canary are added to the object code.

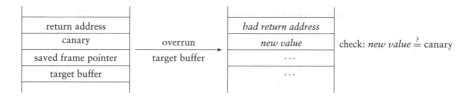

**Figure 14.3: Canary Indicating an Attempted Buffer Overflow Attack on the Stack**

### 14.4.6 Heap Overruns

Because of the prominence of attacks based on stack overflows, designers have invested more effort on protecting the stack than on protecting the heap. The heap is a memory area dynamically allocated by the application. Buffer overrun attacks on the heap are known as *heap overruns*. It is more difficult to determine how to overwrite a specific buffer on the heap, and to determine which other buffers will be overwritten in the process. If you are an attacker, you may not want to crash the system before you have taken over, but even attacks that do not succeed all the time are a threat to the defender.

To take control of execution, an attack has to overwrite some parameter that has influence on the control or data flow. Such parameters can also be found on the heap, for example pointers to (temporary) files and function pointers. Take a vulnerable program that defines a temporary file to write some data to. Create a buffer overrun that overwrites the pointer to the temporary file with a pointer to the target file, e.g. the password file. The program will now access the target file and the attacker can write to the target file. A function pointer `int (*funcptr)(char *str)` allows a

---

[1]Canaries were used in coal mines to detect gas leaks. The death of a canary was a warning for the miners to evacuate the pit.

programmer to dynamically modify a function to be called. On execution the function pointed to by the pointer will be called. When a buffer overrun overwrites the function pointer, a function defined by the attacker will be executed. Exploiting function pointers requires an executable heap.

The attack code could be passed as an argument to the program so that it gets placed on the stack. This method requires an executable stack. Alternatively, the attacker could guess the distance (offset) between the address of the target buffer that will be overrun and the location of the shellcode (/bin/sh) on the heap. This method works with an executable heap. There is a greater probability for the heap to be executable than the stack. Heap overruns were once thought to be of theoretical interest only, but they are occurring now in the wild.

### Lesson

Redirecting pointers is a great way of attacking systems.

### 14.4.7 Type Confusion

Programs written in a type safe (memory safe) language cannot access memory in inappropriate ways. A well-known example is the Java programming language. Each Java object is an instantiation of a class. Only certain operations are allowed to manipulate objects of a given class. The Java Virtual machine (JVM) keeps track of objects in memory by using pointers that are tagged with the class of the object. Static and dynamic type checking should prevent any access that violates the abstractions provided by objects and classes. Automatic garbage collection takes care of further memory management tasks.

A *type confusion* attack manipulates the pointer structure so that two pointers, one with a wrong class tag, point to the same object. Thus, this object can also be manipulated by parties that may access the 'wrong' type. Consider, for example, a trusted object $A$ of type $Tr$. When an attacker manages to have the pointer for some other untrusted object $X$ of type $Un$ point to the same buffer in memory, the trusted object $A$ can be modified as if it were of type $Un$ (Figure 14.4). Often (but not always) a type confusion attack can be extended to compromise the entire system and modify objects at will. Type confusion attacks are rare but they do occur. Sun Security Bulletin # 00218 (18 March 2002) warns of a problem in a JVM implementation. An attack on a mobile phone version of Java[2] was reported in 2004.

Netscape Navigator version 3.0$\beta$5 had a bug that allowed a simple type confusion attack (McGraw and Felten, 1997). (The bug was fixed in version 3.0$\beta$6.) Java allows a

---

[2] Adam Gowdiak: Java 2 Micro Edition Security Vulnerabilities, Hack In The Box Security Conference 2004, Kuala Lumpur, Malaysia.

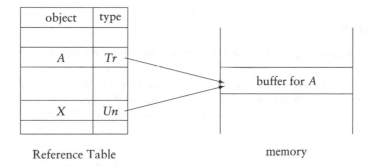

Figure 14.4: Type Confusion Attack

program that uses type $T$ to also use type *array of T*. Array types are defined for internal use only and their names begin with the character [. A programmer-defined classname is not allowed to start with this character. Hence, there should be no danger of conflict. However, a Java byte code file could declare its own name to be a special array type name, thus redefining one of Java's array types.

An ingenious type confusion attack using random memory errors is described by Govindavajhala and Appel (2003). The attack strategy is to create a data structure where a random memory error is likely to change a reference so that it points to an object of the wrong type. For this purpose, create two classes $A$ and $B$:

```
class A {           class B {
  A a1;               A a1;
  A a2;               A a2;
  B b;                A a3;
  A a4;               A a4;
  A a5;               A a5;
  int i;              A a6;
  A a7;               A a7;
};                  };
```

The attack proceeds as follows.

1. Fill the memory with lots of objects of type $B$ and a single object of type $A$ in position $x$. Let all the $A$ fields in the $B$ objects point to this $A$ object.

2. Keep scanning the $B$ objects and checking their $A$ fields until a memory error is detected. Shining a light bulb on the memory chip is a proven way of inducing a memory error.

3. Assume that bit $i$ in the field $a'$ of the object $b'$ has flipped. Create a pointer $r$ of type $A$ and set $r = b'.a'$.

4. Create a pointer $q$ of type $B$ and dereference the $B$ field of $r$ into $q$, i.e. $q = r.b$.

If there is no memory error, $r$ contains the address $x$ and we get the value for $q$ by fetching from address $x + offset$, where $offset$ denotes the distance between the base of an $A$ object and the beginning of the $b$ field. However, there had been a memory error so $r$ contains the address $x \oplus 2^i$ and the fetch for $q$ is from position $(x \oplus 2^i) + offset$. Given the memory layout in the attack, we are likely to get the address $x$ of the sole $A$ object. We now have a pointer $p$ of type $A$ containing $x$ and a pointer $q$ of type $B$ containing $x$. The type confusion attack is complete.

### Lesson

Attacks at the hardware layer can undermine security controls in the layer above.

### 14.4.8 The Mad Hacker

Sometimes, a software developer may step down the levels of abstraction and directly manipulate memory entries. Mistakes can lead to vulnerabilities, as demonstrated by the following story that is of historical interest, also for legal reasons. The operating system affected was ICL's VME/B. This is the sequence of events.

VME/B stored information about files in *file descriptors*. All file descriptors were owned by the user :STD. This created a problem once file descriptors could be classified at different security levels. For this very reason, :STD was not given access to classified file descriptors. In consequence, these descriptors could not be restored during a normal backup. The solution was obvious. A new user :STD/CLASS was created who owned the classified file descriptors. This facility was then included in a routine systems update.

The user :STD/CLASS had no other purpose than owning file descriptors. Hence, it was undesirable and unnecessary for anybody to log in as :STD/CLASS. To make login impossible, the password for :STD/CLASS was defined to be the RETURN key. Nobody could log in because RETURN would always be interpreted as the delimiter of the password and not as part of the password. The setting of the password in the user profile was done by patching hexadecimal code. Unfortunately, the wrong field was changed and instead of a user who could not log in, there emerged a user with an unrecognizable security level. This unrecognizable security level was interpreted as 'no security' so the designers had achieved the opposite of their goal.

There was still one line of defense left. User :STD/CLASS could only log in from the master console. However, once the master console was switched off, the next device opening a connection would be treated as the master console.

These flaws were exploited by a hacker who was managing a VME/B system himself. He thus had ample opportunity for detailed analysis and experimentation. He broke into a number of university computers via dial-up lines during night time when the computer center was not staffed, modifying and deleting system and user files and leaving messages from *The Mad Hacker*. He was successfully tracked, brought to court, convicted (under the UK Criminal Damage Act of 1971) and handed a prison sentence. The conviction, the first of a computer hacker in the United Kingdom, was upheld by the Court of Appeal in 1991.

### 14.4.9 AS/400 Machine Interface Templates

AS/400 (Applications System 400) was an IBM operating system for mid-range computers popular in the financial sector and thought to be reasonably secure. In AS/400, developers had easy access to the layer below the operating system. Machine language programs, written as *machine interface templates*, are not subject to the operating system's security controls. Machine interface templates were originally used by experienced AS/400 developers to increase software performance. However, with this technique it is also possible to *patch* (overwrite) objects to change security settings.

IBM first tried to stop such modifications by removing the offending machine interface commands and using a syntax checker to detect those commands in machine interface templates. This syntax checker referred to a table of legal commands. Once software writers found out how the check was performed, they simply replaced IBM's table with a table containing all original commands. As a next step towards protecting the integrity of the operating system, AS/400 introduced a separation of user state from system state and of user domain from systems domain. System state programs residing in the user domain gave users access to protected software, like a database management system. Technical discussions, further information on AS/400; and general good advice on managing operating system security can be found in Park (1995).

## 14.5 DATA AND CODE

Data and code can be important abstractions when assessing the security of a system. When input that is presented as data gets executed, the abstraction is broken and attacks may be possible. The following examples have in common that the data received as input may not mean what the programmer expected.

### 14.5.1 The rlogin Bug

The format of the Unix **login** command was

$$\textbf{login } [\text{-p}] \ [\text{-h}<\text{host}>] \ [[\text{-f}]<\text{user}>]$$

The -f option 'forces' log in and the user does not have to enter a password. The rlogin command allows users to log in on remote machines. This command has the format

rlogin [-l&lt;user&gt;] &lt;machine&gt;

The *rlogin* daemon takes the first argument in this command and sends the login request to the machine named in the second argument. Some versions of Linux and AIX did not check the syntax of the name field. The request

rlogin -l -froot machine

would then result in

login -froot machine

i.e. a forced login as root at the designated machine. This problem is caused by the composition of two commands. Each command on its own is not vulnerable. Syntax checking by the *rlogin* daemon can prevent this attack.

## 14.5.2 Scripting

Scripting languages are interpreted languages popular for writing web applications. Examples are Perl, PHP, Python, Tcl or Safe-Tcl. CGI (Common Gateway Interface) is a meta-language for translating URLs (uniform resource locators) or *html* forms into runnable programs. These programs can be written in any language that meets a few standard CGI requirements, including those just mentioned. Figure 14.5 describes the fundamental principle of CGI. A client sends a URL or a *html* form to the server, specifying a CGI script and its input argument. This request is transferred to a program that is executed with the user identity of the web server program. The web server may invoke applications like *Server-side Includes (SSIs)*. With SSIs, a document on the server may contain system commands, called *SSI in-lines*. When a client requests such a document, these system commands are evaluated and the result is inserted in the document returned to the client.

○ **Figure 14.5: The Server Runs CGI Scripts**

A simple example may illustrate how CGI scripts can cause damage. A script for sending a file to client could look like

**cat** thefile | **mail** clientaddress

where thefile is the name of the file and clientaddress is the mail address of the client. When a malicious user enters user@address | rm -rf / as the mail address, the server will execute

```
cat thefile | mail user@address | rm -rf /
```

and, after mailing the file to the user, delete all files the script has permission to delete. Like in any other case of controlled invocation, the input to the CGI scripts ought to be filtered. The more powerful the invoked operation is, the more careful you have to be about the input it receives. SSIs can be very powerful. The format of an SSI in-line is

```
<!-#operator arg1="string1" arg2="string2" ... ->
```

The ultimate in flexibility is provided by the operator exec with argument cmd. The SSI in-line

```
<!-#exec cmd="myprogram myparameters" ->
```

passes the string myprogram myparameters to /bin/sh for execution. (This option can be disabled by specifying Options IncludesNOEXEC in the server options.) Malice can come from the program, or from the parameters handed to a perfectly innocent program if myparameters contains a shell escape. The 'unescape' operation gets rid of shell escapes in input coming from the client by commenting out escape characters[3]. The command

```
unescape "string1;string2"
```

returns "string1 \;string2\" . Scripting languages like Perl also do unescaping. However, filters for escape characters have to know all escape characters for the character set in use, which is a nontrivial task, as documented in CERT advisory CA-2000-2.

### 14.5.3 SQL Inserts

SQL is a widely used database query language. Applications may process SQL queries to access a database from within a web page, for example, or to create dynamic web pages for interactive sites. Malformed user input can be processed in a way that defeats the developer's intentions. Consider the following query to a client database:

---

[3] An *escape character* indicates that the data following it is interpreted in a different context.

```
string sql = "select * from client where name = '"+ name +"'"
```

The intention is to deal with queries like `select * from client where name = 'Bob'`. However, when an attacker enters the input `Bob' OR 1=1--`, the query is processed as

```
select * from client where name = 'Bob' OR 1=1--'
```

The argument of the WHERE clause is read as the logical disjunction of "`name = 'Bob'`" and "`1=1`", and `--` is read as the start of a comment. The argument evaluates to TRUE so the disjunction evaluates to TRUE and the entire client database is selected. Another input with malicious impact is `Bob' drop table client --`.

As a countermeasure, we could filter the input for illegal characters and replace them with safe characters. In our example, single quotes (end an argument) could be replaced by double quotes (end the query) so the attacks just described will be blocked. However, this is not very satisfactory as we have only blocked one type of attack and have to know about all illegal characters.

**Lesson**

Do not try to figure out which inputs are bad. Define which inputs are good, e.g. using regular expressions, and only accept good inputs.

## 14.6 RACE CONDITIONS

Race conditions can occur when multiple computations access shared data in a way that their results depend on the sequence of accesses. This could happen when multiple processes or multiple threads in a multithreaded process, as in Java servlets, access the same variable. An attacker can try to exploit a race condition to change a value after it has been checked by the victim but before it is used. This issue is known in the security literature as TOCTTOU (time of check to time of use).

We give a historic example from the 1960s relating to the CTSS, one of the early time-sharing operating systems. This is the start of our story (Corbato, 1991):

> Once, a user found that the password file was given as the 'message of the day'.

What had happened? In CTSS, every user had a unique home directory. When a user invoked the editor, a scratch file was created in this directory. This scratch file had a fixed name, say SCRATCH, independent of the name of the file that was edited. This was a reasonable design decision as a user could only run one application at a time. No one else could work in another user's directory. Therefore, there was no need for providing more than one scratch file for the editor. So far so good. Furthermore, *system* was treated as a user with its own directory. At some stage, several users were working as system managers. It seemed convenient that more than one system manager should be allowed to work (access the system directory) at the same time. This feature was implemented. Now (Figure 14.6),

1. one system manager starts to edit the message of the day: SCRATCH:=MESS,

2. then a second system manager starts to edit the password file: SCRATCH:=PWD,

3. and the first manager stores the edited file, so we get MESS:= SCRATCH = PWD.

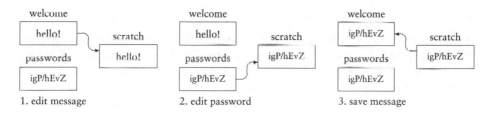

1. edit message          2. edit password          3. save message

◯ **Figure 14.6: Sharing the Scratch File in CTSS**

### Lesson

An *atomic transaction* is an abstraction of an operation that should execute as a single unit. Nothing else can occur while the operation is being executed. This abstraction is implemented using locking mechanisms that protect access to the resources used by the transaction. An example of a locking mechanism is the *synchronized* keyword in Java. Protecting atomic transactions is important in Java as Java is a multithreaded language, but this is a task left to the programmer. The disadvantage of adding synchronization can be a loss of performance.

## 14.7 DEFENSES

We could treat the problems presented individually and look for specific solutions, often limited to a given programming language or runtime system. This would amount to *penetrate-and-patch* at a meta-level. Instead, we should try to identify general patterns. In the case of insecure software, the pattern repeated is of familiar programming abstractions like *variable, array, integer, data and code, address (resource locator)* or *atomic transaction* being implemented in a way that can break the abstraction.

Software security problems can be addressed in the processor architecture, in the programming language we are using, in the coding discipline we adhere to, through checks added at compile time (e.g. canaries) and during software development and deployment.

### 14.7.1 Prevention: Hardware

Many buffer overflow attacks overwrite control information. Such attacks can be prevented by using hardware features to protect control information. Intel's Itanium processor has a separate register for the return address. A processor architecture with a separate *secure return address stack* (SRAS) is described by R.B. Lee *et al.* (2003). When adding protection mechanisms at the hardware layer, there is no need to rewrite or recompile programs. Only some processor instructions have to be modified. However, there are also some drawbacks beyond the need for new hardware. Existing software, e.g. code that places executables on the stack or code that uses multithreading, may work no longer.

### 14.7.2 Prevention: Type Safety

We can prevent software bugs by using a programming language that stops us from making mistakes. *Type safety* guarantees the absence of untrapped errors (Cardelli, 1997). Type safe languages include Java and C#. A language does not have to be typed to be safe, take LISP as an example. Safety can be guaranteed by static checks and by dynamic runtime checks. *Static type checking* at compile time examines whether the arguments an operand may get during execution are always of the correct type. Static type checking is more complicated than dynamic type checking during runtime, but it results in faster execution because the hard work is done in advance.

For practitioners, type safety often means just 'memory integrity'. For theoreticians, it means 'execution integrity' and it is the latter that is more relevant now. With type safety, we are getting close to 'provably secure' software but there are some caveats. Type safety is difficult to prove completely and problems may hide in the actual implementation (section 14.4.7). An even greater challenge is to define precisely what execution integrity means for a given software component (e.g. an operating system). Hence, the type safety properties we usually get are useful to have for security, but do not imply 'security'.

### 14.7.3 Prevention: Safer Functions

As a software developer programming in C or C++, you have to avoid writing code susceptible to buffer overruns. C is infamous for its unsafe string handling functions such as strcpy, sprintf, or gets. Take the specification of strcpy as an example:

```
char *strcpy( char *strDest, const char *strSource );
```

An exception is raised if source or destination buffer are null. The result is undefined if strings are not null-terminated, and there is no check whether the destination buffer is large enough. It is advisable to replace the unsafe string functions by safer functions where the number of bytes or characters to be handled can be specified, like strncpy, _snprintf or fgets. The specification of the function strncpy is

```
char *strncpy( char *strDest, const char *strSource,
  size_t count );
```

Using safer string handling functions does not eradicate buffer overruns on its own. You still have to get your byte counts and your arithmetic right. You have to know the correct maximal size of your data structures. This is straightforward when data structures are used only within a function but may be difficult if data structures are shared between programs. If you underestimate the required length of the buffer your code may become unreliable and crash. Some compilers can be configured to check for unsafe functions.

### 14.7.4 Detection: Code Inspection

Manual code inspection is tedious and error-prone so automation is desirable. Code inspection tools scan the code looking for potential security problems. A tool that uses meta-compilation for C source code is described by Ashcraft and Engler (2002) and Hallem *et al.* (2002). It works as an expert system that incorporates rules for known security issues. The rules look for a pattern of the form

'untrustworthy source → sanitizing check → trust sink'

and raise an alarm if untrustworthy input gets to a sink without proper checks. This pattern can also be used to learn about new rules. If, say, code analysis indicates a check but no sink, then probably the rules are not aware of a particular kind of sink. If this is the case and a new sink is identified, corresponding rules can be added to the rule base. Code-inspection is good at catching known types of problem but does not guarantee that there are no vulnerabilities, or that everything that is flagged as a problem is indeed a flaw. For practical deployment of code analysis tools, it is essential to keep the false alarm rate low.

### 14.7.5 Detection: Testing

Testing is an integral part of software development, normally used to demonstrate the correctness of functionality. In security testing, the situation differs somewhat as we have to show the correctness of security functionality. This implies that we have to have some idea about the potential threats, and the results of a threat analysis should provide input to security testing. Testing cannot prove the absence of errors, but nor do proofs. Proofs only show the absence of those errors we have been looking for in the abstract model used in the proof.

In *white-box testing*, the tester has access to the source code of the components and can use this information for test planning. *Black-box testing* is performed when source code is not available. A famous case of black-box testing is the security analysis of SNMP implementations carried out by the Oulu University Secure Programming Group (see CERT advisory CA-2002-03).

### Lesson

You do not need the source code to observe how memory is used or to test whether inputs are properly checked. It may actually be more helpful to have access to a high-level specification of a software component and of its interfaces than to have access to the source code only.

An important general technique for security testing is *data mutation* (Howard and LeBlanc, 2002). Data mutation sends malformed inputs to the program interfaces. Random inputs are not particularly useful for security testing. They test how unexpected inputs are handled but usually not much code will be exercised as such inputs will be caught by simple input checks or crash the code. (When code crashes, check whether the return address has been overwritten by input data. This indicates that the code is vulnerable to buffer overruns.) Partially incorrect inputs try to get past the first line of defense and exercise more of the code.

For data containers, data mutation might explore the following cases. The container the program is creating already exists. Software may crash if it tries to create a new temporary file that already exists. The container the program tries to access does not exist. Consider e.g. a NULL DACL in Windows. If there is no DACL, the access permissions are not checked and access is granted. The program does not have access to the container, or only has restricted access. Set permissions so that the tested component has no access to the container or only insufficient access rights. Test what happens if the name of the container changes and test the code with filenames that are links to other files.

For data, the test cases should include null (no value; what happens if an input field is empty?), zero, wrong sign (which brought down the Ariane 5 rocket[4]), wrong type, out of bounds input and combinations of valid and invalid data (valid data to get past input checks so that invalid data may actually be processed). Test cases should include inputs that are too long and inputs that are too short. When the application expects a fixed-size input but gets less data, security problems may arise, see e.g. the Sun tarball vulnerability described by Graff and van Wyk (2003). For network code, test cases should include replay of messages from previous protocol runs, out of sync messages, fragmented messages, partially correct protocol runs (to check for something like TCP SYN flooding attacks) and high traffic volumes.

## 14.7.6 Mitigation: Least Privilege

The principle of least privilege applies twofold. When writing code, be sparing with requiring privileges to run the code. If code running with few privileges is compromised, the damage is limited. Least privilege comes into play again when deploying software systems. Do not give your users more access rights than necessary. Do not activate options you do not need.

[4]http://archive.eiffel.com/doc/manuals/technology/contract/ariane/page.html.

The Unix `sendmail` program may illustrate the latter problem. System managers configuring mail systems need to establish that messages arrive at their destination. It would therefore help if the mail configuration on a network node could be checked and modified remotely, without requiring the system manager to log in at that node. For this purpose, `sendmail` includes a *debug* option. When this option is switched on at the destination, the username in a mail message can be substituted by a set of commands which `sendmail` will execute on the destination system. This feature was one point of attack for the Internet Worm (Spafford, 1989).

### Lesson

In the past, software was usually shipped in an open configuration, with generous access permissions and all features activated. It was up to the user to harden the system by removing features and restricting access rights. Today, software is more likely to be shipped in a locked-down configuration. Users have to switch on the features they want to use.

### 14.7.7 Reaction: Keeping Up to Date

When a software vulnerability is discovered, the affected code has to be fixed, the revised version has to be tested, a patch has to be made available and installed by the users for the problem to be fixed, so it is not just the software vendors that have to react to problems found in their products. The user community must also take action, and be aware of the problem in the first place. The investigations in Arbaugh, Fithen and McHugh (2000) show that most exploits of a given vulnerability occur well after countermeasures have been made available. Figure 14.7 is taken from this report. Patches might become a resource for potential attackers as they may give information about the vulnerability that has been removed, which may still persist in other places. Hence, there is a lively discussion about the best strategies for vulnerability disclosure and patch distribution.

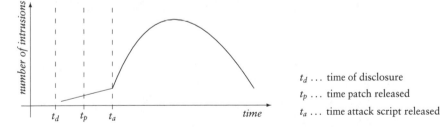

$t_d$ ... time of disclosure
$t_p$ ... time patch released
$t_a$ ... time attack script released

Figure 14.7: Lifecycle of Intrusions (redrawn from Arbaugh, Fithen and McHugh, 2000. © 2000 IEEE)

## 14.8 FURTHER READING

There is now a good choice of books on writing secure software, see e.g. Viega and McGraw (2001), Howard and LeBlanc (2002), Graff and van Wyk (2003), Viega and Messier (2003) and McGraw (2004). Technical details of various buffer overflow attacks are covered by Foster (2005). If you are interested in the stories behind real attacks, try Stoll (1989), Shimomura (1995) and Dreyfuss (1997). These are factual accounts of attacks written for a general audience. You can learn about new attacks through CERT advisories, mailing lists like BugTraq (maintained at http://www.securityfocus.com) and security bulletins from software vendors. The Phrack magazine covers technical details of software vulnerabilities. For those interested in the history of the field, the first paper on computer worms was published by 1982 (Shoch and Hupp, 1982).

## 14.9 EXERCISES

**Exercise 14.1**  Will this while loop ever terminate? If yes, after how many iterations? Would the result change if the variables are unsigned integers instead of signed integers?

```
int i = 1;
int c = 1;
while (i > 0)
{
i = i * 2;
c++;
}
```

**Exercise 14.2**  Give a fix to the flaw in the code for concatenating two strings discussed in section 14.2.2.

**Exercise 14.3**  An alternative design for a canary mechanism places the NULL value just below the return address. What is the rationale for this design decision? When does this method meet its objectives and what are its limitations?

**Exercise 14.4**  What is the flaw in the code snippet below that fills a buffer with zeros? How can the problem be fixed?

```
char* buf;
buf = malloc(BUFSIZ);
memset ( buf, 0, BUFSIZ);
```

**Exercise 14.5**  Unix systems use *environment variables* to configure the behavior of utility programs. A program executing another program can set the environment variables for that program. How could this fact be used in an attack? Which defenses should programmers apply?

**Exercise 14.6**  Consider a memory system that stores free blocks in a double linked list IDX in ascending order of size. A free block P of size S is inserted using the frontlink macro given below. Blocks are taken from the list using unlink. How does this system react when a block that is already in the free list is added again, and removed later?

```
#define frontlink(A, P, S, IDX, BK, FD)
  ...
[1] FD = start_of_bin(IDX);
[2] while ( FD != BK && S < chunksize(FD) )
          {
[3]          FD = FD->fd;
          }
[4] BK = FD->bk;
[5] P->bk = BK;
[6] P->fd = FD;
[7] FD->bk = BK->fd = P;
}

#define unlink(P, BK, FD) {
[1] FD = P->fd;
[2] BK = P->bk;
[3] FD->bk = BK;
[4] BK->fd = FD;
}
```

**Exercise 14.7**  When deploying a web server on a Unix system, how would you set ownership and access permissions on the software components involved applying the principle of least privilege?

**Exercise 14.8**  It has been claimed that full disclosure of software vulnerabilities will improve software security. When a vulnerability is found, which steps have to be taken so that the problem eventually gets fixed at the end user's site? Give a step-by-step analysis discussing important issues that should be taken into account. What are the advantages and/or disadvantages of full disclosure?

# New Access Control Paradigms

The Internet and the World Wide Web have brought a large but overwhelmingly security-unaware population of users into direct contact with new IT applications. Mobile code moves through the Internet and runs on the clients' machines. Electronic commerce promises new business opportunities on a global scale. Once again, we are facing considerable change in the way IT systems are being used. We thus have to question whether the old security paradigms still fit or whether new policies and new enforcement mechanisms are needed.

At the time of writing, this transition phase had not yet come to its end. Some new concepts have emerged but more experience has to be gained before we can give clear advice on the best security strategies to follow in this new environment.

## OBJECTIVES

- Explore new paradigms for access control.
- Explain background and rationale for the move to code-based access control.
- Present stack walking as the main security enforcement algorithm used in code-based access control.
- Give an introduction to the Java security model and the .NET security framework.

## 15.1 INTRODUCTION

The major paradigm in distributed computing before the emergence of the World Wide Web had been the client–server architecture. A client wants to perform computations on a server, so the server authenticates the client to protect itself. Kerberos is a prime example of an authentication service designed for such an environment (section 12.4). This architecture has changed in several core aspects. Computation moves from server to client. When a client looks up a web page, the client's browser will run programs (applets) embedded in the page. The nature of access operations has changed. Instead of simple read/write requests to an operating system or a database, programs are being sent to be executed at the other side. Servers execute scripts coming from the clients. Security aspects of scripting were discussed in section 14.5.2. Clients receive applets from servers and may store session states in cookies (section 15.5). So, what has changed with the World Wide Web?

- The separation of program and data becomes blurred. *Executable content (applets)* is embedded in documents to create interactive web pages that can process user input.

- Computation is moved to the client. Documents contain executable code and clients run on quite powerful machines, so servers can free resources by passing computational tasks to their clients. The client needs protection from rogue content providers.

- As computation moves to the client, the client is asked to make decisions on security policy, and on enforcing security. Users are forced to become system administrators and policy makers.

- The browser becomes part of the TCB.

The Web has also created a new paradigm for software distribution. Software is just one kind of content that can be downloaded from the Internet. Today, particularly updates and patches are distributed in this way. There is though a lesson to be learned from a previous age. In the early days of PCs, software was distributed on floppy disks. Accepting floppy disks from arbitrary sources became a common cause of virus infections. Many organizations learned the hard way that import of floppy disks had to be properly policed. The same risks are present on the World Wide Web and similar protection measures must be taken.

On a more speculative note, we may envisage mobile code moving from machine to machine, collecting information from different places or looking for spare computing resources. Clients need protection from mobile code. Mobile code may need protection from the clients it is running on.

While the World Wide Web has not created fundamentally new security problems, it has changed the context in which security has to be enforced to such an extent that a fundamental rethinking of access control paradigms is necessary. This chapter will explore the changes that are occurring in access control.

### 15.1.1 Paradigm Shifts in Access Control

In the access control model of section 4.2, principals send access requests that have to be authenticated. Security policies authorize principals to access an object. There is a strong underlying assumption that principals by and large correspond to known people. Access control in Unix and Windows builds on this model and implements *identity-based access control* (IBAC). This model originated in 'closed' organizations like universities or research laboratories. This approach to access control is underpinned by some important organizational assumptions. The organization has authority over its members. The members (users) can be physically located. Audit logs point to users who can be held accountable for their actions. In such a setting, security policies refer naturally to user identities and access control seems to require by definition that identities of persons are verified. Biometrics (section 3.7) then appear as a logical step towards stronger identity-based access control.

These assumptions about the organization are correlated to the way access control is typically deployed. Access rules are local. There is no need to search for the rule that applies for the current request or for the credentials a subject has to supply. The rules are stored as ACLs with the objects. The credentials are the UIDs (SIDs in Windows) subjects are running under. Enforcement of rules is centralized. The reference monitor does not consult other parties when making a decision. Permissions apply to simple and generic operations, like read, write or execute. There is a degree of *homogeneity* when setting security policies. The same organization is in charge of defining organizational and automated security policies

### 15.1.2 Revised Terminology for Access Control

For historic reasons, the established terminology for access control is geared towards explaining identity-based access control. In code-based access control, the topic of the next three sections, we do not necessarily ask "who made this statement?" so we either have access control without authentication, or we have to reinterpret authentication and widen its meaning so that it stands for the verification of any externally provided evidence associated with a request (Figure 15.1). Additionally, we might associate local evidence with a request. For example, the request could be part of a current session or the decision whether to grant access could depend on the current date and time. We might let authentication also include the verification of such an association.

Second, we have to find the policy that applies to the request and then check whether the available authenticated evidence is sufficient to grant the request. In a system that uses permissions, we would check whether all *required permissions* are included in the *granted permissions*. This phase could be called *authorization* but it no longer tells us who is entitled to access a resource but rather which evidence has to be provided to gain access.

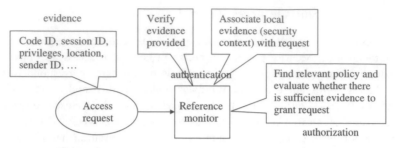

○ **Figure 15.1: Access Control in Open Environment**

To keep the presentation simple, the reference monitor in Figure 15.1 is in charge of all aspects of authentication and authorization. In current practice, these functions are separated and taken care of by different components.

- A policy administration point (PAP) creates the policy.

- A policy decision point (PDP) evaluates the applicable policy and makes an authorization decision.

- A policy enforcement point (PEP) performs access control. It sends decision requests to a PDP and enforces the authorization decisions received.

- A policy information point (PIP) acts as a source of evidence.

## 15.2 CODE-BASED ACCESS CONTROL

The Internet connects us to parties we have never met before. In applications like e-commerce it is often necessary commercially to permit unknown entities access to our systems. Naturally, this should not compromise our own security. We have moved out of closed organizations into an 'open' environment.

- We are dealing with people who are a priori unknown. Their 'identity' can hardly figure in our access rules.

- We may not be able to physically locate other parties.

- We may have no real authority over other parties. Even if we were able to identify the persons responsible for some action, we will not always be able to hold them accountable. They might live in different jurisdictions so that recourse to the legal process would be too slow, cumbersome and expensive to be considered as part of a security strategy. The relationship to customers is in many ways different from the relationship to employees.

In these circumstances user identities are not helpful when setting security policies. In consequence, the source of a request is no longer a useful access control parameter. At the same time, reference monitors do not receive read/write/execute requests but entire programs (applets, scripts). Access control has to decide whether to execute an applet, and which rights to give to the applet in case it is run. The Java sandbox had shown the way to control access based on code instead of user identities. The evidence used in making access decisions can be as follows.

- Code origin: is the code stored locally or does it come from a remote site? If it is remote code, which URL does it come from? We can use the URL to determine a *zone* and define security policies on the basis of zones. As a simple example, we could have separate policies for code coming from our intranet and for code from the Internet.

- Code signature: has the code been digitally signed by a trusted author? In this context, 'trust' simply means that we have made a decision to run code signed by a given author (code distributor) and assign certain privileges to it. This is usually an operational decision and not a judgment about the trustworthiness of the author.

- Code identity: we could decide to give certain approved (trusted) applets specific privileges. A home banking application would be a typical example. We could compute the hash of the applet received and check whether it is on a list of trusted applets. Again, this is likely to be an operational decision and not a technical judgment about the trustworthiness of the applet.

- Code proof: the decision whether to run an applet could be based on specific properties of the code, like the files it can write to or the sites it can connect to. Creating a proof that such a security property holds is a nontrivial task. Thus, the author could provide the proof and the reference monitor would only check the proof when making an access decision. *Proof-carrying code* is still mostly an idea explored by researchers (Necula, 1997). Deciding on useful security properties may actually be more difficult than proving that they hold.

We will refer to this type of access control as code-based access control. *Evidence-based access control* is an alternative term denoting the same concept. To keep security policies manageable, permissions are usually assigned to code sets (assemblies in .NET terminology). Individual software components derive their permissions from the code set they are contained in.

## 15.2.1 Stack Inspection

Subjects act on behalf of principals. In identity-based access control, the principal is a user. When the user logs in, a process is created that runs under the UID of that user. The access rights (permissions) given to that process derive from this UID. Normally, the permissions do not change while the process is running. To effect a change, a new process is spawned that runs under a UID different from that of the parent process. SUID programs in Unix are a typical example.

In code-based access control, when one software component calls another component, the *effective* permissions of the process executing these components will change. The algorithm that determines the effective permissions has to take into account the permissions of the calling component and of the component being called. We have to decide how to assign permissions when a 'trusted' component calls an 'untrusted' component, and vice versa. Consider the following example. Function g has permission to access resource $R$ but function f does not have this permission. Function g calls f and f requests access to $R$ (Figure 15.2, left). Should access be granted? The conservative answer is "no" because f does not have the required permission. However, g could explicitly *delegate* the access right to f. Conversely, let f call g and g request access to $R$ (Figure 15.2, right). Should access be granted? The conservative answer is again "no" because g could be exploited in a *luring attack* (also known as a *confused deputy attack*, section 5.3.5) by f, but g could explicitly *assert* its access right. In both examples, we need to know the entire call chain when making access decisions.

○ **Figure 15.2: Call Chains in Code-based Access Control**

It is customary to refer to components that have been assigned powerful permissions as 'trusted' components. Usually, this does not imply that there exist particularly good reasons to trust that such a component is free of security flaws, but that it needs permissions such as systems privileges to do its job. Similarly, an 'untrusted' component is not so much a component you cannot trust but a component that needs fewer permissions to run.

The Java Virtual Machine and the .NET Common Language Runtime both use a call stack to manage executions. At every function call a new frame is created on the stack. Each frame contains the local state of the function, including the permissions directly granted to it. For the computation of the effective permissions, *lazy evaluation* has so far been the option preferred by software developers. If a function requests access to a protected resource, a *stack walk* is performed to establish whether the caller has the required permissions. The effective permissions of the final caller are computed as the intersection of the permissions of all functions on the call stack (Figure 15.3).

The options for controlled invocation would be severely curtailed if this strategy were strictly adhered to. Therefore, it is usual to provide the option for code to *assert* a permission. The asserted permissions are attached to the current stack frame and removed when returning from that component. The stack walk for a permission terminates when it reaches a frame that asserts the permission and grants this permission. (All frames examined so far also have the permission.) The stack walk continues if there are other

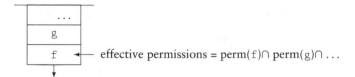

effective permissions = perm(f)∩ perm(g)∩ ...

○ **Figure 15.3: Computing Effective Permissions in a Stack Walk**

required permissions that have not been asserted. Assertion allows 'untrusted' callers to call a 'trusted' method.

Programmers writing components and assigning permissions to components have to consider that untrusted components may take advantage of the functions they implement and build in the appropriate defenses. On the other hand, they also have to consider that permissions may be missing when running their code because the caller has insufficient permissions.

## 15.2.2 History-based Access Control

Stack inspection reuses the call stack for a new purpose, which might get in the way of its original use. In terms of performance, common optimizations might have to be disabled for security reasons. In terms of security, it is difficult to establish precisely the guarantees provided by stack inspection. Security-relevant parameters may not be stored on the stack (see section 14.4.6 on heap overruns). It is thus also hard to relate the security policy enforced by this mechanism to high-level security policies.

We use *tail call elimination* to illustrate the first point. A function call that is the last instruction in a component is called a tail call. Consider the following example.

```
void g()                          void f()
{                                 {
  ...;                              ...;
  f(); // tail call               }
  return;
}
```

Once f() is called, g's frame is not needed anymore and could be overwritten with f's new frame. Eventually, f returns directly to g's caller. The gains of this optimization are particularly significant for recursive functions. With tail call elimination, however, an 'untrusted' caller may leave no tracks on the stack. In our example, let f request an access that requires a permission $p$ that had not been granted to g. Without tail call elimination, the stack walk will raise an exception when it examines g's stack frame.

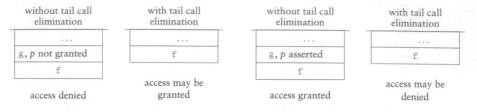

Figure 15.4: Effects of Tail Call Elimination

With tail call elimination, the stack walk will proceed and a situation may arise where access is granted that should be denied (Figure 15.4, left).

On the other hand, a trusted caller may have an asserted permission cancelled. In our example, let f have the permission $p$ and g assert the permission $p$, but assume that some previous caller does not have this permission. Without tail call elimination, the stack walk for $p$ would terminate at g's stack frame and the permission would be granted. With tail call elimination, the stack walk is unaware of the *assert* and may eventually deny access. Here, access is denied although it should have been granted (Figure 15.4, right).

To avoid these shortcomings of stack inspection as a security mechanism, do not be lazy but perform an *eager evaluation* that keeps track of the callers' rights proactively. In history-based access control (Fournet and Gordon, 2003), static permissions $S$ are associated with each piece of code at load time. The current rights $D$ associated with each execution unit are updated automatically at execute time with the rule $D := D \cap S$.

## 15.3 JAVA SECURITY

To surf freely on the Web, users have to be prepared to accept executable content (applets) from any web site that catches their attention. To be prepared, they have to be able to control the actions of applets. Applets are programs interpreted by a virtual machine in a web browser. It is thus natural to let this virtual machine perform access control, constraining applets within a *sandbox*. In addition, the language the applets are written in can make it more difficult to create damage. To make proper use of the access control mechanisms in the execution environment, security policies have to be set correctly.

### 15.3.1 The Execution Model

Java is a type safe object-oriented language. Java source code is compiled to machine independent byte code and stored as class files. Java byte code is similar to an assembly language. A platform-specific virtual machine interprets the byte code, translating it into machine-specific instructions. When running a program, a class loader loads any

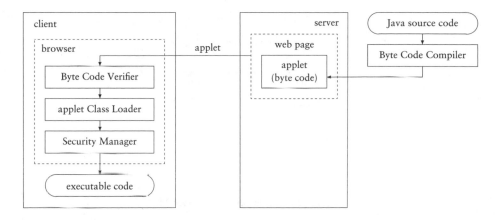

○ **Figure 15.5: The Java Execution Model**

additional classes required. Figure 15.5 shows the typical scenario for using Java applets. The applet is written in Java and compiled to byte code. The byte code is put on a web page, and gets executed by the browser on the client machine. A Java-enabled browser has its own Java Virtual Machine (JVM). A JVM has three security components, Byte Code Verifier, Class Loader and Security Manager. Browsers tend to enforce similar policies but this is by choice, not by necessity. Typical security policies for applets are:

- applets do not get access to the user's filesystem;
- applets cannot obtain information about the user's name, email address, machine configuration, etc;
- applets may only make outwards connections back to the server they came from;
- applets can only pop up windows that are marked 'untrusted';
- applets cannot reconfigure the JVM, e.g. by substituting their own Classes for systems classes.

### 15.3.2 The Java 1 Security Model

The initial Java security model implemented a very simple policy (Figure 15.6). Unsigned applets are restricted to a sandbox. Local code is unrestricted. Since Java version 1.1, signed code is also unrestricted. This basic policy does not provide any intermediate levels of control. It lacks the flexibility to give some additional privileges to 'semi-trusted' applets, e.g. to an applet that is part of a home banking application.

Moreover, the location of code, local or remote, is not a precise security indicator. Parts of the local filesystem could reside on other machines and would then be constrained in the sandbox. Conversely, downloaded software becomes 'trusted' once it is cached or

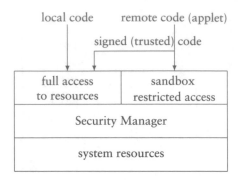

Figure 15.6: The Java 1 Security Model

installed on the local system. For more flexible security policies a customized Security Manager needs to be implemented, a nontrivial task that requires both security and programming skills.

### 15.3.3  The Java 2 Security Model

The Java 2 security model separates policy specification from policy enforcement. It provides a flexible framework for code-based access control, simplifying some aspects of policy enforcement at the same time. A *security policy* grants resource access permissions to code by mapping properties characterizing code to granted permissions. The *Security Manager* is the policy enforcement point called when access to a protected resource is requested. It collects the relevant evidence and invokes the *Access Controller*, the policy decision point making the actual decision.

We can only give a broad overview of the Java 2 security model, concentrating on features of general interest. The four areas covered are language security (byte code verification), securing extensible systems (class loading), policy specification, and policy enforcement. For detailed guidance on using this model you are referred to Gong, Dageforde and Ellison (2003).

### 15.3.4  Byte Code Verifier

The first line of defense is the programming language applets are written in. The language can limit the options for writing malicious applets. Java applets are written in byte code and are expected to honor certain safety properties. The *Byte Code Verifier* analyzes Java class files, performing syntactic checks and using theorem-provers and data flow analysis for static type checking to ensure that these expectations are met before the applet is executed. Verification intends to guarantee properties like the following.

• The class file is in the proper format.

- Stacks will not overflow.

- Methods are called with arguments of the appropriate type and return results of the appropriate type.

- There is no illegal data conversion between types.

- All references to other classes are legal.

- There is no violation of access restrictions; e.g. private fields are not accessible from outside the object.

The Byte Code Verifier reduces the workload for the interpreter, as the properties of code guaranteed by the verification do not have to be checked again at runtime. Byte code verification cannot take care of all security issues so security also depends on the security mechanisms in the runtime environment. Research towards a precise formal description of byte code verification is still ongoing, with the aim to have a full proof that byte code verification offers the guarantees advertised.

## 15.3.5  Class Loaders

The Java platform is an *extensible system*. Classes are loaded on demand as they are needed to resolve links (lazy loading). Class loading is delayed as much as possible to reduce memory usage and improve system response time. There are three types of Class Loader. The *Bootstrap Class Loader* loads system classes that form the core of the virtual machine. Classes loaded in this way have (at the time of writing) unrestricted access to system resources. The Bootstrap Class Loader is platform dependent, usually written in a native language like C, and often loads from the local filesystem. The *Extension Class Loader* loads classes from the installed optional packages (formerly known as extensions). The *Application Class Loader* (once known as the System Class Loader) loads user-defined classes.

When a Class Loader is being instantiated it reads in the byte code, defines the class and assigns it a protection domain (section 15.3.6). Link time checks are performed by the JVM to maintain type safety. Compared to runtime checks, link time checks have the advantage of being performed only once. Every JVM has a class file verifier. The class file verifier makes sure that 'untrusted' classes are safe. Class file verification checks if the constraints of the Java language are respected and that class files have a proper internal structure. Class file verification invokes the Byte Code Verifier.

Each class is uniquely defined by its class type and by its defining Class Loader. Thus, Class Loaders provide separate name spaces for different classes. A browser would load applets from different sources into separate Class Loaders. These applets may contain classes of the same name, but the classes are treated as distinct types by the JVM. *User-definable class loading policies* are supported. A user-defined Class Loader can, for example, specify the how classes are discovered, or assign appropriate security attributes to classes loaded from a given source.

### 15.3.6 Policies

Security policies map attributes of code to *permissions*. Permissions represent system resources and the operations permitted on those resources. The format of a permission is (*name,actions*), e.g. (`/tmp/abc,read`) stands for a read right on file `/tmp/abc`. Permissions are granted to code (granted permissions), and are required to access a resource (required permissions). Java uses only positive permissions. Developers are not restricted to predefined permissions but can define application-specific permissions.

There is a permission class hierarchy. Relationships between permissions are defined by `implies` and `equals` methods. `AllPermission` is a wildcard for all permissions, designed to streamline policy evaluation for entities like system administrators that need many permissions to do their job. `UnresolvedPermission` is a placeholder for permissions that have yet to be resolved, e.g. in case some permission classes have not yet been loaded when a `Policy` object is being constructed. To support policy management, permissions can be collected in *permission sets*.

The security-relevant parameters associated with code are *code source*, consisting of a URL (code origin) and possibly digital certificates (code signers), and *principals* representing users or services. *Protection domains* are an instrument for managing security. Each class is associated at load time with a protection domain. A protection domain contains code source, principal, a reference to the defining Class Loader, static permissions granted to code, and permissions assigned at load time. Protection domains are *immutable* objects, i.e. they cannot be modified once created.

Policies are stored in policy files. A policy file can contain at most one *keystore* entry and an arbitrary number of *grant* entries. The keystore entry tells where to find the public keys of the signers given in the grant entries. A grant entry assigns permissions to a code base, a list of signers and a list of principals. All three fields are optional. It is possible to specify a signer for individual permissions. In this case, the permission is only valid if it is found in a file signed by the nominated signer.

### 15.3.7 Security Manager

The *Security Manager* is the reference monitor in the JVM, invoked at runtime to check whether the process requesting access to a protected resource has the required permissions. To request this check, the program has to call the `checkPermission` method of the Security Manager. This method can be called with the required permission as the only argument or with the required permission and an *execution context*. The execution context captures the content of the execution stack. The `checkPermission` method of the Security Manager in turn calls the `checkPermission` method of the *Access Controller*.

The Access Controller implements a uniform access decision algorithm for all permissions. To compute the granted permissions, the Access Controller examines the given execution context, i.e. the execution stack, and performs a stack walk. Each method on the stack has a class and each class belongs to a protection domain. The protection domain defines the permissions granted to this method. The basic access control algorithm computes the intersection of the granted permissions for all methods in the execution context. It grants access if all methods on the stack have been granted the required permission. This algorithm is extended so that methods can assert permissions by calling the `doPrivileged` method that stops the stack walk at this method ignoring previous callers. Further modifications deal with aspects related to inherited methods and inherited execution contexts.

### 15.3.8 Summary

The approach chosen in the Java 2 security model is called *declarative security*. The writers of application programs declare which permissions are required to access protected resources by including the relevant checks in the code. They have full flexibility in defining application-specific permissions. The administrator deploying the application assigns permissions by specifying security policies. There is a single shared access control algorithm provided by the Access Controller, ensuring consistency in the enforcement of security policies. Application writers need not implement their own application-specific access control logic.

The JVM in a web browser enforces security in a layer above the operating system. Once a user has access to the layer below the security mechanisms, for example by running applications other than the browser, all bets on the integrity of the protection system are off. Furthermore, the Java platform is not secure simply because Java is designed to be a type safe language. Over time, security problems have been found and had to be fixed. Chapter 14 mentioned some incidents related to type safety. In most cases, attacks are launched by breaking the type system. This should be a warning message to anyone trying to build strong security on object-oriented abstractions and hoping that no additional effort is required to tighten the security of the underlying object management system. Making a complex system watertight is a difficult task. The work on securing the Java platform is still ongoing.

## 15.4 .NET SECURITY FRAMEWORK

This section gives a general overview of .NET security features and introduces the terminology used in .NET. A detailed introduction to .NET security is provided by La Macchia *et al.* (2002).

### 15.4.1 Common Language Runtime

The Common Language Runtime (CLR) is a runtime system supporting a number of programming languages such as C#, Visual Basic, managed C++, Visual J# and more.

The Common Language Specification (CLS) specifies general requirements on all .NET languages. The main language is C#, a type safe programming language. The design of C# builds to some extent on experiences gained from using Java. Code written in any of the .NET languages is compiled into MSIL code (Microsoft Intermediate Language). MSIL is conceptually similar to Java byte code. MSIL code is sent to a JIT (just in time) compiler just before it is executed. The CLR loads and executes code, performs security checks, and also automatic garbage collection so programmers do not have to explicitly free or delete objects that are no longer needed. Architecturally, the CLR corresponds to the JVM.

*Managed code* is code compiled to run in the .NET framework and is controlled by the CLR. *Native code*, also called unmanaged code, is code compiled to machine language for a specific hardware platform. Native code is not controlled by the CLR and works at a layer below the CLR. Calls from managed code to native code are security critical, as any guarantees provided by the CLR no longer apply. Particular care has to be taken to check that such a call does not lead to security violations.

An *assembly* is a logical unit of MSIL code. The *metadata* for an assembly provides information including the full assembly name, referenced assemblies, visibility, inherited class, implemented interfaces of each defined class, and information about class members such as methods, fields and properties.

## 15.4.2 Code-identity-based Security

The .NET platform implements code-based access control, called code-identity-based security by La Macchia *et al.* (2002). The basic idea is again to assign different levels of 'trust' to code. To be precise, different permissions are granted to code. Applying the principle of least privilege would be a good reason to do so. Calling code with all permissions 'fully trusted', code with very limited permissions 'untrusted' and code with permissions somewhere in between 'semi-trusted' mixes operational aspects of access control with the reasons why permissions have been assigned in a certain way.

Code-identity-based security refers to code identities. Security policies refer to *evidence* about assemblies, *authorizing* code rather than users to access resources. Evidence is dynamically calculated when code is running. Some pieces of evidence, like the URL of origin of an assembly, are usually not known in advance. *Authentication* of code identity is the process of collecting and verifying evidence about an assembly.

## 15.4.3 Evidence

The evidence about assemblies may include objects from default classes like the site of origin where the assembly has just been loaded from, the URL of origin, the hash of the assembly, an authenticode signature, a strong name signature and a security zone. It is also possible to use any other object as evidence to define application-specific access control. Custom code usually has to be added to process such evidence. Permission Request Evidence states the permissions an assembly must have to run, permissions it may be granted and permissions it must never get.

Evidence can be provided in two ways. It can be given by the entity that launches the assembly. This entity is called the *host* and can either be an unmanaged entity that initiates the CLR, e.g. Internet Explorer, or managed code launching other managed code. This evidence is known as *host-provided* evidence and uses the default classes mentioned above. *Assembly-provided* evidence is provided by an assembly itself using application-specific classes. It cannot override host-provided evidence. Evidence is associated with assemblies and with so-called *app domains* (short for application domains). App domains contain loaded assemblies and provide in-process isolation of executing code. All .NET code has to run in an app domain.

### 15.4.4 Strong Names

Strong names create separate protected name spaces for assemblies from different publishers. The publisher's public key is added to the metadata with other parts of the assembly name. The assembly is digitally signed during compilation and the signature is written into the assembly. This signature can later be verified by the .NET framework, thereby protecting the assemblies in the name space from modification and spoofing. In contrast to authenticode signatures, no certificates are required in this process.

### 15.4.5 Permissions

*Code access permissions* represent rights to access resources or to perform protected operations, such as accessing unmanaged code. Code access permissions provided by the .NET framework are, for example, `FileIOPermission` giving the right to read, append or write files or directories, `EventLogPermission` giving the right to read or write access to event log services, `PrintingPermission` giving the right to access printers and `SecurityPermission` giving among others the right to assert permissions, to call into unmanaged code, and to skip verification. There are numerous built-in permissions of this kind.

*Identity permissions* represent evidence about code identity as permissions so that policies that refer to specific code identities can be defined and enforced. Identity permissions can relate to the publisher of an assembly, its strong name, its site of origin, URL of origin or zone of origin. The `PrincipalPermission` is different from code access permissions and represents a user identity. It is used when defining identity-based security policies. For easier policy management, permissions can be collected in *permission sets*.

Permissions are granted to assemblies by the security policy (section 15.4.6). Required permissions are specified by placing *security demands* in the code. During execution, a security demand will trigger a stack walk to check whether the permission has been granted. *Declarative* demands are stored in the assembly's metadata. They can be reviewed easily by looking at the metadata. Checks will occur at the beginning of a method. JIT-time security actions can only be expressed in declarative form. *Imperative* demands are placed in the code, facilitating more complex security logic that can also handle dynamic parameters (not yet known when the declarative demands are checked) in access requests.

### 15.4.6 Security Policies

The security policy translates evidence into permissions. The main elements in constructing this mapping are *code groups*. A code group consists of a membership condition and a policy statement. The policy statement is in essence the permission set granted if the membership condition holds. The membership conditions check at load time whether evidence provided for an assembly matches given parameters. For example, one might compare zone evidence with a zone stored in membership condition, or compare a hash value of the assembly loaded with a hash value stored in membership condition.

To support policy management, code groups are arranged in hierarchies. Permissions are resolved from the code group root looking for matching children. For an *exclusive code group* assemblies matching such a code group are not evaluated against other code groups and only get permissions from this code group. Furthermore, there are four *policy levels*, Enterprise, Machine, User and Application Domain. A policy level consists of a named permission set, a code group hierarchy and a list of 'full trust' assemblies (to avoid recursive security checks when loading assemblies). Evidence is evaluated against each policy level individually and the results are intersected.

### 15.4.7 Stack Walk

A *Demand* security action triggers a stack walk. In the basic mode, all calling assemblies on the call stack are checked (not the current code making the demand) and need to have the required permission for access to be granted. This algorithm can be modified with *Assert* actions that assert a permission and stop the stack walk. There is also a *Deny* action that terminates the stack walk denying access (raising a security exception). This action is mainly useful during testing. The *PermitOnly* action is equivalent to a *Deny* on all permissions other than the one specified.

### 15.4.8 Summary

.NET security follows the same strategy as Java security. Managed code is written in a type safe language like C#. The CLR verifies IL code to ensure type safety. Code, not users, is authorized to access resources and has to be authenticated when it is being executed. The security enforcement algorithm performs a stack walk. There are numerous means available for structuring security policies and two different styles for expressing required permissions. This is the framework provided. For practical use, you would then need strategies for setting policies and assigning permissions to assemblies. At the time of writing, these are still very much open questions.

## 15.5 COOKIES

We now leave code-based access control and explore other paradigm shifts in access control. Next, we examine security aspects of session management on the World Wide Web. The *http* protocol (hypertext transfer protocol, RFC 1945), originally designed to transfer HTML documents, is the workhorse of the World Wide Web. This protocol is stateless by design. All *http* requests are treated as independent events, even when they come from the same client. Hence, all associated management tasks need to be repeated constantly. For example, if a password is required to access a web page, this password would have to be returned every time you click on this page. This problem was already handled by *http* 1.0 for the duration of a session. The browser would store the password entered at the first request and automatically include it in all further replies to the server.

Applications that involve transactions consisting of several steps, like making a purchase on the web, need to keep the state of the transaction so that they are able to return to a consistent state between client and server in case the flow of the transaction is interrupted. To do so, the state of the transaction is stored by the browser on the client side as a *cookie* (Figure 15.7). The server can retrieve the cookie to learn about the client's current state in the transaction. With cookies, *stateful http* sessions can be created.

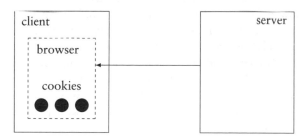

Figure 15.7: Cookies Stored at the Client

Depending on the duration for which cookies are kept, the concept of a session can be extended beyond a single transaction. A service provider could use cookies to manage customer relationships. Customers contact the service provider via *http* requests, but *http* requests do not necessarily identify individual users. The server could thus ask the browser to store persistent cookies that contain the information the server will refer to next time the customer calls.

Are cookies a security problem? Cookies cannot violate the integrity of your system. They are data, not executable code. Individual cookies do not disclose information to the server. After all, the server asks the browser to store the cookie. Usually, cookies are domain specific and servers are only given access to cookies belonging to their domain. In this sense, there is no new confidentiality problem either. We have, however, to consider application-level attacks. The attacker could be the server violating client *privacy* by creating client profiles, combining information from cookies placed by different servers or by observing client behavior over time. The attacker could be a client changing cookies with the intent of gaining some benefits from the server the customer is not entitled to. For example, when the server uses the cookie to store bonus points in a loyalty scheme, a client could increase the score to get higher discounts. This is called a *cookie poisoning attack*. The attacker could be a third party that makes an educated guess about a client's cookie and then uses the spoofed cookie to impersonate the client.

Clients can protect themselves by setting up their browsers to control the placement of cookies. The browsers could ask for permission before storing a cookie, which easily becomes a nuisance, or block cookies altogether. There is also the option of deleting the cookies at the end of a session. The server could protect itself by encrypting cookies. Spoofing attacks are prevented by using proper authentication.

An interesting legal conundrum about cookies is mentioned by Hogben, Jackson and Wilikens (2002). P3P, the Platform for Privacy Preferences, enables web sites to express their data-collection and data-use practices in a standardized machine-readable XML format. In an earlier version of P3P, only policies about retrieving cookies could be expressed. This is reasonable from a technical point of view but is not in accordance with the EU Data Protection Directive. The Directive asks for user consent at the time personal data is written. The Directive addresses privacy concerns originally related to databases holding personal data. When data about a person is recorded on systems belonging to someone else, it makes sense to ask for consent when data is written. Cookies, however, store data pertaining to a person on that person's machine. The sensitive operation is read access by some other party.

## Lesson

Legislation may enshrine old technology. Laws regulating IT are passed to meet the challenges posed by the technology of the time they were drafted. It may happen that lawmakers incorporate assumptions about the use of technology that, with the benefit of hindsight, turn out to apply only to the specific applications of their time. A law may thus not only prescribe the protection goal, which remains unchanged, but also the protection mechanism, which may not be the best option in some novel application.

## 15.6 SPKI

In the old access control paradigm, access rules are stored locally in protected memory. In decentralized access control systems, we can protect the integrity of access rules by cryptographic means. Specifically, we can encode rules in digitally signed certificates. Identity-based access control can be implemented using X.509 identity certificates and attribute certificates as discussed in section 12.5.3.

SPKI, the Simple Public Key Infrastructure (RFC 2692, 2693), is a PKI intended to support authorization schemes that work without user identities. The designers of SPKI postulate that names used in access control have essentially only a local meaning, and that access rights are likely to derive from attributes other than a person's name. So, for the purpose of access control, names are just pointers to access rights (authorizations). A security policy sets the rules in a given domain, e.g. a university department. The names that are used to state the policy must have a meaning locally within the domain, but need not be globally unique.

When there is interaction between domains, we may need to refer to names from other local name spaces. We need globally unique identifiers for name spaces to avoid any confusion about names. Public key cryptography offers an elegant solution to this problem. Public/private key pairs generated at random are unique with extremely high probability, as would be the hash of the public key. The public key of an issuer (or its hash) is then the unique identifier for the name space defined by that issuer. In SPKI terminology, such keys are called *principals*[1]. Name certificates signed with the private key define a name in the local name space.

Access rights are bound directly to public keys through *authorization certificates*. Authorization certificates contain at least an *issuer* and a *subject*, and may also include a delegation bit, authorizations and validity conditions. The issuer signs the certificate and authorizes the subject, i.e. assigns access rights to the subject. Thus, the issuer sets the policy and is the source of authority ('empowerment', in SPKI terminology). The subject is typically a public key, the hash of a key, or the name for a key. The root key for verifying certificate chains is stored in an ACL. Identity certificates that bind a person's name to a key are used for accountability, and could be issued by a CA other than the one issuing authorization certificates (Figure 15.8).

Access rights are assigned to public keys. The holders of the corresponding private keys may delegate (grant) some of their access rights to other subjects by issuing certificates for those rights. Delegation is restricted in two ways. Delegators can only delegate rights they hold themselves. This design decision is justified with the observation that a key holder who may delegate a right without being able to exercise it could just generate

---

[1]The terms principal and subject are used here with a different meaning from that given in Chapter 4.

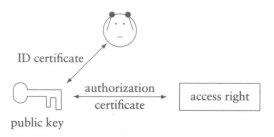

ID certificate

authorization
certificate

access right

public key

Figure 15.8: Certificates in SPKI

a new key pair and delegate the right to that key. Second, a flag indicates whether the access rights in a certificate may be delegated further.

Authorization certificates and ACLs have the same function and differ only in the mode of protection. Certificates are signed by an issuer. ACLs are unsigned and have no issuer. They are stored locally and are never transmitted. Tuples are an abstract notation for SPKI certificates and ACL entries. The algorithm for processing authorizations is expressed in terms of 5-tuples <issuer, subject, delegation, authorization, validity dates>. The issuer is a public key or the reserved word 'Self' for ACLs. The subject is defined as above. The delegation bit is a Boolean value. The authorization field gives application-specific access rights. Validity is defined by a not-before date and a not-after date. The algorithm for evaluating certificate chains takes two 5-tuples as input and gives the result as a 5-tuple. Authorizations and validity periods can only be reduced by the respective intersection algorithms.

```
Input: <Issuer1,Subject1,D1,Auth1,Val1>
          <Issuer2,Subject2,D2,Auth2,Val2>

IF Subject1 = Issuer2 AND D1 = TRUE
THEN output <Issuer1, Subject2, D2,
    AIntersect(Auth1,Auth2), VIntersect(Val1,Val2)>
```

SPKI is a key-centric PKI and an interesting alternative to X.509, at least from the point of certificate theory. SPKI standardizes certain automated policy decisions, e.g. on delegation. Hence, one has to check that these rules match the given organizational policy. Organizational policies are unlikely to be expressed by direct reference to cryptographic keys.

## 15.7 TRUST MANAGEMENT

A subject (as defined in Chapter 4) requesting access to a resource presents a set of *credentials*. Credentials are security evidence. The security policy states which credentials are required for the request to be granted. Three factors contribute to a security decision: the set of credentials granted to the subject; the set of credentials required to gain access; and an algorithm that evaluates whether the required credentials are implied by the granted credentials.

In IBAC, typical credentials are usernames and passwords. Granted and required credentials are found in well-defined places like the subject's access token and an ACL for the object. The algorithm checking whether the granted credentials are sufficient is relatively simple, going through an ACL, granting access once all required credentials have been found and denying access otherwise. The reference monitor does not ask third parties for help when making its decisions.

In open environments, it may become more complicated to find granted and required credentials and third parties may get involved in access decisions. Consider the following hypothetical example. Two telecommunications providers $X$ and $Y$ have a Service Level Agreement that gives customers from $X$ access to the services offered by $Y$. Provider $Y$ will not get a list of all subscribers from $X$, but $X$ issues its subscribers with certificates and gives $Y$ the required verification key. Subscribers from $X$ request services from $Y$ by presenting their certificates. Provider $Y$ calls back $X$ to perform an on-line status check on the certificates, 'deferring' this check to $X$. The reply from $X$ is input to $Y$'s decision.

Trust management is the name adopted by Blaze, Feigenbaum and Lacy (1996) for a more general and flexible approach to access control. For the discussions in this section, we have to redefine parts of our terminology. As in SPKI, principals can be public keys and we can directly authorize actions the keyholder can perform. There is no need to authenticate a user to perform access control. The *actions* a policy regulates are defined in an application-specific action description language. An *assertion* binds a public key to a *predicate* on actions. An assertion is a policy statement that authorizes actions if a digitally signed request to perform those actions can be verified with the public key given in the assertion and if the requested actions satisfy the predicate. Predicates could be written in any safe interpreted language. With predicates, we can specify more sophisticated evaluation algorithms than with ACLs. *Credentials* are digitally signed assertions. They generalize authorization certificates. *Policies* are locally stored assertions. They are the roots of trust (authority). *Trust relationships* reflect policy decisions to accept credentials issued by another party. Trust management provides a common language for policies, credentials and trust relationships. The first trust management system was PolicyMaker (Blaze, Feigenbaum and Lacy, 1996). KeyNote is a trust management system for the Internet (RFC 2704).

It is important to understand what trust means in such a trust management system. When we defer trust to some other party, we make a policy decision to assign to this party the authority to make assertions we will consider when evaluating an action request. In real life, trust relationships may be based on contractual relationships between parties. They may also be based on 'trust' in the colloquial sense of the word, but it is much safer to separate the rationale for entering into a trust relationship (which may have nothing to do with trust) from the operational aspects of a trust management system.

Access requests are evaluated by a Policy Decision Point (a.k.a. *compliance checker* or *trust management engine*) that receives as its inputs a request $r$ and a set of credentials $C$, and refers to the local policy $P$ when answering the question:

> "Does the set $C$ of credentials prove that the request $r$ complies with the local security policy $P$?" (Blaze, Feigenbaum and Lacy, 1996).

Possible answers to this question are "yes", "no", "don't know" or an indication that further checks are required. There is a trade-off between the expressiveness of the predicate language and the complexity of the compliance checker. Depending on the language, compliance checking may turn out to be undecidable. We also have to consider how users find out about the credentials they need to present so that their request complies with the given policy. Should the server provide this information? Should the server publish its policy at all? The policy itself may be sensitive information. Alternatively, there could be an algorithm for users to compute the set of credentials required for their request, or users could refer to a *credential chain discovery service*.

To add a further degree of freedom to our problem, consider the situation in a *federated environment* where several organizations collaborate, but each has its own security policy. There is now no longer a single entity setting the policy. Conflicts between policies are bound to occur. In such a setting you have to consider how conflicts could be resolved, and on the course of action that should be taken if this is not possible.

# 15.8 DIGITAL RIGHTS MANAGEMENT

At the technical level, Digital Rights Management (DRM) is about enforcing vendor policies on a customer machine. This is another departure from the traditional access control paradigm. The policies enforced on a system are no longer set by the owner but by an external party. The adversary is no longer an external party trying to subvert the system but an owner trying to bypass the policy. The security goal is the integrity of the access control system, as interpreted by the external party.

To achieve this goal, you could try to make it difficult for the owner to change the policy settings. If the adversary is assumed to be a technically sophisticated owner, protection mechanisms may have to go down to the hardware level. Alternatively, the content provider could ask for a truthful report about the hardware and software configuration of a target machine before agreeing to a download. This solution could be implemented on a Trusted Platform Module running an attestation protocol (section 12.6).

The challenges described are interesting from a technical point of view. A further technical aspect is the construction of digital *watermarks* that embed information about content owner or customer in the content delivered. The main issues here are the difficulty of removing or modifying watermarks, and their impact on the quality of audio and video content. Whether DRM is a useful basis for business models in content distribution is open to debate.

## 15.9 FURTHER READING

For detailed expositions of Java security and .NET security, refer to McGraw and Felten (1997) and La Macchia *et al.* (2002) respectively. Readers with an interest in the history of the field may consult McGraw and Felten (1997) to learn about problems discovered in the early stages of Java security. As a background on DRM, an entertaining review of the arms race between copy protection and copy programs can be found in Grover (1992). Current research on code-based access control looks at alternatives to stack inspections, see e.g. Fournet and Gordon (2003) and at policy management, see e.g. Besson *et al.*, (2004).

## 15.10 EXERCISES

**Exercise 15.1**  Document the current security settings of your web browser. Where is the security-relevant information stored on your system?

**Exercise 15.2**  Find the cookie file on your system and the options for setting cookie-retention policies.

**Exercise 15.3**  Consider an application that uses predictable cookies to maintain session state. How could an attacker hijack a session of some other user? How could the application be secured?

**Exercise 15.4**  Analyze the performance advantages of storing access rules in certificates and not in ACLs.

**Exercise 15.5**  We could use the hash of an assembly or a digital signature of the assembly as its identity. Examine the relative advantages and disadvantages of these two options.

**Exercise 15.6**  Consider a recursive functions that calls itself $n$ times (as a tail call). Compare the performance of the stack walk when there is no tail call elimination and when there is tail call elimination.

**Exercise 15.7**   Consider a policy that, for reasons of separation of duties, does not allow an entity to exercise the rights it may grant (delegate) to others. How could SPKI be augmented to support such a policy?

**Exercise 15.8**   Give an example of an application where access decisions are deferred to a third party for reasons other than trust.

**Exercise 15.9**   In some circumstances it is desirable to protect mobile code from the system it is running on. To what extent is this goal achievable at all? List the protection properties that could be achieved and those that are inherently impossible to achieve.

# Chapter 16

## Mobility

The first mobile IT service to find wide acceptance was second generation digital cell phone networks. The number of mobile services has since increased, supporting a wider range of applications using different underlying technologies. Mobile services pose new security challenges. Some of these challenges derive from the technology. Messages transmitted over a radio link can be intercepted by third parties. Secure sessions should persist when a device changes its point of attachment. To access a wireless network you do not have to attach a cable to a socket but only need to be within range of an access point. Physical access control to buildings or rooms is no longer an effective barrier keeping unauthorized users out. Other changes derive from the applications. Frequently, the entity offering some service to its subscribers is different from the operator managing the local network used to access these services. The security interests of all three parties, subscriber, network operator and service provider, have to be taken into account, and possibly also the requirements of law enforcement agencies.

## OBJECTIVES

- Examine new security challenges and attacks specific to mobile services.
- Give an overview of the security solutions adopted for different mobile services.
- Show some novel ways of using cryptographic mechanisms.
- Discuss the security aspects of location management in TCP/IP networks.

## 16.1 INTRODUCTION

The first generation analog mobile cell phone systems provided direct dialing, automatic handover between cells, and call forwarding. In the context of security, it is interesting to note that criminals tried to use the latter feature for creating alibis, and that telecommunications experts were then called up by courts to explain why a person who had answered a call at a particular land line number was not necessarily at that place at the time of the call. The simple challenge-response protocol used for authentication transmitted the relevant secrets in the clear so that some networks suffered from a high level of charge fraud. There was also some obfuscation of voice traffic, but no strong protection against eavesdropping, as mentioned in Chapter 1.

## 16.2 GSM

Against this backdrop of low security in the first generation network, the study group Groupe Spéciale Mobile (GSM) of the Conference of European Posts and Telegraphs (CEPT) was founded in 1982 to specify the second generation mobile network. The design goals for this digital network were good subjective voice quality, cheap end systems, low running costs, international roaming, handheld mobile devices, ISDN-compatibility and support for new services like SMS. In 1989, the responsibility for GSM was transferred to the European Telecommunication Standards Institute (ETSI). Phase I of the GSM specification was published in 1990 and GSM was renamed as the Global System for Mobile Communications.

To understand some of the design decisions made, you have to be conscious of the political influences on the development of GSM. An international system has to take into account various national regulations and attitudes to the public use of cryptography. Restrictions on the use of strong cryptography were an issue until the mid-1990s. Moreover, law enforcement authorities requested the possibility to conduct authorized 'wiretaps', in analogy to wiretaps in the fixed network.

The main security goals of GSM are protection against charge fraud (unauthorized use of a service) and the protection of voice traffic and signaling data on the radio channel. Once traffic is in the fixed network, no added cryptographic protection is provided. Also, there is a contribution to physical security. It should be possible to track stolen end devices. This feature is not always implemented[1].

### 16.2.1 Components

Each GSM user has a subscription in a *home network*. The network where a service is requested is called the *visited network* (or serving network). A Mobile Station (MS)

---

[1]At a time when cell phone robberies among school children became a nonnegligible item in the UK crime statistics, service providers were strongly encouraged to implement mechanisms for tracking stolen phones.

(cell phone) consists of the Mobile Equipment (ME) and the Subscriber Identity Module (SIM). The SIM is a smart card chip that performs the cryptographic operations in the MS and stores the relevant cryptographic keys. The SIM may also contain other personal data of the subscriber, like the personal phone book, and gives personal mobility independent of the ME. On the network side, there is the Base Station (BS), the Mobile Switching Center (MSC), the Home Location Register (HLR) of a subscriber, the Authentication Center (AuC) and the Visitor Location Register (VLR). The HLR and VLR manage call routing and roaming information. The AuC manages a subscriber's security-relevant information. The relationship between different network operators is managed through Service Level Agreements (SLAs).

The identifier for a GSM subscriber is the International Mobile Subscriber Identity (IMSI). The subscriber and HLR/AuC share a secret 128-bit Individual Subscriber Authentication Key $Ki$. The SIM stores $Ki$, the IMSI, the TMSI (explained below) and a current 64-bit encryption key $Kc$. The algorithms A3 and A8 (also explained below) are implemented in the SIM. Access to the SIM is controlled by a PIN (personal identification number). After three attempts with a wrong PIN the SIM is blocked. A SIM can be unblocked using a PUK (Personal Unblocking Key).

### 16.2.2 Temporary Mobile Subscriber Identity (TMSI)

When an MS connects to the network it has to identify itself by some means. If a fixed identity is used at each call, the movements of subscribers can be tracked, even if subsequent traffic is encrypted. As a step towards better subscriber privacy, the unencrypted IMSI is sent only when an MS makes initial contact with the GSM network. Thereafter a Temporary Mobile Subscriber Identity (TMSI) is assigned in the visited network and used in the entire range of the MSC. The IMSI is thus not normally used for addressing on the radio path. The VLR maintains a mapping $\langle(\text{TMSI}, \text{LAI}), \text{IMSI}\rangle$ from TMSI and Location Area Identity to IMSI. When the MS moves into the range of another MSC a new TMSI is assigned. When permitted by signaling procedures, signaling information elements that convey information about the mobile subscriber identity are encrypted for transmission on the radio path.

### Lesson

Protection of location information is a security issue specific to mobile services. Fixed identifiers leak information about the movement of a mobile station.

### 16.2.3 Cryptographic Algorithms

GSM uses symmetric cryptography for encryption and subscriber authentication. The use of public key cryptography had been considered, but when decisions were made in the 1980s public key cryptography was not yet a feasible option with the technology of the time. There are three cryptographic algorithms: the authentication algorithm A3, the encryption algorithm A5 used on signaling and user data, and the key generation algorithm A8. These algorithms are not published outside the partners in the GSM Memorandum of Understanding (GSM/MoU), but were eventually leaked or reverse-engineered.

Algorithms A3 and A8 are shared between subscriber and home network. Hence, each network could choose its own algorithms A3 and A8. Only the formats of their inputs and outputs must be specified. A3 and A8 compute a response RES and ciphering key $Kc$ from a random challenge RAND and the key $Ki$. Processing times should remain below a maximum value, e.g. 500 *msec* for A8. Proposals for A3 and A8 are managed by the GSM/MoU. One of the choices for A3/A8 is the algorithm COMP128. This algorithm is weak and susceptible to attacks that retrieve the key $Ki$ from the SIM. With this key, cloned devices could be created. More secure alternatives for A3/A8 are used by circumspect service providers.

Algorithm A5 has to be shared between all subscribers and all network operators. This algorithm has to be standardized. There are two versions, A5/1 and a less secure 'export' version A5/2. Although there are no official public specifications of these algorithms, cryptanalytic attacks against both versions have been published.

### 16.2.4 Subscriber Identity Authentication

Subscriber authentication is triggered by the network at the first network access after a restart of the MSC/VLR or when the subscriber applies for access to a service, like set-up of a mobile originating or terminated call. Authentication is also performed when the subscriber applies for a change of subscriber-related information in the VLR or HLR, like location updating involving change of VLR, or in the event of cipher key sequence number mismatch.

Figure 16.1 describes the message flow during authentication. The initial message from ME to VLR contains a subscriber identity, either TMSI or IMSI. The VLR maps TMSI to IMSI and forwards the IMSI to the HLR/AuC over the fixed subnet. The AuC generates a non-predictable 128-bit challenge RAND and computes the response RES = A3($Ki$,RAND) and a 64-bit encryption key $Kc$ = A8($Ki$,RAND). The triple ⟨RAND,RES,$Kc$⟩ is sent to the VLR. The VLR stores RAND and $Kc$ and passes the challenge RAND on to the MS. The key $Kc$ is only valid within one location area.

In the MS, the response SRES = A3($Ki$,RAND) of RAND is computed in the SIM ('signature' in GSM terminology, but not a digital signature) and transmitted by the MS back to the VLR. The VLR compares SRES and RES. Authentication succeeds if the two values match. To speed up subsequent authentications in a visited network, the AuC sends several triplets ⟨RAND, SRES, $Kc$⟩ to the VLR, which are then used in turn for subscriber authentication.

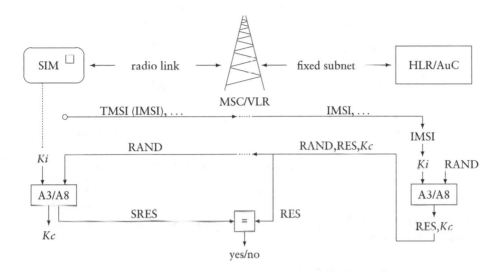

Figure 16.1: Subscriber Identity Authentication in GSM

### 16.2.5 Encryption

Normally, all voice and non-voice traffic on the radio link is encrypted. The infrastructure is responsible for deciding which algorithm to use, or whether to switch off encryption so that no confidentiality protection is afforded. If necessary, the MS signals to the network which encryption algorithms it supports. The serving network then selects one of these that it can support, based on a priority order preset in the network, and signals the choice to the MS.

The *ciphering indicator* feature allows the ME to detect that ciphering is not switched on and to flag this to the user. This feature may be disabled by the home network operator by setting the administrative data field (EFAD) in the SIM accordingly (GSM 11.11). If it is not disabled in the SIM, then whenever a connection is or becomes unenciphered, an indication shall be given to the user (GSM 02.07 version 7.0.0, Release 1998).

The encryption algorithm A5 is a stream cipher applied to 114-bit frames. The key for each frame is derived from the secret key $Kc$ and the current 22-bit frame number (Figure 16.2). Radio links are relatively noisy so a stream cipher is preferable to a block cipher. With a block cipher, a single bit error in the ciphertext affects an entire plaintext frame. In a stream cipher, a single bit error in the ciphertext affects a single plaintext bit. By today's standards a key length of 64-bits is rather short and cryptanalysis of A5 has further reduced the effective key length.

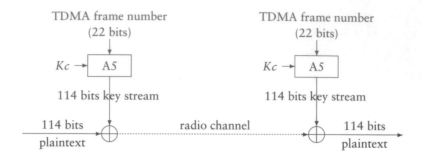

Figure 16.2: Encryption of GSM Frames from MS to MSC

### Lesson

The characteristics of the physical network layer can be relevant for the choice of cryptographic algorithms.

### 16.2.6 Location-based Services

The GSM network records the location of mobile equipment. This information can be used to offer a Location-based Service (LBS) like traffic information for motorists. There are also emergency location services that give the location of an ME making a call to an emergency number. This service is obligatory in some countries, e.g. US laws demand mobile location to an accuracy of 125 m.

### 16.2.7 Summary

Challenge-response authentication in GSM does not transmit secrets in the clear, so one major vulnerability of first generation networks has been removed. Voice traffic is encrypted over the radio link but calls are transmitted in the clear after the BS. There is optional encryption of signaling data but the ME can be asked to switch off encryption. There is some protection of location privacy through the TMSI but attackers can use so-called IMSI-catchers that ask the MS to revert to initial authentication using the IMSI. This attack is possible because the network is not authenticated to the MS. Law enforcement agencies have access to recorded movement data of subscribers. There is a separation of subscriber identity (IMSI) from equipment identity (IMEI) and there are provisions for tracking stolen devices.

The main criticisms of GSM security are directed against the decision not to publish the cryptographic algorithms so that they could be publicly scrutinized, and against the decision to provide only unilateral authentication of the subscriber to the network, but no authentication of the visited network to the subscriber.

An overall assessment of GSM security must look beyond the technical security features. Many cases of GSM fraud attack the *revenue flow* rather than the data flow and do not break the underlying technology. In *roaming fraud* subscriptions are taken out with a home network. The SIM is shipped abroad and used in a visited network. The fraudster never pays for the calls (soft currency fraud) but the home network also has to pay the visited network for the services used by the fraudster (hard currency fraud). There is obvious scope for fraudsters and rogue network operators to collude. In premium rate fraud, unwitting customers are lured into calling back to premium rate numbers owned by the attacker, who uses the existing charging system to get the victim's money. Criminals may also start a premium rate service, make fraudulent calls to their own numbers to generate revenue, collect their share of the revenue from the network operator and disappear at the time the network operator realizes the fraud.

Countermeasures are to be found at the human level, e.g. exercising caution before answering a call back request, in the legal system, e.g. clarifying how user consent has to be sought for subscribers to be liable for charges to their account, and in the business models of network operators. GSM operators have also taken a lead in using sophisticated fraud detection techniques, e.g. based on neural networks, to detect fraud early and limit their losses.

**Lesson**

Do not lose sight of application-level attacks when analyzing the security of a service provided to end users.

# 16.3 UMTS

Work on third generation (3G) mobile communications systems started in the early 1990s. One of those systems is UMTS, the Universal Mobile Telecommunications System. The standardization organization for UMTS is the 3G Partnership Project (3GPP). The Organizational Partners of 3GPP are ARIB (Japan), ATIS (North America, formerly T1), CCSA (China), ETSI (Europe), TTA (South Korea) and TTC (Japan)[2]. The first UMTS specifications were released in 1999. The UMTS security architecture is similar to GSM. Subscribers have a Universal Subscriber Identity Module (USIM) that is part of the user equipment (UE) and share a secret key with the AuC in the home network. The UE requests services from a visited network or a Serving GPRS Support Node (SGSN).

## 16.3.1 False Base Station Attacks

In GSM, the network is not authenticated to the ME. Hence, the ME cannot tell whether requests to use the IMSI for authentication or to switch off encryption are genuine or come from a bogus BS. To address this problem, one might call for mutual authentication

---

[2]Status spring 2005.

between ME and network. There are several reasons that militate against this naïve solution. The ME has a preestablished relationship only with the home network so direct authentication of a visited network is not feasible. Extending the challenge-response protocol to give mutual authentication would not prevent false BS attacks either. The attacker need only wait for authentication with the genuine BS to complete and then take over communications with the ME by sending with a stronger signal than the genuine BS. Furthermore, cryptographic authentication mechanisms are of limited use on noisy channels. Any bit error in a message will cause authentication to fail. So, the longer the authenticated message, the larger is the likelihood that it will be rejected because of a transmission error.

Section 16.3.3 covers the defenses against false BS attacks adopted in UMTS. A deeper discussion of the design rationale for these mechanisms is given by Mitchell and Pagliusi (2003).

## 16.3.2 Cryptographic Algorithms

The authentication functions $f1$ and $f2$ and the key generation functions $f3$, $f4$ and $f5$ can be specific to the service provider. The MILENAGE framework, a recommendation for AKA functions, has a block cipher with 128-bit blocks and 128-bit keys at its core. The encryption algorithm for the radio link and the integrity check algorithm for signaling data on the radio link have to be standardized. UMTS has adopted KASUMI, an eight round Feistel cipher with 64-bit blocks and 128-bit keys. KASUMI is used in a variation of OFB mode for encryption and in a variation of CBC-MAC mode for integrity protection. All algorithms proposed for UMTS are published and have been subject to thorough cryptanalysis.

## 16.3.3 UMTS Authentication and Key Agreement (AKA)

Home network (AuC) and subscriber (USIM) share a secret 128-bit key $K$ and maintain a synchronized sequence number SQN. In response to an authentication request, the AuC generates a random challenge RAND and an expected response XRES=$f2$(RAND,$K$). The AuC also computes a 128-bit cipher key CK=$f3$(RAND,$K$), a 128-bit integrity key IK=$f4$(RAND,$K$), a 48-bit anonymity key AK=$f5$(RAND,$K$), and a MAC of the challenge RAND, the sequence number SEQ, and the Authentication Management Field AMF (which may contain a key lifetime) (Figure 16.3). The AuC then constructs AUTN = ⟨SQN⊕AK,AMF,MAC⟩ and sends the authentication vector ⟨RAND,AUTN,XRES, CK,IK⟩ to the VLR/SGSN, which stores ⟨RAND,AUTN,XRES,CK,IK⟩ for the IMSI and passes RAND and AUTN to the UE.

Upon receipt of RAND and AUTN, the USIM first computes AK=$f5$(RAND,$K$) and SQN=(SQN⊕AK)⊕AK (Figure 16.4). Then the expected message authentication code XMAC is derived from RAND, SQN and AMF, and compared with the MAC value received. This verifies that RAND and AUTN were generated by the home AuC. If there

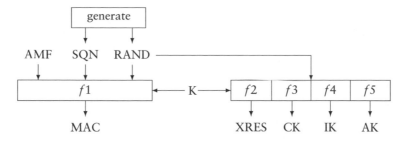

Figure 16.3: Generation of Authentication Vector at AuC

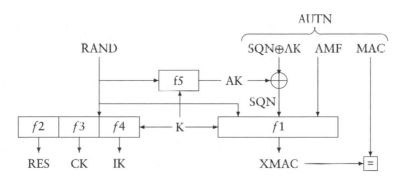

Figure 16.4: Authentication in USIM

is a mismatch, the USIM aborts the protocol run, sending a reject message to the VLR. Otherwise, the USIM continues the protocol and checks that SQN is valid to detect replay attacks. In case this check fails, a synchronization error is signaled to the VLR. False BS attacks are thus prevented by a combination of key freshness and integrity protection of signaling data, not by authenticating the serving network.

Finally, the USIM computes the response RES and the keys CK and IK from the challenge RAND and its secret key $K$, and returns the response RES to the VLR. The VLR compares RES and XRES to authenticate the USIM (Figure 16.5).

## 16.4 MOBILE IPv6 SECURITY

The security problem in GSM and UMTS was access control to services when users are mobile and do not have a preestablished relationship with the operator of the network where the service is delivered. In this section we will use Mobile IPv6 to demonstrate another mobility problem. When a device changes its location, how can other nodes verify that information about the new location of the device is correct? The standard remedy in such a situation is authentication, but we are running into two problems. To

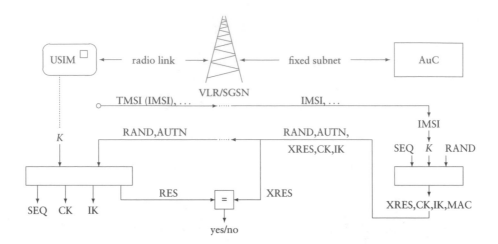

**Figure 16.5: Authentication and Key Agreement in UMTS**

authenticate a message, we have to know the identity of the sender. In IP, the identities are IP addresses. To verify cryptographically that a message comes from a claimed address, we have to reliably associate a cryptographic key with this address. It had been suggested to use a PKI for this purpose, but there is currently no such PKI we could readily use and it is unlikely that this situation will change anytime soon.

Second, data origin authentication does not solve our problem. In the 'old' setting of the wired network, a node could lie about its identity. Alice could claim to be Bob to get messages intended for Bob. A mobile node can lie about its identity and about its location. Alice could claim that Bob is at her location so that traffic intended for Bob is sent to her. This is still a variation of the 'old' attack. Alice could also claim that Bob is at a nonexistent location so that traffic intended for him is lost. Both attacks could be stopped by checking that Bob gave the information about his location.

There is yet another denial-of-service attack. Alice could claim that she is at Bob's location so that traffic intended for her is sent to Bob. In a *bombing attack*, Alice orders a lot of traffic and has it delivered to Bob's location. Verifying that the information about Alice's location came from Alice does not help in this case. The information had come from her, but she was lying about her location.

Bombing attacks are a flow control issue. Data is sent to a victim who has not asked for it. Authenticating the origin of location information does not prevent bombing. It would be more appropriate to check whether the receiver of a data stream is willing to accept the stream. Instead of origin authentication we require an authorization from the destination to send traffic to it. Flow control issues should in principle be handled at the transport layer. It was decided to address this issue at the IP layer because otherwise all transport protocols would have to be modified.

**Lesson**

Mobility changes the rules of the security game. In a fixed network, nodes may use different identities in different sessions (e.g. NAT in IPv4), but in each session the current identity is the location messages are sent to. With mobile nodes, we have to treat identity and location as separate concepts.

### 16.4.1 Mobile IPv6

An IPv6 address specifies a node and a location. A 128-bit Mobile IPv6 (MIPv6) address consists of a 64-bit subnet prefix (location) and a 64-bit interface ID (identity within the location indicated by the prefix). IPv6 addresses of mobile nodes and stationary nodes are indistinguishable. A mobile node is always addressable at its *home address* (HoA), whether it is currently attached to its home link or away from home. The home address is an IP address assigned to the mobile node within its home link. The mobile node and its home agent have a preconfigured IP security association that constitutes a secure tunnel. RFC 3776 specifies the use of ESP to protect MIPv6 signaling between mobile and home agent. While a mobile node is attached to some foreign link away from home, it is also addressable at a *care-of address* (CoA). This care-of address is an IP address with a subnet prefix from the visited foreign link.

### 16.4.2 Secure Binding Updates

The association between a mobile node's home address and care-of address is known as a *binding* for the mobile node. Away from home, a mobile node registers a binding with a router on its home link, requesting this router to function as its *home agent*. Any other nodes communicating with a mobile node are called *correspondent nodes*. Mobile nodes can inform correspondent nodes about their current location using binding updates. The correspondent node stores the location information in a binding cache. Binding updates refresh the binding cache entries. Packets between the mobile node and the correspondent node are either tunneled via the home agent, or sent directly if a binding exists in the correspondent node for the current location of the mobile node.

Binding updates are in essence a network management task, but can be performed by any node. If binding updates cannot be verified, attackers could create havoc with the Internet, including the wired Internet. Not surprisingly, it is a problem if any node can participate in – and interfere with – network management. These security concerns halted work in the IETF on mobile IP for a while. The first attempt at securing binding updates suggested using IPsec. This proposal applies an old solution to a new problem and has serious deficiencies. Security associations would have to be established but IKE is a heavyweight protocol not suited for mobility. A chain of trust between mobile node and correspondent node would have to be constructed in the absence of a global PKI for the Internet.

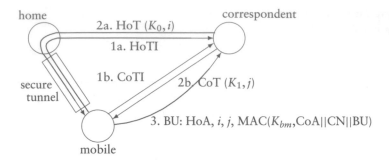

home                    2a. HoT ($K_0, i$)        correspondent
                        1a. HoTI

                        1b. CoTI
secure                              2b. CoT ($K_1, j$)
tunnel
                        3. BU: HoA, $i, j$, MAC($K_{bm}$,CoA||CN||BU)

mobile

○ **Figure 16.6: Binding Updates in Mobile IPv6**

Thus, dedicated protocols are needed for verifying that a node with a claimed identity is in its claimed location. A secure binding update protocol for mobile IPv6 is specified in RFC 3775 (Figure 16.6). The design considerations behind this protocol are explained by Aura, Roe and Arkko (2002). The primary security goals were that mobility must not weaken the security of the IP, and the protection of nodes not involved in an exchange, e.g. nodes in the fixed Internet. The protocol also has several features that should provide resilience against denial-of-service attacks.

In this protocol, the mobile node first sends two *Init* messages to the correspondent (CN), *Home Test Init* (HoTI) via the home network and *Care-of Test Init* (CoTI) directly (steps 1a and 1b). The correspondent replies to both requests independently. A *Home Test* (HoT) message containing a 64-bit home keygen token $K_0$ and a home nonce index $i$ is sent to the mobile node via the mobile's home address (step 2a). A *Care-of Test* (CoT) message containing a 64-bit care-of keygen token $K_1$ and a care-of nonce index $j$ is sent directly to the claimed current location (step 2b). The mobile node uses both keygen tokens to compute a binding key

$K_{bm}$:= SHA1(home keygen token||care-of keygen token),

and the *Binding Update* (BU) authenticated by a 96-bit MAC (step 3)

HoA, $i, j$, HMAC_SHA1($K_{bm}$, CoA||CN||BU)_96.

This protocol does not rely on the secrecy of cryptographic keys but on *return routability*. The correspondent checks that it receives a confirmation from the advertised location. In the threat model assumed, keys $K_0$ and $K_1$ may be sent in the clear on the channels from the correspondent. These keys could also be interpreted as challenges (nonces) that bind identity to location through the binding key $K_{bm}$. In communications security, the term authentication typically refers to the corroboration of a link between an identity of some kind and an aspect of the communications model, like a message or a session (Gollmann, 2003). In this interpretation, binding update protocols provide *location authentication*. The protocol would be vulnerable to an attacker who can intercept both communications links, in particular the wired Internet. If we are concerned about the security of the wired Internet, we could use IPsec to protect traffic between the correspondent and the home agent.

To be resilient against DoS attacks, the correspondent should be stateless in the protocol. That is, it should not need to remember the keys $K_0$ and $K_1$. For this reason, each correspondent node has a secret node key $K_{cn}$ used for producing the keys sent to the mobile node. This key must not be shared with any other entity. Each correspondent node generates nonces at regular intervals. Nonces are identified by an index (indices $i$ and $j$ in Figure 16.6). The keys are obtained as the first 64 bits of MAC values,

$K_0 := \text{HMAC\_SHA1}(K_{cn}, \text{HoA} || \text{nonce}[i] || 0)_{64}$,

$K_1 := \text{HMAC\_SHA1}(K_{cn}, \text{CoA} || \text{nonce}[j] || 1)_{64}$.

After replying the correspondent can discard $K_0$ and $K_1$ because it is able to reconstruct the keys when it receives the final confirmation. The state kept by the correspondent is thus independent of the number of BU requests it receives. Balancing message flows is another provision against denial-of-service attacks. A protocol where more than one message is sent in reply to one message received can be used to amplify DoS attacks. Therefore, the BU request is split in two. The mobile node could send the home address and care-of address in one message but then the correspondent would reply to one BU request with two BU acknowledgments.

### Lesson

In communications security, it is traditionally assumed that passive eavesdropping attacks are easier to perform than active attacks. In mobile systems, the reverse can be true. To intercept traffic from a specific mobile node, one has to be in its vicinity. Attempts to interfere with location management can be launched from anywhere.

## 16.4.3 Ownership of Addresses

Schemes that dynamically allocate addresses should check that a new address is still free. This could be done by broadcasting a query asking whether there is any node on the network already using this address. In a *squatting attack*, an attacker falsely claims to have the address that should be allocated, thereby preventing the victim from obtaining an address in the network.

We will now present a scheme whereby a node can prove that it 'owns' an IP address. This scheme has the interesting feature of not relying on any third party, be it home agent or certification authority. The core idea is have the address owner create a public key/private key pair and uses the hash of the public key as the interface ID in an IPv6 address. To prove ownership of an address, a claim is signed with the private key. The signed claim together with the public key is sent to the correspondent. The correspondent verifies the signature on the claim and checks the link between public key and IP address. The address is the 'certificate' for its public key. Public key cryptography is used without using a PKI.

Cryptographically Generated Addresses (CGAs) as specified in RFC 3972 and by Aura (2003) apply this idea to IPv6 addresses. In this case, the length of the hash value would be limited to 62 bits as two bits of the interface ID are reserved. To forge claims for a given address, an attacker does not have to find the original key pair but only a collision, i.e. a key pair where the public key hashes to the interface ID. The feasibility of finding collisions for 62-bit hash values is too close for comfort so a method for extending the hash has to be found. A CGA has thus a security parameter *Sec* (3-bit unsigned integer) encoded in the three leftmost bits of the interface ID. The security parameter increases the length of the hash in increments of 16 bits. Hash values *Hash1* and *Hash2* for the public key are computed as

Hash1 = SHA-1(modifier||subnet prefix||collision count||public key),

Hash2 = SHA-1(modifier||$0_{64}$||$0_8$||public key).

The $16 \times Sec$ leftmost bits of *Hash2* must be zero. The 64 leftmost bits of *Hash1* become the interface ID, excluding the five fixed bits so that only 59 bits are used. Resistance against collision attacks is proportionate to finding a collision for a $59+16 \times Sec$ – bit hash. To get a *Hash2* value of the required format, the address owner has to do a brute force search varying the modifier, which is a random 128-bit number. The effort for this search amounts to getting a hash with $16 \times Sec$ bits equal to a fixed value (all zeros). The collision count is initialized to 0 and incremented if a collision in the address space is reported. An error is reported after three failures.

The workload of the correspondent is constant. To verify the link between address and public key two hashes have to be computed. To verify a claim, a signature has to be verified. This may, however, become an issue in denial-of-service attacks as signature verification is an expensive operation. CGAs do not stop an attacker from creating bogus addresses from its own public key and any subnet prefix. Thus, CGAs do not prevent bombing attacks. To defend against such attacks, a return routability test may be performed checking whether the receiver is willing to accept traffic.

## 16.5 WLAN

Wireless LAN (WLAN) is a technology for wireless local area networks specified in the IEEE 802.11 series of standards. The security challenges in this application are not primarily consequences of mobility but of wireless network access. Again, the integrity and confidentiality of data transmitted over the air should be protected. Suitable cryptographic algorithms have to be chosen and key management procedures have to be defined. In addition, access to the local network and access to mobile devices has to be controlled. An unprotected WLAN would give an attacker the opportunity to use bandwidth services that will be charged to the network owner, or to use the victim's system as a staging post for attacks against third parties.

A WLAN can be operated in infrastructure mode or in *ad hoc* mode. In infrastructure mode, mobile terminals connect to a local network via *access points*. In *ad hoc* mode, mobile terminals communicate directly. The security discussions in this section will focus on infrastructure mode, and on the access control options at an access point. Each access point has a Service Set Identifier (SSID). An *open* WLAN does not restrict who may connect to an access point. An open WLAN is not necessarily unprotected; security mechanisms could be provided in other protocol layers. Public access points are known as hot spots.

To control access to a WLAN, access points can be configured not to broadcast their SSIDs but to require clients to know the SSID to connect to. The SSID would be the secret necessary to gain access. This approach does not work too well. The SSID is included in many signaling messages where it could be intercepted by an attacker, so it should not be treated as a secret. Also, access points are delivered with a default SSID set by the manufacturer. An attacker could try these default values in the hope, often justified, that they had not been changed. It is moreover possible to configure access points so that only mobile terminals with known MAC (medium access control) addresses are accepted. This attempt at address-based authentication is not very secure. An attacker could learn valid MAC addresses by listening to connections from legitimate devices and then connect with a spoofed MAC address.

It is in general problematic to base access control on information needed by the network to manage connections, such as SSIDs or MAC addresses. Typically, this information has to be transmitted when setting up a connection before security mechanisms can be started. Hence, it is a more promising strategy to let the client establish a connection to the access point and then authenticate the client before giving access to protected services. The Universal Access Mechanism (UAM) shown in Figure 16.7 illustrates this approach. Clients are assumed to have a web browser installed. A client connecting to an access point gets a dynamic IP address from a DHCP server. When the client's web browser is started, the first DNS or *http* request is intercepted and the client is directed via an *https* session to a start page asking for username and password. The web server at the access point controller refers verification of username and password entered to a RADIUS server. Once the client has been authenticated, the access point can apply familiar identity-based access control to the client's requests. Protection of subsequent traffic between client and access point is a separate issue. An analysis of the security provided by this scheme is left as an exercise.

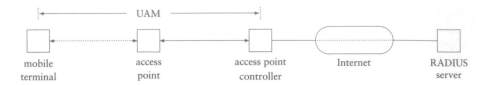

○ Figure 16.7: Hot Spot Access Using UAM and a RADIUS Server

## 16.5.1 WEP

The Wireless Equivalent Privacy (WEP) protocol specified in IEEE 802.11 was proposed to protect the confidentiality and integrity of data passed between mobile terminal and access point, and to authenticate mobile terminals to the network. Authentication is based on a shared secret. So-called preshared secrets are installed manually in all devices that should get access, and in all access points of the network. This solution is suitable for small installations like home networks. Most LANs use the same key for all terminals.

WEP uses a stream cipher for encryption. In a stream cipher, keys must not be repeated as the exclusive OR of two plaintexts encrypted with the same key stream is equal to the exclusive OR of the two plaintexts. The statistical properties of the exclusive OR of two plaintexts can be used for cryptanalysis that reconstructs the two plaintexts and thereby also the key stream. Hence, a 24-bit Initialization Vector (IV) is used to randomize encryption. Sender and receiver have a shared secret 40-bit or 104-bit key $K$. To transmit a message $m$, the sender computes a 32-bit checksum CRC-32($m$), takes the 24-bit IV and generates a key stream with the 64-bit (128-bit) key $K' = \text{IV}||K$ using the stream cipher RC4. The ciphertext $c$ is the bitwise exclusive OR of $(m||\text{CRC-32}(m))$ and the key stream,

$$c = (m||\text{CRC-32}(m)) \oplus \text{RC4}(K').$$

Ciphertext and IV are transmitted to the receiver, who computes $c \oplus \text{RC4}(K') = (m||\text{CRC-32}(m))$ and verifies the checksum. To authenticate a client, the access point sends a 1024-bit challenge in the clear to the client. The client uses the above algorithm to encrypt the challenge with the preshared key, and the access point verifies this response.

The cryptographic mechanisms used in WEP suffer from two major design flaws. First, CRC-32 is a cyclic redundancy check, i.e. a linear function useful for detecting random errors but no defense against targeted modifications. When used in conjunction with the linear encryption operation (exclusive OR) of a stream cipher, it does not offer any real integrity protection. An attacker who only has a WEP ciphertext, but neither key $K'$ nor plaintext $m$, can modify the plaintext as follows. Let $\Delta$ be the intended alteration of the plaintext. The attacker computes $\delta = \text{CRC-32}(\Delta)$ and adds $(\Delta||\delta)$ to the ciphertext, obtaining a valid encryption of the plaintext $m \oplus \Delta$ as

$$(m||\text{CRC-32}(m)) \oplus \text{RC4}(K') \oplus (\Delta||\delta) = (m \oplus \Delta||\text{CRC-32}(m) \oplus \delta) \oplus \text{RC4}(K')$$
$$= (m \oplus \Delta||\text{CRC-32}(m \oplus \Delta)) \oplus \text{RC4}(K'),$$

A second problem is the size of the IV. As long as the secret key $K$ remains unchanged, the IV is the only variable part of the key $K'$. An attacker could observe traffic for a longer period until IVs repeat and then try to reconstruct the key streams and build a table of IVs and corresponding key streams.

On top of these design flaws, there has been progress in the cryptanalysis of RC4. Attacks that find the key $K$ are described by Fluhrer, Mantin and Shamir (2001), and have been further improved since. These attacks retrieve the key byte by byte so a 104-bit key does not offer much more resistance to cracking than a 40-bit key. Some attacks replay encrypted control messages to create more traffic so that they can obtain the amount of data necessary for cryptanalysis.

## 16.5.2 WPA

WEP had comprehensively failed to meet its security goals. WiFi Protected Access (WPA) was designed as a quick preliminary solution that removed the major flaws of WEP prior to a complete redesign of the WLAN security architecture. WPA was required to run on existing WLAN hardware. There are also improved procedures for authenticating the client to the network and for establishing temporary encryption keys dynamically. The Extensible Authentication Protocol (EAP) is a meta-protocol specified in RFC 2284 and IEEE 802.1X that supports multiple authentication methods, such as token cards, Kerberos, one-time passwords, certificates and public key authentication.

For integrity protection, CRC-32 was replaced by a message integrity code (MIC) called Michael. The length of the IV has doubled to 48 bits. The Temporal Key Integrity Protocol (TKIP) creates a key hierarchy. Client and access point need to have a long-term Pairwise Master Key (PMK). For each connection new Pairwise Transient Keys (PTKs) are derived from the master key and used for protecting traffic between mobile terminal and access point. When WPA is deployed with preshared master keys (WPA-PSK), the PMK is computed with the key generation function PBKDF2 (RFC 2898) as

$$PMK = PBKDF2(passphrase, SSID, SSID\ length, 4096, 256).$$

The inputs are a secret passphrase (20 characters are recommended), the SSID of the access point, and the length of the SSID. This input is hashed 4096 times and a 256-bit key is returned. The algorithm computing a PTK takes the PMK, the MAC address of both devices, and nonces generated by both devices as its inputs. Nonces are transmitted in the clear.

WPA-PSK is vulnerable to password guessing attacks. The attacker records the messages exchanged when the victim connects to the WLAN. Then, the attacker guesses a passphrase and computes a master key PMK' for the passphrase guessed and the known (intercepted) values SSID and SSID length, and a transient key PTK' from PMK' and the intercepted MAC addresses and nonces. Encrypted messages that had been recorded are decrypted with the candidate key PTK'. If the result is meaningful plaintext, the guess of the passphrase is correct with very high probability.

Given the design constraints, the WPA security mechanisms are not as strong as one might wish from a cryptographic perspective, but WPA is still a definite improvement on WEP.

### 16.5.3 IEEE 802.11i – WPA2

A complete redesign of WLAN security mechanisms has been specified in the standard IEEE 802.11i, published in 2004. This standard is also known as WPA2. In WPA2, the stream cipher RC4 has been replaced by AES in CCMB mode, i.e. counter mode with CBC-MAC mode. WPA2 requires new hardware.

## 16.6 BLUETOOTH

Bluetooth is a technology for wireless *ad hoc* networks, initially envisaged for short-range communications (up to 10 m) between personal devices like a PC, keyboard, mouse, printer, headset or other peripherals, forming a Personal Area Network. Such a local *ad hoc* network does not require a sophisticated key management infrastructure. A security association between two devices can be established manually by *pairing*, i.e. the user entering a common PIN on both devices.

For cryptographic protection of traffic between the devices, a 128-bit link key is derived from the PIN. The link key is used for later authentication between devices. Authentication is performed in a challenge-response protocol, similar to GSM authentication. Temporary communication keys for encrypting messages are derived from the shared PIN, the PIN length, a random value generated by the sender, and the receiver's address. Authentication of devices is the basis for access control. The objects of access control are the services (dial-in, file transfer) offered on a device.

The Bluetooth security architecture was designed for Personal Area Networks. As Bluetooth applications and also Bluetooth technology, e.g. extending the range of communications, are changing, new security architectures will have to be developed. For Bluetooth applications, application-level attacks that exploit weaknesses in the software configuration of the devices have to be considered. Attacks like Bluesnarf retrieve personal data from devices with flawed implementation of access control. Roaming profiles of users can be established when Bluetooth devices are configured to broadcast their identities on request.

## 16.7 FURTHER READING

This chapter has described various mobile and wireless technologies with a focus on security issues of general interest. Further interesting security issues of great practical relevance not covered in this chapter relate to more specific aspects of individual technologies. A detailed discussion of GSM and UMTS security is given by Niemi and Nyberg (2003). GSM standards are managed by ETSI (`http://www.etsi.org`), the UMTS specifications by the 3GPP (`http://www.3gpp.org`). Mobility issues in TCP/IP networks are discussed in various IETF working groups. The current status of these discussions can be found on the respective IETF web sites (`http://www.ietf.org`). WLAN security is specified in IEEE 802.11. The official Bluetooth membership site is (`http://www.bluetooth.org`).

## 16.8 EXERCISES

**Exercise 16.1**  Telephone service providers have to deal with complaints from customers who claim not to have made a call (to a premium rate number) that appears to have been made from their phone. What kind of protection measures could be offered to address such problems?

**Exercise 16.2**  Discuss the issues that arise when wiretaps in a mobile system with international roaming should be authorized.

**Exercise 16.3**  Let a 128-bit MAC be used for message authentication on a channel with an error rate of 1:1000. What is the probability to reject a message because of a transmission error when the message length is 1Kbit, 2Kbit and 1KByte? What are the probabilities when the bit error rate rises to 1:100? For both bit error rates, what are the probabilities when a 32-bit MAC is used?

**Exercise 16.4**  Nodes that have established a session at the transport layer are changing their IP address during the session. How could a session be protected at the IP layer in such a situation? Give an analysis of the general security problems a solution to this problem has to address, and of proposals currently discussed in the IETF.

**Exercise 16.5**  What effort is required from the address owner to create a valid CGA in comparison to the effort for an attacker for values $Sec$ = 1,2,3 when the computation of a hash value takes $1\mu sec$?

**Exercise 16.6**  Consider a busy access point that sends 1500-byte packets at the IEEE 802.11b data rate of 11Mbit/s. How long would an attacker have to wait for IVs to start repeating? If IVs are generated randomly, how long does an attacker have to wait on average for the first collision (two packets encrypted with the same IV)?

**Exercise 16.7**    The WEP challenge-response protocol sends challenges in the clear and encrypts the responses. Would it make any difference if the challenges were encrypted and the responses sent in the clear?

**Exercise 16.8**    Describe an attack whereby WEP-encrypted IP packets are re-routed to a destination chosen by the attacker.

**Exercise 16.9**    Give a comparison of the security services provided by UAM and 802.1X with EAP (RFC 2284).

# Chapter 17

## Database Security

A database does not merely store *data*, it provides *information* to its users. Database security should therefore not only be concerned with the protection of sensitive data, it should also look into mechanisms that allow users to retrieve information in a controlled manner. This remark highlights the two topics that distinguish database security from operating system security. You should control access to information more than access to data, and you should definitely focus control on the subjects requesting access, not withstanding the fact that the protection of data remains an important issue.

### OBJECTIVES

- Analyze the security issues that are specific to database systems.
- Understand how views can be used for access control in a relational database.
- Appreciate the problem of protecting information in statistical databases.
- Examine the potential interactions between security mechanisms in the database management system and in the underlying operating system.

## 17.1 INTRODUCTION

A database is a collection of data, arranged in some meaningful way. A *database management system (DBMS)* organizes the data and gives users the means to retrieve information. If access to information were completely uncontrolled, a database would render a less useful service because you would quite likely (be forced to) refrain from putting certain data into the database. For example, databases often hold information about individuals, be it employee records in a company, student records in a university or tax records with the Inland Revenue. Many countries have enacted *privacy* legislation putting an organization maintaining such a database under an obligation to protect personal data. Therefore, from early on database security had an important place within computer security. It had a special place, because database security is different from operating systems security. Here is the argument to back up this claim.

Operating systems manage *data*. Users invoke operating systems functions to create a file to delete a file or to open a file for read or write access. None of these operations considers the content of a file. Quite appropriately, the same is true for access control decisions made by an operating system. These decisions depend on the identity of the user, permissions defined for the file, access control lists, security labels etc., but not on the content of the file. This is not due to some fundamental security theorem, it is simply a reasonable engineering decision.

Entries in a database carry *information*. Database users perform operations that consider the content of database entries. The most typical use of a database is perhaps a database search. Hence, it is fitting that the access control decisions made by a DBMS also consider the content of database entries. A popular example is a salaries database where salaries above a given threshold should be kept confidential. In summary, database security is placed more towards the user end of the man–machine scale (Figure 17.1).

Figure 17.1:  The Place of Database Security on the Man–Machine Scale

At first sight, protecting sensitive information in a database looks easy. In the salaries database, you simply add to the query statement a condition that checks the amount of the salary. If you know which data to protect, this approach is certainly feasible.

However, an intruder may be interested in many different pieces of information. The range of possible sources of information is:

- exact data: the values stored in the database;
- bounds: lower or upper bounds on a numerical value like a salary can already be useful information;
- negative result: e.g. if a database contains numbers of criminal convictions, then the information that a particular person does not have zero convictions is sensitive;
- existence: the existence of data may already be sensitive information;
- probable value: being able to guess some information from the results of other queries.

In the end, you have to defend yourself against all eventualities. Protecting information becomes even more tricky if the database permits statistical queries. A statistical query would for example return the sum of all salaries or the mean of all salaries. A clever combination of such queries can reveal the information you want to protect. This topic will be taken up in section 17.4.

You have been warned about the many routes through which sensitive information may leak from your database. You should, of course, take security seriously but not lose sight of the fact that your database has to serve some useful purpose. Too restrictive policies, denying access to data although no sensitive information is disclosed, reduce the value of the database. You thus have to strive for *precision*, i.e. protecting sensitive information while revealing as much nonsensitive information as possible.

Database entries carry information about entities external to the computer system, like stock levels in a warehouse, examination results of students, balance of bank accounts, or available seats on a flight. Database entries should correctly reflect these external facts. Database security incorporates application-specific integrity protection to achieve:

- *internal consistency*: the entries in the database obey some prescribed rules. For examples, stock levels cannot fall below zero;
- *external consistency*: the entries in the database are correct. For example, the stock levels indicated in the database match the stock levels in the warehouse. The DBMS can help to avoid mistakes when updating the database but you cannot rely on the DBMS alone to keep the database in a *consistent state*. This property is also called *accuracy*.

In the layered model of section 2.4, the DBMS can be placed in the services layer on top of the operating system. The DBMS has to meet database-specific security requirements that are not dealt with by the operating system. The DBMS can enforce security in conjunction with protection mechanisms within the operating system or on its own when there are no adequate controls in the operating system or when it becomes too cumbersome to involve the operating system. Moreover, the DBMS can be a tool for defining security controls in the application layer. Figure 17.2 captures

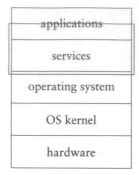

○  **Figure 17.2:  Location of Database Security**

the fact that database security includes security mechanisms at quite different layers of abstraction.

## 17.2 RELATIONAL DATABASES

Among the various models for organizing a database, the relational model is today the most widely used. Once more, we assume that you are familiar with the underlying concepts and give only a brief introduction to relational databases. A detailed exposition is given by Date (1990).

> **Relational Database**   A relational database is a database that is perceived by its users as a collection of *tables* (and tables only).

This definition of a relational database refers to its perception by the users and not to its physical organization. This also happens to be the appropriate level of abstraction to discuss database security.

Formally, a relation $R$ is a subset of $D_1 \times \cdots \times D_n$ where $D_1, \ldots, D_n$ are the *domains* on *n attributes*. The elements in the relation are *n*-tuples $(v_1, \ldots, v_n)$ with $v_i \in D_i$, i.e. the value of the *i*-th attribute has to be an element from $D_i$. The elements in a tuple are often called *fields*. When a field does not contain any value, we represent this by entering a special *null* value in this position. The meaning of null is 'there is no entry' and not 'the entry is unknown'.

The relations in Figure 17.3 could be part of a travel agent's database. The relation *Diary* has four attributes, name, day, flight and status, with the domains:

- name: all valid customer names;
- day: the days of the week, Mon, Tue, Wed, Thu, Fri, Sat, Sun;

| Name | Day | Flight | Status |
|------|-----|--------|--------|
| Alice | Mon | GR123 | private |
| Bob | Mon | YL011 | business |
| Bob | Wed | BX201 | |
| Carol | Tue | BX201 | business |
| Alice | Thu | FL9700 | business |

| Flight | Destination | Departs | Days |
|--------|-------------|---------|------|
| GR123 | THU | 7:55 | 1 - 4 - |
| YL011 | ATL | 8:10 | 1 2 3 4 5 - 7 |
| BX201 | SLA | 9:20 | 1 - 3 - 5 - |
| FL9700 | SLA | 14:00 | - 2 - 4 - 6 - |
| GR127 | THU | 14:55 | - 2 - 5 - |

Figure 17.3: The Relations *Diary* and *Flights*

- flight number: flight numbers, two characters and up to four numerals;
- status: business or private.

The standard language for describing how information in a relational database can be retrieved and updated is SQL, the *Structured Query Language* (International Organisation for Standardization, 1992). The SQL operations for data manipulations are:

- SELECT: retrieves data from a relation,

```
SELECT Name, Status
      FROM Diary
      WHERE Day = 'Mon'
```

returns the result

| Name | Status |
|------|--------|
| Alice | private |
| Bob | business |

- UPDATE: update fields in a relation,

```
UPDATE Diary
      SET Status = private
      WHERE Day = 'Sun'
```

marks all journeys on a Sunday as private trips.

- DELETE: deletes tuples from a relation,

```
DELETE FROM Diary
      WHERE Name = 'Alice'
```

deletes all of Alice's journeys from *Diary*.

- INSERT: adds tuples to a relation,

```
INSERT INTO Flights (Flight,Destination,Days)
     VALUES ('GR005', 'GOH', '12-45-')
```

inserts a new tuple into *Flights* where the field *Departs* is still unspecified.

In all cases, more complicated constructions are possible. It is not the purpose of this book to explain all the intricacies of SQL and we will only give one example for demonstration. To find out who is going to Thule, run:

```
SELECT Name
     FROM Diary
     WHERE Flight IN
          ( SELECT Flight
                    FROM Flights
                    WHERE Destination = 'THU' )
```

Relations are often visualized as *tables*. Attributes correspond to the columns in the table, using the names of the attributes as *headings* for the columns. The rows in the table correspond to the tuples (*records*) in the database. In the relational model, a relation cannot contain links or pointers to other tables. A relationship between tables (relations) can only be given by another relation. In a relational database, different kinds of relations may exist.

- *Base relations*: also called real relations, are named and autonomous relations; they exist in their own right, are not derived from other relations, and have 'their own' stored data.
- *Views*: are named, derived relations, defined in terms of other named relations; they do not have stored data of their own.
- *Snapshots*: like views, are named, derived relations, defined in terms of other named relations; they have stored data of their own.
- *Query results*: the result of a query; they may or may not have a name; they have no persistent existence in the database *per se*.

For example, a snapshot of the *Diary* table that tells who is traveling when is defined by:

```
CREATE SNAPSHOT Travellers
    AS SELECT name, day
       FROM   Diary
```

## 17.2.1 Database Keys

In each relation, we have to be able to identify all tuples in a unique way. Sometimes, a single attribute may be used as such an identifier. There may even be a choice of attributes which could serve for this purpose. On the other hand, it also may happen that we need more than one attribute to construct such a unique identifier.

A *primary key* of a relation is a unique and minimal identifier for that relation. A primary key $K$ of a relation $R$ has to fulfill the following conditions.

1. Uniqueness: at any time, no tuples of $R$ have the same value for $K$.

2. Minimality: if $K$ is composite, no component of $K$ can be omitted without destroying uniqueness.

In the relation *Diary*, the combination of *name* and *day* can serve as the primary key (assuming that customers only go on one journey per day.) In the relation *Flights*, the primary key is the flight number.

Every relation must have a primary key, as no relation may contain duplicate tuples. This follows directly from our formal definition of a relation. When the primary key of one relation is used as an attribute in another relation, then it is a *foreign key* in that relation. In our example, the flight number as the primary key in the relation *Flights* is a foreign key in the relation *Diary*.

## 17.2.2 Integrity Rules

Within a relational database, you can define integrity rules that enforce *internal consistency* and help to maintain *external consistency (accuracy)*. Most of these rules will be specific to the application, but there are two rules which are inherent to the relational database model.

**Entity Integrity Rule**  No component of the primary key of a base relation is allowed to accept nulls.

This rule allows us to find all tuples in the base relations. The tuples in the base relations correspond to 'real' entities and we would not represent such an identity in the database if we could not identify it.

**Referential Integrity Rule**  The database must not contain unmatched foreign key values.

A foreign key value represents a *reference* to an entry in some other table. An unmatched foreign key value is a value which does not appear as a primary key in the referenced table. It is a reference to a nonexisting tuple.

In addition to these two rules, further application-specific integrity rules may be desirable. Those integrity rules are important because they keep the database in a useful state. Typically, you would use them to do the following.

- *Field checks:* to prevent errors on data entry. In our example, we can guard against the insertion of arbitrary values in the status attribute of the *Diary* relation through a rule checking that the value entered is either *business* or *private*.

- *Scope checks:* in statistical databases, you may want rules for checking that the results of queries are computed over a sufficiently large sample. Looking ahead to the *Students* relation of Figure 17.4, you could define a rule that returns a grade average 67 by default if the sample size is not larger than three.

- *Consistency checks:* entries in different relations may refer to the same aspect of the external world and should therefore express a consistent view of this aspect. In our example, we can check the day a customer travels against the scheduled departure days of their flights. Alice's flight on Monday on GR123 is consistent with the fact that this flight departs on Mondays and Thursdays. Carol's booking on Tuesday on BX201 is inconsistent with the fact that this flight leaves on Mondays, Wednesdays and Fridays. An integrity rule comparing the respective fields could have stopped the travel agent from making this mistake.

Integrity rules of this kind are controls in the application layer. The DBMS provides the infrastructure for specifying and enforcing such rules. For example, an *integrity trigger* is a program that can be attached to an object in the database to check particular integrity properties of that object. When an UPDATE, INSERT or DELETE operation tries to modify such an object, this program is triggered and performs its check.

We will pursue this topic no further than pointing to potential clashes between confidentiality and integrity. When the evaluation of an integrity rule requires access to sensitive information, you face the dilemma of either evaluating the rule incompletely (and incorrectly) to protect the sensitive information, or leaking some sensitive information to maintain consistency of the database.

## 17.3 ACCESS CONTROL

To protect sensitive information, the DBMS has to control how users can access the database. To see how controls could be implemented, you should remember that access to a database can be considered at two levels, which are:

- data manipulation operations on base relations;
- compound operations like views or snapshots.

Go back for a moment to section 2.4.1. You can look at access control from two directions, using rules that:

- restrict the operations available to a user;
- define the protection requirements for each individual data item.

In a DBMS, controls on compound operations regulate how users can work with the database. On the other hand, checks on the manipulation of base relations protect the entries in the database. By deciding on the type of access operations you want to control, you also influence the focus of the policies to be enforced. Conversely, the focus of your policies will suggest which type of operations to control. Whatever option you choose, there are two properties you ought to aim for.

- *Completeness:* all fields in the database are protected.

- *Consistency:* there are no conflicting rules governing the access to a data item.

A security policy is consistent if there is no element in the database which can be accessed in different ways which result in different access control decisions. Legitimate access requests should not be prevented nor should there be ways of circumventing the specified access policy.

### 17.3.1 The SQL Security Model

The basic SQL security model follows a familiar pattern. It implements discretionary access control based on three entities.

- *Users:* the users of the database; the *user identity* is authenticated during a logon process; the DBMS may run its own logon or accept user identities authenticated by the operating system.

- *Actions:* include SELECT, UPDATE, DELETE and INSERT.

- *Objects:* tables, views and columns (attributes) of tables and views; SQL3 further includes structured user-defined data types.

Users invoke actions on objects and the DBMS has to decide whether to permit the requested action. When an object is created, a user is designated as its owner and initially only the owner has access to the object. Other users first have to be issued with a *privilege*. The components of a privilege are:

$$(\text{grantor, grantee, object, action, grantable})$$

The two mainstays of the SQL security models are privileges and views. They provide the framework for defining application-oriented security policies.

### 17.3.2 Granting and Revocation of Privileges

In SQL, privileges are managed with the operations GRANT and REVOKE. Privileges refer to particular actions and can be restricted to certain attributes of a table. In our example, we allow two travel agents, Art and Zoe, to inspect and update parts of the *Diary* table by:

```
GRANT SELECT, UPDATE (Day,Flight)
     ON TABLE Diary
     TO Art,Zoe
```

Privileges can be selectively revoked.

```
REVOKE UPDATE
      ON TABLE Diary
      FROM Art
```

A further feature is the granting of the right to grant privileges, implemented in SQL by the GRANT *option*. For example, with

```
GRANT SELECT
      ON TABLE Diary
      TO Art
      WITH GRANT OPTION
```

travel agent Art may in turn grant privileges on the *Diary* table to Zoe,

```
GRANT SELECT
      ON TABLE Diary
      TO Zoe
      WITH GRANT OPTION
```

When the owner of the *Diary* table revokes the privileges granted to Art, all the privileges granted by Art also have to be revoked. Thus, revocation has to *cascade* and the information necessary to do so has to be maintained by the database system.

You should also note that once other users have been granted access to data, the owner of the data cannot control how information derived from this data is going to be used, even if there is still some control over the original data. You can read data from a table and copy this data into another table without requiring any 'write' access to the original table.

### 17.3.3 Access Control through Views

Views are derived relations. The SQL operation for creating views has the following format.

```
CREATE VIEW view_name [ ( column [, column ] ... ) ]
      AS subquery
      [ WITH CHECK OPTION ];
```

You could implement access control in a relational database by granting privileges directly for the entries in base relations. However, many security policies are better expressed through views, and through privileges on those views. The subquery in the view definition can describe quite complex access conditions. As a simple example, we construct a view that includes all business trips in the example relation *Diary*.

```
CREATE VIEW business_trips AS
      SELECT * FROM Diary
      WHERE Status = 'business'
      WITH CHECK OPTION;
```

Access control through views can properly be placed in the application layer. The DBMS only provides the tools for implementing the controls. Views are attractive for several reasons.

- Views are flexible and allow access control policies to be defined at a level of description that is close to the application requirements.
- Views can enforce context-dependent and data-dependent security policies.
- Views can implement controlled invocation.
- Secure views can replace security labels.
- Data can be easily reclassified.

Application-oriented access control can be expressed through views like

```
CREATE VIEW Top_of_the_Class AS
      SELECT * FROM Students WHERE Grade <
      (SELECT Grade FROM Students WHERE Name = current_user());
```

to display only those students whose grade average is less than that of the person using the view, or

```
CREATE VIEW My_Journeys AS
      SELECT * FROM Diary
      WHERE Customer = current_user();
```

to display only those journeys booked by the customer using the view. Discretionary access control can be implemented by adding the access control table to the database. Views can now refer to this relation. In this way, you can also express access control based on group membership as well as policies regulating the users' rights to grant and revoke access rights.

Furthermore, views can define or refer to security labels. In our example, business flights to Thule can be marked as confidential by creating the view:

```
CREATE VIEW Flights≥CONFIDENTIAL AS
      SELECT * FROM Diary
      WHERE Destination = 'THU' AND Status = 'business';
```

Controlling read access through views poses no particular technical problem other than capturing your security policy correctly. The situation is different when views are used by INSERT or UPDATE operations to write to the database. First, there exist views that are not updatable because they do not contain the information that is needed to maintain the integrity of the corresponding base relation. For example, a view that does not contain the primary key of an underlying base relation cannot be used for updates. Second, even if a view is updatable, some interesting security issues remain. A travel agent who only has access to the *Diary* database through the view business_trips sees

| Name | Day | Flight | Status |
|-------|------|--------|----------|
| Bob | Mon | YL011 | business |
| Carol | Tue | BX201 | business |
| Alice | Thu | FL9700 | business |

Should the travel agent be allowed to update the view with the following operation?

```
UPDATE business_trips
      SET Status = 'private'
      WHERE Name = 'Alice' AND Day = 'Thu'
```

The entry for Alice would then disappear from view. As a matter of fact, in this case the update will not be permitted because the definition of the view has specified the CHECK option. If the definition of a view includes WITH CHECK OPTION, then UPDATE and INSERT can only write entries to the database that meet the definition of the view. If the CHECK option is omitted, *blind writes* are possible.

A view is not only an object in the SQL security model; it can also be seen as a program. When a view is evaluated with the privileges of its owner rather than with the privileges of the user invoking the view, then you have another method of implementing controlled invocation.

The access conditions in a view have to be specified within the limits of SQL. If this proves too restrictive, software packages (stored procedures) written in a more expressive language are another option for the DBMS to provide controlled access to the database. Again, users are granted execute privilege on the package which runs with the privileges of its owner.

## Lesson

Controlled invocation can be found at any layer of a computer system. It is a principle equally useful in microprocessors and DBMSs.

So far we have presented the aspects that make views a useful security mechanism. Naturally, views have also their disadvantages.

- Access checking may become rather complicated and slow.

- View definitions have to be checked for 'correctness'. Do they really capture the intended security policy?

- Completeness and consistency are not achieved automatically; views may overlap or may fail to capture the entire database.

- The security-relevant part of the DBMS (the TCB) will become very large.

Views are suitable in a 'normal commercial' environment. They can be tailored to the application and require no modification of the DBMS. Definition of views then is part of the general process of defining the structure of the database so that it best meets the business requirements.

It may, however, become difficult to determine for individual data items who has access. Therefore, views are less suitable in situations where it is deemed necessary to protect the data items, rather than control the users' actions.

## 17.4 STATISTICAL DATABASE SECURITY

Statistical databases raise security issues that so far have hardly been investigated in this book. The distinctive feature of a statistical database is that information is retrieved by means of *statistical (aggregate) queries* on an attribute (column) of a table. The aggregate functions in SQL are:

- COUNT: the number of values in a column;

- SUM: the sum of the values in a column;

- AVG: the average of the values in a column;

- MAX: the largest value in a column;

- MIN: the smallest value in a column.

The *query predicate* of a statistical query specifies the tuples that will be used to compute the aggregate, the *query set* is the tuples matching the query predicate. In a nutshell, statistical databases pose the following security problem.

- The database contains items of data that are individually sensitive. Direct access to data items is therefore not permitted.

- Statistical queries to the database are permitted. By their very nature, these queries read individual data items.

In such a setting it becomes possible to *infer* information and we will show that it is no longer sufficient to police access requests individually. We are also taking a more pragmatic view of information flow. The confidentiality models in Chapters 8 and 9 tried their best to stop any information flow whatsoever. In a statistical database, there must be some information flow from the data items to their aggregate. We can only try to reduce it to an acceptable level.

| Name | Sex | Program | Units | Grade Ave. |
|------|-----|---------|-------|------------|
| Alma | F | MBA | 8 | 63 |
| Bill | M | CS | 15 | 58 |
| Carol | F | CS | 16 | 70 |
| Don | M | MIS | 22 | 75 |
| Errol | M | CS | 8 | 66 |
| Flora | F | MIS | 16 | 81 |
| Gala | F | MBA | 23 | 68 |
| Homer | M | CS | 7 | 50 |
| Igor | M | MIS | 21 | 70 |

○ **Figure 17.4: The Relation *Students***

The *Students* database in Figure 17.4 will provide the examples in this section. Statistical queries on all attributes are allowed but individual entries in the *Units* and *Grade Ave.* columns cannot be read directly. The statistical query

```
Q1 : SELECT AVG(Grade Ave.)
     FROM   Students
     WHERE  Programme = 'MBA'
```

computes the grade average of all MBA students. The *query predicate* in the example is `Programme = 'MBA'`.

### 17.4.1 Aggregation and Inference

Two important concepts in statistical database security are aggregation and inference. *Aggregation* refers to the observation that the sensitivity level of an aggregate computed over a group of values in a database may differ from the sensitivity levels of the individual elements. You will mostly meet scenarios where the sensitivity level of the aggregate is lower than the levels of the individual elements. The reverse is true when the aggregate is sensitive executive information derived from a collection of less sensitive business data.

The aggregate is another relation in the database, e.g. a view, so you can use the security mechanisms proposed in this chapter to control access to the aggregate. However, an attacker can exploit the difference in sensitivity levels to obtain access to the more sensitive items. The *inference problem* refers to the derivation of sensitive information from nonsensitive data. The following types of attack have to be considered.

- *Direct attack*: the aggregate is computed over a small sample so that information about individual data items is leaked.
- *Indirect attack*: this attack combines information relating to several aggregates.
- *Tracker attack*: this is a particularly effective type of indirect attack.
- *Linear system vulnerability*: this takes tracker attacks a step further, using algebraic relations between query sets to construct equations which yield the desired information.

## 17.4.2 Tracker Attacks

We will now demonstrate how to employ statistical queries to elicit sensitive information from our *Students* relation. Assume that we know that Carol is a female CS student. By combining the legitimate queries

```
Q1 : SELECT COUNT(*)
     FROM   Students
     WHERE  Sex = 'F' AND Programme = 'CS'

Q2 : SELECT AVG(Grade Ave.)
     FROM   Students
     WHERE  Sex = 'F' AND Programme = 'CS'
```

we learn from Q1 that there is only one female CS student in the database so the value 70 returned by Q2 is precisely her grade average. The problem here is that the selection criteria define a set containing only one element. You could therefore allow a statistical query only if it covers a sufficiently large subset. However, we could simply query the complement by negating the selection criteria and obtain the same result as before from the difference between the result of the query applied to the entire database and the result of the query applied to the complement of the set we are really interested in. You therefore have to demand that not only the set of tuples considered by a query but also its complement are sufficiently large.

Unfortunately, even this is not good enough. Assume that each query set and its complement must contain at least three elements. The sequence of queries

```
Q3 : SELECT  COUNT(*)
     FROM    Students
     WHERE   Programme = 'CS'


Q4 : SELECT  COUNT(*)
     FROM    Students
     WHERE   Programme = 'CS' AND Sex = 'M'


Q5 : SELECT  AVG(Grade Ave.)
     FROM    Students
     WHERE   Programme = 'CS'


Q6 : SELECT  AVG(Grade Ave.)
     FROM    Students
     WHERE   Programme = 'CS' AND Sex = 'M'
```

returns the values Q3: 4, Q4: 3, Q5: 61, Q6: 58. All queries take into account a sufficiently large set of tuples so they are not prohibited. However, by combining the four results we compute Carol's grade average as $4 \cdot 61 - 3 \cdot 58 = 70$.

You may feel that we were lucky in this case and were only able to construct this set of queries because Carol was the single female CS student. We will now show how to set up an attack in a systematic way. First, we need a tracker.

> A query predicate $T$ that allows the tracking down of information about a single tuple is called an *individual tracker* for that tuple. A *general tracker* is a predicate that can be used to find the answer to any inadmissible query.

Let $T$ be a general tracker and let $R$ be a predicate that uniquely identifies the tuple $r$ we want to probe. In our example, the predicate is Name = 'Carol'. We make two queries to the database using the predicates $R \vee T$ and $R \vee \mathrm{NOT}\,(T)$. Our target $r$ is the only tuple used by both queries. To make sure that both queries are admissible, we choose $T$ so that the query set and its complement are large enough for the query to be permitted. A final query over the entire database gives us all the data to complete the attack. In our example:

```
Sex = 'F' AND Programme = 'CS'
```

is an individual tracker for Carol and Programme = 'MIS' is one of many general trackers. We proceed with the queries

```
Q7 : SELECT  SUM(Units)
     FROM    Students
```

```
        WHERE   Name = 'Carol' OR Programme = 'MIS'

Q8 : SELECT  SUM(Units)
     FROM    Students
     WHERE   Name = 'Carol' OR NOT (Programme = 'MIS')

Q9 : SELECT  SUM(Units)
     FROM    Students
```

and receive Q7: 75, Q8: 77 and Q9: 136. So Carol must have passed $(75 + 77) - 136 =$ 16 units. Experience has shown that almost all statistical databases have a general tracker.

## 17.4.3 Countermeasures

The analysis of statistical inference attacks has dominated the early literature on database security. Since then, researchers have shifted their attention to other areas, less because complete and watertight solutions have been found and implemented than because they had to acknowledge the limits of countermeasures against inference attacks. Given those limitations, what can you realistically do about the inference problem?

First, you would suppress obviously sensitive information. This implies that you know which information is sensitive, which hopefully will be the case, and that you know how this information can be derived. At least, you would check the size of the query set before releasing the result of a statistical query.

Next, you could disguise the data. You could randomly swap entries in the database so that an individual query will give a wrong result although the statistical queries would still be correct. Alternatively, you could add small random perturbations to the query result so that the value returned is close to the real value but not quite correct. As a drawback, these techniques reduce precision and usability. You would not want to randomly swap values in a medical database.

Some aggregation problems can be eased by taking care with the design of the database schema (Lunt, 1989). A *static* analysis of the structure of the database can reveal sensitive relationships between attributes. Such attributes are then placed in separate tables. A user with access to one table only is no longer able to correlate the attributes. Of course, a user with access to all relevant tables is still in a position to do so but as the database manager you can be more *precise* when allocating privileges. In our example, the relationship between names and academic performance is sensitive. We replace the table *Students* by two tables, linked by a student identity number (Figure 17.5).

The first table can now be classified at a sufficiently high level so that only authorized users can link names and academic performance.

| Name | ID | | ID | Sex | Programme | Units | Grade Ave. |
|-------|------|--|-------|------|------------|--------|-------------|
| Alma  | B13  | | B13   | F    | MBA        | 8      | 63          |
| Bill  | C25  | | C25   | M    | CS         | 15     | 58          |
| Carol | C23  | | C23   | F    | CS         | 16     | 70          |
| Don   | M38  | | M38   | M    | MIS        | 22     | 75          |
| Errol | C12  | | C12   | M    | CS         | 8      | 66          |
| Flora | M22  | | M22   | F    | MIS        | 16     | 81          |
| Gala  | B36  | | B36   | F    | MBA        | 23     | 68          |
| Homer | C10  | | C10   | M    | CS         | 7      | 50          |
| Igor  | M20  | | M20   | M    | MIS        | 21     | 70          |

○ **Figure 17.5: Students Table Split into Two Tables**

Finally, observe that inference problems are caused not so much by single queries but by a clever combination of several queries. You could therefore track what the user knows. Possibly this gives the best security but it is also the most expensive option. User actions are recorded in an audit log and you perform a *query analysis* to step in if a suspicious sequence of queries is detected. Of course, in the first place you have to know what constitutes suspicious behavior. To tighten your protection even further, your query analysis will have to consider what two users, or a group of users, know together.

## 17.5 INTEGRATION WITH THE OPERATING SYSTEM

When you look at a database from the position of the operating system, you see a number of operating system processes and the memory resources that keep the data entries. In many respects, the DBMS has similar duties to the operating system. It has to stop users from interfering with each other, and with the DBMS.

If you do not want to duplicate effort, you could give these tasks to the operating system. In such a set-up, the DBMS runs as a set of operating system processes. There are system processes for general database management tasks and each database user is mapped to a separate operating system process (Figure 17.6). Now, the operating system can distinguish between users and if you store each database object in its own file, then the operating system can do all the access control. The DBMS only has to translate user queries into operations the operating system understands.

Allocating an individual operating system process to every database user wastes memory resources and does not scale up to large user numbers. Hence, you need processes that handle the database requests of several users (Figure 17.7). You save memory but the

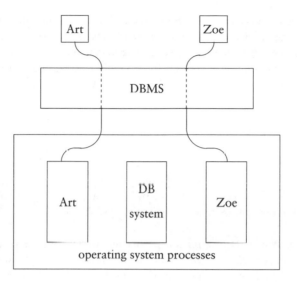

Figure 17.6: Isolation of Database Users by the Operating System

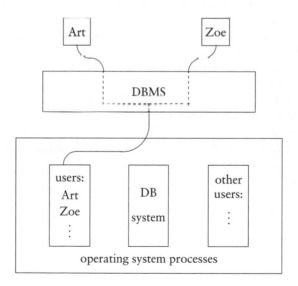

Figure 17.7: Isolation of Database Users by the DBMS

responsibility for access control now firmly rests with the DBMS. Similar considerations apply to the storage of database objects. If the objects are too small, having a separate file for each object is wasteful. Once the operating system has no access control functions with respect to database users, you are free to collect several database objects in one operating system file.

## 17.6 PRIVACY

Many organizations will for legitimate reasons store personal data about their customers, such as name, address, age, credit card numbers, meal preferences or other consumer habits. Data of this kind is usually protected by law. Compliance with legal and regulatory constraints is an important issue when maintaining such data.

International recommendations for the protection of personal data are the *OECD Guidelines on the Protection of Privacy and Transborder Flows of Personal Data*. These guidelines state eight protection principles where the *data subject* is the individual the data refers to and the *data controller* is the person who maintains the database.

1. Collection Limitation Principle: there should be limits to the collection of personal data; data should be obtained by lawful and fair means and, where appropriate, with the knowledge or consent of the data subject.
2. Data Quality Principle: personal data should be relevant to the purposes for which it is to be used, accurate, complete and up to date.
3. Purpose Specification Principle: the purposes for which personal data is collected should be specified.
4. Use Limitation Principle: personal data should not be disclosed or used for purposes other than those specified, except with the consent of the data subject or by the authority of law.
5. Security Safeguards Principle: personal data should be protected by reasonable security safeguards.
6. Openness Principle: there should be a general policy of openness about developments, practices and policies with respect to personal data.
7. Individual Participation Principle: an individual should have the right to obtain confirmation of whether or not the data controller has data relating to him/her, to challenge data relating to him/her and to be given reasons if such a request is denied.
8. Accountability Principle: a data controller should be accountable for complying with measures which give effect to the principles stated above.

Another important document is the EU Directive[1] on the protection of individuals with regard to the processing of personal data and on the free movement of such data. EU directives are not laws but have to be transformed into national law by EU member

[1] EU Directive 95/46/EC of the European Parliament and of the Council of 24 October 1995.

states. The Directive has a strong emphasis on user consent. Users should 'opt in' to indicate that they agree that their data is stored. The alternative is an 'opt out' policy where data subjects have to state explicitly that data should not be kept.

In the US, data protection is addressed by sectoral laws. For example, HIPAA, the Health Insurance Portability and Accountability Act of 1996, is a federal law protecting patients' medical records and other health information provided to health plans, doctors, hospitals and other health care providers. The Act took effect in 2003 and had a considerable impact on database security, and on IT security in general.

## 17.7 FURTHER READING

If you need to revise the relational database model, consult Date (1990). A substantial collection of material on database security has been compiled by Castano *et al.* (1994). An earlier but still very useful book on database security by Denning (1982). This book is in particular a good reference for statistical database security. A further useful source on this topic is by Lunt (1989). All major database vendors maintain web pages with information on their products and with good introductions to database security.

## 17.8 EXERCISES

**Exercise 17.1** Consider an accounts database with records *(customer name, account number, balance, credit rating)* and the following types of user, *customer, clerk, manager*. Define an access structure, e.g. through views, so that:

- customers can read their own account;
- clerks can read all fields other than *credit rating* and update *balance* for all accounts;
- managers can create new records, read all fields and update *credit rating* for all accounts.

**Exercise 17.2** Consider a database of student records that contains student names and the marks for all courses in the program. Lecturers are provided with a view that shows all students on their course whose paper has not been marked yet. Should this view be defined WITH CHECK OPTION? Suggest general criteria for deciding whether to use the CHECK OPTION.

**Exercise 17.3** All statistical queries on the *Students* relation (Figure 17.4) must have at least three tuples in their query set. Only AVG-queries on the attribute Grade Ave. are allowed. Find a new general tracker and construct a tracker attack on Homer's grade average.

**Exercise 17.4**   In database security, you have seen examples of security controls placed in the application layer. What are the problems with this approach?

**Exercise 17.5**   Consider a database where aggregates are placed at a higher sensitivity level than the data items they are derived from. A user privileged to access the data items can potentially compute the aggregate by accessing the data items individually. How can you defend against such an attack?

**Exercise 17.6**   You are given a database where access rights can be defined separately for each row in a table. Access control shall use the security mechanisms of the operating system. What are the consequences of this design decision with respect to the way the database objects are stored in operating system files? (As a yardstick, consider an operating system that uses 100 bytes of administrative data for each file and a database with 10 m. records.) Is this a viable design decision?

# Bibliography

Abu El-Asa, Ahmed, Martin Aeberhard, Frank J. Furrer, Ian Gardiner-Smith, and David Kohn (2002) *Our PKI-Experience*. SYSLOGIC Press, Birmensdorf, Switzerland.

Adams, Anne and Martina Angela Sasse (1999) Users are not the enemy. *Communications of the ACM*, **42**(12):40–46.

Alberts, C. and A. Dorofee (2003) *Managing Information Security Risks*. Pearson Education Inc., Boston, MA.

Alpern, B. and S. Schneider (1985) Defining liveness. *Information Processing Letters*, **21**(4):181–185.

Amoroso, E. (1994) *Fundamentals of Computer Security Technology*. Prentice Hall, Englewood Cliffs, NJ.

Anderson, J. (October 1972) Computer security technology planning study. Technical Report 73–51, US Air Force Electronic Systems Technical Report.

Anderson, Ross (2001) *Security Engineering*. John Wiley & Sons, New York.

Arbaugh, William A., William L. Fithen and John McHugh (2000) Windows of vulnerability: a case study analysis. *IEEE Computer*, **33**(12):52–59.

Arceneaux, J. (October 1996) Experiences in the art of security. *Security Audit & Control–Review*, **14**(4):12–16.

Aresenault, Alfred W. and Sean Turner (November 2000) Internet X.509 Public Key Infrastructure – Roadmap. Internet Draft draft-ietf-pkix-roadmap-06.txt. http://www.ietf.org.

Ashcraft, Ken and Dawson Engler (2002) Using programmer-written compiler extensions to catch security holes. In *Proceedings of the 2002 IEEE Symposium on Security and Privacy*, pages 143–159.

Ashley, Paul M. and Mark Vandenwauver (1999) *Practical Intranet Security*. Kluwer Academic Publishers.

Atkins, D., P. Buis, C. Hare, R. Kelley, C. Nachenberg, A.B. Nelson, P. Phillips, T. Ritchey, T. Sheldon and J. Snyder (1997) *Internet Security*. New Riders, Indianapolis, IN, 2nd edition.

Aura, Tuomas (2003) Cryptographically generated addresses (cga). In W. Mao C. Boyd, editor, *Proceedings ISC'03, LNCS 2851*, pages 29–43. Springer-Verlag.

Aura, Tuomas, Michael Roe and Jari Arkko (December 2002) Security of Internet location management. In *Proceedings of the 18th Annual Computer Security Applications Conference*, pages 78–87.

Baker, D.B. (September 1996) Fortresses built upon sand. In *Proceedings of the New Security Paradigms Workshop*, pages 148–153.

Bejtlich, Richard (2000) Interpreting network traffic: a network intrusion detector's look at suspicious events. In *Proceedings of the 12th Annual Computer Security Incidence Handling Conference*, Chicago.

Bell, D.E. and L.J. LaPadula (1996) MITRE technical report 2547 (secure computer system): Volume II. *Journal of Computer Security*, 4(2/3):239–263.

Bell, David and Leonard LaPadula (1975) Secure computer system: unified exposition and Multics implementation. Technical Report ESD-TR-75-306, The MITRE Corporation, Bedford, MA, July 1975.

Bellare, Mihir and Phillip Rogaway (1994) Entity authentication and key distribution. In D.R. Stinson, editor, *Advances in Cryptology – CRYPTO'93, LNCS 773*, pages 232–249. Springer-Verlag.

Bellare, Mihir and Phillip Rogaway (1995) Optimal asymmetric encryption padding. In A. De Santis, editor, *Advances in Cryptology – Proceedings Eurocrypt 94, LNCS 950*, pages 92–111. Springer-Verlag.

Bellare, Mihir, Ran Canetti and Hugo Krawczyk (1996) Keyed hash functions and message authentication. In N. Koblitz, editor, *Advances in Cryptology – Proceedings Crypto 96, LNCS 1109*, pages 1–15. Springer-Verlag.

Bellovin, S. (1989) Security problems in the TCP/IP protocol suite. *ACM Computer Communications Review*, 19(2):32–48, April.

Bellovin, Steve M. and Michael Merritt (1990) Limitations of the Kerberos Authentication System. *ACM Computer Communications Review*, 20(5):119–132.

Bellovin, Steve M. and Michael Merritt (1992) Encrypted key exchange: password-based protocols secure against dictionary attacks. In *Proceedings of the 1992 IEEE Symposium on Security and Privacy*, pages 72–84.

Berstis, D. *et al.* (1978) IBM System/38 addressing and authorization. Technical Report GS80-0237, IBM System/38 Technical Development.

Besson, Frédéric, Tomasz Blanc, Cédric Fournet and Andrew D. Gordon (2004) From stack inspection to access control: a security analysis for libraries. In *Proceedings of the 17th IEEE Computer Security Foundations Workshop*, pages 61–75. IEEE Computer Society.

Biba, K.J. (1977) Integrity consideration for secure computer systems. Technical Report ESD-TR-76-372, MTR-3153, The MITRE Corporation, Bedford, MA, April.

Bieber, P., J. Cazin, P. Girard, J.-L. Lanet, V. Wiels and G. Zanon (2000) Checking secure interactions of smart card applets. In F. Cuppens *et al.*, editors, *ESORICS 2000, LNCS 1895*, pages 1–16. Springer-Verlag.

Bird, R., I. Gopal, A. Herzberg, P. Janson, S. Kutten, R. Molva and M. Yung (1995) The KryptoKnight family of light-weight protocols for authentication and key distribution. *IEEE/ACM Transactions on Networking*, 3(1):31–41, February.

Blakely, B. (1996) The emperor's old armour. In *Proceedings of the New Security Paradigms Workshop*, pages 2–16, September.

Blaze, Matt, Joan Feigenbaum and Jack Lacy (1996) Decentralized trust management. In *Proceedings of the 1996 IEEE Symposium on Security and Privacy*, pages 164–173.

Bleichenbacher, Daniel (1998) A chosen ciphertext attack against protocols based on RSA encryption standard PKCS # 1. In H. Krawczyk, editor, *Advances in Cryptology – Crypto 98, LNCS 1462*, pages 1–12. Springer-Verlag.

Brewer, D.F.C. and M.J. Nash (1989) The Chinese Wall security policy. In *Proceedings of the 1989 IEEE Symposium on Security and Privacy*, pages 206–214.

Brickell, Ernie, Jan Camenisch and Liqun Chen (2004) Direct anonymous authentication. In B. Pfitzmann *et al.*, editors, *Proceedings of the 11th ACM Conference on Computer and Communications Security*, pages 132–145. ACM Press.

Brown, Keith (2000) *Programming Windows Security*. Addison-Wesley.

BSI (2003) IT baseline protection manual. Technical report, Bundesamt für Sicherheit in der Informationstechnik, Bonn, Germany, October.

Camenisch, Jan (2004) Better privacy for Trusted Computing Platforms. In P. Samarati *et al.*, editors, *ESORICS 2004, LNCS 3193*, pages 73–88. Springer-Verlag.

Canadian System Security Center (1993) *The Canadian Trusted Computer Product Evaluation Criteria*, Version 3.0e.

Cardelli, Luca (1997) Type systems. In *Handbook of Computer Science and Engineering*, Chapter 103. CRC Press.

Castano, S., M. Fugini, G. Martella and P. Samarati (1994) *Database Security*. Addison-Wesley, Reading, MA.

CCIB (2004a) *Common Criteria for Information Technology Security Evaluation*, Version 2.2.

CCIB (2004b) *Common Methodology for Information Technology Security Evaluation – Part 2: Evaluation Methodology*, Version 2.2.

CCITT (1988) *The Directory – Overview of Concepts, Models and Services*, CCITT Rec X.500.

Cheswick, William R., Steven M. Bellovin and Aviel D. Rubin (2003) *Firewalls and Internet Security: Repelling the Wily Hacker*. Addison-Wesley, Reading, MA, 2nd edition.

Chokhani, S. (1992) Trusted product evaluations. *Communications of the ACM*, 35(7):64–76, July.

Clark, D.R. and D.R. Wilson (1987) A comparison of commercial and military computer security policies. In *Proceedings of the 1987 IEEE Symposium on Security and Privacy*, pages 184–194.

CNSS (2003) *National Policy on the Use of the Advanced Encryption Standard (AES) to Protect National Security Systems and National Security Information*, June. CNSS Policy No. 15, Fact Sheet No. 1.

Commission of the European Communities (1991) *Information Technology Security Evaluation Criteria (ITSEC)*, Version 1.2.

Commission of the European Communities (1993) *Information Technology Security Evaluation Manual (ITSEM)*.

Corbato, F.J. (1991) On building systems that will fail. *Communications of the ACM*, 34(9):72–81, September.

Cowan, Crispan, Calton Pu, Dave Maier, Jonathan Walpole, Peat Bakke, Steve Beattie, Aaron Grier, Perry Wagle, Qian Zhang and Heather Hinton (1998) StackGuard: automatic adaptive detection and prevention of buffer-overflow attacks. In *Proceedings of the 7th USENIX Security Symposium*, pages 63–78.

Curry, D.A. (1992) *Unix System Security*. Addison-Wesley, Reading, MA.

Daemen, Joan and Vincent Rijmen (1999) AES proposal: Rijndael. Technical report, September, AES Algorithm Submission.

Date, C.J. (1990) *An Introduction to Database Systems – Volume I*. Addison-Wesley, Reading, MA, 5th edition.

Daugman, John (1993) High confidence visual recognition of persons by a test of statistical independence. *IEEE Transactions on Pattern Analysis and Machine Intelligence*, 15(11):1148–1161.

Denning, D.E., T.F. Lunt, R.R. Schell, W.R. Shockley and M. Heckman (1988) The SeaView Security Model. In *Proceedings of the 1988 IEEE Symposium on Security and Privacy*, pages 218–233.

Denning, Dorothy E. (1982) *Cryptography and Security*. Addison-Wesley, Reading, MA.

Denning, Dorothy E. and Giovanni M. Sacco (1981) Timestamps in key distribution protocols. *Communications of the ACM*, 24(8):533–536.

Diffie, Whitfield , Paul C. van Oorschot and Michael J. Wiener (1992) Authentication and authenticated key exchanges. *Designs, Codes and Cryptography*, 2:107–125.

Diffie, Whitfield and Martin E. Hellman (1976) New directions in cryptography. *IEEE Transactions on Information Theory*, 22:644–654.

Dobbertin, Hans (1996) Cryptanalysis of MD4. In D. Gollmann, editor, *Fast Software Encryption, LNCS 1039*, pages 53–69. Springer-Verlag.

Dreyfuss, S. (1997) *Underground*. Reed Books.

Eichin, M.W. and J.A. Rochlis (1989) With microscope and tweezers: an analysis of the Internet virus of November 1988. In *Proceedings of the 1989 IEEE Symposium on Security and Privacy*, pages 326–343.

ElGamal, Tahir (1985) A public key cryptosystem and a signature scheme based on discrete logarithms. *IEEE Transactions on Information Theory*, 31(4):469–472.

Ellis, J.H. (1970) The possibility of non-secret encryption. Technical report, CESG, January http://www.cesg.gov.uk/about/nsecret/home.htm.

Ellison, Carl M., Bill Frantz, Butler Lampson, Ron Rivest, Brian M. Thomas and Tatu Ylonen (1999) *SPKI Certificate Theory*, September, RFC 2693.

England, P., B. Lampson, J. Manferdelli, M. Peinado and B. Willman (2003) A trusted open platform. *IEEE Computer*, 36(7):55–62.

Erlingsson, Úlfar and Fred B. Schneider (2000) IRM enforcement of Java stack inspection. In *Proceedings of the 2000 IEEE Symposium on Security and Privacy*, pages 246–255.

European Computer Manufacturers Association (1993) Secure information processing versus the concept of product evaluation. Technical Report ECMA TR/64, December.

Feldmeier, D.C. and P.R. Karn (1990) UNIX password security – ten years later. In *Advances in Cryptology – CRYPTO'89, LNCS 435*, pages 44–63. Springer-Verlag.

Ferbrache, D. and G. Shearer (1992) *UNIX Installation Security and Integrity*. Blackwell Scientific Publications, Oxford.

Fluhrer, Scott R., Itsik Mantin and Adi Shamir (2001) Weaknesses in the key scheduling algorithm of RC4. In Amr M. Youssef and S. Vaudenay, editors, *Proceedings SAC 2001, LNCS 2259*, pages 1–24. Springer-Verlag.

Ford, W. (1994) *Computer Communications Security* Prentice Hall, Englewood Cliffs, NJ.

Foster, James C., (2005) *Buffer Overflow Attacks*. Syngress Publishing, Rockland, MA.

Fournet, Cédric and Andrew D. Gordon (2003) Stack inspection: theory and variants. *ACM Transactions on Programming Languages and Systems*, 25(3):360–399, May.

Framer, D. and E. H. Spafford (1990) The COPS security checker system. In *The Summer Usenix Conference*, Anaheim, CA.

Garfinkel, Simson, Gene Spafford and Alan Schwartz (2003) *Practical Unix & Internet Security*. O'Reilly & Associates, Sebastopol, CA, 3rd edition.

Gasser, M. (1988) *Building a Secure Computer System*. Van Nostrand Reinhold, New York. http://www.acsac.org/secshelf/book002-html.

Gasser, M. (1990) The role of naming in secure distributed systems. In *Proceedings of the CS'90 Symposium on Computer Security*, pages 97–109, Rome, Italy, November.

Gasser, M., A. Goldstein, C. Kaufman and B. Lampson (1989) The digital distributed system security architecture. In *Proceedings of the 1989 National Computer Security Conference*.

Gligor, V.D. (1984) A note on denial of service in operating systems. *IEEE Transactions on Software Engineering*, 10(3):320–324, May.

Goguen, J.A. and J. Meseguer (1982) Security policies and security models. In *Proceedings of the 1982 IEEE Symposium on Security and Privacy*, pages 11–20.

Gollmann, Dieter (2003) Authentication by correspondence. *IEEE Journal on Selected Areas in Communications*, 21(1):88–95, January.

Gong, Li (1999) *Inside Java 2 Platform Security*. Addison-Wesley, Reading, MA.

Gong, Li, Mary Dageforde and Gary W. Ellison (2003) *Inside Java 2 Platform Security*. Addison-Wesley, Reading, MA, 2nd edition.

Govindavajhala, Sudhakar and Andrew W. Appel (2003) Using memory errors to attack a virtual machine. In *Proceedings of the 2003 IEEE Symposium on Security and Privacy*, page 154–165.

Graff, Mark G. and Kenneth R. van Wyk (2003) *Secure Coding*. O'Reilly & Associates.

Granville, Andrew (2005) It is easy to determine whether a given integer is prime. *Bulletin (New Series) of the American Mathematical Society*, 42(1):338.

Grover, D. (ed.) (1992) *The Protection of Computer Software – its Technology and Applications*. Cambridge University Press, Cambridge, 2nd edition.

Hadfield, L., D. Hatter and D. Bixler (1997) *Windows NT Server 4 Security Handbook*. Que Corporation, Indianapolis, IN.

Halevi, Shai and Hugo Krawczyk (1999) Public-key cryptography and password protocols. *ACM Transactions on Information and System Security*, 2(3):230–268, August.

Hallem, Seth, Benjamin Chelf, Yichen Xie and Dawson Engler (2002) A system and language for building system-specific, static analyses. In *Proceedings of PLDI 2002, June 17–19, 2002, Berlin, Germany*, pages 69–82. ACM Press.

Hansen, P. Brinch (1973) *Operating Systems Principles*. Prentice Hall, Englewood Cliffs, NJ.

Harrison, M.A., W.L. Ruzzo and J.D. Ullman (1976) Protection in operating systems. *Communications of the ACM*, 19(8):461–471, August.

Hellman, M.E. (1980) A cryptanalytic time-memory trade-off. *IEEE Transactions on Information Theory*, 26(4):401–406.

Hennessy, J. and D. Patterson (2002) *Computer Architecture – A Quantitative Approach*. Morgan Kaufmann, San Mateo, CA, 3rd edition.

Hogben, Giles, Tom Jackson and Marc Wilikens (2002) A fully compliant research implementation of the P3P standard. In D. Gollmann *et al.*, editors, *Computer Security – ESORICS 2002, LNCS 2502*, pages 104–120. Springer-Verlag.

Housley, Russell, Tim Polk, Warwick Ford and David Solo (2002) *Internet X.509 Public Key Infrastructure – Certificate and Certificate Revocation List (CRL) Profile*, April, RFC 3280.

Howard, Michael and David LeBlanc (2002) *Writing Secure Code*. Microsoft Press, Redmond, WA, 2nd edition.

Howard, Michael, Jon Pincus and Jeanette M. Wing (2003) Measuring relative attack surfaces. Technical Report CMU-CS-03-169, Carnegie Mellon University, Pittsburgh, PA.

International Organization for Standardization (1989) *Basic Reference Model for Open Systems Interconnection (OSI) Part 2: Security Architecture*. Geneva, Switzerland.

International Organization for Standardization (1991) *Information technology – Security Techniques – Entity Authentication Mechanisms; Part 1: General Model*. Geneva, Switzerland, September. ISO/IEC 9798-1, Second Edition.

International Organization for Standardization (1992) *ISO/IEC 9075: Information Technology – Database Languages – SQL*. Geneva, Switzerland.

International Organization for Standardization (1997) *Information technology – Open Systems Interconnection – The Directory-Authentication Framework*. Geneva, Switzerland, June. ISO/IEC 9594-8 – ITU-T Rec X.509 (1997 E).

International Organization for Standardization (2001) *Information Technology – Code of Practice for Information Security Management*. Geneva, Switzerland.

Kahn, D. (1967) *The Codebreakers*. Macmillan Publishing Company, New York.

Kang, M.H., A.P. Moore and I.S. Moskowitz (1998) Design and assurance strategy for the NRL pump. *IEEE Computer*, 31(4):56–64, April.

Karger, P.A. (1991) Implementing commercial data integrity with secure capabilities. In *Proceedings of the 1991 IEEE Symposium on Research in Security and Privacy*, pages 130–139.

Karger, P.A., M.E. Zurko, D.W. Bonin, A.H. Mason and C.E. Kahn (1990) A VMM security kernel for the VAX architecture. In *Proceedings of the 1990 IEEE Symposium on Research in Security and Privacy*, pages 1–19.

Karger, Paul A. and Roger R. Schell (2002) Thirty years later: lessons from the Multics security evaluation. In *Proceedings of ACSAC 2002*, pages 119–148.

Kohl, J. and C. Neumann (1993) *The Kerberos Network Authentication Service (V5)*, September, Internet RFC 1510.

Krawczyk, Hugo, Mihir Bellare and Ran Canetti (1997) HMAC: keyed-hashing for message authentication. Technical report, February, RFC 2104.

La Macchia, Brian A., Sebastian Lange, Matthew Lyons, Rudi Martin and Kevin T. Price (2002) *.NET Framework Security*. Addison-Wesley Professional, Boston, MA.

Lamport, L. (1979) Constructing digital signatures from a one way function. Technical Report CSL-98, SRI International Computer Science Laboratory, October.

Lamport, L. (1985) Checking secure interactions of smart card applets. In M.W. Alford *et al.*, editors, *Distributed Systems: Methods and Tools for Specification: An Advanced Course, LNCS 190*, pages 119–130. Springer-Verlag.

Lampson, B. (1974) Protection. ACM *Operating Systems Reviews*, 8(1):18–24, January.

Lampson, Butler, Martín Abadi, Michael Burrows and Edward Wobber (1992) Authentication in distributed systems: theory and practice. ACM *Transactions on Computer Systems*, 10(4):265–310, November.

Landwehr, C. (1983) The best available technologies for computer security. *IEEE Computer*, 16(7):86–100.

Lang, Ulrich and Rudolf Schreiner (2002) *Developing Secure Distributed Systems with CORBA*. Artech House, Norwood, MA.

Laprie, J.-C. (1992) *Basic Concepts and Terminology*. Springer-Verlag, Vienna.

Lee, Ruby B., David K. Karig, John P. McGregor and Zhijie Shi (2003) Enlisting hardware architecture to thwart malicious code injection. In *Proceedings of the International Conference on Security in Pervasive Computing (SPC-2003), LNCS 2802*, pages 237–252. Springer-Verlag.

Lee, T.M.P. (1991) Using mandatory integrity to enforce "commercial" security. In *Proceedings of the 1991 IEEE Symposium on Research in Security and Privacy*, pages 140–146.

Lipton, R.J. and L. Snyder (1978) On synchronization and security. In R.D. Demillo *et al.*, editors, *Foundations of Secure Computation*, pages 367–385. Academic Press, New York.

Lunt, T.F. (1989) Aggregation and inference: facts and fallacies. In *Proceedings of the 1989 IEEE Symposium on Security and Privacy*, pages 102–109.

Lunt, T.F., D.E. Denning, R.R. Schell, M. Heckman and W.R. Shockley (1990) The seaview security model. *IEEE Transactions on Software Engineering*, 16(6):593–607.

MacKenzie, D. and G. Pottinger (1997) Mathematics, technology, and trust: formal verification, computer security, and the U.S. Military. *IEEE Annals of the History of Computing*, 19(3):41–59.

Manger, James (2001) A chosen ciphertext attack on RSA Optimal Asymmetric Encryption Padding (OAEP) as standardized in PKCS # 1 v2.0. In J. Kilian, editor, *Advances in Cryptology – Crypto 2001, LNCS 2139*, pages 230–238. Springer-Verlag.

Matsumoto, Tsutomu (2002) Gummy and conductive silicon rubber fingers – importance of vulnerability analysis. In Y. Zheng, editor, *Advances in Cryptology – Asiacrypt 2002, Queenstown, New Zealand, LNCS 2501*, pages 574–575. Springer-Verlag.

McGraw, G. and E.W. Felten (1997) *Java Security*. John Wiley & Sons, New York.

McGraw, Gary (2004) *Exploiting Software: How to Break Code*. Addison-Wesley.

McLean, J. (1987) Reasoning about security models. In *Proceedings of the 1987 IEEE Symposium on Security and Privacy*, pages 123–131.

McLean, J. (January 1990) The specification and modeling of computer security. *IEEE Computer*, 23(1):9–16.

McLean, J. (1994) Security models. In J. Marciniak, editor, *Encyclopedia of Software Engineering*. John Wiley & Sons, New York.

Menezes, Alfred J., Paul C. van Oorschot and Scott A. Vanstone (1997) *Handbook of Applied Cryptography*. CRC Press, Boca Raton, FL.

Miller, B.F., L. Frederiksen and B. So (December 1990) An empirical study of the reliability of Unix utilities. *Communications of the ACM*, 33(12):32–44.

Miller, S.P., B.C. Neuman, J.I. Schiller and J.H. Saltzer (1987) Section E.2.1: Kerberos authentication and authorization system. Technical report, MIT Project Athena, Cambridge, MA.

Mitchell, Christopher J. and Paolo S. Pagliusi (2003) Is entity authentication necessary? In B. Christiansen *et al.*, editors, *Security Protocols, 10th International Workshop, Cambridge, LNCS 2845*, pages 20–33. Springer-Verlag.

Mitnick, Kevin D. and William L. Simon (2002) *The Art of Deception*. John Wiley & Sons, Indianapolis, IN.

Morris, R. and K. Thompson (November 1979) Password security: a case history. *Communications of the ACM*, 22(11):594–597.

Morris, R.T. (February 1985) A weakness in the 4.2BSD Unix TCP/IP Software. Bell Labs Computer Science Technical Report.

National Institute of Standards and Technology & National Security Agency (1992) *Federal Criteria for Information Technology Security*, Version 1.0.

NCSC (1987) *Trusted Network Interpretation*, NCSC-TG-005, Version 1.0.

NCSC (April 1991) *Trusted Database Management System Interpretation*, NCSC-TG-021.

Necula, George C. (January 1997) Proof-carrying code. In *Proceedings of the 24th ACM SIGPLAN-SIGACT Symposium on Principles of Programming Langauges (POPL '97)*, pages 106–119, Paris.

Needham, R.M. (1992) Later developments at Cambridge: Titan, CAP, and the Cambridge Ring. *Annals of the History of Computing*, 14(4):57.

Needham, R.M. and M.D. Schroeder (1978) Using encryption for authentication in large networks of computers. *Communications of the ACM*, 21(12):993–999.

Nelson, R.P. (1988) *The 80386 Book*. Microsoft Press.

Neumann, J. von, (1993) First draft of a report on the EDVAC (M.D. Godfrey (ed.)). *Annals of the History of Computing*, 15(4):27–75.

Niemi, Valtteri and Kaisa Nyberg (2003) *UMTS Security*. John Wiley & Sons, Chichester.

Organick, E.I. (1972) *The Multics System: An Examination of Its Structure*. MIT Press, Cambridge, MA.

Park, J.S. (1995) *AS/400 Security in a Client/Server Environment*. John Wiley & Sons, New York.

Pfleeger, C.P. and S. Lawrence Pfleeger (2003) *Security in Computing*. Prentice Hall, Englewood Cliffs, NJ, 3rd edition.

Preneel, B., B.B. Van Rompay, S.B. Örs, A. Biryukov, L. Granboulan, E. Dottax, M. Dichtl, M. Schafheutle, P. Serf, S. Pyka, E. Biham, E. Barkan, O. Dunkelman, J. Stolin, M. Ciet, J.-J. Quisquater, F. Sica, H. Raddum and M. Parker (February 2003) Performance of optimized implementations of the NESSIE primitives. Technical report, Version 2.0. http://www.cryptonessie.org.

Ptacek, Thomas H., and Timothy N. Newsham (1998) Insertion, evasion, and denial of service: eluding network intrusion detection. Technical report, Secure Networks, Inc.

Rivest, Ron, Adi Shamir and L. Adleman (1978) A method for obtaining digital signatures and public-key cryptosystems. *Communications of the ACM*, 21(2):120–126.

Russel, D. and G.T. Gangemi Sr (1991) *Computer Security Basics*. O'Reilly & Associates, Sebastopol, CA.

Saltzer, J.H. (1974) Protection and the control of information sharing in Multics. *Communications of the ACM*, 17:388–402.

Samalin, S. (1997) *Secure Unix*. McGraw-Hill.

Sandhu, R.S. (November 1993) Lattice-based access control models. *IEEE Computer*, 26(11):9–19.

Sandhu, R.S., E.J. Coyne, H.L. Feinstein and C.E. Youman (February 1996) Role-based access control models. *IEEE Computer*, 29(2):38–47.

Schaefer, Marvin (2004) If A1 is the answer, what was the question? An edgy naïf's retrospective on promulgating the Trusted Computer Systems Evaluation Criteria. In *Proceedings of ACSAC 2004*, pages 204–228.

Schellhorn, Gerhard, Wolfgang Reif, Axel Schairer, Paul Karger, Vernon Austel and David Toll (2000) Verification of a formal security model for multiapplicative smart cards. In F. Cuppens *et al.*, editors, *ESORICS 2000, LNCS 1895*, pages 17–36. Springer-Verlag.

Schneider, Fred B. (2000) Enforceable security policies. *ACM Transactions on Information and System Security*, 3(1):30–50.

Schneier, B. (1996) *Applied Cryptography*. John Wiley & Sons, New York, 2nd edition.

Schroeder, M. and J.H Saltzer (1972) A hardware architecture for implementing protection rings. *Communications of the ACM*, 15(3):157–170.

Shimomura, T. (1995) *Takedown*. Martin Secker & Warburg Ltd.

Shoch, John F. and Jon A. Hupp (September 1982) The "worm" programs – early experience with a distributed computation. *Communications of the ACM*, 25(3):172–180.

Shoup, Victor (2001) OAEP reconsidered. In J. Kilian, editor, *Advances in Cryptology – Crypto 2001, LNCS 2139*, pages 239–259. Springer-Verlag.

Sibert, O., P.A. Porras and R. Lindell (1996) An analysis of the Intel 80x86 processor architecture and implementation. *IEEE Transactions on Software Engineering*, 22(5):283–293, May.

Smith, Martin (1993) *Commonsense Computer Security*. McGraw-Hill, London.

Spafford, E.H. (1989) Crisis and aftermath. *Communications of the ACM*, 32(6):678–687, June.

Spitzner, Lance (2003) Honeypots. http://www.tracking-hackers.com, May.

Stallings, William (2003) *Cryptography and Network Security*. Prentice Hall, 3rd edition.

Sterne, Daniel F. (1991) On the buzzword "Security Policy". In *Proceedings of the 1991 IEEE Symposium on Research in Security and Privacy*, pages 219–230.

Stoll, C. (1989) *The Cuckoo's Egg*. Simon & Schuster.

Swift, Michael M., Anne Hopkins, Peter Brundrett, Cliff Van Dyke, Praerit Garg, Shannon Chan, Mario Goertzel and Gregory Jensenworth (2002) Improving the granularity of access control for Windows 2000. *ACM Transactions on Information and System Security*, 5(4):398–437.

UK ITSEC Scheme (1991) *Description of the Scheme*, March, UKSP 01.

United Nations (1999) *International Review of Criminal Policy – United Nations Manual on the Prevention and Control of Computer-related Crime*. New York.

US Department of Commerce, National Bureau of Standards (1977) *Data Encryption Standard*, December, NBS FIPS PUB 46.

US Department of Commerce, National Institute of Standards and Technology (2000) *Digital Signature Standard (DSS)*, January, FIPS PUB 186–2.

US Department of Commerce, National Institute of Standards and Technology (2001) *Advanced Encryption Standard (AES)*, November, FIPS 197.

US Department of Defense (1985) *DoD Trusted Computer System Evaluation Criteria*, DOD 5200.28-STD.

US Department of Defense (1987) *Industrial Security Manual for Safeguarding Classified Information*, June, DOD 5220.22-M.

Van der Putte, Ton and Jeroen Keuning (2000) Biometrical fingerprinting recognition: don't get your fingers burned. In Josep Domingo-Ferrer *et al.*, editors, *Smart Card Research and Applications*, pages 289–303. Kluwer Academic Publishers.

Viega, John and Gary McGraw (2001) *Building Secure Software*. Addison-Wesley, Boston, MA.

Viega, John and Matt Messier (2003) *Secure Programming Cookbook for C and C++*. O'Reilly & Associates.

Wahbe, R., S. Lucco, T.E. Anderson and S.L. Graham (1993) Efficient software-based fault isolation. In *Proceedings of the Symposium on Operating System Principles*.

Ware, W. (1979) Security controls for computer systems. Technical Report R-609-1, Rand Corp Tech Report, October.

Weissman, C. (1992) BLACKER: security for the DDN, examples of A1 security engineering trades. In *Proceedings of the 1992 IEEE Symposium on Research in Security and Privacy*, pages 286–292.

Wilkes, M.V. (1968) *Time-sharing Computer Systems*. Elsevier, New York.

Wu, Thomas (1999) A real-world analysis of Kerberos password security. In *Proceedings of the 1999 Network and Distributed System Security Symposium*. Internet Society, February.

Zwicky, Elizabth D., Simon Cooper and D. Brent Chapman (1995) *Building Internet Firewalls*. O'Reilly & Associates, Sebastopol, CA, 2nd edition.

# Index

# Index

374      INDEX

Wireless Equivalent Privacy (WEP)
    322–323
Wireless LAN (WLAN)   320–324
wiretap   234, 308
worm   258, 279
WPA (see WiFi Protected Access)
WPA2   324

write-once memory (WROM) (see
    memory)
wrapper   109–110

## X
X.509   225–227
    certificate (see certificate)

UNIVERSITY OF WALES, NEWPORT
LIBRARY AND INFORMATION SERVICES
ALLT-YR-YN